*The Politics of Finance
in Developing Countries*

A volume in the series

Cornell Studies in Political Economy

EDITED BY PETER J. KATZENSTEIN

A full list of titles in the series appears at the end of the book.

The Politics of Finance in Developing Countries

Edited by

STEPHAN HAGGARD,
CHUNG H. LEE, *and*
SYLVIA MAXFIELD

CORNELL UNIVERSITY PRESS

Ithaca and London

First published 1993 by Cornell University Press.

International Standard Book Number 0-8014-2892-0 (cloth)
International Standard Book Number 0-8014-8130-9 (paper)
Library of Congress Catalog Card Number 93-28589
Printed in the United States of America
Librarians: Library of Congress cataloging information
appears on the last page of the book.

⊗ The paper in this book meets the minimum requirements of the
American National Standard for Information Sciences—Permanence
of Paper for Printed Library Materials, ANSI Z39.48-1984.

Contents

CONTENTS

Contributors

LESLIE ELLIOTT ARMIJO is Assistant Professor in the Department of Political Science at Northeastern University.

TUN-JEN CHENG is Assistant Professor in the Department of Government at the College of William and Mary.

BYUNG-SUN CHOI is Associate Professor in the Graduate School of Public Administration at Seoul National University, Republic of Korea.

RICHARD DONER is Associate Professor in the Department of Political Science, Emory University.

STEPHAN HAGGARD is Professor in the Graduate School of International Relations and Pacific Studies, University of California, San Diego.

LAURA A. HASTINGS is Assistant Professor in the Department of Political Science at the University of Pittsburgh.

PAUL D. HUTCHCROFT is a doctoral candidate in the Department of Political Science, Yale University, and Academy Scholar for International and Area Studies at Harvard University.

CHUNG H. LEE is Professor in the Department of Economics at the University of Hawaii and Research Associate at the East-West Center.

CONTRIBUTORS

ANDREW J. MACINTYRE is Senior Lecturer and Deputy Dean on the Faculty of Asian and International Studies at Griffith University, Australia.

SYLVIA MAXFIELD is Associate Professor in the Department of Political Science at Yale University.

DANIEL UNGER is Assistant Professor in the Department of Government at Georgetown University.

Preface

The origins of this project reside in our collective dissatisfaction with the literature on the role of finance in development. Since the mid-1980s, Chung Lee has wrestled with the question of why countries such as Korea and Taiwan could couple rapid economic growth with relatively underdeveloped and "repressed" financial systems. Did the financial system really hinder the growth of the East Asian newly industrializing countries, or was there in fact some elective affinity between government intervention in financial markets and rapid economic growth? Though of obvious importance, this question had been sidestepped in the economic literature owing to the relative neglect of the allocative function of financial systems: how different financial systems affect the flow of resources among different sectors and activities. In articles in *Economic Development and Cultural Change* (with Seiji Naya) and *World Development,* Lee drew on the work of Oliver Williamson on the properties of hierarchies to suggest how government intervention in the allocation of resources might be efficient. These observations were clearly of relevance to the debate over the role of the state in the development process.

Stephan Haggard had been approaching similar questions from the angle of political economy. Dissatisfied with dominant explanations of East Asian development, he sought to explore the politics of export-led growth in his book *Pathways from the Periphery* (Cornell University Press, 1990). That work and collaboration with Tun-jen Cheng and Chung-in Moon focused largely on industrial and trade policy. But through a collective research project on the political economy of the debt crisis and the influence of two close colleagues and friends, Jeffry Frieden and Sylvia Maxfield, Haggard became increasingly interested in the political economy of finance. Why did countries pursue the financial market policies they did? In particular, what political and institutional factors determined the effectiveness and efficiency of state intervention in financial markets?

In 1989, Haggard visited the East-West Center at Chung Lee's invitation to work on a proposal concerned with the political economy of financial markets in developing countries. That proposal and the idea for a comparative project were discussed at an initial workshop at the East-West Center in April 1990. In attendance were Shigeyuki Abe, Thomas Cargill, Jeffry Frieden, Joseph Grunwald, Rolf Luders, Manuel F. Montes, Sang Woo Nam, Seiji Naya, James Roumasset, and Philip Wellons. Initially, the project was to be limited to East and Southeast Asia, but it was realized that additional intellectual leverage could be gained by comparing East Asia's experience with that of some major Latin American countries. At this point, Rolf Luders provided assistance in securing financial support from the International Center for Economic Growth for the Latin American studies.

We then went about the task of putting together a research team. Our approach was to bring together economists and political scientists to write complementary country monographs. Eight countries were chosen for analysis: Brazil, Chile, Mexico, South Korea, Taiwan, the Philippines, Thailand, and Indonesia. The economists focused on the economic determinants and effects of credit allocation policies. The papers by the political scientists, collected in this volume, examined financial market policy, with particular attention to two issues: the use of preferential credit as a policy instrument and the politics of financial market liberalization.

The project received generous financial support from the Korean Development Institute (KDI) and the Asian Development Bank (ADB). We are particularly thankful to the president of KDI during this period, Bon-Ho Koo, and to Sang Woo Nam for coordinating relations between KDI and the East-West Center. We also thank Hakchung Choo, chief economist at the ADB during this period, for his suppport. The East-West Center graciously and efficiently hosted two meetings to review the papers, the first in November 1990 and the second in October 1991. For their support at the center, we thank Seiji Naya, former director of the Resource Systems Institute, and Bruce Koppel, vice president for Research and Education.

The political scientists benefited greatly from the chance to interact with the economists who wrote parallel country studies: Eduardo Suarez (Mexico); Luis Felipe Lagos (Chile); Daniel Gleizer (Brazil); Manuel F. Montes (the Philippines); Wing Thye Woo (Indonesia); Sang Woo Nam (Korea); Tein-Chen Chou (Taiwan); and Robert Muscat (Thailand). We are also thankful for the useful comments we received at these meetings from David Cole, Betty Slade, Jeffry Frieden, Nathaniel Leff, Yung Chul Park, Joseph Ravalo, and James Roumasset.

At the October 1991 meeting, Haggard and Sylvia Maxfield began discussions on the conclusion, drawing on the initial project outline and ideas that Maxfield had developed in her book *Governing Capital: International Finance and Mexican Politics* (Cornell University Press, 1990) and in the first draft of her essay on Mexico. Jeffry Frieden subjected various drafts to criticism, which managed to be both withering and constructive at the same time, and Nancy Nieman provided useful insights. Haggard and Maxfield subsequently had the opportunity to present their ideas to a conference on capital account convertibility at the Organization for Economic Cooperation and Development in Paris in June 1992. Our thanks to Bernhard Fischer and Helmut Reisen, organizers of the conference, and the participants, particularly Silvio Borner, Colin Bradford, Peter Kenen, John Williamson, and Charles Wyplosz for their encouragement.

At Cornell University Press, we thank Roger Haydon for his interest and are particularly grateful for the extremely thoughtful comments of an anonymous outside reviewer. We also thank Janis Togashi for her editorial assistance, Ann Takayesu for typing the manuscripts, and Mendl Djunaidy for her help in organizing and managing this project.

STEPHAN HAGGARD

San Diego, California

CHUNG H. LEE

Honolulu, Hawaii

SYLVIA MAXFIELD

New Haven, Connecticut

PART I

INTRODUCTION

CHAPTER ONE

The Political Dimension of Finance in Economic Development

STEPHAN HAGGARD AND
CHUNG H. LEE

The developing world's debt problems, the growing integration of financial markets, and the pervasiveness of financial crises generated a strong revival of interest in developing country financial systems in the 1980s.[1] Traditionally, the literature on finance and development focused on the effect of interest rates on savings mobilization and the relationship between financial and macroeconomic policy. The crises of the 1980s added a new set of questions to the agenda, including the management of foreign indebtedness and the liberalization and internationalization of financial markets.

Though there has been an explosion of literature on the politics of the debt crisis, relatively little theoretical or empirical work has been done on the political economy of finance in developing countries.[2] Yet the governments of developing countries are typically deeply involved in the allocation of financial resources, both through state-owned banks

---

[1] For recent reviews of the issues, see World Bank, *World Development Report, 1989: Financial Systems and Development* (New York: Oxford University Press, 1989); and Maxwell J. Fry, *Money, Interest, and Banking in Economic Development* (Baltimore: Johns Hopkins University Press, 1988).

[2] Among the exceptions are Jeffry Frieden, *Debt, Development, and Democracy: Modern Political Economy and Latin America, 1965–1985* (Princeton: Princeton University Press, 1991); Sylvia Maxfield, *Governing Capital: International Finance and Mexican Politics* (Ithaca: Cornell University Press, 1990); and Jung-en Woo, *Race to the Swift: State and Finance in Korean Industrialization* (New York: Columbia University Press, 1991). On the advanced industrial states, major studies include John Zysman, *Government, Markets, and Growth: Financial Systems and the Politics of Industrial Change* (Ithaca: Cornell University Press, 1983); Frances McCall Rosenbluth, *Financial Politics in Contemporary Japan* (Ithaca: Cornell University Press, 1989); and Louis W. Pauly, *Opening Financial Markets: Banking Politics on the Pacific Rim* (Ithaca: Cornell University Press, 1988).

and through their regulation of private financial intermediaries. Such intervention raises three issues for political analysis.

The first question concerns the conditions under which governments are drawn to intervene in financial markets. Some states, such as Korea, have exercised pervasive control over financial markets, by means including state ownership of banks. In other countries, including Thailand, the government's role in the allocation of credit is substantially smaller and the private financial community is correspondingly more significant. What accounts for this cross-national variation? Is intervention motivated by efforts to correct market failures? Is it the outcome of rent-seeking activity? Or does it come in response to other constraints, such as changes in the cost and availability of capital?

The second set of questions concerns the efficiency of government intervention in financial markets.[3] Economists generally argue that intervention leads to a misallocation of resources, except where it acts to correct quite specific market failures. Even where such a role is initially justified, however, it can give rise to rent-seeking behavior. This stylized portrait of government failure, inefficiency and corruption certainly fits some countries, such as the Philippines. But it does not fit the newly industrializing countries of East Asia as well. Korea and Taiwan both combined rapid growth with government allocation of credit. Was such intervention a drag on growth that would have otherwise been higher, or were these states distinguished from their developing country counterparts precisely by their capability to use targeted credit policies efficiently? If so, what political and institutional factors allowed planning authorities to focus on the social gains of the investments being supported and to guarantee that those activities were pursued?

A third set of questions, discussed in more detail in the conclusion by Stephan Haggard and Sylvia Maxfield, surrounds the liberalization of financial markets. The governments of developing countries have come under strong economic and political pressures from trading partners and international financial institutions to reduce the government's role in the allocation of credit and to open financial markets to greater foreign participation. Governments have embraced these objectives with varying degrees of enthusiasm. Some countries, such as Chile, undertook sweeping experiments in financial market liberalization. Indonesia was also precocious in liberalizing its capital account. In most other countries, the process of domestic liberalization has been gradual and halting, and internationalization of financial markets is just beginning. Under what conditions are governments motivated to initiate

[3]This question is addressed in more detail in Chung H. Lee and Stephan Haggard, eds., *Government, Financial Systems, and Economic Development*: vol. 2, *Efficiency and Allocation* (forthcoming).

liberalization attempts, and what determines the pace and scope of these efforts?

In this introduction, we frame these questions in more detail by reviewing some of the main lines of debate on financial markets and financial market policy in the economics literature. We argue that the debate over the relationship between finance and development has gone through three phases. In the early post-World War II period, development economists justified government intervention in financial markets. In a first major round of controversy, the neoclassical revival challenged this view and underlined the costs of financial "repression." But just as market-oriented orthodoxy appeared ascendant, new theoretical and empirical work once again raised questions about the benefits of liberalizing financial markets.

We show that at each stage, the positions taken by the protagonists in these debates rested in critical ways on underlying, but usually unexamined, institutional and political assumptions. The arguments of the early interventionists implicitly relied on a strong and capable state. By contrast, proponents of the neoclassical revival generally assumed that the state was incompetent, and they drew on rent-seeking arguments to buttress that claim. Drawing on a transactions costs framework, we show that there are theoretical reasons why government allocation of credit might be efficient. The actual operation of such programs, however, will depend on two political factors: the power and organization of relevant social groups and the extent to which institutional arrangements, including the integrity and cohesion of the state apparatus itself, allow them to gain access to and control over the decision-making process.

I. The Debate on "Financial Repression":
Round One

The early literature on finance and development, inspired by the seminal work of Ronald I. McKinnon and Edward S. Shaw,[4] juxtaposed two ideal-typical financial systems: a "repressed" financial system and a free-market financial system. In a "repressed" financial system, the government maintains artificially low interest rates. Because this induces an excess demand for credit, the government is drawn into the process of rationing financial resources among competing uses. These preferential credit schemes constitute the central empirical focus of this

[4]Ronald I. McKinnon, *Money and Capital in Economic Development* (Washington, D.C.: Brookings Institution, 1973); and Edward S. Shaw, *Financial Deepening in Economic Development* (New York: Oxford University Press, 1973).

volume. We define them as government-directed programs that provide lending to "targeted" sectors, activities, classes of firms, or individual companies in quantities and at interest rates that would not be provided by existing financial institutions acting independently of government guidance.

Preferential credit can be extended through a variety of mechanisms. The most direct is through state-owned commercial or development banks. The government can also influence the behavior of private financial intermediaries through interest rate ceilings, through controls on the lending practices and portfolios of banks, through the extension of loan guarantees, and, more indirectly, through a broad array of regulations that affect entry and the scope of bank business.

The controversy over financial repression has gone through an evolution. In the immediate postwar period, development economists defended government intervention in finance on the grounds of market imperfections. Credit markets in most developing countries were small, undiversified, and unable to adopt the longer-term perspective required to underwrite some socially profitable investments. Lowering the returns to financial assets, it was argued, had the beneficial effect of encouraging higher levels of real investment, higher capital/labor ratios and productivity, and thus higher growth.[5]

Historical experience also showed that a number of successful late developers, including Germany and Japan, had manipulated their financial systems to achieve the goals of industrialization.[6] Indeed, the very concept of a development "strategy" hinged on the government playing a central role in resource mobilization. As Albert O. Hirschman writes in his *Strategy of Economic Development,* "Development depends not so much on finding optimal combinations for given resources and factors of production as on calling forth and enlisting for development purposes resources and abilities that are hidden, scattered, or badly utilized."[7]

The initial line of attack against government intervention centered on the effects of financial repression on resource mobilization. Because preferential lending schemes were financed through controls on deposit rates, they implied a disincentive to saving. Given that developing

[5] James Tobin, "Money and Economic Growth," *Econometrica* 33, no. 4 (1965): 671–84.

[6] The classic statement is Alexander Gerschenkron, "Economic Backwardness in Historical Perspective," in his *Economic Backwardness in Historical Perspective: A Book of Essays* (Cambridge: Harvard University Press, 1962). See also Rondo Cameron, ed., *Banking in the Early Stages of Industrialization: A Study in Comparative Economic History* (New York: Oxford University Press, 1967).

[7] Albert O. Hirschman, *The Strategy of Economic Development* (New Haven: Yale University Press, 1958), p. 5.

countries were constrained in their capacity to borrow internationally—at least until the 1970s—and as there were clear limits on the availability of aid, low domestic savings meant low investment and thus low growth.

The empirical evidence on the relationship between the liberalization of interest rates and aggregate savings proved controversial, however; although a number of studies found positive relationships, others found the effects to be small or nonexistent.[8] Yet the neoclassical defense of liberalization was by no means limited to its effects on aggregate savings. Financial repression also had effects on the growth and competitiveness of the financial sector and on allocative efficiency. Subsidized credit lowered the cost of capital and thus led to the adoption of overly capital-intensive techniques, with implications for both equity and employment.[9] Preferential credit schemes could also reinforce other policy biases, such as the emphasis on import substitution in manufacturing over export-oriented manufacturing or agriculture. Analysts typically pointed to Latin American and African countries for evidence supporting this argument against financial repression.[10]

A close reading of the literature on financial repression suggests that the critique rested in no small measure on a political economy analysis as well.[11] Advocates of intervention in financial markets implicitly assumed a competent, informed, and "strong" government whose motives were to maximize social welfare by offsetting and correcting market imperfections. Yet models of rent seeking and regulatory cap-

[8] Studies on Korea, which played centrally in McKinnon's original analysis, by Dowling and van Wijnbergen show little clear relationship between financial liberalization and aggregate savings; financial savings increase, but this increase comes as a result of diversion from informal markets. See J. M. Dowling, Jr., *Domestic Resource Mobilization through Financial Development: Korea* (Manila: Asian Development Bank, 1984); and Sweder van Wijnbergen, "Stagflation Effects of Monetary Stabilization Policies: A Quantitative Analysis of South Korea," *Journal of Development Economics* 10, no. 2 (1982): 133–69. For overviews that stress the conflicting nature of the findings on the effects of interest rates on savings, see Alberto Giovannini, "The Interest Elasticity of Savings in Developing Countries: The Existing Evidence," *World Development* 11, no. 7 (1983): 601–7; and Deena R. Khatkhate, "Assessing the Impact of Interest Rates in Less Developed Countries," *World Development* 16, no. 5 (1988): 577–88. For more positive assessments, see Fry, *Money, Interest, and Banking*, p. 146; Alan Gelb, "A Cross Section Analysis of Financial Policies, Efficiency, and Growth," World Bank PRP Working Paper no. 202 (Washington, D.C., 1989); and Yoon-je Cho and Deena Khatkate, *Lessons of Financial Liberalization in Asia: A Comparative Study*, World Bank Discussion Paper no. 50 (Washington, D.C., 1989).

[9] For a discussion of these issues with reference to the newly industrializing countries, see Stephan Haggard, *Pathways from the Periphery: The Politics of Growth in the Newly Industrializing Countries* (Ithaca: Cornell University Press, 1990), chap. 9.

[10] See Fry, *Money, Interest, and Banking*, pp. 143–53, 410–17; and Jacques Polak, *Financial Policies and Development* (Paris: Development Centre, Organisation for Economic Co-Operation and Development [OECD], 1989), especially chap. 3.

[11] As Fry writes in summarizing the role of government intervention in financial markets, "Vested interests have ensured that entry barriers are maintained and competition from direct markets is suppressed." Fry, *Money, Interest, and Banking*, p. 322.

7

ture suggested that government intervention was more likely to reflect pressures emanating from powerful groups capable of extracting policy favors: in different countries, these might include rising manufacturing groups, the banking sector, or simply personalistic networks tied to top executive officials.[12] Misallocation of resources could result not only from rent-seeking pressures from social groups but also from the fact that allocative decisions were made by bureaucrats who lacked appropriate incentives and information.

Opponents of state intervention in general and of financial repression in particular argued that these negative allocative effects and perverse political incentives could be eliminated through liberalization. In a typical series of articles in this vein from the early 1980s, Maxwell Fry argued that raising real interest rates would ration out low-yielding investments, increase the average efficiency of investment, and thus increase the rate of economic growth.[13] Domestic financial market reform was also seen as a crucial prerequisite for opening the capital account and allowing greater entry of foreign financial intermediaries, which promised additional economic gains.[14]

The advocates of liberalization also deployed political economy arguments in their favor. If credible, interest rate reform would undercut the incentive to lobby for preferential credit. Opening the capital account would impose needed discipline both on the financial sector and on macroeconomic policy.[15] Freeing capital movements would put downward pressure on interest rates—an aim of intervention in the first place—and would render inflationary policies untenable.

The rent-seeking model was plausible, but it suffered from two flaws—one empirical, the other theoretical. Despite the extensive theoretical work on rent seeking and the invocation of "vested interests" to explain distortions in financial markets, there was surprisingly little empirical work examining the politics of financial market policy. Few studies bothered to ask whether financial market policy was in fact a result of political pressures or whether it sprang from economic constraints or the projects of state officials.

[12] On rent-seeking activities, see Jagdish Bhagwati, "Directly-Unproductive Profit-seeking (DUP) Activities," *Journal of Political Economy* 90, no. 5 (1982): 988–1002.

[13] Maxwell J. Fry, "Models of Financially Repressed Developing Economies," *World Economy* 10, no. 9 (1982): 731–50, "Saving, Financial Intermediation, and Economic Growth in Asia," *Asian Development Review* 2, no. 1 (1984): 82–91, and *Money, Interest, and Banking.*

[14] For a review of the debate on capital account convertibility, see Bernhard Fischer and Helmut Reisen, *Towards Capital Account Convertibility,* OECD Development Centre Policy Brief no. 4 (Paris, 1992).

[15] For a review of the issues, see James A. Hanson, "Opening the Capital Account: A Survey of Issues and Results," World Bank Policy Research Working Papers, WPS 901 (Washington, D.C., May 1992).

A second flaw was the inability to account for variations across countries in terms of the extent or nature of government intervention in financial markets. Though some developing countries had severely distorted financial markets, in others, such as Thailand, government intervention was lighter. As the 1980s unfolded, an unexpected development occurred that cast further doubt on a simple rent-seeking model: more and more middle-income developing countries experimented with financial liberalization. How did reformers in these countries overcome resistance from politicians, bureaucrats, and rent seekers, who presumably had a vested interest in seeing such policies sustained?

II. The Debate on Liberalization: Round Two

In the 1980s, the theoretical pendulum swung once more, as several lines of empirical analysis emerged to challenge the case for financial liberalization.[16] The neoclassical approach to the East Asian newly industrializing countries came under increasing fire from those arguing that the state had played a constructive, even pivotal, role in their development. These cases suggested that intervention in financial markets could be efficient and growth-promoting, at least under certain conditions. The extensive postmortem on the radical liberalization efforts in the Southern Cone of Latin America reached the complementary conclusion that liberalization could have devastating costs in the absence of an appropriate regulatory framework. A small body of work on the industrial organization of the financial sector went farther, underlining how liberalization had unanticipated effects under the conditions of industrial and financial concentration that are typical of most developing countries. Each of these lines of debate raised crucial questions for political analysis.

The State in East Asian Growth

The debate about the rapid growth of the East Asian newly industrializing countries (NICs)—Korea, Taiwan, Singapore, and Hong

[16] There were also important theoretical developments that carried a similar implication, though a full discussion is beyond the scope of this chapter. In an important article, Stiglitz and Weiss argued that the problems of adverse selection, moral hazard, and contract enforcement are innate characteristics of financial markets. As a result, credit rationing is characteristic of *all* financial markets, including "free" ones. See Joseph E. Stiglitz and Andrew Weiss, "Credit Rationing in Markets with Imperfect Information," *American Economic Review* 71, no. 3 (1981): 393–410. For his reflections on these conclusions for intervention in developing countries, see J. Stiglitz, "Financial Markets and Development," *Oxford Review of Economic Policy* 5, no. 4 (1989): 55–68.

9

Kong—has been well rehearsed and need not be outlined here in detail.[17] In general, there are two competing explanations. On the one hand, neoclassical interpretations attribute the NICs' success to relatively stable macroeconomic policies and outward-looking development strategies that provided unbiased incentives to both exports and import substitutes. Where the government did play a more active role, it was generally to offset the effect of already existing price distortions. When intervention went further—as in the efforts in Korea, Taiwan, and Singapore to upgrade their industrial structures in the 1970s—it was usually misguided.

The critics of this position have argued that the state has played a much more active role, by means including the financial system. This criticism has taken two somewhat different tacks. One is to challenge the neoclassical approach head on by advancing reasons why government intervention does, in fact, contribute to economic development. With reference to the use of the financial system, Robert Wade argued that government intervention increased financial savings in the banking system, held real savings within the country for use by domestic investors, and gave the government a powerful tool for effecting industrial policy.[18] Colin I. Bradford noted that the cost of investment goods in the rapidly growing East Asian NICs was low compared with other developing countries; financial market policies were clearly one reason for this outcome.[19] Alice Amsden showed that financial subsidies were critical not only to spurring investment but also to overcoming particular costs associated with an export-oriented strategy, including those of devaluation in import-dependent economies and the high degree of uncertainty in entering foreign markets.[20]

A second line of attack on the neoclassical position attempted to show how the broader institutional and political milieu in the East Asian NICs contributed to relatively efficient outcomes. Chalmers Johnson, who pioneered this line of thinking with reference to Japan, focused on the interactive relationship between government and business, the

---

[17] For a statement of the neoclassical position, see Bela Balassa, *The Newly Industrializing Countries in the World Economy* (New York: Pergamon, 1981). Among the critics are Chalmers Johnson, *MITI and the Japanese Miracle: The Growth of Industrial Policy, 1925–1975* (Stanford: Stanford University Press, 1982); Alice Amsden, *Asia's Next Giant: South Korea and Late Industrialization* (New York: Oxford University Press, 1989); Robert Wade, *Governing the Market: Economic Theory and the Role of Government in East Asian Industrialization* (Princeton: Princeton University Press, 1990); and Haggard, *Pathways from the Periphery*.

[18] Robert Wade, "East Asian Financial Systems as a Challenge to Economics: Lessons from Taiwan," *California Management Review* 27, no. 4 (1985): 106–26.

[19] Colin I. Bradford, Jr., "NICs and the Next-Tier NICs as Transitional Economies," in *Trade and Structural Change in Pacific Asia*, ed. Colin I. Bradford, Jr., and William H. Branson (Chicago: University of Chicago Press, 1987).

[20] Amsden, *Asia's Next Giant*, pp. 143–44.

relative autonomy of the technocrats, and their commitment to a form of planning that was market-conforming.[21] Haggard emphasized the role of the state in solving collective action problems associated with economic policy reform, including through the exercise of authoritarian power.[22] Wade argued that the one-party state was crucial for Taiwan's development, and Amsden's study of Korea referred succinctly to the power of the state to "discipline" the private sector.[23]

(AUTHORIT-ARIAN POWER)

Proponents of what might be called the "institutional" approach to East Asian capitalism have not always been theoretically clear about why these distinctive government-business relationships are efficient. Yet the analytic tools for constructing such a defense are available in the literature on transactions costs and industrial organization.[24]

As Oliver Williamson has argued, markets are superseded by organizations when the latter are more efficient in carrying out economic transactions.[25] For example, because financial transactions are especially subject to moral hazard and costly contract enforcement, firms develop their own internal capital markets for the purpose of allocating financial resources; such internal capital markets are a crucial feature of the multidivisional structure of the large modern enterprise. With its capacity for strategic planning, monitoring, and control, the M-form structure can effectively reallocate cash flows among its subunits to high-yield uses.

Williamson suggests a number of reasons why such a hierarchical arrangement might be efficient.

(1) Hierarchy extends the bounds on rationality by permitting the specialization of decision making and economizing on communication expense. Direct channels of communication may be more efficient than reliance on parametric signaling that takes place in the market.
(2) Hierarchy reduces opportunism as it permits additional incentives and control techniques to be brought to bear in a more selective manner.
(3) Hierarchy reduces uncertainty by permitting interdependent units to adapt to unforeseen contingencies in a coordinated way.

---

[21] Chalmers Johnson extends the ideas he developed in *MITI and the Japanese Miracle* to the NICs in "Political Institutions and Economic Development: The Business-Government Relationship in Japan, South Korea, and Taiwan," in *The Political Economy of the New Asian Industrialism,* ed. Fred Deyo (Ithaca: Cornell University Press, 1987).

[22] Haggard, *Pathways from the Periphery,* chap. 2.

[23] Wade, *Governing the Market,* pp. 228–55; and Amsden, *Asia's Next Giant,* pp. 144–46.

[24] For a further elaboration of the arguments that follow, see Chung H. Lee, "The Government, Financial System, and Large Private Enterprises in the Economic Development of South Korea," *World Development* 20, no. 2 (1992): 187–97.

[25] The following draws on Oliver Williamson, *Markets and Hierarchies: Analysis and Antitrust Implications* (New York: Free Press, 1975) and *The Economic Institutions of Capitalism* (New York: Free Press, 1985).

(4) Hierarchy permits small-number bargaining indeterminacies to be resolved by fiat.

(5) Hierarchy improves information by extending the constitutional powers to perform an audit, thereby narrowing the information gap that obtains between government and business under conditions of parametric signaling.

(6) Hierarchy may provide opportunities for a less calculating or mistrustful atmosphere and thus allow for the convergence of objectives between various units.

Just because a hierarchical system of credit allocation *can* be efficient does not mean that it necessarily *is*. One reason why hierarchical systems of credit allocation within the firm are efficient is because the enterprise as a whole is subjected to competitive pressures from the markets in which it operates.

What is commonly called financial "repression" is, in effect, a hierarchical system of credit allocation. The government performs the role of the general office, and enterprises receiving credit perform the role of divisional subunits. In the East Asian NICs, government intervention with credit allocation was efficient precisely because these countries adopted relatively outward-oriented development strategies and were thus subjected to competitive pressures from the world markets. That is, "discipline" was ultimately provided by the market.

Yet it is plausible that features of the political system also matter in this regard; we focus here on two. The first is the political power and interests of those social groups who are likely *demandeurs* of preferential credit. As Haggard and Maxfield emphasize in the conclusion, the social base of support for interventionist policies varies across countries depending on the relative size, organization, and financial needs of the manufacturing sector. Although demand for subsidized credit was relatively weak in Thailand, it was extremely strong in Korea.

Yet the ability of rent-seeking groups to get their way depends crucially on the interests of politicians and the structure of government institutions. Three cases can be distinguished. In countries in which macroeconomic instability has constituted a serious political liability in the past, politicians may delegate macroeconomic policy to relatively insulated central banks and finance ministries, which, in turn, are less likely to intervene in financial markets. In cases where growth and the need to pay off specific clients are deemed more important, governments are, of course, more likely to use financial policy for political ends. The success of such intervention will then hinge on the cohesion and insulation of the industrial policy machinery. In Korea, government policy was pervasive, but the bureaucracy was generally strong and able to extract a quid pro quo from the private sector in the form of sustained high levels of investment. On the other hand, Paul D. Hutchcroft's analysis of the Philippines (Chapter Six) provides an example of the opposite extreme: a weak state which has been thoroughly penetrated by social forces and which as a result is unable to use credit policy to achieve broader social objectives.[26]

The Southern Cone Experiences

The experiences of the Southern Cone countries (Argentina, Chile, and Uruguay) with financial liberalization and internationalization played an important role in demonstrating that reduced government intervention does not in itself guarantee an efficient financial market.[27] The reasons for the failure of these experiments are numerous but can be divided into two broad categories: the macroeconomic and the microeconomic and regulatory.

Macroeconomic policy played a key role in undermining the Southern Cone experiments with financial liberalization. Fiscal, monetary, and wage policies resulted in an appreciation of the real exchange rate and high spreads between domestic and dollar-denominated assets; these effects on the exchange rate were only aggravated by the inflow of funds associated with an opening of the capital account. Appreciating real exchange rates further encouraged increased indebtedness and leverage in dollars but also contributed to severe financial crises when continued overvaluation became untenable. When massive devaluations occurred, the local-currency cost of debt service soared, firms failed, and the quality of bank portfolios declined precipitously. A consistent refrain in the literature on the Southern Cone experiences is that for financial liberalization to work, a country must have macroeconomic stability.[28]

As Maxfield emphasizes in her essay on Mexico (Chapter Eight), the political economy of macroeconomic policy and that of the govern-

---

[26] See Peter Evans, "The State as Problem and Solution: Predation, Embedded Autonomy, and Structural Change," in *The Politics of Economic Adjustment,* ed. Stephan Haggard and Robert Kaufman (Princeton: Princeton University Press, 1992).

[27] For overviews of the debate, see Vittorio Corbo and Jaime de Melo, "Liberalization with Stabilization in the Southern Cone of Latin America: Overview and Summary," *World Development* 13, no. 8 (1985): 863–66, and "Lessons from the Southern Cone Policy Reforms," *World Bank Research Observer* 2, no. 2 (1987): 111–42; Joseph Ramos, *Neoconservative Economics in the Southern Cone of Latin America* (Baltimore: Johns Hopkins University Press, 1986); and Alejandro Foxley, *Latin American Experiments in Neo-conservative Economics* (Berkeley: University of California Press, 1983).

[28] See, for example, Michael Dooley and Donald Mathieson, "Financial Liberalization in Developing Countries," *Finance and Development* 24, no. 3 (1987): 31–34.

13

ment's stance toward financial markets are closely linked.[29] Governments—including those of Thailand, Taiwan, and Mexico—with strong and conservative central banks for some of their history are also governments that tend to eschew the use of preferential credit programs. Governments placing an emphasis on growth over stability are likely to exhibit both a tendency toward expansionist macroeconomic policy and a reliance on preferential credit; Korea and Brazil both provide examples. The cases of Chile before 1973 (Chapter Seven) and Indonesia before 1966 (Chapter Five) demonstrate how "preferential" finance can emerge by default as controlled interest rates are not adjusted to inflation.

Yet high inflation also increases the opportunity costs of maintaining such programs, increases the differentials among different market segments, including the black market, and thus increases the countervailing political pressures on the government for policy adjustments. As Haggard and Maxfield argue in the conclusion, large-scale changes in financial market policies, such as those in Indonesia (1966–1970), Brazil (1964), and Chile (1974–1975) follow economic crises and are typically associated with stabilization programs. These programs, in turn, are often initiated following changes of government or even political regime. More gradual reform paths, such as those seen in Korea and Taiwan in the 1980s, are more typical in settings showing less macroeconomic as well as political volatility.

The Southern Cone countries, particularly Chile, raised a second issue that is germane to the political economy of financial markets: the nature of the regulatory environment. As Laura A. Hastings argues (Chapter Seven), Chile was typical of many developing countries in having an industrial structure in which large "groups" were integrated across financial and manufacturing activities. Financial liberalization, reduced barriers to entry, and privatization gave rise to a new generation of conglomerates heavily oriented toward financial activities. The freeing of interest rates led manufacturing firms within the groups to pressure affiliated banks to provide credit. In the short run, these funds went not to real investment but were used to bid up stock and real estate prices. Bank portfolios became increasingly concentrated in related clients, and when those companies failed, nonperforming assets accumulated. Ultimately, and ironically, the state had to step in once again, renationalizing companies and refinancing insolvent banks. This problem would not have arisen if adequate prudential regulation had been in place.[30]

---

[29] See, for example, Stephan Haggard and Robert Kaufman, "The Political Economy of Inflation and Stabilization in Middle-Income Countries," in Haggard and Kaufman, *Politics of Economic Adjustment.*

[30] Hugh T. Patrick, "The Financial Development of Taiwan, Korea, and Japan: A

One reason for the absence of adequate regulation is the weak capacity of the state; in low-income countries, in particular, the absence of an appropriate institutional infrastructure is a component of the larger syndrome of underdevelopment. Yet the largest regulatory failure in the cases examined took place not in Indonesia, the poorest country, but in Chile, which has a long tradition of competent civil service and bureaucratic strength. This suggests that it is not the *capacity* to regulate that is the most significant political variable but the *willingness* to do so. Clearly, a political economy perspective is required to understand why the Pinochet government pursued such a radically laissez-faire reform program, one that included but was by no means limited to financial market policy.

Industrial Organization and Financial Market Outcomes

The first round of debate on financial repression did not pay particular attention to financial market *institutions*. Several strands of recent literature have emphasized in different ways that industrial organization, including especially the degree of concentration of both industry and finance, is an important factor in determining the effects of liberalization.[31]

As we have already noted with reference to Chile, many developing countries are characterized by the existence of highly concentrated groups that are diversified across both industrial and financial activities.[32] If interest rates are liberalized in such a setting, banks within the group will aggressively seek funds in order to channel resources to group companies. In the absence of effective regulation, financial abuses and increased concentration of credit toward group firms can result.

Framework for Consideration of Issues," Paper presented at the Conference on Financial Development in Japan, Korea, and Taiwan, Institute of Economics, Academia Sinica, Taipei, August 27–28, 1990.

[31] An additional aspect of the industrial organization of finance that is not addressed extensively here concerns the existence and operation of informal credit markets. Neostructuralist critiques of orthodox stabilization policies have pointed out that the existence of such markets will have important consequences for liberalization efforts. See, for example, Michael Bruno, "Stabilization and Stagflation in a Semi-Industrialized Economy," in *International Economic Policy, Theory, and Evidence*, ed. Rudiger Dornbusch and Jacob Frenkel (Baltimore: Johns Hopkins University Press, 1979); Lance Taylor, *Structuralist Macroeconomics: Applicable Models for the Third World* (New York: Basic Books, 1983); and van Wijnbergen, "Stagflation Effects of Monetary Stabilization Policies," and "Credit Policy, Inflation, and Growth in a Financially Repressed Economy," *Journal of Development Economics* 13, no. 1 (1983): 45–65.

[32] Nathaniel H. Leff, "Capital Markets in the Less Developed Countries: The Group Principle," in *Money and Finance in Economic Growth and Development*, ed. Ronald I. McKinnon (New York: Dekker, 1976); and Vicente Galbis, "Financial Sector Liberalization under Oligopolistic Conditions and a Bank Holding Company Structure," *Savings and Development* 10, no. 2 (1986): 117–41.

Similar problems can arise where the financial sector itself is concentrated and is able either economically or politically to deter entry. In such settings, liberalization of rates can provide new opportunities for collusion and oligopolistic pricing. Even the opening of the capital account may not lead to a convergence of world and domestic interest rates if the financial sector is dominated by a small number of firms and if substantial market or policy barriers to entry remain.

A crucial theme that recurs throughout the case studies is that concentration has important consequences for the *political* dynamics of financial market policy as well. Concentration—whether within the financial sector, among favored borrowers, or as reflected in the group structure—clearly increases the power of the concentrated segment of the private sector vis-à-vis the government. This occurs not only because the small number of players eases collective action problems but also because of the capacity to blackmail the government, and the central bank in particular, during periods of distress. In Chapter Two, Byung-Sun Choi shows how the dependence of large groups, or *chaebol*, on government finance in Korea became a source of political strength in policy debates over interest rates, preferential credit schemes, and financial market policy more generally. In countries where banks face difficulties as a result of lax regulation, corruption, or past preferential credit policies, as was the case in the Philippines, they are well positioned to extract concessions from the central bank.

It can be argued that these problems of concentration are themselves the result of prior government intervention and that they could be solved by liberalization and reducing barriers to entry. But this assumes away the problem to be explained, that is, the political power of private sector actors to influence government policy in order to maintain privileged market positions.

III. AN OVERVIEW OF THE VOLUME

The case studies in this book examine the politics of finance in eight middle-income developing countries in East Asia and Latin America. The findings concerning the political economy of liberalization are discussed in more detail in the conclusion by Haggard and Maxfield. Here, we introduce the cases briefly by highlighting some of the main arguments about the political origins and efficiency of preferential credit programs.

We begin with Korea and Taiwan as they have been central to the debate over the role of the state in the success of the East Asian NICs. Choi shows that finance has been a crucial tool of government policy in Korea (Chapter Two). He concurs that it contributed to the country's rapid economic growth, but he points out that close business-government relations contributed to a highly concentrated industrial structure dominated by chaebol. This concentration ultimately gave the chaebol substantial leverage over financial market policy.

Tun-jen Cheng's analysis of Taiwan in Chapter Three presents an illuminating contrast. As in Korea, the Kuomintang (KMT) government controlled the financial system. It proved extremely cautious, however, in using finance as a tool of industrial policy. Cheng traces the difference to two features of Taiwan's economic and political development. The hyperinflation of the late 1940s—which contributed to the KMT's loss of the mainland—instilled in the leadership a strong aversion to inflation. This aversion had a crucial institutional correlate. In contrast to Korea, where finance was subordinated to industrial policy, financial market policy in Taiwan was placed under the control of a conservative central bank.

Yet the rationale for a cautious use of the financial instrument also had to do with the desire to restrain the emergence of big capital that could pose a challenge to the KMT's political monopoly. In Korea, the government used finance to forge close political links with big business; in Taiwan, the KMT sought to counter big business by favoring other social groups, including small and medium-sized firms and farmers. Both Choi and Cheng portray the state as relatively strong and cohesive, though Choi sees the strength of the Korean state eroding over time. Yet differences in the bases of social support resulted in different financial market outcomes. Not until the 1980s, as a result of both the costs of financial repression and international pressures, do financial market policies in the two countries once again converge around a cautious liberalization strategy.

The study by Richard Doner and Daniel Unger (Chapter Four) shows that like Taiwan, Thailand represents a case of a relatively low degree of intervention in financial markets. They emphasize both the demand and the supply sides of the policy equation. In contrast to Korea, Thailand lacked a strong manufacturing coalition that would constitute a demandeur for preferential credit. Although they have expanded significantly, manufacturing interests have generally been linked to commercial banking groups, which themselves remain tied to agroexport interests. Moreover, the very proliferation of business interests and the fragmented nature of the Thai political elite make preferential credit policies politically risky. Doner and Unger also emphasize the supply side of the political market, however. As in Taiwan, though for different historical reasons, a conservative central bank controls financial market policy. The central bank is characterized by a high degree of autonomy, cohesion, and prestige, and as a result, it has substantial power vis-à-vis the private sector, other state agencies, and parliamentary pressures.

Andrew MacIntyre's study of Indonesia (Chapter Five) also demonstrates how concerns about bases of political support and opposition can determine patterns of credit allocation. Unlike in Korea, where manufacturing interests were prominent, preferential credit in Indonesia favored the agricultural sector, particularly rice farmers. Though MacIntyre emphasizes that Suharto's New Order regime was relatively insulated from direct societal pressures, he interprets this pattern as a political strategy designed to demobilize a potentially volatile rural sector. Yet even with the apparent political strength of the Suharto regime, the state apparatus itself exhibits substantial differences from the cohesive economic policy-making machinery in Taiwan and Thailand. MacIntyre points out that technocratic actors have had influence despite disagreements among them but that preferential credit was ultimately not an effective policy tool because of substantial diversion to the political elite itself. These financial resources were, in turn, used to sustain patronage networks. MacIntyre concludes that financial market policy in Indonesia has been driven less by social demands or by a clear strategic vision carried by technocrats than by the patrimonial nature of the state itself.

The Philippines (Chapter Six) stands at the extreme of the Asian cases in terms of the incoherence of its economic policy in general and its policy toward finance in particular. Like MacIntyre, Hutchcroft attributes this to the weak and patrimonial nature of the Philippine state. Yet Indonesia and the Philippines also present several important contrasts. In Indonesia, the tendency toward patrimonialism was partly checked by some degree of delegation of decision-making authority to technocrats. Moreover, the Indonesian government had successfully "managed" any immediate social challengers to its political dominance. In the Philippines, Hutchcroft argues, such delegation did not take place, in large part because of the enduring power of the oligarchy. As Hutchcroft concludes, "The Philippine state is more often *plundered* than *plunderer*." Public policy was almost wholly captured by the interests of a narrow elite, thus resulting not only in abuses of public finances but in the private banking sector as well.

We begin the analysis of the Latin American cases with Hastings's study of Chile (Chapter Seven). At the time that preferential credit policies were first initiated in the interwar period, Chile showed striking similarities to the Philippines; policy was controlled by a relatively narrow oligarchy. These forces remained potent in the postwar period, though economic policy was also increasingly driven by shifting elec-

toral and coalition politics. The politicization of financial policy culminated in the socialist experiment of Salvador Allende, when state
controls over the financial system reached their peak.

The Pinochet regime initiated the most sweeping financial market
liberalization in any of the eight country cases. Some elements of the
new regime, such as the privatization of the banks and the opening of
the capital account, gained favor with large segments of the private
sector. Yet, as Hastings argues, the attempt to construct a sectoral story
is strained; one must see the reform episode in the light of the unusual
degree of political autonomy enjoyed by the Pinochet government,
including that from major segments of the private sector. This autonomy became evident when the banking system collapsed in the early
1980s and the government quickly moved to rein in the new financial
groups that emerged during the heyday of the liberal experiment.

Maxfield's study of Mexico (Chapter Eight) shows that financial policy
in that country exhibits broad swings between growing intervention
(1934–1954, 1970–1982) and periods during which the government
took a more liberal stance (1954–1970, 1982 to the present). She argues
that, in general, the demand for preferential credit from the private
sector is relatively weak because of the political strength of the financial
sector and the close integration of financial and industrial interests.
Since 1954, swings in policy have been related to international constraints and their effect on the power of different state actors. A major
balance-of-payments crisis in 1954 enhanced the strength and independence of the central bank, which favored credit controls but primarily for macroeconomic reasons. When lending constraints were
somewhat relieved in the 1970s, both by access to borrowing and as a
result of the oil boom, the president and spending agencies could use
credit policy for political and development ends. When balance-of-
payments constraints returned in the 1980s, however, conservative
forces once again gained strength, and the government began to retreat
from involvement in financial markets.

Leslie Elliott Armijo's study of Brazil (Chapter Nine) divides the
period from 1945 to 1991 into two subperiods. In the first period,
access to external financing, a comparatively strong state apparatus,
and a low degree of integration between banks and industrial firms
granted the government substantial leeway in formulating financial
market policy. Despite conflicts between "liberals" and "interventionists"
within the government, the latter tended to win. Armijo argues that
this was in part because of the sectoral pressures arising from past
patterns of intervention, but she gives greater weight to ideological
factors and the strong backing from the military for the interventionist
policy project. After 1980, however, this structural and ideological con-

figuration breaks down as a result of political liberalization, economic crisis, and, finally, democratization. These new pressures undermined the preexisting consensus on Brazil's economic model, though they did not succeed in creating consensus around a new one.

The conclusion by Haggard and Maxfield draws on theoretical literature in political economy to synthesize the project findings. They begin with a sectoral approach that focuses on the demand for preferential credit coming from the manufacturing sector; this goes some way in explaining variation across the country cases both in the extent of intervention and in the sectors receiving credit. Yet there are interesting anomalies. For example, the sharp differences between Korea and Taiwan can be explained only partly by differences in industrial structure. Chile presents even more grave challenges to a pure sectoral model, because as we have argued, liberalization efforts were launched over the objections of their previous beneficiaries.

Haggard and Maxfield contend that a sectoral argument must be coupled with an examination of the institutional characteristics of the state, including the power and political interests of the executive and the insulation of the policy-making apparatus. Politically insulated states are better able to control rent seeking, but unless insulation is accompanied by delegation to bureaucratic agencies, then "strong" states can exploit their power for the purpose of predation and patrimonialism.

Haggard and Maxfield argue that external economic and political constraints have influenced major changes in financial market policy, including the current trend toward liberalization. Yet despite the increasing pressures for liberalization, distinctive institutional and political arrangements continue to shape financial market policies in the developing world. They conclude by suggesting how these institutional patterns might influence policy advice. Liberalization may be an appropriate strategy where distortions are particularly large and institutions for formulating a coherent industrial policy strategy are weak. But these conditions do not hold across all developing countries, particularly middle-income countries, which suggests that there is continuing room for government to influence the allocation of financial resources as a component of a more comprehensive strategy for longer-term growth.

PART II

ASIA

Chapter Two

Financial Policy and Big Business in Korea: The Perils of Financial Regulation

Byung-Sun Choi

In the pursuit of economic development, the government's creation of economic rents for certain segments of business is of critical importance. It can be a source of a variety of evils, including political and bureaucratic corruption. But wisely used, the creation of rents can be a convenient and powerful policy instrument in eliciting business cooperation and support for government policies. Furthermore, it can increase capital formation in the country if it effects a redistribution of income from consumption to investment activities.

In Korea, regulated finance has represented the most important source of economic rents since the mid-1960s, thus enabling the government to utilize it as the most powerful industrial policy instrument.[1] In fact, it has been used as the fundamental tool with which Korean policymakers induced business cooperation and compliance in their efforts to promote exports and economic growth. Without it, the country may not have been able to carry out the rapid and continued industrial restructuring that has characterized its growth.

But the use of finance for the purpose of industrial development exacted a high price as well, turning finance into a highly politicized area. By having encouraged the growth of big business with subsidized credit as a shortcut to economic growth, the government has come to be increasingly influenced in its decision making by big business. This mutually dependent relationship between government and big

[1]On the political-economic characteristics of industrial adjustment in a country with the credit-based financial system, see John Zysman, *Governments, Markets, and Growth: Financial Systems and the Politics of Industrial Change* (Ithaca: Cornell University Press, 1983).

business is what Michael Barzelay calls "strategic interdependence."[2] Thus, the economic performance and international competitiveness of big business—the major beneficiary of cheap credit—have become factors that circumscribe the parameters of the government's financial policy.

Financial regulation has also created perverse incentives for business and financial institutions. The government's financial regulation has led big business to depend for too long on debt financing. This policy may have been a necessity in the early stages of Korea's economic development, and while the economy boomed, debt financing did not pose a major problem. But when it slowed, debt-ridden firms fell back on the government for relief. The government has had no choice but to respond favorably, even though the provision of financial relief has only nurtured continued dependence on debt.

Moreover, insofar as it is the government that has been ultimately responsible for credit allocation decisions, the problem of moral hazard on the part of the commercial banks has been serious. When banks accumulated nonperforming debts, the government could not help but rescue them. As a result, it has proved difficult for the government to break out of a vicious circle of financial regulation. As will be highlighted in this chapter, the "restructuring"—in effect, the bail out—episodes, which recurred in 1969–1970, 1972, 1979–1981, and 1986–1988, exemplify this cycle.

In addition to the vicious circle of financial regulation, vested business interests in the maintenance of cheap credit have put formidable obstacles in the way of financial liberalization. Although financial regulation began with the benign objective of overcoming imperfections of the capital market, debt-based industrial development has itself created an obstacle to financial liberalization as major beneficiaries of cheap loans have developed a vested interest in the low-interest regime. Since the early 1980s, commercial banks have been privatized and entry barriers to domestic and foreign banks have been lowered, but the underlying financial structure and the way in which business is conducted have remained very much unchanged.

This chapter analyzes the history of Korea's financial policy through the lens of government-business relations. Section I traces the government's involvement in the regulation and management of the financial system and examines the reasons for this involvement. In particular, I examine the close relationship between major political changes, such as the seizure of power by the military and the initiation of the *Yushin*

[2] Michael Barzelay, *The Politicized Market Economy: Alcohol in Brazil's Energy Strategy* (Berkeley: University of California Press, 1986), chap. 3.

(Revitalizing Reform) Constitution, and changes in the country's broad economic strategy and its financial market policy.

Section II, examines at the microlevel the relationship between business strategy and the pattern of preferential credit. The discussion shows how the development strategy of the government and the diversification strategies of the firms were closely linked through preferential credit policies. Control over finance appears to have provided the government with leverage over private sector decision making, whereas firms appear to have responded to government directives. But this relationship between the government and business changed in the 1970s, when large *chaebol* groups came to dominate the economy, effectively constraining the government's ability to make economic policy.

The final section examines the constraints on financial market liberalization. Financial crises and competitive pressures in the financial markets acted as a powerful spur to liberalization. Moreover, big business was largely favorable to the liberalization agenda. Yet the government was also bound by the legacies of past patterns of intervention, including the political power of the largest groups. The government was ultimately responsible for the highly leveraged and ultimately weak financial position of a number of major firms; moreover, this weakness was reflected in the deteriorating condition of bank balance sheets. As a result, despite its preferences, the government found it extremely difficult to extricate itself fully from intervention in the credit markets, and its liberalization drive proved to be only partial.

I. Origins of Financial Regulation

The Financial System before 1961

A modern financial system came into existence in Korea during Japanese colonial rule (1910–1945). With independence, the Japanese-owned banks were turned over to the government. But major restructuring of the financial system was undertaken only in 1950, based on a financial reform plan prepared by American advisers. Reflecting the prevailing notion that the central bank should be independent, the plan envisioned a highly liberal financial system in Korea.[3] But its implementation was stalled with the outbreak of the Korean War. During the war, as the Ministry of Finance (MOF) took over monetary policy, the autonomy and independence of the Bank of Korea (BOK) were severely compromised. Initially, commercial banks were to be privatized, but they fell subject to tight government control as well.

[3] A. I. Bloomfield and J. P. Jensen, *Banking Reform in South Korea* (New York: Federal Reserve Bank, 1951).

25

After the war, the government further strengthened its control over the financial system in support of reconstruction efforts. The government established long-term development banks, such as the Korea Development Bank (KDB) and the Korea Agriculture Bank. But these specialized banks depended heavily on the BOK for resources, and their lending policies were dictated by the government.[4] The government privatized four commercial banks. Major chaebol groups acquired the controlling shares of the commercial banks and monopolized bank loans.[5] The loan decisions of the commercial banks were also heavily influenced by political interference by the Syngman Rhee government, which used rents generated by low-interest loans to finance its political activities.

Throughout the 1948–1961 period, the government pursued an import-substituting industrialization policy. The government tried to channel financial resources to selected industrial sectors through a rediscount policy and a system of prior loan approval. The major beneficiaries were such industrial sectors as textiles, chemical products, food, machinery, and metal products. To take advantage of reconstruction-related foreign aid, which was a major source of funds for both the government budget and bank lending programs, the government assured importers of financing at low interest rates. Given the severe foreign exchange shortage in this period, this import financing represented a great boon to already privileged importers, which were mostly large firms with strong political connections.

Major Financial Restructuring in the Early 1960s

The military coup of 1961 toppled the democratic government that had been established following the Student Revolution in the previous year. The Park Chung Hee government set economic development as the top national priority and reorganized the financial system in support of economic development plans. It nationalized commercial banks by repossessing the shares held by large stockholders, which were mostly big business owners who had been accused of illicit wealth accumulation in the aftermath of the Student Revolution. Instead of punishing the

---

[4] These specialized banks' share of credit increased rapidly. By the end of 1955, the KDB's share alone accounted for over 40 percent of total bank lending. David C. Cole and Yung Chul Park, *Financial Development in Korea, 1945–1978* (Cambridge: Harvard University Press, 1983), p. 52.

[5] In response to public concern about economic concentration by chaebol, the government placed restrictions on the upper limit of ownership and transfer of bank shares among large shareholders. But these restrictions rendered futile all six successively held auctions in 1956. Only after those restrictions were significantly relaxed was the privatization move completed in 1957.

accused leading businessmen as criminals or appropriating their illicit wealth outright, Park took this opportunity to elicit their support for and active participation in the government's newly drafted economic development plan. The accused business leaders gave up their equity shares in the banks to the government but received promises of financing.

Moreover, by amending the Bank of Korea Act in May 1962, Park made it clear that it was the government, not the central bank, that was ultimately responsible for monetary and financial policy.[6] As a result, the BOK was relegated to the status of a virtual rubber stamp for MOF decisions and served as a ready source of government debt financing when necessary.[7]

In addition, in 1962 the government set up a number of specialized banks including the Central Federation of Agricultural Cooperatives, the Medium Industry Bank (MIB), the Citizens' National Bank, and the Central Federation of Fisheries Cooperatives. The establishment of the first two banks reflected the military government's coalitional politics aimed at bringing farmers and businessmen of medium-sized and small firms, who had both been left outside the banking institutions that were monopolized by big business in the 1950s, into the new coalition.[8]

But the most notable change in this period was the authorization of the KDB to borrow funds from abroad and guarantee foreign commercial loans. This authorization represented the military government's willingness to rely on foreign capital as a major source of financing for economic development, particularly given the fact that the level of foreign aid continued to decline.[9] The military leaders clearly understood the implications of changing U.S. foreign aid policy.[10] It was under these circumstances that the Korean government

---

[6] On the controversies since 1957 over the constitutionality of the Bank of Korea Act, see Byong Kuk Kim, *Central Banking Experiment in a Developing Economy*, Korean Studies Series, vol. 12 (Seoul: Korean Research Center, 1965), pp. 77–90.

[7] During the 1950–1962 period, a maximum of 97 percent and a minimum of 86 percent of total financing of government debt consisted of borrowing from the BOK. Byong Kuk Kim, *Central Banking Experiment*, p. 105 (table 6–1).

[8] Tun-jen Cheng, "Political Regimes and Development Strategies: South Korea and Taiwan," in *Manufacturing Miracles: Paths of Industrialization in Latin America and East Asia*, ed. Gary Gereffi and Donald L. Wyman (Princeton: Princeton University Press, 1990), pp. 153–61.

[9] From 1958 on, the amount of foreign aid began to decline sharply. In 1959, foreign aid amounted to $222.2 million, in 1961 it was $207 million, and in 1965 it was $134 million. See Anne O. Krueger, *The Developmental Role of the Foreign Sector and Aid* (Cambridge: Harvard University Press, 1979).

[10] For background material on the change in the U.S. commitment, see David C. Cole and Princeton N. Lyman, *Korean Development: The Interplay of Politics and Economics* (Cambridge: Harvard University Press, 1971), p. 90.

promulgated the Law of Guaranteeing Foreign Loans in July 1962. The government granted tax concessions for foreign borrowing and sent an economic mission abroad to attempt to secure financing for major projects included in the Five-Year Plan. The government also sped up the "normalization" of Korea-Japan relations, despite strong national political protest against it, because Japan was the most promising source of foreign capital and technology at the time.[11]

The government policymakers' turn toward foreign loans changed the role of Korean banks and the attitude of business greatly. Domestic banks became facilitators and guarantors of external finance, but they did not actually intermediate between foreign lenders and domestic borrowers; foreign loan negotiations were managed by the Economic Planning Board (EPB). The banks basically issued the guarantees on instruction from the government and took little responsibility for evaluating either the economic or the financial feasibility of the projects for which guarantees were extended. As a result, the banks had little basis for being held responsible for bad loans.

Big business turned to foreign borrowing as a new, rich ground for economic rent seeking. By the early 1960s, as foreign aid declined and the multiple exchange rate system was abolished, the two traditional grounds of rent seeking—preferential foreign exchange allocation and import licensing—had given way to domestic and foreign credit.[12] It was for this reason that foreign borrowing was so often embroiled with political and bureaucratic corruption; during the 1960s, a number of financial scandals erupted that involved kickbacks to the government from foreign loans.

Interest Rate Reform and the Boom and Bust of Foreign Borrowing, 1965–1971

The interest rate reform of September 1965 doubled the annual time deposit rate from 14 to 30 percent and created a "negative spread" between the commercial banks' low lending rates and high deposit rates. This reform marked a watershed in the history of financial policy in Korea. It brought forth a nearly sevenfold increase in total bank deposits over the four years from 1965 through 1969. In addition, the financial reform contributed to a massive inflow of foreign loans that were guaranteed by the KDB and commercial banks.[13] The outstanding

[11] For a detailed description of Korea-Japan talks and their political repercussions, see Cole and Lyman, *Korean Development*, pp. 98–118.

[12] Leroy P. Jones and Il Sakong, *Government, Business, and Entrepreneurship in Economic Development: The Korean Case* (Cambridge: Harvard University Press, 1980), p. 273.

[13] Total foreign loan guarantees almost doubled in 1966 and were nearly equal to total

balance of foreign loans increased tenfold from $210 million in 1965 to $2,250 million in 1970. The gap between international and domestic interest rates, which could equal as much as 20 percentage points per year, prompted private investors to rush for foreign capital as a new and profitable source of financing.[14] Moreover, the upsurge of foreign borrowing entailed a corresponding demand for domestic credit as operating capital; the government responded to this surge by allowing foreign cash loans for this purpose.

Finally, the interest rate reform turned foreign borrowing into a new policy instrument at the disposal of the government.[15] Of course, economic development based on foreign borrowing created monetary policy problems. But thanks to high interest rates, the additional money supply created by the increase in foreign exchange reserves could be successfully sterilized. The government could absorb the excess money supply in the form of time deposits and, at the same time, turn them into domestic credit.[16]

While foreign borrowing boomed, private sector investment grew rapidly. The gross investment ratio rose from 15 percent of GNP in 1965 to 28.8 percent in 1969. But the economic boom triggered by foreign borrowing did not last for very long. From around 1969, foreign loan repayments began to rise rapidly. The increase in foreign exchange reserves almost stopped, and large firms dependent on foreign loans began to run into severe financial difficulties.

The economic stabilization policies that the government adopted under International Monetary Fund (IMF) surveillance in the wake of the 1969 presidential and general elections pushed many business firms, both large and small, to the brink of bankruptcy. Under these circumstances, the government undertook in 1969 a restructuring of those firms dependent on foreign loans. Among eighty-six firms that borrowed heavily from abroad, thirty were subject to the restructuring plan. The "restructuring" was in effect a bailout. The government directed the concerned banks to turn bad loans into equity or reschedule them and to provide the additional new loans needed to meet repayments.

---

outstanding domestic bank loans. From 1968 on, commercial banks assumed a significant role in the guaranteeing activity. Cole and Park, *Financial Development in Korea*, p. 62 (table 12).

[14] Soon Chough, *Han'guk Kyongjeui Hyonshilgwa Chinro* [The realities and the future course of Korean economy] (Seoul: Bibong Press, 1981), p. 194.

[15] L. Harris, "Financial Reform and Economic Growth: A New Interpretation of South Korea's Experience," in *New Perspectives on the Financial System*, ed. L. Harris et al. (London: Croom Helm, 1988).

[16] Kyu Dong Lee, *Kyongjenonliwa Choch'aekpungto* [Economic logic and policy practices] (Seoul: Chongusa, 1982), pp. 61–63.

*The August 3, 1972, Emergency Decree and Heavy Industrialization,
1972–1979*

Despite the bailout, the financial distress of large firms persisted.[17]
The 18 percent devaluation in 1971 dealt a severe blow to firms that had
borrowed heavily from abroad. In these circumstances, many large
firms began to turn to the unregulated money markets.[18] At that time,
major private moneylenders had the power to drive even large chaebol
firms to bankruptcy by turning in commercial bills they held to the
banks. Rumors circulated about the bankruptcy of certain large firms,
which threatened a chain of bankruptcies of smaller firms dependent on
them.

The Federation of Korean Industries (FKI), an association of influential business leaders in Korea, held daily meetings to avoid this outcome. They pleaded with the government for the conversion of short-
term curb market loans into long-term bank loans, a reduction of the
corporate tax burden, and a lowering of interest rates. After private
and public talks with leading businessmen, President Park came to the
conclusion that ordinary policy measures alone would not suffice in
cushioning the financial burden of debt-ridden firms and curbing the
expansion of the private money markets. He thus ordered the presidential economic staff to prepare clandestinely a set of emergency
measures.[19] The measures, announced as the Presidential Emergency
Decree for Economic Stability and Growth of August 3, 1972, was
historical. It placed a moratorium on all private loans incurred by
firms.[20] Loans exceeding three million won were rescheduled for repayment over five years after a three-year grace period at below the
current interest rate. Curb loan lenders had the option to switch their
loans into equity shares. Loans made by large stockholders or executives
to their firms were converted mandatorily into stocks. Short-term bank
loans held by business firms were replaced by long-term loans at an 8

[17] The ratio of net equity to total assets of manufacturing firms rose from 51.6 percent
in 1965 to 24.2 percent in 1972. To put it differently, the debt/equity ratio rose from
83.7 percent in 1965 to 313.4 percent in 1972. See the BOK, *Financial Statements Analysis*
(Seoul: BOK, 1978).

[18] Cole and Park, *Financial Development in Korea,* p. 160.

[19] For a detailed description of the background of the August 3, 1972, emergency
measures, see Chungryum Kim, *Han'guk Kyongjechongch'aek Samsipnyunsa: Hoegorok*
[Thirty-year history of Korea's economic policy: Recollections] (Seoul: Chungan Ky-
ongjeshinmunsa, 1990), pp. 255–69.

[20] The total amount of curb market loans reported in a one-week period amounted to
345.6 billion won, which was equivalent to 80 percent of the money supply and 34 percent
of the outstanding domestic credit held by the banking sector. See MOF, *Chaejong Ku-
myung Samsipnyonsa* [Thirty-year history of fiscal and monetary policy] (Seoul: MOF,
1978), p. 155.

percent annual interest rate. Needless to say, the measure relieved all firms, large and small, of financial difficulties in one fell swoop.

With a view to justifying the extraordinary measure that went against the interests not only of private moneylenders and savers at large, however, the government also began to put pressure on large firms to go public through a newly enacted Corporation Disclosure Promotion Law. But the underdeveloped capital market, which had been plagued by stock price manipulation by large shareholders, and the reluctance on the part of big businesses frustrated this policy initiative.[21]

Also in an effort to bring the unregulated money markets under control by creating new financial intermediaries, the MOF enacted the Short-Term Financing Business Act of 1972 and began to encourage the establishment of a variety of nonbank financial intermediaries (NBFIs), including investment and finance companies, mutual savings firms, and general finance companies. The greater freedom in managing their financial resources provided the NBFIs with a competitive edge vis-à-vis the banking institutions. Permitted to offer higher deposit interest rates, they could expand their market share rapidly.[22] As institutional investors and underwriters, they also played an important role in the stock market. For these reasons, many major chaebol came to acquire controlling shares of NBFIs by the late 1970s.

As David C. Cole and Yung Chul Park note, the August 3 emergency decree was "significant in that it marked the end of the partial financial liberalization policy the government had initiated with the reforms in 1965 and a complete return to the financial repression of previous years."[23] But, even more significant, the decree firmly set the precedent that the government would take extraordinary measures to relieve the financial burden of firms at the expense of banks and the public at large.

In any case, the emergency decree helped pave the way for the government's heavy and chemical industrialization drive in the 1970s, the success of which hinged so much on the availability of cheap long-term capital. Indeed, as the heavy and chemical industrialization drive began, the government felt the need to strengthen further its control over banks. It thus established more specialized state-run banks and ear-

[21] The number of firms that went public remained at 42 until 1969. In view of the recalcitrance on the part of big business, President Park issued a special directive in May 1974 to urge them to go public. Only after that time did the number of disclosed firms rise significantly, reaching 128 in 1974 and 355 in 1979.

[22] Their share of total deposits rose from about 14.3 percent in 1974 to 23.9 percent in 1979 and 42.4 percent in 1984, thus shrinking the share of the banking sector. See Yoon Je Cho and David C. Cole, "The Role of the Financial Sector in Korea's Structural Adjustment," Development Discussion Paper no. 230, Harvard Institute for International Development, May 1985, pp. 9–11.

[23] Cole and Park, *Financial Development in Korea*, p. 159.

marked a portion of commercial bank funds as "policy loans" that were channeled toward key heavy industry sectors. Policy loans proliferated in the 1970s, limiting the discretion of the banks' asset management. Increased financial segmentation and discretionary credit allocation was not confined to domestic financial resources either. Continued foreign borrowing and further constrained the allocation of domestic credit, for the government was compelled to supply adequate working capital for the successful operation of the projects financed by foreign loans.

With this selective and discretionary credit allocation system, the government could channel greater financial resources toward "strategic" heavy and chemical industries. The high rate of economic and export growth and the significant deepening of the industrial structure and the composition of exports in the 1970s can be traced to this policy of selective credit allocation. But the ever greater control of the financial system produced devastating results by the late 1970s. During the 1970s, the financial structure of the chaebol grew weaker as they spread their capital over a wider range of industrial activities, in part as a result of rivalry among chaebol groups for government financing. These groups faced severe difficulties during the recession of the early 1980s that followed the second oil price increase and the downturn in major export markets. The political vacuum and turmoil created by the assassination of President Park in October 1979 made the prospects for heavy industrialization even more bleak and uncertain. The chaebol could not even secure capital to meet their operating and foreign loan repayment needs. Banks, which had already begun to accumulate a stock of nonperforming debts, were not in a position to respond effectively to the chaebol demands.[24] In this situation, the new government in the early 1980s made another round of massive industrial-restructuring attempts. Before discussing these new attempts, however, it will be helpful to analyze the politics of preferential credit in the 1960s and the 1970s in greater detail.

II. THE POLITICS OF PREFERENTIAL CREDIT

The politics of preferential credit has changed over time in Korea as the relationship between government and business has shifted from the supremacy of the state over business to a strategic interdependence between the two. From 1961 through the mid-1970s, the government

---

[24] As of 1984, nonperforming debts accounted for 9 percent of total credit outstanding by five commercial banks, reaching 1.65 times their equity. See Joong Woong Kim, "Sanopbaljongwa chongch'aekkumyung" [Industrial development and policy loans], in *Korea Development Research* (Spring 1986), p. 58.

retained substantial power over business, reflected in part by the government's control over credit allocation. Credit was channeled in part to ongoing import-substituting activities but primarily to exporters on an automatic approval basis; this nondiscretionary approach in and of itself reduced the weight of political factors in credit allocation. Beginning in the early 1970s with the institution of the heavy industrialization policy, the government allocated preferential credit to large manufacturing firms. Not only did the heavy industrialization drive favor large-scale, capital-intensive sectors and projects, but the government also began to discriminate among exporters on the basis of size. Larger general trading companies that were tied to major chaebol received favored access to credit. This policy led to further expansion of larger firms, which, in turn, increased their power. This then altered the politics of preferential credit. This section analyzes the interaction between export and industrialization policies on the one hand and the politics of credit allocation on the other.

Export Promotion and Export Financing

The shift in the trade and industrialization regime from import substitution to export promotion in the mid-1960s brought a major change in Korea's credit allocation policy. The system of short-term export financing was streamlined in February 1960 into its modern form and remained effective until 1972.[25] The heart of the system was the automatic approval of loans by commercial banks to those who had received export letters of credit (L/C).

Initially, the program covered the costs of production or domestic purchase of export goods. But its coverage expanded rapidly over time to cover sales to the UN forces in Korea in 1961; exports on a D/P (documents against payment), D/A (documents against acceptance), or consignment basis in 1965; construction services rendered to foreign governments or their agencies in 1967; imports of raw materials and intermediate goods for export use or purchase from local suppliers in 1967; costs involved in the preparation of agricultural and fisheries products in 1969; and so on. Each of these export-financing schemes was operated according to its respective regulations until they were unified into a Regulation on Export Financing in 1972. A new "export-financing ceiling system" was also adopted in 1976 to provide financing on the basis of past export performances for a certain period of time.

[25] For more detail on export-financing systems before 1961, see Wontack Hong, *Trade, Distortions, and Employment Growth* (Seoul: Korea Development Institute, 1979), pp. 117–18; and the MOF, *Han'gukui Kumyungjongch'aek* [Financial policy in Korea] (Seoul: MOF, 1979), pp. 212–15.

Under this system, exporters (or producers) eligible to apply for this type of export financing were restricted to those whose past year's exports exceeded $30 million as of 1979; thus, the system favored established exporters.

This expansion of coverage exemplified the government's high responsiveness to the changing demands of exporters. Exploration of new export opportunities and diversification of export products and services were immediately rewarded in this fashion. Probably the most important conduit through which changing demands of exporters were communicated to the central policymakers was the Monthly Expanded Meetings for Export (later Trade) Promotion, in which the president and all economic cabinet members participated and to which leading businesspeople were regularly invited. The meeting was prepared by the Ministry of Commerce and Industry (MCI), the ministry most attentive to the interests of exporters and of business in general.

These short-term loans were granted at preferential interest rates that declined over time. Commercial banks could obtain rediscounts from the BOK. The automatic short-term export financing thus constituted a major source of the rapid growth of money supply, as export volume increased rapidly over time. When inflationary pressures mounted and the government was forced to restrict the money supply, it was the nonexport sectors that had to bear the brunt of monetary restraint.

In addition to short-term loans, export producers have been granted various kinds of preferential long-term foreign and domestic loans both for capital investments and for operations. Unlike in short-term export financing, long-term facility loans were not provided automatically but had to be approved by specialized banks (such as the KDB and the MIB) and commercial banks. Usually, the MCI was involved in the process. The MCI almost always retained the right to examine the appropriateness of loan applications and to issue recommendations to the banks concerned. When foreign loan guarantees were involved, the EPB stepped into the loan allocation process. Sometimes, a committee consisting of officials from related ministries was established, as was the case for the export industry equipment loans introduced in 1973. In most of these cases, the MCI has specified the industrial sectors eligible to receive such loans.

Heavy Industrialization and Selective Credit Allocation

The heavy and chemical industrialization drive in the 1970s once again brought a significant change in the government-business relationship and in the politics of credit allocation. The push toward heavy industrialization represented Park's resolve to develop a defense industry as a reaction to the dwindling U.S. military commitment to Korea, to respond to protectionism in the world trading system, and to sustain the high economic growth momentum built in the previous decade. But the more direct impetus for heavy industrialization in Korea was political. President Park Chung Hee, who had barely won the 1971 presidential election, proclaimed martial law in October 1972, banned political activity, closed the universities temporarily, and imposed press censorship. Under the pretext of meeting the growing military threat from North Korea, the U.S. plan to withdraw its ground forces, and the deteriorating world trading environment, he undertook a constitutional reform.

The new Yushin Constitution was meant to strengthen Park's authoritarian rule of the country. In the face of strong opposition, Park justified the illegitimate constitutional change at a press conference in January 1973 by presenting a bold vision of "$10 billion worth of exports and a $1,000 per capita income by the early 1980s" as a midterm goal of the Yushin regime.[26] At the same time, he proclaimed that the government would direct all energies to the development of heavy and chemical industries in an effort to achieve those goals.

The task of mobilizing and channeling massive financial resources toward heavy industrial sectors called for strong political intervention in the traditional technocratic economic policy-making structure of Korea.[27] To spearhead the heavy industrialization drive, President Park created in May 1973 the Heavy and Chemical Industry Promotion Committee and the Planning Council as its standing committee. Based on the President's strong mandate and direct involvement, the Planning Council became the new center of economic decision making concerning heavy industrialization policies. New development plans and investment projects were jointly initiated by private firms, concerned ministries (in most cases, the MCI), and the Planning Council. Economic decision making was short-circuited through the council and the second economic secretary directly to the president, frequently bypassing the EPB and the prime minister's office.

As a result, the EPB's formal authority to coordinate economic policy decisions related to heavy industries diminished. The EPB tried to check this trend by subjecting investment projects and proposals to

[26] Per capita GNP and exports in 1972 were $295 billion and $16.2 billion, respectively, in current prices.

[27] For a detailed analysis of the changes in the economic policy-making structure, see Byung-Sun Choi, "Institutionalizing Liberal Economic Order: The Strategic Management of Economic Change," Ph.D. diss., Harvard University, June 1987, chap. 3.

strict feasibility studies. But President Park's personal sanction of major investment projects and his selection of private businesspeople who would undertake them frustrated the EPB's efforts. The EPB and the MOF's plan to coordinate allocation of investment resources had to be revised almost constantly, though it was already based on increasingly opaque guidelines.

One of the strategic components of the heavy and chemical industry development plan was industrial targeting. Iron and steel, machinery, nonferrous metals, electronics, shipbuilding, and petrochemical industries were selected as "strategic industries." The promotion of basic industries such as steel and petrochemicals was required for developing the defense industry and ensuring a more stable supply of these key materials. Defense industry–related interests prevailed in selecting nonferrous metals industries (such as aluminum, copper, zinc, and lead), which are highly import-dependent and energy-intensive. The selection of the electronic and shipbuilding industries was motivated by another strategic consideration, namely, that these relatively labor-intensive industries could gain competitiveness within a short period of time.

Because of the high market risks and uncertainties involved in making huge investments in technologically unfamiliar lines of business, however, even the major chaebol groups were unwilling and reluctant to participate in the state-led heavy industrialization drive. To induce the chaebol to invest actively in these sectors, therefore, the government needed to turn them into "privileged sectors." In other words, the government needed to assure the private sector that once they committed resources, the government would support them by all means.

In short, President Park's extraordinary commitment to heavy industrialization and his apparent control over actual investment decisions were meant to reduce the "strategic uncertainty" involved in heavy industry investments. As long as private investors acquiesced to the political leadership's vision of the desired politico-economic order, they could secure the resources and support necessary to make otherwise highly risky business undertakings profitable.[28] In this way, the government and private investors forged a "strategic interdependence" in the sense that private investors could now reasonably expect that they could influence the government's economic policy-making.

The primary source of heavy industries' long-term investment capital was the KDB. It provided long-term loans, underwrote corporate bonds and stocks, and guaranteed foreign loans. The KDB's share of total

---

[28] For a differentiation between market uncertainty and strategic uncertainty and the use of these concepts in analyzing private investors' decision making, see Barzelay, *Politicized Market Economy*, chap. 3.

Table 2.1. Share of heavy and chemical industries in total manufacturing measured by various indicators (percent), 1976–1978

Share	1976	1977	1978
Of value added	46.8	48.5	48.8
Of output	49.5	50.4	51.4
Of bank credit	54.2	56.4	59.5
(deposit money banks and Korea Development Bank)			
Investment	74.2	75.4	82.5
Share of policy loans in total bank loans	56.6	55.7	68.7

Source: Sang-woo Nam, "Korea's Stabilization Efforts since the Late 1970s," Korea Development Institute Working Paper 84-05, March 1984, p. 10.

equipment investment lending, which had declined since the mid-1960s, rose from 40.3 percent in 1972 to 44.7 percent in 1975 and 49.6 percent in 1979.[29] Another new financial institution was the Export-Import Bank of Korea, which provided medium- and long-term financing for domestic exporters and foreign importers of Korea's heavy industry goods and underwrote export insurance for domestic corporations and financial institutions.

To finance huge capital investments, the government further tightened its control over the financial system. The easiest and surest way to channel funds to specific sectors was to earmark a portion of all commercial bank lending as "policy loans" through the creation of a National Investment Fund. By 1980, there were more than thirty different sector-specific loan funds, including export financing, and raw material import financing as well as funds for the defense industry, regional industry promotion, medium- and small-scale enterprises, and equipment investment in export industries.

Such expansion of preferential policy loans resulted in a sharp increase in their share of total bank credit from less than 40 percent in 1971 to 68.7 percent in 1978.[30] Thanks to preferential policy loans, more than 77 percent of total manufacturing investment during 1976–1978 was undertaken in the heavy and chemical industries, which accounted for only about 50 percent of total manufacturing output (Table 2.1). As of the end of 1978, the outstanding balance of various policy loans for the heavy and chemical industries constituted 92.8 percent of total loans to the manufacturing sector.[31]

In addition to domestic credit, the government guaranteed foreign

[29] KDB, *Han'guksanopunhaeng Samsipnyonsa* [Thirty-year history of the Korea Development Bank] (Seoul: KDB, 1984), p. 850.

[30] Sang-woo Nam, "Korea's Stabilization Efforts since the Late 1970s," Korea Development Institute Working Paper 84–05, March 1984, p. 8.

[31] Soogil Young, "Sanopjongch'aekui Kibongwajewa Chiwonshich'aekui Kaepyonbangan" [Basic issues of industrial policy and a scheme for rearranging assistance system], Korea Development Institute Research Report 82–09, December 1982, p. 48.

loans in these privileged sectors. From 1973 to 1979, the EPB channeled toward the heavy and chemical industries $3.8 billion (of which $172.5 million was in public loans), which is equivalent to 32 percent of total foreign loans, whose payments were guaranteed by the KDB and other banking institutions. From 1977 onward, the trend accelerated, with these industries accounting for more than 80 percent of total foreign loans and for all public foreign loans in the manufacturing sector. This left less than 20 percent of total foreign lending for light industries.

Financial Policy and the Chaebol's Growth Strategies

Of course, it is not easy to specify which side—the government or big business—actually controlled Korea's credit allocation policy because their interactions have been so closely intertwined. Some initiatives, such as the initial export push and the move into heavy and chemical industries, no doubt came from the government, which, compared with other governments in this volume, had a relatively sophisticated planning capability. Yet, it is clear that big business and the chaebol stood to benefit heavily from the credit allocation system.[32] In particular, as the chaebol and big business grew in size and economic weight, their direct and indirect influence on the government's credit allocation policy grew; this is evidenced by the major changes in the government's credit policies, which matched closely with the diversification strategies of chaebol.

For example, the government has since 1975 designated certain firms as general trading companies, which are all owned by the largest chaebol. The establishment of general trading companies had several policy objectives: (1) strengthening overseas marketing capabilities, (2) seeking economies of scale, and (3) acting as agents for medium- and small-scale producers. The government granted these general trading companies preferential treatment in international bidding, loosened restrictions on their importation of raw materials, and provided funds for the stockpiling of finished export goods.

Moreover, the government's use of past export performance as a criterion for the renewal of status as a general trading company, led chaebol to rely heavily on and actively seek merger and acquisitions of

[32] The bank loans provided to the thirty largest chaebol groups (676 firms) amounted to 19,704 billion won, or 26.9 percent of the total, in 1988. This figure compares with their share in 1985 of manufacturing sales of 40.2 percent; manufacturing exports, 41.3 percent; and manufacturing employment, 17.6 percent. *Dong-A Ilbo*, September 3, 1988. On the other hand, the ratio of bank credit (except loan guarantees) to total assets of the thirty largest chaebol groups reached 22.3 percent on average, ranging from 45.6 percent of Hanil Synthetic Fiber to 7 percent of Lotte. For more details, see *Maeil Kyungje Shinmun*, July 19, 1988.

medium- and small-scale enterprises in broad lines of business. As a result, the number of medium- and small-scale firms merged or acquired by the ten general trading houses increased from 96 in 1976 to 208 in 1979.[33] The same corporate growth strategy was repeated in the overseas construction industry, another major recipient of preferential credit in the late 1970s and early 1980s. It is noteworthy that the vigorous pursuit of mergers and acquisitions of medium- and small-scale enterprises has usually been made in new industries to exploit the changing emphasis of the government's credit allocation policy.

The close match between the changes in the government's industrial policy emphasis and the diversification strategies of chaebol may be a strong indication that the government actively created market pressures that would compel big businesses to adjust to changing economic conditions. By controlling the allocation of credit, the government could support new growth sectors. Insofar as they have represented the cutting edge of structural change, chaebol enjoyed an ever greater reservoir of preferential credit.

In controlling the allocation of credit to facilitate industrial adjustment, the government, for political reasons, has not overtly withheld preferential credit from sectors such as agriculture and textile, that had been favored in the past; the objective of shifting the emphasis of credit policy has been achieved in a more subtle way. Even in periods of stabilization, chaebol would suffer little from the credit crunch because they had already diversified lines of business and credit allocation was made by sector, not by enterprise. Thus, some lines of business belonging to chaebol would always benefit from special treatment. One result, however, was that the number of industries that received preferential credit continued to grow, and the structure of Korea's preferential credit system became increasingly complicated over time. This fragmented and extremely complicated structure of preferential credit may have encouraged credit diversion into untargeted activities such as real estate.[34]

The corollary of this argument is that other enterprises engaged in only a single line of business would bear the brunt of the credit crunch if that line happened to be the one dropped from the list for policy loans. Although the commercial banks have been required to make available a minimum of 30 percent of their total loans to small- and medium-scale enterprises to offset these biases, banks have tended to ignore this regulation. Neither has the government ever punished the commercial banks for their noncompliance. Furthermore, as they were

[33] Dong-Sung Cho, *Han'gukui Chaebol Yongu* [A study of chaebol in Korea] (Seoul: Maeil Kyungje Shinmunsa, 1990), pp. 194–97.
[34] Joong Woong Kim, "Sanopbaljongwa," p. 58.

39

granted almost automatically, policy loans severely constrained the central bank's capacity to control liquidity and thus contributed to inflationary pressures.

Chaebol's active participation in the financial industry has also enhanced their privileged position in the preferential financial system. Because they have been allowed to acquire controlling shares of nonbank financial intermediaries since the 1970s and because they could increase their equity holdings in commercial banks directly and indirectly after their privatization in the 1980s, they could not only borrow much of their working capital from the NBFIs but they could also influence the decision making of the commercial banks. Moreover, they utilized idle funds through the NBFIs under their control.

III. THE POLITICS OF FINANCIAL MARKET LIBERALIZATION

The policy legacies of the heavy industrialization drive in the 1970s were immense. In particular, the excessive and duplicative investments made by chaebol in major heavy industry sectors were problematic. Heavy industry plants exhibited surplus capacity owing to insufficient demand in Korea and in export markets; many other large investment projects had long lead times and required additional capital for loan repayment and operational purposes. But banks were not in a position to respond to these demands, which entailed high risks.

Two Restructuring Episodes Leading to Reform

Under these circumstances, the Chun Doo Hwan government attempted to restructure the excessive and duplicative investments made by rival chaebol groups by fiat. During 1980–1981, the government initiated a restructuring program toward such industrial sectors as power generation and heavy construction equipment, heavy electrical equipment, electronic-switching systems, and diesel engines, in which the financial problems were most pronounced. Despite the unusual threat to the concerned firms that the government would no longer support future projects unless they complied with government directives, the restructuring attempt failed.

Certainly the economic planners' inconsistent restructuring guidelines and the protests by foreign lenders and joint venture partners contributed to this failure. But a more fundamental reason for the failure consisted in the highly politicized heavy industrialization drive itself. Since excessive investments in the heavy industry sectors were made under the government's direction, private investors knew that terminating financial assistance would be disastrous not only for themselves but also probably more so for the political leadership, who would have to accept the political cost of massive layoffs. In fact, the government was never fully able to enforce the threat of terminating credit.

The Chun government's other attempt at improving the financial structure of big business in September 1980 showed even more clearly the perils of the highly politicized financial system. The government obligated firms and business groups (or their owners) that owed bank loans of ten billion won (for a firm) and twenty billion won (for chaebol) to report all landholdings to the banks and to sell land unrelated to the main line of business.[35] In addition, the largest twenty chaebol groups were required to divest minor lines of business.[36] The government declared that it would no longer provide relief loans unless firms complied with government directives. Although this policy was undertaken in the name of ameliorating the extremely high level of economic concentration, its real motive was to strengthen the new government's control of the chaebol. But this attempt failed to produce visible results.[37]

The lesson to policymakers from these two unsuccessful and frustrating attempts was clear enough: direct and selective intervention by the government in the allocation of financial resources generated only more difficult problems for both big business and the banks. In particular, it became clear that banks could not be held accountable for bad loans.

Looking ahead, the financial system itself was also a problem, frustrating the government's pursuit of a stable economic growth policy. Under the prevailing regime of low interest rates and the consequent excess demand for funds, economic stabilization policies could not be sustained because of political pressures from business. Given the extremely weak financial structure of big business, economic stabilization would result only in an increase in bad loans, necessitating a further supply of relief loans and thereby undermining stabilization efforts.

This experience and the tremendous frustration felt by government

---

[35] The number of firms that were subjected to the measures was 1,217, most of which were owned by thirty to forty of the largest chaebol groups.

[36] According to a report of the Bank Surveillance Board, the largest twenty-six business groups owned 540 firms. The largest five business groups owned 139 firms (Hyundai, 60; Lucky, 53; Daewoo, 48; Hyosung, 39; and Samsung, 39). *Dong-A Ilbo*, October 25, 1980.

[37] Certainly, this attempt met with many technical difficulties. For example, how business-unrelated land was to be separated was a controversial issue. Moreover, only chaebol could buy such land in a short period of time. No less controversial was the question of how to single out the main line of business in the extremely diversified lines of business.

policymakers during the difficult period of economic adjustment in the early 1980s became a boon to economic policymakers who believed in the efficiency of a free-market economy. The political leadership was thus persuaded to undertake a wide-ranging economic policy reform effort.[38] Financial liberalization was only a part of this effort, but it was especially significant in that it implied the most fundamental change in government-business relations.

The position of big business on the reform was mixed. On the positive side, they saw financial liberalization as a means of limiting the government's intervention in economic decision making.[39] As demonstrated in the aforementioned restructuring episodes, businesspeople abhorred the situation in which their fate was at the disposal of government policymakers' fickle political judgments. In addition, to meet its rapidly increasing capital needs more flexibly, big business felt a need to own and control financial institutions. On the negative side, concern was expressed about the increase in interest rates that would follow financial liberalization. Thus big business favored a gradual transition to the more liberalized regime.

Naturally enough, the BOK, commercial banks, and other financial intermediaries welcomed the financial liberalization policy; the recovery of autonomy was what they had long desired. Under the existing oligopolistic structure of the financial industry, the banks might well have favored the status quo. But given that the government's intervention had continuously weakened their autonomy and profitability, they stood for financial liberalization. For the foreign bank subsidiaries, financial liberalization meant an expanded space for their operations. Finally, the media and academic circles made a strong case for financial liberalization. Unlike other actors, they tended to view the liberalization as a means to assure a more equitable allocation of financial resources and to eliminate political corruption and bureaucratic interference in the financial system and the economy in general.

In sum, there existed no disagreement among interested parties about the ultimate goal of financial liberalization; every party could expect some benefit. The actual implementation process was not smooth, however. Neither was the progress uniform in three different areas of financial liberalization: privatization of commercial banks, the deregulation of entry and business boundaries, and the freeing of interest rates and credit allocation. Speedy and remarkable progress was made in privatization and entry regulation, whereas the freeing of

[38] For an analysis of these broad economic policy changes in the 1980s, see Choi, "Institutionalizing a Liberal Economic Order," chap. 6.

[39] Unch'an Chung, *Keumyung Kaehyukron* [Discourse on financial reform] (Seoul: Pummunsa, 1991), p. 41.

interest rates was bogged down, policy loans reappeared, and the presidents of the privatized banks continued to be appointed by the government. It is thus useful to review the three major components of financial liberalization separately.

Privatization of Commercial Banks

The first move toward financial liberalization was to privatize the commercial banks.[40] Immediately after the inauguration of the Chun Doo Hwan government in 1980, the MOF reported to the president that it would privatize one of the five nationwide commercial banks in 1981 and prepare for continued privatization of the remaining banks. In doing so, it added, it would take precautionary measures to prevent the monopolization of financial resources by chaebol and to protect depositors.[41]

The primary objective of the privatization was to let banks have owners who would pay attention to the efficiency of banking operations. But a fiscal consideration also played a role. The selling off of government-owned equities would contribute to government revenue in a period of fiscal austerity. Furthermore, it was expected that the supply of "good stocks" would stimulate the stock market.

In April 1981, the MOF announced that it had selected Hanil Bank as its first target. The privatization of Hanil Bank satisfied the stated policy objectives. Of the five banks to be privatized, Hanil Bank displayed the best managerial performance and thus had the most promising prospects for successful divestiture. In addition, its equities were more widely distributed than were those of other banks, which was important in light of the sad experience of privatization in the 1950s, when chaebol acquired the controlling shares of privatized banks.

As expected, however, when the divestiture of government equities of Hanil Bank was completed in June 1981, two major chaebol groups acquired the controlling shares. This was partly due to the restricted bidding; the MOF imposed a minimum equity ratio standard on firms that would be eligible to participate in the auction. In view of the auction results, the issue of amending the General Banking Act became controversial. Major disputes centered on imposing an upper limit on the share a single company or individual could own, limiting credit to a single beneficiary (or firm), and designing mechanisms to enforce "responsible" bank management. The fate of heavily indebted big business

[40] The share of equities of commercial banks that the government owned at the time of privatization ranged from 20 to 30 percent.
[41] MOF, "Measures for Deregulating Commercial Banks," *Kyongjeanjonghwa Shich'ackjaryojip* [Collected reports on economic stabilization policy measures] (Seoul: KDI, 1981), pp. 699–718.

43

hinged greatly on these prospective provisions and regulations. Under these circumstances, while the MOF delayed the introduction of the amendment to the assembly, the opposition party submitted its more restrictive amendment to the National Assembly, to which the Federation of Korean Industries was strongly opposed.

In the meantime, as the economy continued to slacken and as business suffered from the stabilization policy, successive privatizations were deadlocked. By this time, the MOF had come to the conclusion that a hasty implementation of the privatization plan would backfire, given that the commercial banks were rapidly accumulating nonperforming debts. Instead, the MOF decided to roll back various government regulations and directives. These moves reflected the then conventional view that what was more important than privatization was the government's commitment to allow privatized banks real autonomy and to discontinue its traditional role of caretaker.

To give the deposit banks more freedom in managing their financial resources and thereby to boost their operating profits, the MOF gradually lowered the required reserve ratio to 3–5 percent in 1981, compared with the average rate of 23 percent in 1979. In January 1982, the MOF switched the method of controlling the money supply from direct credit controls (credit ceilings and quotas to individual banks) to the indirect reserve requirement method, with a view to increasing autonomy in fund use.

Little progress was made until May 1982, when the largest curb market scandal broke. Chang Yong Ja, a woman distantly related by marriage to President Chun (her husband's brother was Mrs. Chun's uncle), and her husband had netted a huge sum, approximately $300 million, by trading promissory notes in the curb market. Four commercial banks were involved. This incident dealt a severe blow to the public's confidence in the Chun government. The opposition demanded President Chun's resignation. In the face of this challenge, the president replaced the prime minister and the finance minister swiftly, thus providing an unexpected opportunity for the advocates of speedier financial liberalization that were based in the EPB. These individuals now came to occupy the upper echelons of the MOF, which had generally been opposed to the idea of rapid financial liberalization.

The new finance minister began to push financial liberalization forcibly. As a first move, he announced a sharp reduction in interest rates by an average of 4 percentage points to stimulate the economy and eliminated the preferential interest rates applied to policy loans, including even export financing. The elimination of preferential interest rates on export loans, which was partly motivated by trade disputes with the United States on export subsidies, represented a big stride toward the reduction of policy loans.

Second, the finance minister resumed the previously deadlocked privatization of the three commercial banks: Korea First Bank and the Bank of Seoul and Trust Company in 1982 and the Chohung Bank in 1983. In this latter move, the government, mindful of speeding up the process, eased the minimum equity ratio of firms eligible to bid. Thus, with the Commercial Bank of Korea already in private hands since 1972, the privatization of all five leading commercial banks was completed. But on the occasion of this privatization move, large chaebol came to acquire controlling shares of the commercial banks indirectly through holdings of shares by the nonbank financial intermediaries under their control.

In December 1982, the National Assembly passed an amendment to the General Banking Act. The MOF initially planned to allow large firms to acquire a maximum 10 percent share of a privatized bank, thus making it possible for three or four big firms to control the bank. But in the process of consultation with the ruling Democratic Justice party, which insisted that the limit should be further reduced to 5 percent to prevent any individual or business group from exercising managerial control of the privatized bank, the MOF retreated and agreed to a maximum ownership by any single shareholder of 8 percent. The revised act also limited loan guarantees and acceptances for a single beneficiary to a maximum of 50 percent of a bank's net worth.

Entry Deregulation and the Conflict between Banks and NBFIs

To promote competition in the banking industry and to strengthen its links to international financial markets, the MOF has lowered entry barriers significantly since 1981. As a result, the number of foreign bank branches that opened in Korea increased sharply in both 1981 and 1982.[42] The MOF licensed two joint venture commercial banks—the Shinhan Bank, capitalized by Korean businesspeople residing in Japan, in July 1982 and the KorAm Bank, subscribed to by the Bank of America and major companies in Korea, in March 1983. In 1985, the MOF permitted foreign bank branches to make use of rediscount facilities at the Bank of Korea for export financing and to enter the trust business. And since 1986, foreign banks have been entitled to make use of rediscount facilities for all their operations.

Because of continued deregulation of entry for local banks, the num-

---

[42] In 1987, fifty-seven foreign bank branches accounted for 10.8 percent in total assets and 63.3 percent in foreign exchange loans of all deposit banks. See Chung, *Keumyung*, pp. 113–14.

ber of commercial banks increased from seven in 1985 to ten in 1990. The Citizen's Bank was privatized in 1990, and in 1991, two commercial banks were created through a merger and conversion of several investment and finance companies. As a result, there are now thirteen nationwide commercial banks in Korea. Currently, Korea Foreign Exchange Bank is in the process of being turned into a commercial bank.

What is notable in regard to entry deregulation is the conflict between commercial banks and nonbank financial intermediaries. As noted in Section I, Korea's financial system bifurcated after the August 3, 1972, emergency decree, and NBFIs grew up alongside commercial banks. Allowed relatively greater freedom, the NBFIs witnessed rapid growth in the 1970s and have largely been owned by chaebol groups, which have also controlled six general financing companies, partly financed by foreign capital (Table 2.2).

The Association of National Investment and Finance Companies (ANIFC), established by the NBFIs in 1979, has long pressed for financial deregulation. Its aim was to secure for NBFIs a position from which to compete squarely with the banking institutions. It successfully persuaded the government to eliminate the discriminatory tax rate on the interest earned through short-term financing companies in 1980. The curb market incident in 1982, which made this market the target of a government crackdown, helped the ANIFC to advance its position. Within months after the incident, the MOF lowered entry barriers to the nonbank financial industry. As a result, the number of NBFIs, such as investment and finance companies and mutual savings and finance companies, increased conspicuously. Within a year, twelve new short-term finance companies and fifty-seven mutual finance companies were chartered.[43] Again, most of them were owned or controlled by major chaebol groups, which saw NBFIs as an excellent source of financing in a period of sustained economic stabilization.

As the share of domestic deposits of the NBFIs increased rapidly, however, the commercial banks began to press the government to allow them to extend the boundaries of their business.[44] In 1982, the MOF allowed commercial banks to engage in the sale of commercial bills that they themselves discounted. Because this change pitted the banks directly against the NBFIs, which had fewer regional branches and weaker public reputations, the ANIFC was strongly opposed to this change. Nonetheless, the MOF continued to allow new business—such as factoring, credit cards, trust, and the repurchase of government and public bonds—to banks. Furthermore, in 1984 the negotiable certifi-

---

[43] Yung Chul Park, "Economic Stabilization and Liberalization in Korea, 1980–1984," in BOK, *Monetary Policy in a Changing Financial Environment* (Seoul: BOK, 1985), p. 95.
[44] BOK, *Financial System in Korea* (Seoul: BOK, 1985), pp. 48–50.

Table 2.2. Market shares of types of financial institutions 1976–1989 (percentage)

	Loans				Average rate of increase[a]	Deposits				Average rate of increase[a]
	1976	1980	1985	1989		1976	1980	1985	1989	
Deposit money banks	68.2	62.2	53.6	49.9	24.7	74.7	66.3	48.5	36.6	23.1
Nonbank financial institutions	31.8	37.8	46.4	50.1	32.2	25.3	33.7	51.5	63.4	39.6
Development institutions	16.6	19.2	17.1	9.0	21.9	0.8	0.9	0.5	0.6	26.5
Savings institutions	7.3	8.8	14.0	22.1	39.1	12.4	15.7	20.5	28.9	38.8
Investment companies	7.1	6.7	8.8	9.0	30.1	8.2	10.9	17.0	18.7	38.6
Life insurance companies	0.8	3.1	6.5	10.0	54.6	3.9	6.2	13.5	15.2	44.3

Source: BOK, Financial System in Korea (Seoul: BOK, 1990).
[a]Represents annual rate of increase from 1976 to 1989.

cate-of-deposit (CD) business was allowed to all commercial banks. In 1985, new savings deposits and household installment savings deposits, which are high-yielding deposit schemes for households, were opened to all banks.

In the face of the continued extension of banks' business, the ANIFC requested further deregulation, except for regulation of entry, in the entire financial sector. The MOF grudgingly agreed but established a commercial paper (CP) market for investment and finance companies and merchant banking corporations in 1981, right after the privatization of Hanil Bank, and for large securities companies in 1984. The cash management account (CMA), a Korean version of the money market account in the United States, was introduced in 1984 for investment and finance companies and merchant banking corporations.

In 1985, because of the structural depression in overseas construction and ocean-shipping industries, many domestic firms in these sectors began to accumulate nonperforming debts, which placed an enormous burden on the related banks.[45] In the face of this crisis, the government prepared measures to facilitate industrial restructuring. Most important, the MOF revised the Tax Reduction and Exemption Law to grant tax privileges to banks and prospective owners, and it revised the Bank of Korea Act to provide cheap "special loans" to the banks involved. In the meantime, the government felt a need to boost deposits at banks and thus permitted banks to provide high-yielding deposit programs while lowering the deposit and lending rates of the NBFIs.

As a result, bank deposits increased considerably, whereas deposits of NBFIs declined abruptly. This triggered a heated debate on the direction of the restructuring of the financial industry. On the one hand, the Federation of National Banks (FNB) argued that the differences in the financial regulation of banks and NBFIs retarded the growth of banks and suppressed their profitability, and it pressed for further deregulation of business boundaries based on the general banking concept. On the other hand, the ANIFC stressed that the MOF should broaden the business boundaries of the NBFIs to allow them to compete squarely with banks.

Generally siding with the FNB, the FKI maintained that to make investment capital cheap and abundant, financial liberalization should favor banks. Reflecting the fact that many NBFIs are under the control of chaebol, however, the FKI emphasized the importance of screening investment projects and the application of differential interest rates on

[45] As of July 1988, the total amount of nonperforming assets, which should be written off by default, owned by seven nationwide commercial banks and seventeen local banks reached 250 billion won (about 3.3 billion dollars, estimated at 750 won per dollar). See *Maeil Kyungje Shinmun*, July 23, 1988.

the basis of the soundness of the project.[46] The FKI's position contrasted with that of the Korea Chamber of Commerce and Industry (KCCI), the representative of small and medium-sized businesses. The KCCI maintained that the distinction between banks and NBFIs should be preserved,[47] pitting the short-term finance companies, against banks.

The issue of the restructuring of the financial industry was handed over to the new democratic government that assumed office in 1988. In a report prepared in that year, the MOF envisioned a further deregulation of entry into the financial industry in the spirit of the general banking system. At the same time, however, the MOF declared that it would promote the conversion of NBFIs into banks or other forms of NBFIs and the mergers between them. And, most recently, in October 1990, the MOF promulgated the Law Regarding the Conversion and Merger of Financial Institutions in anticipation of the opening up of Korea's financial market to foreign participation. Currently, a significant reshuffling of the NBFIs is underway.

The privatization and deregulation measures outlined thus far may leave the impression that the privatized commercial banks now enjoy a certain degree of autonomy. It should be remembered, however, that even after privatization, the government continues to appoint bank presidents and executive board members through "consultation" with the banks and that major operational decisions of the banks continue to be under government scrutiny and "administrative guidance."

The Freeing of Interest Rates and the Discontinuing of Policy Loans

Despite the fact that the freeing of interest rates constitutes an integral part of financial liberalization, little progress has been made on this front (see Table 2.3). The fundamental reason for this delay is that Korea's business is highly leveraged, with high capital costs and high levels of indebtedness.[48] Moreover, the term structure of borrowing has been extraordinarily skewed toward the short term, though short-term loans have become long-term through continuous rollovers.[49] In this situation, a small change in short-term interest rates would result in a significant change in the financial position of business.

[46] FKI, *Mingan Kyungjebaekso* [Private sector's white paper on the economy] (Seoul: FKI, 1985), pp. 8–11.
[47] KCCI, *Chayukiopjuuiui Ch'angdalul wuihan Cheon* [Suggestions for the development of free enterprise system] (Seoul: KCCI, 1985), pp. 87–101.
[48] In 1988 the average debt ratio of Korean manufacturing firms was 296.0, compared with the ratios for firms in Taiwan of 84.3; Japan, 243.0; and the United States, 138.2. BOK, *Kiop Kyonyong Bunsok* [Analysis of financial status of firms] (Seoul: BOK, 1989), p. 22.
[49] The share of operating funds in total bank loans hovered between 74 and 78 percent during 1982–1988. BOK, *Yearly Economic Statistics* (Seoul: BOK, various years).

Table 2.3. Regulated and market interest rates, 1970–1991 (year average, percent)

	Regulated rates		Market rates		Average borrowing cost (manufacturing)	Consumer inflation rate	Real GNP growth	M₂ growth rate
	Bank 1-year time deposit	General bank loans	Corp. bond yield	Curb rate				
1970	22.8	24.0	—	49.8	14.7	15.4	7.6	—
1975	15.0	15.5	20.1	41.3	11.3	25.4	6.4	27.0
1976	15.5	16.5	20.4	40.5	11.9	15.3	13.1	29.2
1977	15.8	17.3	20.1	38.1	13.1	10.0	9.8	37.0
1978	16.7	17.7	21.1	41.2	12.4	14.5	9.8	39.3
1979	18.6	19.0	26.7	42.4	14.4	18.2	7.2	26.8
1980	22.7	23.4	30.1	44.9	18.7	28.7	−3.7	25.8
1981	19.3	19.8	24.4	35.3	18.4	21.6	5.9	27.4
1982	10.9	12.5	17.3	30.6	16.0	7.1	7.2	28.1
1983	8.0	10.0	14.2	25.8	13.6	3.4	12.6	19.5
1984	9.1	10.6	14.1	24.8	14.4	2.3	9.3	10.7
1985	10.0	11.5	14.2	24.0	13.4	2.5	7.0	11.8
1986	10.0	11.5	12.8	23.1	12.5	2.8	12.9	16.8
1987	10.0	11.5	12.8	23.0	12.5	3.0	13.0	18.8
1988	10.0	11.5	14.5	22.7	13.0	7.1	12.4	18.8
1989	10.0	11.5	15.2	19.1	13.6	5.7	6.8	18.4
1990	10.0	11.5	16.4	18.7	—	8.6	9.0	21.2
June 1991	10.0	11.5	18.6	—	—	10.1	—	18.4

Sources: BOK, *Monthly Bulletin,* and *Financial Statements Analysis* (Seoul: BOK, various years).

For these reasons, the government has been extremely reluctant to free interest rates. Of course, the government has experimented with partial interest rate liberalization from time to time by allowing banks and the NBFIs to provide various kinds of new deposit programs and lending services. But the government's impact on interest rate liberalization has been minimal.[50]

Instead, the government has continued to reduce the gap between the formal administrative interest rates and the unregulated market interest rates. For example, as the inflation rate fell remarkably in the mid-1980s because of the successful implementation of economic stabilization policies, real interest rates rose significantly. Taking advantage of their relatively greater freedom in setting interest rates, the NBFIs came to form a "third" money market in the 1980s, distinct from either the regulated money market or the unregulated private market, and thus served the function of bridging the interest rate gap between these two markets. Actual interest rates have been drawn closer to the market interest rates as the NBFIs and banks have continued to charge high commissions and rely on such illegal banking practices as "forced savings," a mechanism under which borrowers are forced to deposit a considerable part of their loans at creditor banks or NBFIs at the time of lending. But the restrictive monetary policy geared to economic stabilization and the increase in lending rates have persistently caused problems for business in general and big business in particular. Under these circumstances, big business attempted to expand its control of NBFIs and pressed for the adoption of a differential lending rate system based on the creditworthiness of the borrowers.

In May 1988, under new government leadership and in view of the inevitable liberalization of the capital market, the MOF decided to speed up interest rate liberalization. According to its plan, the MOF would first gradually liberalize the lending rates of commercial banks and NBFIs and adopt a prime rate system. It would then delay the liberalization of the deposit rates of banks and NBFIs until the MOF was certain that this action would not disrupt existing market shares. Instead, the ministry would accentuate the liberalization of interest rates on corporate bonds, finance bonds, negotiable CDs, CP, and other savings programs such as the CMA.

From December 1988 on, the MOF began to put its liberalization plan into practice. But in anticipation of a sudden hike in interest rates, it increased the money supply at the same time. In the wake of the general election in April 1989, as the rate of inflation went up, the MOF took the extraordinary measure of absorbing money by forcing banks

[50]Chung, *Keumyung,* pp. 286–87.

to roll back loans. This episode indicated clearly the extreme difficulty of liberalizing interest rates given the high indebtedness of business and the instability of financial markets.

In reducing policy loans, another important area of financial liberalization, the government made no progress at all. The share of policy loans in total bank credit outstanding fell from 68.2 percent in 1980 to 62.1 percent in 1982. But the share rose again to 67.9 percent in 1983, 69.9 percent in 1984, and 70.5 in 1985, and it has continued to stay at this level.[51] One important reason for this is the growing demand for policy loans as a result of democratization since 1988. From the mid-1980s on, the government has tended to make specialized banks such as the KDB bear the brunt of policy loans. But there exists an evident limit without replenishing the banks' capital. As a result, commercial banks have invariably been called on to provide policy loans, though the MOF has not insisted that banks comply with government plans to channel financial resources to specific sectors and policy purposes.

An Aberration: Recent Restructuring Attempts

Probably the most important roadblock in the course of financial liberalization has been the existence of financially unhealthy firms (*Pusilgiop*). Most of these firms are the by-products of the heavy industrialization drive in the 1970s and some of them are the "structurally depressed" industries such as overseas construction and ocean shipping of the 1980s. Given that these firms were accumulating large nonperforming debts, the government decided to undertake another massive industrial restructuring effort. The MOF revised the Tax Reduction and Exemption Law in 1985 to grant tax privileges to banks or prospective owners, and it revised the Bank of Korea Act to authorize its provision of special BOK loans to commercial banks. This restructuring took place in six episodes between May 1986 and February 1988. Among seventy-eight firms subjected to rationalization, fifty-seven firms changed hands, nineteen merged, and the remaining two were liquidated.[52] The government directed the concerned banks to reschedule the repayments of their debts and to grant new credit as "seed money." Total financial assistance and tax benefits provided to such

[51] Joong Woong Kim, "Sanopbaljongwa," p. 54.
[52] In selecting firms to be subjected to industrial rationalization, the government used the following somewhat ambiguous criteria: (1) structurally depressed industries necessitating industrial restructuring, (2) minor lines of businesses under the control of chaebol needing streamlining, and (3) firms continuously accumulating nonperforming debts.

firms amounted to 11,418 billion won (about 14.27 billion dollars, estimated at the exchange rate of 800 won per dollar).

As in the previous restructuring attempts in the late 1960s and the early 1970s, the episode in the 1980s again confirms the vicious circle of financial repression in Korea and the underlying logic of continued government intervention in the financial system. Insofar as the government was ultimately responsible for the accumulation of nonperforming debts in the banking system, it could not avoid rescuing the banks. In addition, because of the problem of moral hazard, the government could not entirely abdicate its control over the financial system.

In the early years of the Sixth Republic, however, the restructuring attempt became the target of political attack by the opposition parties. They contended that it was a prime example of the politics-industry nexus (*chungkyungyuchak*) in Korea and charged that in the process of selecting new owners for the restructured firms, the government promoted a further concentration of economic power in the hands of big business.

The phenomenon of the "monopolization" of financial resources by large chaebol groups was alarming. For example, bank loans provided to the thirty largest chaebol (which include a total of 676 firms) amounted to 19,704 billion won, or 26.9 percent of total bank loans, whereas these groups accounted for 40.2 percent of manufacturing sales, 41.3 percent of manufacturing exports, and 17.6 percent of manufacturing employment. Moreover, they have taken up a lion's share of the financing facilities of the NBFIs. In addition, they have multiplied the number of firms under their control mainly through mutual stock exchange in violation of the Anti-Monopoly and Fair Trade Law. At the same time, the financial structures of chaebol have grown weaker. The ratio of bank credit (excluding loan guarantees) to total assets of the thirty largest chaebol groups reached 22.3 percent on average. Accordingly, the government has since April 1988 further strengthened its grip on bank credit to the chaebol groups.

Over three decades, the Korean government has used finance as a major industrial policy instrument. The mechanism to induce big business to invest in sectors that the government regards as strategic or important has invariably been through selective credit allocation. In the mid-1960s, the government adopted a system of export financing to make big business turn its eyes to foreign markets, although these loans were nondiscretionary and benefited all exporters. To meet rapidly growing demand by big business' for capital, the government opened a new avenue for foreign capital inflow via foreign loan guarantees intermediated by the specialized state banks and commercial banks. In the 1970s, to induce chaebol groups to invest in heavy and chemical industry sectors, the government deepened financial regulation. There was little space left for banks to exercise discretion.

Over time, as these large business groups grew further in size and political strength, the nature of the business-government relationship changed accordingly. Their large size has now become a liability to policymakers as the viability of big business has turned into a matter of great importance to the nation's economic stability and employment. In addition, with the establishment of a pluralistic political system in Korea, chaebol groups' influence on policy-making has become stronger because they are now a potent political force.

With the Korean economy becoming increasingly complex and with economic concentration and political corruption being blamed on financial policy, the government launched a serious attempt toward financial liberalization in the early 1980s. The process of financial liberalization has, however, proved difficult. In the first place, the government could not abdicate financial control abruptly. As continued industrial adjustment is necessary to meet the challenges posed by democratization and foreign pressure to open the Korean market, the government has been forced to intervene continuously in the financial market. The most recent restructuring episode in 1986–1988 exemplified the government's policy predicament. In addition, big business, though generally favoring financial liberalization, has never been prepared to give up the privileges that it enjoyed, particularly with regard to the price and availability of finance. Moreover, big business has now evolved into a financial interest group itself, as it has continued to expand its ownership and control of most of the NBFIs and, to a considerable degree, banks.

The recent opening of the financial market in Korea to foreign participation should accelerate the process of financial liberalization. As of early 1993, however, internationalization has been gradual. More important, the basic political relationship between big business and the government—the most vital aspect of financial liberalization in the Korean context—remains largely intact.

CHAPTER THREE

Guarding the Commanding Heights:
The State as Banker in Taiwan

TUN-JEN CHENG

The case of Taiwan poses the puzzle of the "dog that did not bark." Because of the nature of Taiwan's decolonization and the Kuomintang regime's relocation from the mainland, the state had direct control over the financial system from the beginning of the postwar period. Had it wanted to, the leadership could have used preferential credit to shape the industrial structure, as was done in Korea and France. The unwillingness, rather than inability, to use credit as a principal instrument of industrial policy also separates Taiwan from Thailand, the Philippines, and Mexico, where the financial sector is not under the government's direct control.

Savings mobilization has been successful in Taiwan. Like Japan and Singapore, Taiwan financed most of its development through domestic savings, although U.S. aid played a decisive role in import substitution during the 1950s. Capital mobilization in Taiwan was the result of successful stabilization in the 1950s and the continuous pursuit of orthodox macroeconomic policies, that is, positive interest rates, cautious monetary policy, and a balanced budget.[1] Steady export expansion

I thank David Cole, Rich Doner, Jeff Frieden, Stephan Haggard, Laura Hastings, Chung Lee, Sylvia Maxfield, and Yung Chul Park for their useful comments on earlier versions of this essay.

[1] Economic stabilization in the early 1950s was the result of many factors, including currency reform, shipment of central bank's gold reserve to Taiwan, U.S. aid, and, in particular, the introduction of a high interest rate policy. The last measure was an innovative departure from conventional wisdom at that time. Positive real interest rates induced risk-averse savers, in contrast with Korea, where financial repression as well as inflationary deficit financing forced the savers to opt for the risky curb market, whereas the government came to rely on foreign borrowing. See S. C. Tsiang, "Exchange Rates, Interest Rates, and Economic Development," in *Quantitative Economics and Development,*

during the 1960s and 1970s led to the accumulation of foreign exchange surpluses after 1980, which made Taiwan second only to Japan
in its reserve holdings and created a capital glut.[2] Yet borrowers still
have a hard time obtaining funds, which suggests possible allocative
inefficiency in Taiwan's financial sector.

As the other chapters in this volume demonstrate, Third World governments often channel savings away from consumption and commerce
to the manufacturing sector and regulate interest rates to reduce the
cost of capital for producers. Taiwan is no exception, as evidenced by
its dualistic financial structure and the gap between interest rates in
the formal market, which are controlled by the government, and interest rates in the black market. Because of excess demand in the organized financial sector, credit is, by definition, rationed.

Taiwan's credit policy, however, differs from those in most Third
World countries in several aspects. The real lending rates in Taiwan
were not so severely repressed as in many other lesser-developed countries (LDCs), notably its competitor South Korea.[3] Moreover, although
Taiwan's credit policy was deliberately used to promote specific industries or even specific firms during the import substitution industrialization (ISI) period of the 1950s, this was not the case during the
subsequent export promotion period until very recently. Policy loans
were broadly targeted to support exports or anti-inflationary import
packages; industry-specific loans were rare. When established, industry-
specific loans were distributed through conservative commercial banks

ed. L. R. Klein, N. Nerlove, and S. C. Tsiang (New York: Academic Press, 1980); and
R. J. Irvine and R. F. Emery, "Interest Rates as an Anti-inflationary Instrument in Taiwan,"
National Banking Review, September 1966.

[2] See Bela Balassa and John Williamson, *Adjusting to Success: Balance of Payments Policy
in the East Asian NICs* (Washington, D.C.: Institute for International Economics, 1987);
and Maxwell J. Fry, "Should Taiwan Reduce Its Current Account Surplus?" 1988, Mimeographed. Taiwan's "surplus capital" is effectively exported, yet its per capita GNP
is still low relative to other developed nations, and the rate of return for domestic
investment is still higher than that on overseas portfolio investment. One important
reason Taiwan's central bank holds large amounts of foreign exchange is political. Diplomatic isolation and the need for weapons procurement, which cannot be planned
because the People's Republic of China has done its utmost to prevent any party from
selling even defensive arsenals to Taiwan, require that funds be available for emergency
diplomatic-security purposes.

[3] Sheng-tae Hsiau, "Taiwan min-ying kung-yeh li-si fu-dan zi she-shi" [A preliminary
analysis of the burden of interest payment for private enterprises in Taiwan], in *Taiwan
huo-pi yu chin-jung lun-wen-chi* [An anthology of money and finance in Taiwan], Cheng-
hsiung Chiu, ed. (Taipei: Lien-chin, 1975), pp. 336, 343–47; and Wen-lung Chen, "Comments on Interest Rates," in *Chai jin cheng tse ta ban lun* [The grand debate on financial
and economic policies] (Taipei: Industrial-Commercial Times, 1982), pp. 161–63. Hsiau
points out that because of the ultraconservatist lending policy in the organized financial
sector, the transaction costs, including the costs of speed money and paperwork, for
getting a loan are high. Hence, interest rate differentials between the formal market and
the black market are overstated.

and often failed to reach the targeted sector. Although Korea had set up a comprehensive system of investment banking and specialized banks as soon as the economy shifted from ISI to export-led industrialization in the mid-1960s, Taiwan's leadership was slow in commissioning development banks for industrial promotion, much to the disappointment of some technocrats. The government did finance new or expanded state-owned enterprises (SOEs) for industrial "deepening" during the 1970s. The channeling of credit to SOEs, however, reflected the low-risk nature of such lending and the political calculation of restraining the growth of private capital as much as it did a strong industrial policy.

To accelerate industrial upgrading, the government began in 1982 to authorize strategic industry loans managed by development banks. But this sector-specific credit facility accounted for only 4.3 percent of total loans dispensed by state-owned banks in 1988. Moreover, these loans were soon overshadowed by special-purpose loans, notably for the purchase of domestically produced machinery, automation for industrial upgrading, and antipollution equipment. These loans are for broad functional categories and are not geared toward specific industries or toward a particular set of "stellar" firms. Whether financing of this sort is good or bad is a subject of debate; whatever the assessment, such credit policy is extremely light by Korean or French standards.

This chapter examines the allocative decisions and institutional structure of the financial sector in Taiwan, focusing on the role of credit rationing in industrial promotion. The emphasis is not on consequences of policy, but on policy choice per se. The basic contention is that a political logic undergirded the government's credit policy and the makeup of the financial sector in Taiwan. Economic technocrats proposed a highly preferential credit policy and argued for a limited but specialized role for the state in the financial sector, but actual institutional design and credit policy followed the political calculus of the KMT regime leadership. The political elite of the KMT regime perceived inflation as a primary cause for their defeat on the mainland and viewed the formation of private indigenous economic power as a challenge to their hegemony in Taiwan. Financial institutions and policy were strongly conditioned by the regime's perennial obsession with macroeconomic stability and the effort to restrain big capital while forging linkages to other social groups, such as small and medium-sized firms, farmers, and state employees.

The lesson of hyperinflation on the mainland was most noticeably reflected in the power given to the central bank relative to spending ministries, especially industrial planning authorities. The leadership's propensity for economic orthodoxy had an institutional correlate in strong central bank control over monetary and financial policies. In-stitutionalized orthodoxy constrained the technocrats who advocated preferential credit for rapid expansion and transformation of industry. Lending policy and the control of loanable funds have been used to maintain price stability.

Licenses for institutional expansion were primarily issued to state-owned banks, and sometimes to foreign bankers and overseas Chinese capitalists, but rarely to indigenous capitalists. This preference order fully reflected the regime's distrust of indigenous capitalists, who, until 1991, had been barred from any place in the core of the banking sector and instead relegated to a marginal role in the financial periphery. Both credit policy and state ownership of the banking sector were used to guard against the overconcentration of private capital.

There is no economic reason for a state monopoly in Taiwan's bank-ing sector. Banks are by nature a public institution, which calls only for state regulation and oversight of their activities. The Gerschenk-ronian logic of late development does provide a rationale for the state's presence in the financial sector, namely, to facilitate industrial invest-ment and adjustment, but this view calls only for a development bank or central bank rediscounting to private banks,[4] not the state's total control of the banking sector.

State ownership of banks may facilitate control of the money supply and the capital account, especially outward flows, but it is not a necessary condition for macroeconomic stability. A responsible fiscal policy, a conservative monetary policy, and the autonomy of the central bank from the Ministry of Finance are more relevant to inflation control than is direct state management of the banking system. Acute fiscal deficits and the abuse of monetary authority caused the inflation spiral that contributed greatly to the collapse of the KMT regime on the main-land.[5] Indeed, it was state domination of the previously private banking sector beginning in the mid-1930s that made deficit financing possible.

The political ideology of the KMT provides a clue to its leaders' interest in guarding the commanding heights against the private sector. The KMT regime was, like many other Third World regimes, an au-thoritarian one, but its ruling party was similar to a Leninist regime, carrying an ideology of statist capitalism, *min sheng chu i* (the principle of people's livelihood), a doctrine invented in the 1920s by Sun Yatsen, the founding father of modern China. As espoused by the KMT re-

[4] John Zysman, *Governments, Markets, and Growth* (Ithaca: Cornell University Press, 1983), chap. 1.
[5] See Shun-hsin Chou, *The Chinese Inflation, 1937–1949* (New York: Columbia University Press, 1963); and Kia-ngau Chang, *The Inflationary Spiral: The Experience in China, 1939–1950* (Cambridge: MIT Press, 1958).

gime, however, min sheng chu i is eclectic, ill-defined, and subject to various interpretations. Although it enunciates the guideline of promoting state capital and restraining private capital, min sheng chu i specifically prescribes state ownership in natural monopolies such as utilities and defense-related industries, but not in other areas, including the banking sector. The onset of the cold war and the alliance with the United States, in particular, led the KMT regime to promote private capital.

The KMT regime's concern about the concentration of private capital was inspired less by Sun Yatsen ideology than by coalitional calculations. The KMT regime was, until recently, an "alien" regime controlled by minority mainlanders and surrounded by Taiwanese society. On the mainland, the KMT leadership was always leery of big private financiers, who, despite their social ties to the political elite, had not been submissive to the state's expansive financial policy. The KMT's relocation to Taiwan and its inheritance of Japanese property reversed the party's prewar dependence on the private sector. The regime, however, found itself in an alien society. Eighty-five percent of the inhabitants were native Taiwanese, who were shut out of the political arena but allowed to pursue economic activities. The other 15 percent of the population were emigrating mainlanders, mostly state employees and the military. Through land reform and the elimination of the landlord class, the KMT acquired a rural political base, which made it possible to run local elections and at the same time extract agrarian surplus to support industrial development. In the urban areas, the regime's coalitional partners were less clear-cut. Although the mainlander-dominated state sector was the KMT's main support base, the burgeoning new middle class and the rapidly growing Taiwanese-dominated business sector were politically more difficult to capture. Having dismantled the indigenous landlord class, the KMT regime had every incentive to avoid the formation of big native capital.

Credit allocation can be a political instrument of control over big capital, as is vividly shown in the case of Korea. Due to the subethnic cleavage and the alien nature of the KMT regime, however, the government was more inclined to prevent the rise of big capital altogether rather than to control it. This propensity was best illustrated by the government's initial reliance on SOEs and the later creation of new SOEs in sectors such as upstream petrochemicals, where private initiatives were suppressed. By allocating credit to SOEs, the government limited the flow of resources to the private sector.

State ownership of the banking system created a number of problems, however. Because state bankers were held personally responsible for their portfolios and had minimal information on borrowers' activities, the risk of default and the availability of collateral became the principal determinants of credit allocation. Until recent years, credits were thus rationed not according to industrial policy goals but according to the size and ownership of enterprises, with SOEs coming first, followed by big enterprises and small and medium-sized enterprises (SMEs).

This ultraconservative policy on the part of state banks created a number of difficulties. First, several recent studies have shown that the ranking of firms in terms of the efficiency of capital use runs exactly the other way, with SMEs being the most efficient, big enterprises less so, and SOEs the least efficient.[6] Second, to offset the advantage accruing to SOEs and larger enterprises, the government did periodically undertake more targeted lending, with SMEs and farmers being the main beneficiaries. Finally, this policy has led directly to the bending and breaking of rules on the part of private financiers. To guarantee that the SMEs could raise financing, the government has tolerated the informal financial sector and even supported its development, for example, by enforcing private lending through the instrument of a post-dated check.

As it had highly risk-averse state bankers, Taiwan's financial sector was immune from the problem of nonperforming debt seen in Korea. The extralegal and even illegal practices of private financial institutions, however, have been a severe problem. Scandals in private lending not only sent shock waves through the organized financial sector but also drew widespread criticism of state domination of finance. Inefficiency of the financial sector was especially salient and pronounced after 1986 under conditions of excess liquidity, which was a result of chronic trade surpluses, and pressure from Taiwan's trade partners for large-scale currency appreciation. More than anything else, the excess liquidity associated with the surpluses impelled the government to commit itself to financial liberalization in the late 1980s. Political liberalization and the gradual ascent of indigenous capitalists in the political process made it difficult for the leadership to continue to inhibit the demands for greater private sector participation in financial markets. The reform was primarily crisis-driven, however, the inadequacy of the existing financial institutions and the mounting extralegal or illegal financial transactions lent support to liberal economists, foreign bankers, and technocrats who echoed private business's demand for financial liberalization. The aversion to the rise of native financial capitalists eroded, but the way the government designed financial liberalization revealed

---

[6]J. D. Shea and P. S. Kuo, "The Allocative Efficiency of Banks' Loanable Funds in Taiwan," in *Proceedings of the Conference on Financial Development in Taiwan* (Taipei: Institute of Economics, Academia Sinica, 1984).

that the regime's obsession with the concentration of capital still lingered.

In the next section, I analyze changes in credit policy through Taiwan's postwar development history, linking the evolution of financial institutions with the stages of industrialization. In Section II, I examine the behavioral consequences of state domination of the financial sector, that is, risk aversion by state bankers and rule breaking by private bankers. In the final section, the structural and situational imperatives for financial liberalization are discussed.

I. THE INTENT OF CREDIT POLICY AND THE DESIGN OF FINANCIAL INSTITUTIONS

Four phases of industrial development can be identified in postwar Taiwan: import substitution industrialization in the 1950s, the initial stage of export promotion in the 1960s, industrial deepening in the 1970s, and industrial diversification in the 1980s. Technocrats proposed to expand and use financial institutions in ways that would meet the changing needs of these different stages of industrialization. Actual financial development, however, especially the ownership pattern of banking institutions, and credit policies have reflected the political leadership's concern with macroeconomic stability and its anxiety toward the creation of an indigenous capitalist class rather than the technocrats' conception of industrial policy. Financial institutions and policies were designed to curtail inflation and to keep industrialists from controlling financial markets. Reconstructing the history of institutional development and policy change in the financial sector allows us to examine how political calculations impinged on technocratic rationality.

Import Substitution Industrialization

Defeated on the mainland in 1949 by the Communists, the KMT regime retreated to Taiwan with a wide array of state-owned financial institutions. Apart from the Bureau of Central Trust, which would manage external trade, and the China Insurance Company, the remaining financial institutions were initially not activated, including the state-controlled postal savings and the "big four banks," namely, the central bank, the Bank of China, the Bank of Communication and the Farmer's Bank. A well-functioning financial sector had already developed in Taiwan under Japanese colonial rule and was reorganized upon Taiwan's decolonization. In 1946 the Taiwan administration—staffed by KMT expatriates—nationalized three commercial banks (Chang-hwa, Hua-nan, and the Taiwan Industrial-Commercial, which was re-named in 1951 as the First), reorganized the Bank of Taiwan (originally the Taipei branch of the Bank of Japan), merged twelve private in-surance companies into two state-owned insurance companies (Taiwan Life and Taiwan Casuality), and initiated the state-owned Taiwan Mu-tual Loans and Savings Company to absorb capital from private credit clubs. The administration also formed a Land Bank (based on the colonial Dai-Ichi Kangyo Bank) and a new Cooperative Bank in 1946, both of which were active in the agricultural sector, with the former playing a significant role in land reform. Overshadowed by the state sector, the private sector was barely visible on the periphery of the financial sector, being active only in credit cooperatives (which since their inception in the 1910s had served local commerce) and seven local mutual loans and savings associations (which were established between 1948 and 1952). Credit cooperatives (CCs) and mutual loans and sav-ings (MLS') are areas where the informal financial sector, such as private credit clubs, crept in.

The Bank of Taiwan was the nerve center of the sector. As the largest commercial bank, it accounted for one-third of total bank deposits and lending in the 1950s and performed the function of the central bank, issuing currency and serving as the lender of last resort. Lending by state-owned banks went mostly to the state sector for social investment and the expansion of SOEs; banks were more timid in lending to the private sector for fear of rekindling inflation. The Bank of Taiwan, however, acted like an industrial bank in the 1950s, extending pref-erential interest rate loans to SOEs and the ISI industries, especially textiles. Because of criticisms from the American aid agency, Chinese-American economists, and KMT elites in the Legislative and Control yuans, the preferential rate loans from the Bank of Taiwan to the private sector were discontinued in 1956 and those to SOEs, in 1961.[7]

K. Y. Yin, Taiwan's foremost economic architect during this period and an electrical engineer by training, promoted ISI and nurtured a crop of private capitalists through his concurrent control of three key organizations: the U.S. Aid Commission; the External Trade Board, which controlled imports and agrarian export earnings through the Bureau of Central Trust (which was headed by Yin as well); and the Industrial Commission, which approved industrial projects.[8] The major

---

[7] Hsing Mo-huan, "Taiwan," in *Taiwan and the Philippines: Industrialization and Trade Policies,* ed. John H. Power, Geraldo P. Sicat, and Hsing Mo-han (London: Oxford University Press, 1971), pp. 224–25.

[8] See Yen-chuan Yen, *Chao-nien chi tai-wan* [Early postwar Taiwan] (Taipei: Times Cultural, 1989), p. 64. Accused of corruption, Yin left office in 1955 and did not resume office until 1957.

instrument for ISI was not the lending policy of the Bank of Taiwan, however, but the allocation of foreign exchange and the control of industrial permits. The loanable funds in the banking system at that time were not yet significant; most bank deposits were from the government and American aid funds.

The Initial Push for Industrial Exports

The principal function of the financial sector in the 1950s was to support the import of capital goods. The U.S. aid agency and the revamped local financial institutions were sufficient to perform this import-financing function. The shift from ISI to export-led industrialization, as well as the expected termination of U.S. aid, led the government to expand the financial sector in the early 1960s. There were four new aspects to the sector: (1) the reopening of the central bank, (2) the establishment of specialized financial institutions for industrial development, (3) the limited entry of foreign banks, and (4) the controlled expansion of the private financial sector. The first two reforms were recommended by foreign advisers, including Chinese-American economists,[9] the third reform was assisted by the departing foreign aid agency, and the last reform was a response to demands from the private sector.

The central bank, restored in 1961, was subordinated to the president rather than the premier. The head of the bank was appointed by the president for a term of five years and was not accountable to the Legislative Yuan. Insulated from the legislative power and directives of the premier or minister of finance, the bank was primarily entrusted with the task of financial stability, though assistance in economic development was also listed as a goal of the bank. Deriving its policies directly from the president, the central bank espoused economic orthodoxy. Not until the revision of the Central Bank Law in 1979 was the central bank subjected to scrutiny by the premier. The governor of the bank continues to maintain his autonomy vis-à-vis the Legislative Yuan, however, and enjoys a five-year appointment.

Seven special financial institutions were either established or reopened in the 1960s. First, the postal savings system, introduced by the KMT regime on the mainland in 1930, resumed operations in Taiwan in 1962 and turned out to be a very successful enterprise. Second, the Bank of China was restored in 1961 to manage foreign exchange trans-

---

[9]S. C. Tsiang, "Taiwan chi li-lu wen-ti" [On Taiwan's interest rates], in *Taiwan ho bi yu jin zong lun wen chi* [Papers on Taiwan's money and finance], ed. Cheng-hsiung Chiu (Taipei: Lien-Jing, 1975), p. 322.

actions.[10] Third, the Bank of Communication—initiated in 1923 on the mainland—was reestablished as a development bank and assigned the task of supplying long- to medium-term loans to industry.[11] Fourth, the China Development Corporation (CDC), a new development financial institution, came into being in 1959. The CDC was to channel funds to new ventures as part of the preparation for the post-U.S. aid era. Endowed with some aid funds and a small amount of equity and expected to receive some government support and to secure development loans from abroad, the CDC would provide long- and medium-term loans, as well as seed capital and guarantees for new industrial undertakings. It was incorporated as a private institution—with 75 percent local, 10 percent government, and 15 percent foreign capital—so as to avoid the administrative constraints imposed on state-owned banks and to facilitate capital inflow. When new firms succeeded, the CDC would divest its share for other projects. In short, the CDC was not a deposit-taking financial company but a semipublic developmental institution using equity participation from major banks and the private sector to promote new enterprises. Fifth, a stock exchange was also created to facilitate the supply of capital. Unfortunately, this capital market remained miniscule and speculative. Finally, the Farmers Bank was restored in 1967 to assist agricultural specialization, while the city of Taipei, immediately after being turned into a municipality, formed the City Bank of Taipei in 1969 to serve as its fiscal agent.

To promote exports and to gain access to the international capital market, six foreign banks were admitted. These banks were the Dai-Ichi Kangyo from Japan; the City Bank, Bank of America, and American Express Bank from the United States; the Bank of Bangkok from Thailand; and the Philippines Metropolitan Bank and Trust Company. The Dai-Ichi Kangyo Bank facilitated trade between Taiwan and Japan, which had been transacted on a barter basis in the 1950s. With strong ties to overseas Chinese, the Bank of Bangkok and the Philippines Metropolitan Bank helped Taiwan export to Southeast Asian markets. The three American banks were reportedly not keen to enter Taiwan at that time; their introduction was not a result of bargaining for re-

[10] Originally established in 1905 by the imperial government, the Bank of China later became an independent private institution for Shanghai financiers and then came under the nationalist government's control after the 1935 reform. See Park M. Coble, Jr., *The Shanghai Capitalists and the Nationalist Government, 1927–1937* (Cambridge: Council on East Asian Studies, Harvard University, 1985), p. 185. In 1971, this bank was reconstituted as a private institution under the new name of the China International Commercial Bank (CICB) to escape possible confiscation by the Chinese Communist regime.

[11] Tso-jong Wang, *Wo Men Ju He Chuang Tsao Ching Chi Chi Chi* [How we created the economic miracle] (Taipei: China Times, 1978), p. 63. The development fund for this bank would be based on the proceeds from the privatization of state-owned enterprises.

ciprocity but rather of American government assistance and persuasion. Planning to terminate its aid, the American aid agency helped Taiwan open a window to the international capital market via the introduction of three leading American banks to Taiwan.[12]

Requests from domestic capitalists for private participation in the banking sector came in the wake of the 1958–1961 economic reform for export promotion.[13] Criticisms of conservative state-owned commercial banks and recommendations for their privatization were widespread among industrialists, legislators, foreign advisers, and even government officials.[14] The government did not respond to these requests and criticisms; rather, it restored its own banks originally established on the mainland. To draw political support from and to facilitate trade with overseas Chinese, however, the government licensed the Overseas Chinese Commercial Bank (OCCB) in 1960 and permitted the Shanghai Savings and Commercial Bank (SSCB) to resume its operations in 1965. Proposed in the first united overseas Chinese patriotic conference in 1957, the OCCB was incorporated by Chinese in Malaya, the United States, and Japan.[15] Having suspended its business on the mainland and reincorporated in Hong Kong in 1952, the SSCB, a renowned private bank in prewar China, recemented its ties with the KMT regime.[16] These two private banks were allowed entry because of their expertise, overseas trade links, and, in the case of the OCCB, its political loyalty. Both banks were authorized to handle foreign exchange and, the OCCB, unsoldered gold and silver as well.[17]

Price stability, export promotion, and the newly refurbished financial institutions contributed to a great leap forward in savings during the 1960s. Household deposits increased from 25 percent of total deposits in the 1950s to 55 percent in the late 1960s. Savings and term deposits as a percentage of total deposits gradually increased from around 26 percent during the 1950s to 50 percent by the end of the 1960s.[18] The

---

[12] Interview in Taipei with a leading economist, April 3, 1991.

[13] Executive Yuan, Republic of China, *Yangminsang Hui Yi Tzi Liau Huei Ben* [Proceedings of Yaninsang conferences] (Taipei: Executive Yuan, 1961), p. 30.

[14] R. F. Leonard, F. L. Deming, and Chester Morrill, *Comments and Recommendations on Central Banking in the Republic of China* (Taipei: Central Bank of China, 1961), pp. 45, 90.

[15] *Independent Evening News*, July 13, 1958, p. 4.

[16] Shong-ling Yaw, *Chen Kuan-pu de i sheng* [The life of K. P. Chen] (Taipei: Chuan-chi wen-huseh, 1984), chap. 14.

[17] Although shut off from the core of the financial sector, the indigenous capitalists were admitted to the insurance industry. Between 1961 and 1963, ten new property and casuality insurance companies and seven life insurance companies were licensed. These new and private insurance companies were to help mobilize savings and support exports but were not expected to transgress the "reserved domains" of the two state-owned insurance companies, SOEs, civil service, and labor insurance firms.

[18] Fu-chi Liu, "Taiwan yu tun huo pung chang tau jing ji wun ting ti jing jung fa jang"

size of the curb market and the gap between official rates and black market rates began to drop after the mid-1950s as inflation was brought under control. Deposits grew and several big black market scandals made savers more risk-averse and wary of the black market.[19] Savings began to flow into the government-controlled financial system. As the supply of foreign exchange increased, black market premia also decreased.

The shift of development strategy from ISI to export promotion at the turn of the 1960s was coupled by a shift in emphasis from the expansion of the state sector to the expansion of the private sector in manufacturing. There was a parallel shift in the allocation of bank credit, which began to substitute for U.S. aid as the primary capital source for investment. After the economic reform in 1958–1961, the share of loans and discounts advanced to private firms, as compared with SOEs, rose sharply (see Table 3.1). Bank credit went primarily to export financing, which was introduced by the Bank of Taiwan in 1957, expanded by the central bank and nearly all commercial banks in 1962, and also supplied by local branches of foreign banks after 1978. Export financing was universal (not industry-specific) and automatic (extended to any firm with export-shipping documents). Using standardized technology and abundant labor and exploiting the growing presence of foreign buyers, export-oriented, assembly-type, and small-scale local firms began to emerge. These manufacturing firms—mostly in garments, toys, and plastic goods—had low start-up costs that could be met by rural credit co-ops and borrowing in the informal market. But the provision of working capital and export financing assisted these firms' growth.

In comparison with short-term export financing, the amount of development financing through the two major institutions, the Bank of Communication and the CDC, was lackluster. Although chartered as a development bank, the Bank of Communication functioned as an ordinary commercial bank. The promised development fund did not materialize as SOEs were never divested. This special bank thus competed with commercial banks for deposits and short-term lending and was also subject to supervision by the profit-minded Ministry of Finance (MOF) and other bureaucratic agencies. The record of development financing from the CDC was equally disappointing. The CDC became very profit-oriented rather than geared toward policy objectives. It was never turned into an important agent for capital inflow because SOEs

[Taiwan's financial development: From inflation to economic stability], in *Taiwan huo-pi yu chin-jung,* ed. Cheng-hsiung Chiu, pp. 57–59.
[19] Fu-chi Liu, "Taiwan yu tun huo," p. 56.

Table 3.1. Breakdown of lending of all financial institutions, 1961–1990 (percent)

Year	Government	SOEs	Private sector
1961	21.3	25.2	53.5
1962	16.4	26.9	56.7
1963	17.3	20.1	62.7
1964	15.9	17.6	66.5
1965	13.9	15.2	70.9
1966	13.0	14.3	72.7
1967	12.4	13.9	73.7
1968	11.6	12.2	76.2
1969	10.0	12.4	77.6
1970	8.3	13.0	78.2
1971	5.6	14.1	80.3
1972	4.7	12.9	82.8
1973	3.8	10.6	85.2
1974	4.5	13.3	82.1
1975	3.3	14.9	81.8
1976	3.9	15.1	80.9
1977	3.2	14.7	82.1
1978	2.9	13.0	84.1
1979	2.5	14.8	82.6
1980	2.1	17.9	80.0
1981	2.6	19.0	78.5
1982	3.3	19.2	77.4
1983	2.9	16.5	80.5
1984	2.4	14.2	83.4
1985	2.3	13.0	84.7
1986	2.2	11.7	86.1
1987	1.3	8.4	90.3
1988	1.6	6.0	92.4
1989	7.0	5.3	87.7
1990	6.3	5.5	88.2

Source: Central Bank of China, Economic Research Division, *Monthly Financial Statistics* (Taipei: Central Bank of China, April 1991), p. 57.

got their funding directly from abroad and the state seemed to prefer foreign direct investment to foreign borrowing.

Development financing to the private sector focused on former import substitution industrialists in textiles, glass, and plastics, which were slightly more capital-intensive and were produced on a large scale. But the amounts were limited. Long-term financing accounted for 23 percent of total lending in 1955; its share increased to only 27 percent in 1968,[20] despite the sharp increase in term deposits and savings. Credit policy in the first decade of export-oriented growth centered only on export financing rather than industrial financing, contrary to what the technocrats had originally envisioned.

[20] Fu-chi Liu, "Taiwan yu tun huo," p. 65.

Industrial Deepening

At the turn of the 1970s, some economic planners began to call for industrial upgrading and deepening. The emphasis on export processing could not be sustained, it was believed, because diminishing surplus labor and increasing wages would mean declining competitiveness. On the demand side, Taiwan faced slowed growth and increasing protectionism in the West. The first step to industrial upgrading, according to technocrats, was to deepen the industrial base by pursuing backward linkages in intermediate and upstream production which might make downstream production more competitive and secure and which might also broaden the base for exports.

Technocrats again urged the divestment of state-owned banks to finance industrial upgrading by the private sector and, only in the case of entrepreneurial failure, by the public sector. Liberal economists proposed a thorough financial liberalization—particularly the deregulation of interest rates—to improve the efficiency of state-owned banks. In 1970, Finance Minister K. T. Li (a physicist by training), who emerged as the spokesman for the technocrats, proposed to privatize one bank as a trial.[21] Meanwhile, the private sector began to push hard for a place in the nonbank financial sector, such as investment, trust, and credit companies.

The moment of technocratic planning for industrial deepening was unfortunately also a moment when the regime was reassessing the state-business relation.[22] Party ideologues and SOE managers began to articulate their concerns about the emergence of a capitalist class. After a good decade of rapid economic growth, the private sector clearly dwarfed the public sector in industrial production. The political leadership thus vetoed private undertakings in the upstream petrochemical industry. As the private sector's equity participation in heavy industry was not forthcoming, the government assumed the main task of industrial deepening and marched into shipbuilding, integrated steel making, machinery, and nonferrous metal industries. At the same time, the government decided to overhaul the country's infrastructure, which was strained to the limit during the rapid export expansion of the 1960s. The industrial undertakings mentioned above, combined with the seven infrastructure projects—one airport, one railway electrifi-

[21] Shi-kang Wen, "Yin hang ti chu lu" [The way out for the banking sector], in *Wei jih chang jing chi kai hsing chu* [Creating a self-strengthening economy] (Taipei: Lien-jing, 1980), pp. 179–80. The idea was for the state to vacate from the commercial banking sector and concentrate on development banking only.

[22] Tun-jen Cheng, "Political Regimes and Development Strategies: Korea and Taiwan," in *Manufacturing Miracles: Paths of Industrialization in Latin America and East Asia*, ed. Gary Gereffi and Donald Wyman (Princeton: Princeton University Press, 1990).

cation, one new railway, two harbor projects, one freeway, and one nuclear power plant—yielded the "ten major projects."

Under these circumstances, the government naturally did not endorse the idea of privatization of the banks. For industrial upgrading, in 1973 the Executive Yuan did establish the Development Fund, which would assist high-technology development and important industries in the private sector, as well as public investment in areas where the private sector was deficient. The government allocated NT $200 million to the Bank of Communication and the Bank of China, which together with their own capital would supply long-term loans for industry and exports.[23] These policy loans, however, were absorbed by SOEs engaged in the ten projects listed above. Because of the government's fiscal burden and lack of private subscription, state-owned steel and shipbuilding plants were undercapitalized and became very dependent on bank credit lines. Postal savings redeposited in the central bank were often allocated to commercial banks, which then extended special loan facilities to SOEs. As Table 3.1 shows, the total loans and discounts advanced to the public sector after 1973 increased once again at the expense of the private sector. The nexus between SOEs and state-controlled finance became even tighter, though; for reasons that will be detailed below, state-owned banks continued to advance loans to leading private enterprises.

Beginning in 1970, the balance of payments began to show a surplus, and throughout the 1970s, these surpluses accumulated, despite the recession of 1974 and 1975. Foreign exchange surpluses were deposited abroad, making Taiwan a capital-exporting developing country. In 1973, Premier Sun Yun-hsuen had proposed to set aside US $400 million in foreign exchange reserves to import machinery, raw materials, and key consumption goods. In 1979 the president also ordered the central bank to allocate US $600 million for a loan facility for the same purpose. The former was obviously motivated by macroeconomic considerations of economic stability,[24] whereas the latter was politically motivated to regain the confidence of the business after the shock of the U.S. derecognition of Taiwan. In both cases, the loan facilities were underutilized.[25]

Two other types of policy loans for the private sector were more active, however. They were targeted at small and medium-sized enterprises and the agricultural sectors. Premier Chiang Ching-kuo explicitly

---

[23] K. T. Li, "Public Finance and Economic Development," *Industry of Free China* 34 (December 1970): 2–4.

[24] *Independent Evening News*, January 8, 1973.

[25] *Independent Evening News*, April 22, 1973; and Tso-jong Wang, *Chai jing wen chun hsu pen* [Essays on finance and economy II] (Taipei: Times, 1982), pp. 333–36.

endorsed special treatment for these sectors, arguing that credit allocation should be "fair and reasonable."[26] The special fund for SMEs had a long history, dating back to 1954, and was used to aid small firms by providing medium- to long-term financing at below-market interest rates. Its origin was the small and medium-sized enterprise assistance loans financed by the Sino-American Fund. Between 1965 and 1969, some one hundred promising firms received support.[27] But the value of small business loans remained small until the central bank drastically enriched it with NT $1 billion, distributed by various banks. In the midst of the 1974 oil crisis, the government also established a credit guarantee fund to assist small firms. This guarantee fund in the amount of NT $450 million was a great success. In 1976, the Small and Medium Enterprise Bank was established to assist small and medium-sized enterprises during the period of financial distress following the oil crisis and to promote mergers and rationalization. Although few mergers were recorded, credit support for SMEs was hence institutionalized.

The evolution of agricultural policy and the development fund tailored for the rural sector is beyond the scope of this chapter.[28] After 1971 the rural sector was turned from one that was squeezed into one that has been heavily subsidized. Moreover, the new agricultural policy has maintained a living standard comparable with the urban standard. As a result of the new agricultural policy, Taiwan's rural credit cooperatives have emerged as one of the richest types of financial institutions in the country.

Via the forum of the Provincial Assembly, the private sector frequently demanded a share in the banking sector. The government usually responded with a promise to study the divestment of state-owned banks rather than with the promise to allow any new financial institutions, but there was some innovation in the financial system in the 1970s.[29] In the early 1970s, the government issued six permits for indigenous capitalists to create trust and investment companies (TICs). Essentially a kind of investment bank, private TICs were, in the eyes of technocrats, a good solution to the problem of longer-term lending given the government's unwillingness to divest SOEs or state-owned commercial banks. Expected to attract the investors who were unwilling to deposit in low-yielding bank accounts but who were without access

[26] *Independent Evening News*, May 28, 1973.

[27] Jung Chang, "Taiwan zi chong shiau chi yeh ying han yu chong shiau chi yeh zong zhi wen ti" [Small business banks and the financing of small and medium enterprises in Taiwan], *Bank of Taiwan Quarterly* 34, no. 3 (1983): 12.

[28] Joseph A. Yager, *Transforming Agriculture in Taiwan* (Ithaca: Cornell University Press, 1988), chap. 6.

[29] *Independent Evening News*, August 24 and 29, 1967.

or expertise to invest in the stock market, TICs could complement rather than compete with the commercial banking sector.

TICs were primarily a concession that the political leadership made to "patriotic" overseas Chinese.[30] In 1972, the government issued a special permit to overseas Chinese to initiate a new bank, United World Chinese Commercial Bank, following the resolution of the World Chinese Financial Conference in 1971. Proposed by a leading Filipino Chinese who later became its chairman, the bank cast its shareholding net wide to collect the support of overseas Chinese for the KMT regime, which was suffering from diplomatic setbacks.[31]

The government also admitted many foreign banks to Taiwan. Ten foreign banks—eight from the United States, one from the United Kingdom, and one from Canada—established their branches or representative offices in Taiwan between 1972 and 1976. On the one hand, this second round of arrivals of foreign financial institutions was due to foreign capital's demand for access. On the other hand, the government permitted foreign financial institutions in order to forge economic and, hopefully, political ties between Taiwan and the United States, one of the very few important allies remaining after Taiwan was forced to withdraw from the United Nations in 1971 and to sever formal diplomatic ties with Japan and other major Western countries in 1972.

To give local capitalists their due share in the banking sector and to promote SMEs, the provincial government—controlled Taiwan Mutual Loans and Savings Company was transformed into the Taiwan Medium Enterprise Bank (TMEB) in 1976, whereas the other seven private and local companies of this genre were turned into regional medium-sized enterprise banks (MEBs) between 1977 and 1979. There was a suggestion for reorganizing mutual loans and savings companies into all-purpose citizen's banks to serve regional communities.[32] The government, however, finally decided to commission these companies into specialized banks serving industrial and business communities only.

To allow state-owned banks some degree of discretion in setting interest rates and to facilitate the creation of a money market, the government helped establish three "private" bills finance companies (BFCs) between 1976 and 1978. Set by market conditions, interest rates in the money market have correlated closely with black market rates. This market signal permitted the central bank to delimit a band within

[30]Hsieu-ying Jiang and Ming-chi Kuo, "Jian-chai sa-tan ti jin-yuen wang-kuo" [Financial kingdom on the sand], *Commonwealth*, November 1, 1985, p. 93.

[31]*Central Daily News*, July 30, 1973, p. 3.

[32]Chun-nan Pai, "New Bank Law and the Establishment of the Specialized Banking Institutes," in his *Huan Dang Jong De Jing Jhi* [The world economy in transition] (Taipei: Commonwealth, 1984), p. 110.

71

which interest rates could be fixed by individual banks. Although private institutions on paper, two of the three BFCs were controlled by SOEs, state-owned banks, and the KMT-owned Central Investment Company, which also monopolized the loan facility for the growing stock exchange market.

Among the three new functional institutions—TICs, new banks, and BFCs—TICs were expected to be the most instrumental to industrial upgrading. Although new banks and BFCs proved to be a success, however, TICs turned out to be more of a problem than a solution. What TICs were allowed to do was never clear to begin with. In the end, TICs competed with banks for short-term funds and, on the lending side, funneled the resources to speculative activities, notably real estate, and often to enterprises affiliated with the owners of TICs. As in the Philippines, this contributed to a financial crisis, which I will discuss in the next section.

Industrial Diversification

By the late 1970s, economic technocrats were again calling for industrial upgrading. The pursuit of heavy and chemical industrialization (HCI) in the 1970s was blunted by the first oil crisis in 1974. A cautious approach to HCI and lack of cooperation between the public and private sectors left Taiwan with an economy that was still based largely on light industry, in contrast with the South Korean economy. Economic technocrats called for an integrated effort to promote industrial diversification into high value-added and technology-intensive industries, rather than capital-intensive, basic ones. Economic technocrats also called for joint public-private efforts to assume the task of industrial upgrading. Following a national economic conference in 1980 planned by newly appointed Minister of Economic Affairs Y. T. Chao (a mechanical engineer by training), two industries were identified as "strategic" to further industrial development: machinery and information science. Later, biotechnology and materials were added to the list of strategic industries.

The financial sector underwent another round of restructuring, but only partly to pursue the new industrial policy. In January 1979, the Export-Import Bank was formed to promote high-credit risk exports, in particular, machinery exports, and the Bank of Communication was recommissioned as a development bank. In 1982, TMEB was chartered as a development bank as well. These two development banks continued to be evaluated by the same criteria as other commercial banks, however. During the early 1980s, the floodgate of foreign banks was open again. But the influx of foreign banks was unrelated to the new industrial policy. Their presence in Taiwan was in part a response to foreign financiers' demand to have a role in the rapidly growing financial sector and in part due to the government's attempt to expand nonpolitical ties with other countries after the United States withdrew its formal recognition in 1979.

With the injection of budgetary support, the Development Fund became very active after 1982. Its size reached NT $30 billion in 1988, of which half was from budgetary sources and half from investment returns. Sixty percent of the Development Fund was used for long-term lending, and 40 percent was for equity participation. Its twenty-five investment items are quite comprehensive, covering everything from electronics to petrochemicals and investment companies. The fund also invested in two venture capital companies, which lent heavily to the electronics industry, both semiconductors and computers, and industries housed in the Hsinchu Science Park, partly with the objective of recruiting young overseas Chinese who were science- or engineering-trained entrepreneurs in Silicon Valley in California for new ventures in Taiwan.

A second major source for development financing is postal savings. Before February 1982, postal savings were redeposited in the central bank. Since then, new deposits have been routed to the Bank of Communication (40 percent), the Land Bank (25 percent), TMEB (25 percent), and the Farmers' Bank (10 percent).[33] The Land Bank and the Farmers' Bank were assigned the task of renovating the agricultural sector; the other two banks were to finance industrial upgrading. Credit policy in support of industrial diversification included several components. The first consisted of new credit facilities for strategic industries through the Bank of Communication and took the form of long-term, low-interest rate loans. The second component, a credit facility for "key industries," financed broad types of investment in antipollution devices and automation, the purchase of locally produced machinery and software, and projects supported by Council of Economic Planning and Development (CEPD). This loan facility is primarily for big enterprises. The third loan facility for small and medium-sized firms was also drastically improved in the 1980s.[34] As mentioned, 25 percent of postal savings flowed to the TMEB. In 1982, a low-interest development loan for small and medium-sized enterprises was established with an

[33] Since October 1984, 25 percent of new postal savings deposits have flowed to the central bank. The remainder is still earmarked for use by the above-listed four banks.
[34] Tai-ying Liu, "Taiwan chong shiau chi yeh tou zhi whang jing chi yen iau" [Investment environment for Taiwan's small and medium enterprises], *Bank of Taiwan Quarterly* 34, no. 3 (1983): 101. In 1981 there was a big boost from the central bank in the amount of NT $3 billion.

amount of NT $16 billion. Of this amount, 25 percent was financed by the Development Fund and 75 percent was financed by the TMEB. This facility is for upgrading small and medium-sized firms in the "strategic" sectors through the purchase of automated and locally produced machinery and through technology development and market exploration in important export sectors.

General Observations

The above analysis of the evolution of financial institutions clearly shows that the political elite in the government has been carefully guarding its dominance in the financial sector by controlling entry to the sector. To meet the growing need for financial services, the regime leadership would do its utmost to expand the state sector before considering any new private institutions. Moreover, although indigenous capitalists, overseas Chinese, and foreign bankers all demanded entry to the financial sector, the leadership granted permission in the following order: foreign banks, overseas Chinese banks, and finally, domestic private financial institutions.

Although foreign banks and overseas Chinese were minor partners in commercial banking, local capital was treated as a marginal partner in the periphery of the financial sector until 1991. Local capital's call for entry to the financial sector was echoed by both economists and technocrats. Yet, local capital gained only four small footholds in the financial sector at a rate of one each decade (see Table 3.2): urban CCs as a colonial legacy, MLSs in the early 1950s, insurance companies in the early 1960s, and TICs in the early 1970s.[35] Moreover, the operation of these institutions was highly restricted. Each MLS company was limited to a single region only, though in that region, it had a monopoly. Insurance companies and TICs were not territorially restricted, but their licenses were issued by special permission and no new permits were issued after 1962. Each CC was confined to a locality, though market entry was open even in the same locality.[36] In consequence, the private sector's shares in assets, deposits and loans of financial institutions remained small (see Table 3.3).

The pecking order for entry into the financial sector might reflect the "economic value" of the three segments of capital. Foreign bankers

---

[35] The credit departments of farmers' associations and fishermen associations are private, but these financial institutions are agents of government-owned specialized banks and government's agricultural administration.

[36] Kuei Chang, "Taiwan hsin yung he cho sheuh fa jang jie duan lun" [On the stages of the development of Taiwan's credit cooperatives], *Local Finance* (Taipei: Taipei Provincial Government, 1990).

Table 3.2. Entry into the financial sector by local capitalists, 1909–1991

Period	Institutions	Number
1909–	Credit co-ops	
1948–1952	Mutual loans and savings	7[a]
1961–1963	Insurance companies	17
1971–1972	Trust and investment companies	7
1976–1978	Bills exchange companies	3[b]
1977–1979	Existing MLSs turned into local medium-sized business banks	7[a]
1991	Commercial banks	15[c]

[a] These seven companies are regional and limited to a district, whereas the government-owned Taiwan Medium Enterprise Bank (TMGB) is islandwide.

[b] Local private capitalists dominate in only one of the three bills exchange companies; the largest and dominant shareholder for the other two companies is the KMT.

[c] New commercial banks are limited to five branches only and are not allowed to deal with foreign exchange transactions or, in the initial three years, with securities.

could transfer modern banking expertise to the local financial sector. Overseas Chinese financiers, mainly from Southeast Asia, could promote Taiwan's trade with that market, where Taiwan often tested its products before venturing into North America. Indigenous financiers had neither the expertise nor the overseas networks. Their economic utility was not insignificant, however. The CCs, as deeply entrenched, grass-roots-level financial institutions, were a savings mobilization machine. The MLSs were initially the government's linkages to the informal financial sector and later turned into special banks for small and medium-sized enterprises. The insurance industry was a savings- and trade-promoting sector, whereas TICs facilitated financial deepening and, hence, assisted industrial deepening.

The regime's preference order for new private institutions was less a function of their economic value than of political risk and the bargaining power the three groups of capitalists possessed vis-à-vis the KMT regime. Foreign banks were politically safe and not predisposed to challenging the legitimacy of the KMT regime. Their operations could also be restricted, as they usually are in the Third World. And, because of their unfamiliarity with local conditions, they were not in direct competition with state-owned banks. Their presence also buttressed Taiwan's external economic linkages, which have been important substitutes for lost diplomatic ties.

New banking licenses were a reward for overseas Chinese political support of the KMT regime. Although unlikely to side with Taiwan's domestic opposition, overseas Chinese capitalists could threaten to switch loyalty from the KMT regime to the Chinese communist regime. Moreover, residing abroad and beyond the reach of the legal power of the KMT's martial law, overseas Chinese could be an "offshore

Table 3.3. Total assets of financial institutions, 1961–1991 (percent)

Institution	1961	1966	1971	1976	1981	1986	1990	1991
Central bank	21.6	23.9	22.8	21.8	21.7	27.3	27.3	20.2
Depository institutions	76.0	71.2	69.1	68.0	65.5	57.1	57.1	63.0
Domestic banks	62.9	54.3	53.0	52.9	47.2	40.6	40.6	42.4
Foreign banks	0.7	1.4	2.7	4.5	5.0	2.2	2.2	2.3
SME banks	2.4	3.4	3.1	2.2	3.3	4.0	3.9	5.8
Credit co-ops	5.9	6.8	6.4	5.3	5.7	5.3	5.3	7.3
Rural credit co-ops	4.1	5.3	3.9	3.1	4.4	5.1	5.1	5.4
Other financial institutions	2.4	5.0	8.1	10.3	12.9	15.6	15.6	16.8
Trust/investment company	1.0	1.7	1.7	3.4	3.4	1.9	1.8	3.4
Postal savings	0.7	1.9	5.0	5.7	7.6	11.5	11.5	9.2
Life insurance company	0.2	0.9	1.0	0.9	1.2	1.7	1.7	3.2
Property insurance company	0.5	0.5	0.4	0.3	0.4	0.3	0.3	0.3
Bills finance company				0.1	0.2	0.2	0.2	0.3
Securities finance company					0.1	0.1	0.1	0.4
Total	100.0	100.0	100.0	100.0	100.0	100.0	100.0	100.0

Sources: Central Bank of China, *Monthly Financial Statistics* (Taipei: Central Bank of China, various years).

opposition," freely criticizing the KMT government. Finally, overseas Chinese have had their representatives in the Legislature and National Assembly, as well as a captured organization in the government, namely, the Overseas Chinese Affairs Commission under the Executive Yuan.

The exclusion of the private sector from the financial commanding heights was also attributable to the fundamental political exigencies that the KMT regime faced in postwar Taiwan, namely, an alien and minority mainlander-controlled regime governing a capitalist economy that was primarily populated by the Taiwanese. State ownership in the banking sector prevented family-controlled, predominantly native Taiwanese industrial groupings from gaining financial power.[37] Keeping industrial capital insulated from the banking sector had the effect of discouraging concentration of the private sector.

Domination of the banking sector enabled the KMT regime to control credit directly and more easily maintain financial stability than if banks were privately owned. Indirect implementation of monetary policy requires government trust of private financiers, an element that was lacking in the KMT regime. Private banks during the final years of the wartime period (1943–1945) colluded with merchants, collected rents from credit allocation, hoarded commodities for speculation, and profited from inflation.[38] Currency reform during the civil war period (1946—1949) received little cooperation from the suspicious financial capitalists. These cumulative experiences with hyperinflation on the mainland led the KMT regime to conclude that private banking would create too much risk for economic stability.

If credit policy was characterized by an overriding concern with economic stability, support for industrial development was also evident. Until recent years, credit allocation has favored production over consumption and commerce. Industry-specific credit policy was apparent in the brief stage of ISI during the 1950s but was soon superseded by credit policies targeted at broad goals that included export promotion, industrial upgrading, and pollution control. Revived in the 1980s to nurture strategic industries, sector-specific credit policy was small in size, comprising only 4.4 percent of total government loans, and constantly came under criticism from economists. Although export loans were accessible and widely used, development financing—either sectoral, specific, or functional—became available to the private sector only recently, and many loan facilities were underutilized. Development financing was never a salient feature of Taiwan's financial system.

[37] Diana Yin, "Interview with Governor Yu," in *Decision Makers* (Taipei: Commonwealth, 1982).
[38] Editorial, *Central Daily News*, May 26, 1983.

Although industrial sector-specific credit policy was rare and controversial, credit support for two other broad sectors, agriculture and SMEs, had been long-lasting and immune from attack. The rural sector has been one of the regime's bases for political support. Never favored by bankers, SMEs are too important politically to be left entirely on their own. Their prosperity and growth mitigate the trend toward industrial concentration and keep the option of self-employment in industry and commerce open for labor and farmers. SMEs have also been the KMT regime's political partners in local elections. Hence SME loans were the only targeted loans that were never suspended. And the informal sector from which SMEs obtained much of their capital was never suppressed, stern laws against underground financial activities notwithstanding.[39]

The general approach to industrial credit support made good politics. The regime granted few privileges to specific industries, loans went to many rather than to a few firms, and government banks basically provided general economic support rather than attempting to shape the industrial structure through credit policy, with the partial exception of a few strategic industries. The beneficiaries of strategic industrial policy loans were young engineers–turned–entrepreneurs in the electronics industry and little educated apprentices–turned–entrepreneurs in the machinery industry. Both were new capitalists unrelated to established industries. These new entrepreneurs basically had small and medium-sized enterprises, which is why the financing scheme for strategic industries concocted by the technocrats was endorsed by the political leadership.

II. Behavioral Consequences of State Domination in the Financial Sector

State ownership and control of the financial sector was instrumental to the pursuit of two political objectives, namely, price stability and prevention of the creation of big indigenous financiers. But state ownership also generated two microlevel problems: perennially conservative lending by state bankers and pervasive rule bending by private financial institutions. The former had the effect of increasing the inefficiency of the financial sector, whereas the latter resulted in scandals and even crises. These problems were inherent in the incentive structure of a state-dominant financial sector.

[39] Yung-jen Huang et al., *Taiwan ti shia jing jung wen ti* [Problems regarding Taiwan's underground finance] (Taichung: Center for Research and Training on Local Finance, 1983).

Table 3.4. Sources of domestic borrowing by private enterprises, 1965–1988 (percent)

Year	Financial institutions	Money market	Curb market
1965	55.8	n.a.	44.2
1970	62.4	n.a.	37.6
1975	70.0	n.a.	30.0
1980	55.0	8.9	36.1
1981	52.8	11.7	35.5
1982	53.4	13.4	33.2
1983	54.9	14.3	30.8
1984	54.7	15.1	30.2
1985	51.7	13.3	35.1
1986	50.6	8.4	41.0
1987	56.2	6.7	37.1
1988	63.3	6.3	30.4

Source: Central Bank of China, *Flow of Funds in Taiwan District* (Taipei: Central Bank of China, 1989).

Risk Aversion of State Banks

State-owned banks in Taiwan function more like pawnshops than like modern financial institutions.[40] Bank credits are rationed according to the degree of presumed risk inferred from the ownership and size of enterprises or according to the extent to which enterprises can provide collateral to secure a loan. The preference order is SOEs, then big enterprises, and finally small and medium-sized enterprises, with consumers rarely receiving credit. Even large private enterprises rely on the curb market for a very significant part of their borrowings (see Table 3.4).

Why are state banks run like pawnshops? State bankers are given very limited freedom in banking operations, yet they assume significant responsibility for the loans they make. Moreover, the regulatory and legal framework for the business sector is so lax that it is difficult and costly for state bankers to develop a monitoring capacity. With little reliable information about a firm's financial condition, it is only rational for state bankers to direct loans first to state-owned enterprises and then to big enterprises.

Banks in Taiwan have not been allowed to be aggressive in lending. Prudential regulation was very strict for commercial banks during the 1950s and 1960s; the bank law limited unsecured loans to 25 percent of total deposits, the duration of credit lending to six months, and the duration of secured loans to one year. For savings banks, industrial

[40] Henry A. Ralph, "Impediment to Modern Banking in Taiwan," *Industry of Free China* 34 (September 1970): 9–16.

banks, and the savings sections of commercial banks, a loan with more than a one-year maturity was to be strictly secured. These regulations gave state bankers little room to practice long-term financing. These statutory requirements on the type of loans a bank could advance were relaxed in 1968 and largely removed in 1975,[41] but managerial freedom was still lacking.[42] State-owned banks are under the control and supervision of fifteen agencies of the central and provincial governments, which precludes managerial innovation. The three leading commercial banks are owned by the Ministry of Finance, managed by the Department of Finance of the Taiwan Provincial Government, supervised by the central bank, overseen by the Control Yuan, audited by the Legislative Yuan and the Provincial Assembly, budgeted by the Director-General of Auditing, Budget and Statistics, and under the Personnel Bureau of the Executive Yuan for personnel management. For every bank, the appointment of top-level personnel, for example, the president or chairperson, needs approval from at least six agencies, whereas budgets need approval from four agencies.[43]

The most restrictive aspect of these regulations are standards and procedures for writing off bad loans.[44] The Control Yuan, which has investigative power, "defines all public deposits with state-owned banks as 'public property' so that any loss of principal of a loan becomes a matter for investigation and assignment of fault."[45] As all banks are state-owned individual bank officers are by definition civil servants, and face administrative sanctions and even criminal punishment for any loans they make that later become nonperforming; thus, they meet strong disincentives against risky lending. The concern over possible personal liability for bad loans and the obsession with earnings makes bank officers risk-averse, valuing the default-proof SOEs and collateral-rich big enterprises in the private sector, while avoiding any unsecured lending. In brief, the bank officers allocate funds based on the consideration of security, not the rate of return.

Even if state bankers were free from bureaucratic constraints, they

[41] Jane Kaufman Winn, "Banking and Finance in Taiwan: The Prospects for Internationalization in the 1990s," 1991, Mimeographed, p. 17.

[42] Robert Wade, "East Asian Financial Systems as a Challenge to Economic Orthodoxy: Lessons from Taiwan," *California Management Review* 27, no. 4 (1985).

[43] Ralph, "Impediment to Modern Banking," n. 40. The Control Yuan is one of the five branches of the central government and is the organization with the duty of overseeing government officials.

[44] Kuo-shu Liang, "Financial Reform, Trade, and Foreign Exchange Liberalization in the Republic of China," in *Proceedings of Conference on Economic Development in the Republic of China on Taiwan* (Taipei: Chung-Hua Institution for Economic Research, 1987), p. 328.

[45] Jane Kaufman Winn, "Creditors' Rights in Taiwan: A Comparison of Corporate Reorganization Law in the United States and the Republic of China," *North Carolina Journal of International Law and Commercial Regulation* 13, no. 3 (1988): 422.

would still be hesitant to deviate from the conservative approach to credit allocation. Banks are expected to verify information supplied by their clients, monitor the activities of firms, and assess projects that bank loans are supposed to finance. The existing disclosure regulations and practices in Taiwan, however, are not conducive to information collection. Legally, all companies should file financial statements with the minister of economic affairs on an annual basis, and all listed public companies should file biannually with the Security Exchange Commission financial statements that should be certified by accountants, boards of directors, and supervisors and be publicly disclosed.[46] But as very few companies are public, financial statements from most companies—if they are filed at all—are not in the public domain and are available to the minister of economic affairs but not to bankers or analysts.

In fact, financial statements from most companies—in general, small and medium-sized firms—simply do not exist, as they do not keep business records. The tax code permits the tax inspectors to use the average rate of the specific industry as a base to levy taxes on companies without complete business records, thus indirectly condoning poor bookkeeping.[47] Where company data are available, it might not be filed with the ministry of economic affairs (MOEF) as required. Ministry statistics showed that in 1980, 72.7 percent of all registered companies did not file financial statements, and 27.7 percent of big corporations did not have a certified financial statement.[48]

The problem of insufficient information is further aggravated by the fact that the data that clients supply to their banks are often unreliable. According to a legislator, most companies keep three books: one for taxation, one for the banks, and one for themselves; the first set is underreported and the second is inflated.[49] Even documents certified by public accountants are not always credible. The ready access to informal financial markets for working capital makes it nearly impossible to assess the financial conditions of a client.

Without complete and accurate financial statements and reliable credit reporting, bank officers can neither monitor credit diversion nor sanction clients for the misuse of funds until a company really falls into financial distress. Creditors used postdated checks and personal guarantees to secure their loans. As a result, criminal penalties for bad

<hr>

[46] Legislative Yuan, *Gon si fa hsu cheng an* [Legislative debates on corporate law revision] (Taipei: Legislative Yuan, 1984), p. 354.

[47] Winn, "Creditors' Rights in Taiwan," p. 420 n. 45.

[48] Legislative Yuan, *Gon si fa hsu cheng an*, p. 47 n. 46. Yet court records in Taiwan were accessible only to litigants and counsel, thus making it impossible to assess the credit condition of a suspect client.

[49] Legislative Yuan, *Gon si fa hsu cheng an*, p. 53.

checks and collateral became the major method for protecting creditors' rights.[50]

Risk-averse state bankers are not corruption-free; whenever there is credit allocation, rents are inevitable. Rents can be captured by the bank itself, by the bankers, or by the borrowers. Forced compensatory deposits by a loan grantee are one way the bank receives some portion of the rent, as this deposit means that the borrower pays a higher interest rate than the loan contract indicates. The rest of the rent is split between bank officers and loan recipients, depending on the size of the kickbacks. Corruption, however, does not necessarily mean non-performing loans. Some risk-averse bankers were corrupt, but because they collected kickbacks from firms with collateral, the size of nonperforming loans in Taiwan's banking sector remained small.

Risk-taking Private Financiers

State dominance in finance did not leave much space for private financiers. Those who were admitted to the sector, however, did their utmost to expand and easily went beyond what they were licensed for. Those firms without a foothold in the financial sector used extralegal methods to attract savers. Except for MLSs, which were owned by politically co-opted Taiwanese elites at the provincial level and above, the other areas of financial activity open to private financiers all ran into problems. A comparative examination of the government's strategy for managing crises reveals its differential political calculations for various subsets of capitalists.

Trust and Investment Companies

The original policy intent of allowing private TICs was to broaden the stock market, facilitate the development of the longer-term credit market, and underwrite financial transactions, in brief, to combine merchant banking with investment banking.[51] As it developed, TICs began to compete with banks for short-term financing, which is clearly a deviation from what they were expected to do. They were tightly restricted in raising funds yet were given many functions to perform; hence, once they had attracted funds, they could become very aggressive.[52] Instead of attracting long- and medium-term investment funds,

[50] Legislative Yuan, *Gon si fa hsu cheng an,* p. 610.
[51] Ching-Ing Hou Liang and Michael T. Skully, "Financial Institutions and Markets in Taiwan," in *Financial Institutions and Markets in the Far East,* ed. Michael T. Skully (New York: St. Martin, 1982), pp. 183–84.
[52] The state-owned Bureau of Central Trust was involved in many lines of business that the government hesitated to allow private TICs to pursue. The privileges of the Central Trust prevented the government from enacting a law governing TICs' activities.

TICs used higher interest rates to lure short-term depositors. As deposits built up, TICs were consequently compelled to go into risky investments so as to get a higher yield. Instead of mediating long-term investments, the TICs finessed the regulations to specialize in short-term financing, portfolio investment, and real estate speculation. Moreover, many TICs indulged in lending and investing in their affiliated industrial firms far beyond the permitted level, a practice also outlined by Paul Hutchcroft in his contribution to this volume on the Philippines. Five out of six private TICs that came into being in the early 1970s were owned by leading business groups.

In terms of assets, TICs grew faster than any other financial institution except for the postal savings system. Out of the TICs emerged a new crop of local financiers who were fierce and even predatory. They absorbed deposits at a high cost and were thus driven to high-yield yet rather risky real estate and stock exchange transactions. The state had encouraged foreign participation to make sure that TICs would function legally and under a strict audit system. Two of the six TICs—the Asia and the Cathay—lacked foreign participation, however, and both experienced difficulties.

The Tenth Credit Co-op (TCC) Scandal

The TCC was the paramount case of private financiers growing beyond the government's control and blatantly disregarding regulations. Because the financial crisis caused by the TCC in 1985 was the largest one the government has faced since 1949, this case deserves a detailed analysis.

Formerly the colonial Taipei CC, the TCC came under the management of the Tsai Wan-chun family in 1957. The Tsais—petty merchants by origin, as were most new native entrepreneurs who emerged in the 1950s—turned the TCC into the largest credit co-op in the 1970s. This success was primarily due to their pioneering a one-dollar savings account campaign (which won the heart of Chiang Kai-shek) and their takeover of three distressed CCs (as they are persuaded to do by the government) during the shake-up period of 1969–1972. By the early 1980s, the Tenth Credit Co-op had surpassed Shanghai Savings and Commerical Bank and most of the private regional Medium Enterprise Banks in terms of deposits.

Rule evasion began in 1966, when the Tsai brothers took turns as head of the TCC. After 1974, a disproportionately high share of total lending went to Tsai family enterprises, especially those in plastics, construction, and home electrical appliances.[53] This lending was illegal;

[53] Control Yuan, "A Report on Investigation on the Tenth Credit Co-op Scandal," *World Journal*, August 15, 1985.

regulations prohibited CCs from extending loans to corporations, not to mention large-scale lending to firms within one conglomerate. Moreover, most of the financial transactions were executed by using the names of employees, often without their cognizance. Through such illegal means, about half of the total deposits of NT $17 billion was funneled to the Cathay group. Like the Cathay Insurance Company, the TCC had been instrumental in financing the Tsai family's acquisition of many financially depressed companies. The rapid growth of the Cathay group via mergers alerted the political leadership, prodding the Tsai family to partition its wealth. A son of the founder of the group inherited the TCC, which was the most prestigious firm of the group, and Cathay Plastics, the leading industrial but money-losing firm of the group. Uncles took insurance companies and construction companies and formed separate business groups.

The management problems with the TCC were akin to those of the Asia TICs. Most of the TCC's funds were diverted to support family-owned enterprises as well as real estate speculation in suburban areas. When the real estate market turned sluggish and the corporate debt of Cathay Plastics accumulated, cash flow problems emerged, leading to a run on TCC, which an emergency loan from the goverment in the amount of NT $30 billion in early 1985 failed to stop. When the MOF severed credit lines, the TCC and Cathay Plastics collapsed altogether. The insolvency of the TCC and Cathay Plastics triggered a chain reaction, affecting the Cathay TIC, many deposit-taking industrial giants (especially Tatung Electronics), as well as the operation of three BFCs, which absorbed many commercial bills endorsed by the TCC or the Cathay TIC. Badly damaged, the Cathay TIC was taken over by a bank consortium and later sold. As a result of the TCC scandal, a good score of MOF top officials were censured, and two ministers resigned.

Rule violation by the Cathay group was also analogous to that of the Asia TIC group except that the former, under the restrictive regulations on credit cooperatives, more systematically used the names of employees for the diversion of funds. The downfall of the Cathay group, however, can also be attributed to political misjudgments. Armed with three financial institutions—TCC, Cathay Insurance, and Cathay TIC—the Cathay group began to make political investments in the late 1970s, sending two members in a row to the Legislative Yuan under the KMT ticket and establishing close personal ties with high officials in the Ministry of Finance. The political investments of the group created the expectation of instant and unconditional government relief in the case of financial distress. If the Asia TIC was rescued, why not Cathay? But, although the Asia TIC group as a leading overseas Chinese business in Taiwan was an economic liability to the regime, it was a political asset, that signaled the solidarity between overseas Chinese and the KMT regime. In contrast, the Cathay group was not only an economic threat but also a political liability to the regime, precisely because of its political connection to the KMT. The initial motivation for "political investment" was to buy protection. The access to the legislature and the factional alignment with other young legislators in the Subcommittee on Finance, however, led the Tsai family to exercise its newly discovered political leverage to affect the agenda and direction of the Banking Law revisions. The coupling of predatory behavior in both the private and public domains could not fail to alarm the KMT leadership, whose disapproving comments served as a cue for the MOF's abandonment of the TCC and the Cathay TIC, even at the risk of braving a financial crisis.

Underground Investment Companies (UICs)

Several hundred UICs emerged after 1985 to attract surplus capital that could not be absorbed, and was sometimes even refused, by financial institutions. Such "indigestion" was caused by sticky interest rates in the state-owned banks and, in the wake of the above-mentioned Asia TIC, TCC, and Cathay TIC scandals, the overcautiousness of the financial institutions in general. By 1989, UICs had attracted an estimated NT $200–300 billion of capital,[54] which was about 15 to 23 percent of the national budget for that year. These funds were funneled into the speculative real estate market and the volatile stock market; many UICs were, in effect, Ponzi schemes.

UICs did not escape the attention of the MOF, which was still haunted by the TCC crisis. UICs were initially not prosecuted, however, because most investors were from low-income mainlander military households in the exclusive "military residential compounds" and delivered votes en bloc for the KMT during the election.[55] The ownership and management of UICs were either from or were intimately connected to the military. The exponential growth of UICs, however, impelled the government to intervene in 1988. On the one hand, the government resorted to persuasion and education to caution the investors from falling into the Ponzi trap and therefore pleading for a government bailout. On the other hand, the government, under a new premier and a new team of financial administrators, decided to use a revision of the Banking Law to authorize the prosecution of UIC owners. The legislative election in December 1988, as well as the bargaining

---

[54] Cheng-i Lin, "Shey yang ta cheu-i-zi lau-hu" [Who fed this big tiger?], *Hsin-hsin-wen* [The journalists], July 17, 1989, p. 36.

[55] Ming-tau Chang, "Those Office-Holders are Experts in Blame-Avoidance," *Hsin-hsin-wen* [The journalists], July 17, 1989, p. 43.

between the legislators and the government, delayed the revision of the Banking Law. It was only after the election and the promulgation of the Banking Law in July 1989 that the government began to close down UICs.

III. Financial Liberalization

The negative consequences of state ownership and control have been major themes of public policy debates in Taiwan throughout the postwar period, making financial liberalization an issue that any new minister of finance must address. Paradoxically, liberalization requires the establishment of prudential regulation, which was not needed in the past because of direct state control of the banking sector. In the context of Taiwan, it also means privatization of state-owned commercial banks as well as lifting the ban on new domestic entry into the banking sector.

Advocates of financial liberalization in Taiwan came from three main sources. First, neoclassical economists pushed for deregulation, notably interest rate decontrol. Second, foreign banks demanded national treatment and urged prudential regulation. Third, local businesses, with the assistance of some leading technocrats, requested the divestment of state-owned banks and the establishment of new private banks. These three sources of pressure emerged in the listed order, but their effects were cumulative in that they pointed in the same direction, though they were not targeted at the same measures. The fundamental reason for the liberalization, however, has less to do with these actors' advocacies than with the explosive and volatile pressures in the financial markets after the unanticipated and large-scale currency appreciation. It was this appreciation that exposed the weakness of the overly controlled, archaic financial institutions.

Neoclassical Economists

Neoclassical economists had long urged interest rate decontrol. Although the high-interest rate policy was instrumental to successful stabilization in the 1950s, once inflation was brought under control, interest rates were lowered to reduce the costs of production. Neoclasical economists opposed this low-interest rate policy on textbook grounds. Low rates to industry, especially the SOEs, were a disguised subsidy that led to waste, credit expansion, the diversion of loanable funds to low-or nonproductive purposes, and eventually a high rather than low cost of production.[56]

[56] Tsiang, "Taiwan chi li-lu wenti," n. 10; Shea and Kuo, "The Allocative Efficiency of

The deregulation of interest rates started in the second half of the 1970s, following the collective recommendation of five influential economists from Academia Sinica in 1974, all of whom had a strong neoclassical bent and were foreign university–based. As a preparation for interest rate decontrol, a money market was created in 1976, again on the suggestion of economists in Academia Sinica, to channel short-term capital away from the curb market and to become a barometer of market interest rates. As seen from the increasing amount of transactions, the money market was successful, albeit the major players remained banks rather than TICs, insurance companies, credit unions, trust funds, and industry.[57] The money market served as a guideline for interest rate deregulation, which was completed in four steps. Before to 1975, both deposit rates and lending rates were fixed by the central bank. The first step for decontrol was the central bank's authorization of the Interest Rate Committee of the Banks' Association to set the ceiling and floor (or the band) of loan rates; the central bank still retained control over deposit rates and the right to approve lending rates. During the second step which lasted from 1975 to 1980, the amplitude of loan rates was enlarged, and interbank call loans as well as certificate-of-deposit rates were free to fluctutate. The market rates in the money market proved to be a good guide for the equilibrium rates. The third step was to abolish ceiling and floor rates for lending in 1985 and 1986; the floor rate for deposits was also abolished. Finally, in 1989, interest rates on both the lending and deposit sides were totally liberalized.

The Complaints of Foreign Banks

Foreign banks did not fight for their entry to Taiwan; they were invited, following the derecognition of Taiwan by the United States in 1979. The liberalization of the foreign exchange market was not due to foreign banks' pressure either: it was the central bank's unilateral, and rather unexpected, decision in response to the buildup of reserves. Foreign banks did demand two things: national treatment and prudential regulation. The influx of foreign banks in the early 1980s easily saturated a profitable market where they had comparative advantages, namely, export financing and syndicated loans to secured customers such as SOEs. The appreciation of the Taiwan dollar against the U.S. dollar

---

Banks' Loanable Funds," n. 7; and J. D. Shea, "Financial Development in Taiwan: A Macro Analysis," Paper presented at the Conference on Financial Development in Japan, Korea, and Taiwan, Institute of Economics, Academia Sinica, Taipei, 1990.

[57] Mu-tsai Chen, "Taiwan ho bi shi chang chi jian tau" [An examination of Taiwan's money market], in *Taiwan ti jin zong fa zang* [Financial development in Taiwan], ed. Zong-hsiang Yu and Ke-chi Liu (Taipei: Academia Sinica, 1985), pp. 193–94.

after 1985 and the decontrol of the outflow of foreign exchange in 1987 also undermined one of the foreign banks' functions, that is, importing cheap foreign capital to exploit high lending rates in Taiwan. Foreign banks took collective action to demand more business opportunities as well as national treatment, notably the permission to raise funds in local currency. The government has been resisting these demands.[58]

Being victims of insufficient prudential financial regulation, foreign banks were the most articulate advocates for regulatory reform. They were initially active in export financing and the comfortable exchange markets. As these two markets became extremely competitive in the 1980s, foreign banks ventured into local credit markets. Aggressive lending under conditions of unreliable accounting and credit-reporting systems resulted in snowballing nonperforming debt in the second half of the 1980s.

Post-Crisis Prudential Regulation

What really led to the improvement of prudential financial regulations was not the pressure of foreign banks, however, but rather financial crisis. After weathering the TCC crisis, the government overhauled its regulations on the asset side of private financial institutions. The CC, as a type of institution, was maintained, but the size of each CC was trimmed to ten-thousand members only; membership was limited to the general public, not business firms; and lending was targeted at small commerce and not small industrial firms.[59] For TICs, direct investment in the manufacturing sector was prohibited, as was investment in real estate and the use of trust funds in portfolio investment. Yet the TICs' lending was no longer limited to the manufacturing sector.[60]

Regulation of financial institutions' liability to depositors had been lacking because of the predominant state ownership in banks and the implicit assumption of insurance in the case of bank failure. After the TCC scandal, the government used administrative guidance to limit employee deposit taking to 20 percent of the total assets of a company

[58] This issue also prevails in Hong Kong. Among the developed countries, the demand for national treatment is still an issue. Japan, for example, extends national treatment to foreign banks, but the interlocking shareholding among its corporations and the long and arduous process of application for branches have the effect of preventing foreign banks from effectively competing with domestic banks. See U.S. Department of the Treasury, *National Treatment Study: Report to Congress on Foreign Government Treatment of U.S. Commercial Banking and Securities Organizations* (Washington, D.C.: Department of the Treasury, 1986).

[59] *Central Daily News*, June 5 and 10, 1985.

[60] *Central Daily News*, May 14, 1985.

and to restrict the service to company employees only.[61] The demand deposits of TICs were also outlawed. Most important, the TCC scandal activated the Central Deposits Insurance Corporation under the MOF and the central bank. The financial crises also upgraded the MOF's ability to supervise banking, and the attempt to curtail UICs led to the revision of the Banking Law that lifted the ban on the formation of new banks. All this preparatory work laid some foundation for financial liberalization.

Divestment of State-owned Banks and New Private Banks

The reform of the existing state-owned banking institutions, most notably, interest rate deregulation, had long been used as an alternative to their divestment or the lifting of the ban on private banks. The influx of foreign banks since the early 1980s also served as an additional option for the government to stimulate competition. The arrival of foreign banks, in fact, might even have convinced the government to block the entry of potential new local banks so as to foster state banks' growth into internationally competitive national banks. Premier Yu pointed out that privatization could only fragment the banking sector and render it unable to compete internationally.[62] Moreover, the TCC case strengthened arguments against privatizing the financial sector.

These carefully crafted arguments washed away in the second half of the 1980s, and the government finally decided to divest state-owned banks in 1989 and, according to the new Banking Law, lift the ban on new banks. The decision to divest three state-owned commercial banks was primarily a palliative to an overly securitized and speculative economy. As the stock market was booming, divestment of state-owned banks and, for that matter, SOEs (especially in utilities and basic industries) could increase the supply of stocks and stabilize the market. Selling SOEs and government banks would also bring an instant profit, a very tempting proposition for a government that was beginning to suffer from budget deficits now that welfare spending was up but industrial investment was slowing down.

The divestment of state-owned banks is easier to explain than is the lifting of bans on new bank entry. Why did the government, after four decades of resistance, finally decide to accept new private banks? In appearance, the government commitment to opening up the banking sector was a concession to newly elected legislators on the Finance

[61] *Central Daily News*, February 27, 1985.
[62] Yin, "Interview with Governor Yu," p. 24 n. 38; and see also *Central Daily News*, May 26, 1983.

Committee—many of whom were from the private sector—in exchange for their support of a speedy passage of the revised bank law, which would legalize the MOF's crackdown on UICs. In actuality, however, the liberalization of the banking sector was attributable to a number of structural factors.

The internationalization of Taiwan's financial sector during the 1980s required that national financiers be dynamic and strong rather than bureaucratic and conservative. Although the government first decontrolled interest rates and then foreign exchange transactions, thus appearing to follow the ideal sequence of liberalization,[63] restrictions on domestic financiers were not removed before the foreign players were let in. After the advance of foreign banks in Taiwan, there was a growing realization that responsible local financiers should have been fostered *before* internationalization of the whole sector. It simply became undefensible to continue to repress indigenous financiers once the restrictions imposed on foreign and overseas Chinese bankers were being rapidly removed.

In addition the capital glut problem became very acute, fully exposing the inefficiency of the banking sector. Business borrowing from the informal sector had been gradually increasing after 1985. Forty percent of bank deposits in 1987 were not lent out.[64] Much of this sort of inefficiency in the banking sector is attributable to the state control of the sector. Yet, the state's capacity to inhibit private financial activities proved to be extremely limited. The government could penalize the irresponsible financiers, as the TCC case illustrates, but only at a heavy cost, and this punitive action did not solve the problem of financial intermediation at all. When financial control created gross inefficiency yet failed to contain the growth of private capitalists, then financial decontrol and the establishment of a regulatory regime to allow the competition of private capitalists became the only way out of the mess and instability in the unregulated segments of the market. In short, financial reform was primarily crisis-driven.

Finally, democratization and the Taiwanization of the KMT leadership—the latter symbolized by the assumption of Dr. Lee Teng-hui as president—has facilitated the policy shift since the mid-1980s. Democratization means, among other things, accountability and thus tends to make political elites avoid blame. Economic liberalization has the effect of displacing the responsibility for economic failure. The growing Taiwanization of the leadership of the KMT regime, through,

[63] Ronald I. McKinnon, "Monetary Stabilization in LDCs," in *Liberalization in the Process of Economic Development,* ed. Lawrence Krause and Kim Kihwan (Berkeley: University of California Press, 1991).

[64] *Economic Daily,* May 30, 1988, p. 3.

made it possible to redefine the regime's relationship to local capital. Big capitalists should no longer be feared and isolated from the financial sector. Originally there were many proposals to restrict big capitalists from capturing new financial institutions.[65] The idea of admitting numerous small citizen-type banks, however, eventually gave way to a policy that favored big capitalists organizing big banks with their own risk capital. Such a policy shift can be seen from the restrictive regulations on new banks promulgated by the MOF. These include the requirement that 20 percent of shares be open to public subscription, a low number of branches, the exclusion from foreign exchange transactions and stock trading for the initial three years, and high capitalization requirements. The new law prohibits kinship ties between supervisors and management, prohibits bank managers from ownership of stock-trading or other financial institutions, and imposes high capital requirements.[66]

According to the original plan, new banks would be formed after three state-owned commercial banks were divested. The divestment plan was only partially executed, however, the MOF sold its shares, whereas the provincial government resisted liquidating its majority shareholdings. One can foresee that increasing budget deficits will force the government to attempt divestment of the three state-owned commercial banks again. All nineteen applicants for new bank licenses were affiliated with big businesses.[67] The Ministry of Finance turned down only four applicants, despite advice for a more concentrated banking sector and thus for the prevention of American-style bank failures. Given that SMEs are highly dependent on the curb market, SME banks, and credit co-ops, new banks will be forced to cater to big businesses, which pits new banks against state-owned banks and, after the initial three-year period, against foreign banks as well.[68] The high rate of approval for new banking licenses indicates a policy of avoiding the fostering of "national champions" and instead permitting market forces to weed out the inefficient new players. In addition, the minister of

[65] These proposals included limiting individual shareholding to 5 percent, denying of voting rights for shares held by an individual that exceed 10 percent of the total shares, requiring a 30 percent versus the preexisting 20 percent profit-retention ratio, requiring two-thirds of shares to be open to public subscription, and low paid-in capital regulations so as to reduce entry barriers to banking businesses. *Central Daily News*, April 28, 1986, July 20, 1989, November 11, 1989, and July 13, 1990. See MOF, *Guidelines for New Banks* (Taipei: MOF, 1990).

[66] See MOF, *Guidelines*, June 21, 1990.

[67] Langyang Bank claimed to represent the public of I-Lan County. A scandal in mid-1991, which led to the resignation of a prominent minister of communication from that county, showed that even this bank was designed and controlled by big business.

[68] Julian Baum, "Banking on Big Business," *Far Eastern Economic Review*, April 4, 1991, pp. 36–37.

finance has moved to transform CCs into banks and is in favor of issuing new banking licenses. The regime's obsession with avoiding the concentration of big capital lingers on.

The KMT government owned the banking system but has not been very aggressive in using selective credit policy to shape Taiwan's industrial structure. Both the degree of financial repression and the extent of preferential credit allocation are lighter than those found in South Korea. Financial policy in Taiwan might reflect the importance of neoclassical economists such as those housed in Academia Sinica. As advisers to the government, these economists have frequently issued joint statements or proposals for economic liberalization, including financial deregulation and privatization. It appears that neoclassical economists' views prevented the government leadership from wholeheartedly embracing policy proposals by the technocrats in charge of industrial development, who are generally engineers and scientists by training.

Just as the government leadership ignored the technocrats' proposals, however, it did not always heed the economists' advice either. The leadership of the KMT regime resisted the temptation of using preferential credit to shape the industrial structure primarily as a result of a political calculation for maintaining a stable macroeconomic environment as well as for guarding against the rise of big indigenous financiers. Preferential credit could be an instrument of control over big capital, but coalitional calculations dissuaded the alien KMT regime from allowing big capital to emerge or to control the levers of finance. Taiwan's financial institutional structure also fully reflected the political leadership's obsession with these two objectives. Neoclassical economists may be heeded, but only when their prescriptions are compatible with the objectives of the political leadership.

CHAPTER FOUR

The Politics of Finance in Thai Economic Development

RICHARD DONER AND

DANIEL UNGER

Over the last thirty years, the Thai economy has grown rapidly while becoming more diversified and outward-oriented. Yet Thailand differs from other industrializing countries in the limited degree to which its state officials have intervened in the economy, either to influence relative factor prices or to provide rents to themselves or their political allies.

Thailand's status as an outlier is especially marked in the financial sphere where monetary authorities have maintained positive interest rates, mandated few credit allocation requirements, and imposed only loose controls on international capital movements. State-owned financial institutions play only a modest role in the banking system. To the small degree that state officials have pursued an interventionist industrialization strategy, they have tended to rely on fiscal rather than financial policy tools.

This combination of low levels of financial repression and strong growth rates suggests a puzzle that is the principal focus of this chapter. Thailand is surrounded by successful examples of more dirigiste approaches to industrial development. Even in the absence of a compelling, or even plausible, economic rationale, the quest for political survival and rents can encourage intervention in financial markets. How can we account for the fact that Thailand was practicing the orthodoxy of the 1990s in the 1960s? Unlike those in other cases in this volume, our challenge here is to identify the political forces behind the Thai state's "hands-off" posture.

We are grateful for comments from George Viksnins, Bob Muscat, Chung Lee, and, especially, Stephan Haggard and Sylvia Maxfield.

93

In Sections I–V, we trace the evolution of Thailand's financial system through the mid-1980s to identify the demand and supply factors explaining the country's relatively liberal credit regime. On the demand side, pressures for preferential credit were muted by the nature of political competition (small number of players), the state's easy access to adequate levels of revenue (through taxing the goods and services consumed by Chinese immigrants and the export of the commodities they controlled), and, perhaps most important, the interests of dominant private actors (concentrated in externally oriented commercial and financial activities).

This is not to deny that important actors, both public and private, did try to stimulate industrial growth in Thailand. But this industrial promotion took the form of extensive use of fiscal incentives. The existence of these alternative fiscal policy instruments may have served to dampen demands for preferential credit policies. The fact that financial authorities did not institute such policies in coordination with fiscal incentives, however, may reflect either the limited extent of demand for credit preferences or institutional features that worked to channel demand toward fiscal rather than financial instruments.

Hence, the final element in our explanation of Thailand's unusually liberal credit system concerns the institutional and political factors that weakened the potential supply of preferential credit. Our major institutional emphasis here is on the Thai central bank (The Bank of Thailand) (BoT): its relatively autonomous position within the Thai state, its tradition of macroeconomic conservatism, and its high level of cohesion and expertise. A second point involves the ways in which major political actors in Thailand accommodated themselves to the parameters of political competition as defined first by foreign colonial powers and, subsequently, by the sharp redirection of state economic policies in the late 1950s associated with Marshal Sarit Thanarat (1957–1963).

This cross-national perspective should not obscure the fact that, although restrained by most comparative standards, Thai officials have, in fact, intervened extensively in various factor markets. In addition to tariffs, Board of Investment officials offered a broad range of incentives to certain firms, especially large manufacturing operations. Most critical for the purposes here, monetary officials maintained lending and deposit rate ceilings and limited entry by new firms into the financial sector. Further, not all financial markets have functioned smoothly. The formal sector in Thailand has continued to vie with the informal sector, a long-term capital market is only now emerging, secondary capital markets have been all but nonexistent, and a market in equities has only recently begun to emerge.[1] In Section VI we explore

---

[1] For details, see Robert J. Muscat, "Thailand," Paper presented at the conference on

efforts to resolve these problems through financial liberalization in a context of political instability during the late 1980s and early 1990s.

The recent reform episode highlights the societal and political bases of central bank strength. The central bank's ability to restrain the growth of preferential credit reflects not only its own expertise and cohesion but also underlying political arrangements and private sector interests. Indeed, the BoT's policy preferences have been largely consistent with those of Thailand's most powerful business interests, which have been linked to the country's commercial banks.

I. The Early Bases of a Noninterventionist State

Thailand's aversion to state-sponsored preferential credit can be traced to the late nineteenth and the early twentieth centuries. Weak domestic pressure for agricultural modernization, external constraints, a general fear of foreign debt, and growing domestic participation in agricultural trade and finance all acted to discourage an active developmental role for the state. These preferences can be seen most clearly in the nineteenth-century decision by Siamese elites not to invest in large-scale irrigation and to neglect agricultural extension and research services.[2] Such measures could have increased Thai rice exports, but the interests of traditional elites did not encourage such initiatives. Equally if not more important, external factors prompted the state to devote scarce resources to other priorities. Beginning in 1855, a series of unequal treaties limited import duties and export taxes, with Thailand regaining its fiscal autonomy only in 1926. The potential danger to Thailand's sovereignty tempered any tendency toward expansionary financing and foreign indebtedness. Further, the threat of European territorial and commercial expansion enhanced the perceived value of railroad construction, the development of armed forces, and the creation of exchange reserves relative to irrigation projects. With the ex-

---

Government, Financial Systems, and Economic Development, Honolulu, Hawaii; and David Robinson, Yangho Byeon, and Ranjit Teja, *Thailand: Adjusting to Success—Current Policy Issues* (Washington, D.C.: IMF, 1991), pp. 20–22.

[2]Thailand was known as Siam until 1939, when, to bolster irredentist territorial claims against French Indochina linked to a broader pan-Thai movement, the country's prime minister changed the name to Thailand. Unless otherwise noted, this section (to 1942) draws on Ian Brown, *The Elite and the Economy in Siam, c. 1890–1920* (Singapore: Oxford University Press, 1988); David Feeny, *The Political Economy of Productivity: Thai Agricultural Development, 1800–1975* (Vancouver: University of British Columbia Press, 1982); James C. Ingram, *Economic Change in Thailand since 1850* (Stanford: Stanford University Press, 1955); G. William Skinner, *Chinese Society in Thailand: An Analytical History* (Ithaca: Cornell University Press, 1957); and T. H. Silcock, "Money and Banking," in *Thailand: Social and Economic Studies in Development*, ed. T. H. Silcock (Singapore: Donald Moore, 1967).

ception of locally sponsored cement production, the few state industries collapsed.

Owing to these decisions, the country's early financial institutions focused on trade, not project financing, under European and, subsequently, Chinese control. Thailand's earliest financial institution was the Privy Purse Bureau, the core organization of the king's economic activities that invested in real estate, railways, and rice milling. European banks established from 1888 to 1897 reduced the Privy Purse's role in rice and dominated tin mining and teak harvesting.

But European banking also provided the basis for the gradual emergence of overseas and local Chinese banks. The foreign banks relied on Chinese compradors to solicit business and guarantee loans. At the same time, the Chinese resisted further Western encroachment into rice milling and were able to maintain a strong position in the rice export business. These agroexport activities provided the impetus for the creation of local Chinese financial institutions as Chinese rice millers and exporters in Bangkok created four small banks to finance their business.[3]

European banks, however, controlled exchange operations critical to local Chinese rice millers. In 1902, the banks refused all exchange business in protest of a Siamese currency revaluation. Indeed, as early as 1890, British financial advisers were discouraging the Ministry of Finance from creating a Siamese bank to counter European dominance.[4] This generated an early nationalist response by the finance minister, who complained that European domination of exchange operations had squeezed the blood from Thai traders, suggesting that Thai nationalism at the time encompassed the immigrant Chinese as well as ethnic Thais. By 1904, the ministry opted to establish a private bank—the Siam Commercial Bank (SCB)—to serve the non-European population and to break the British domination of Bangkok's exchange business. The SCB operated under the management of the finance minister. But the institution went under the name of "Book Club" to avoid a loss of face should the bank fail and to prevent sabotage by competing European interests. Three of the bank's four local directors were Chinese, and from 1910 to 1913, the bank was managed by the founder of the Chino-Siam Bank, an institution closely tied to rice-milling operations.

[3] Brown, *Elite and the Economy in Siam*, p. 109; Paanee Bualek; *Wikhraw Naithun Thanakan Phanith Khong Thai Phaw Saw 2475–2516* [Analysis of Thai commercial banking capitalists] (Bangkok: Social Science Research Institute, Chulalongkorn University, 1986), pp. 16–17; and Silcock, "Money and Banking," p. 182.

[4] This and the following paragraph draw on Ingram, *Economic Change in Thailand*, pp. 153, 172; and Brown, *Elite and the Economy in Siam*, pp. 127, 128, 136–37.

A combination of external factors and domestic interests also help to explain early preferences for orthodox fiscal and monetary policies. Such preferences stemmed in part from the Siamese elite's recognition that foreign debt problems had prompted the colonization of Thailand's neighbors. The country's general economic success during the late 1800s and early 1900s also encouraged monetary conservatism and a developmentally passive state. Rice cultivation expanded, and rice exports grew twenty-fivefold from 1874 to 1930. This growth occurred without major infrastructure investments. Although foreign goods wiped out local crafts and Thailand became increasingly reliant on foreign markets and funds, external shocks did not destabilize the Thai economy until the interwar depression. Rice export revenues and taxes on opium, spirits, gambling, and the lottery compensated for the loss of government revenue because of the unequal treaties.

This economic growth did not generate coalitional shifts and political instability with the potential to create popular pressure for increased state spending. The Siamese elite's rural wealth was based largely on control of labor rather than land. And as slavery was modified and eventually abolished in 1905, ethnic Thais expanded rice cultivation by clearing new land rather than raising productivity. Chinese immigrants controlled the financial and commercial functions critical to rice cultivation and marketing. Market forces thus did not generate mass protests or a bourgeois-led movement for reform. The Chinese provided revenues for but did not constitute any direct threat to the Siamese ruling elite.

Until World War II, then, Thailand's combination of stable coalitional arrangements, ample trade-related foreign exchange revenues, and external constraints encouraged conservative fiscal policy and a very modest growth of state financial institutions.

II. BANK OF THAILAND AND GROWTH OF COMMERCIAL BANKING, 1942–1957

External challenges surrounding World War II led to the creation of the Bank of Thailand. The central bank sustained Thailand's tradition of fiscal conservatism and achieved the objectives for which it was designed, that is, preserving Thai sovereignty during the war and stabilizing the country's economy after Japan's defeat. Benefiting from its cohesion, its nationalist status, and its influence over the country's booming export trade, the BoT achieved significant influence within the Thai state. Its position vis-à-vis the country's expanding commercial banks was considerably less dominant. Economically, the latter were critical to the country's export trade. Politically, they gained leverage as supporters of competing cliques.

The direct origins of the BoT lay in efforts to safeguard Thai independence. Japan, which occupied Thailand in 1941, asked the Thai government to establish a central bank with Japanese advisers and department heads. The Thais feared Japanese control of a Thai central bank, and Prince Viwat, the financial adviser, consequently argued that Thailand already had a central bank and that a new institution was unnecessary. The "bank" to which Viwat was referring was the National Banking Bureau, established in 1940 to manage certain government loans, control foreign exchange, and train financial officials. Thais quickly expanded the bureau's functions and established the BoT in 1942.[5]

The 1942 act establishing the bank and an emergency decree in the following year emphasized control over inflation by maintaining reserve requirements and credit restraints. Following political pressure against financial discipline, the emergency decree was repealed after only a few weeks. A new banking law in 1945 set clearer banking standards and specified the BoT's supervisory functions. The minister of finance, who named the central bank governor, had the formal power to scrutinize books and suspend licenses. The BoT itself had the power to determine the legal ratio of cash reserves to deposits, to fix interest rates paid on deposits, and to restrict the distribution of profits until capital and reserves reached an assigned proportion of all assets.

But the central bank never used most of the powers granted in the 1945 act and failed to dampen inflation immediately. The bank failed in its bid to offset the inflationary impact of government bond sales to the BoT by getting the commercial banks to hold government securities. And when the government attempted to reduce the money supply in 1956 by encouraging the purchase of government bonds, it raised the interest rate on them to 8 percent but did not attempt to raise the banks' legal reserve ratios. This also weakened BoT efforts to increase commercial bank dependence on the central bank.

The BoT also paid little attention to development financing during the early postwar period. Owing to the traditional Thai aversion to expansionary financing, high rates of currency inflation during the war, and a combination of foreign exchange shortages and huge pent-up demand for foreign consumer goods after the war, the bank focused on stabilization.[6] Although inflationary episodes persisted in the mid-

[5] Bualek, *Wikhraw Naithun*, p. 53; and Silcock, "Money and Banking," p. 179. Unless otherwise noted, the following discussion draws on Silcock, "Money and Banking," pp. 190–95.

[6] Inflation was in part the result of large expenditures made by Japanese occupation

1950s, by 1951 the BoT had succeeded in replenishing foreign exchange reserves, which was facilitated by strong external demand for Thai exports, an effective system of multiple exchange rates, and limits on infrastructural programs to restrain imported capital goods.

The central bank gained leverage relative to other parts of the bureaucracy during the 1950s. The BoT enjoyed high status as a result of its having deterred Japanese domination and maintained its own professional integrity during a war. To encourage its independence, the government placed the BoT outside normal bureaucratic control and granted its personnel salaries that were significantly higher than those in the civil service. The quality of the bank's leaders and its linkages with the IMF and World Bank (which it joined in 1949) also strengthened the bank's position. The BoT was able to use consultations with and loans from these institutions to limit corruption and inflationary spending.

Earnings from the country's multiple exchange rate system (in operation until 1955) also strengthened the BoT's influence. The bank made substantial profits on the margins between the prices at which it purchased foreign exchange from exporters and those at which it sold to commercial banks. These funds were significant (equal to 12 percent of government revenues in 1954) but were not included in the government budget. Because government agencies often ran deficits during this period and could tap into these funds only through negotiations with the BoT, the latter had some power to check inflationary spending.[7]

Paralleling the expansion of central bank activities was a growth of domestic commercial banks. Before the outbreak of World War II, twenty commercial banks operated in Thailand. Four were colonial branches of European banks; three belonged to overseas Chinese banks; and the rest were family-run enterprises belonging to Chinese rice millers and exporters.[8] The latter tended to be small exchange banks organized by Chinese groups, often working through trade associations. These banks functioned to avoid the foreign exchange losses suffered by Chinese exporters working with Western banks and to ensure that benefits from the rice trade did not flow to other groups.

The financial sector was restructured in 1932, when a group of civilian and military officers known as the People's Party overthrew the

---

forces through baht notes issued in exchange for yen credits. Ingram, *Economic Change in Thailand*, pp. 163–65.

[7] Silcock, "Money and Banking," p. 190; and W. M. Corden, "The Exchange Rate System and the Taxation of Trade," in Silcock, *Thailand*, p. 155.

[8] The following draws on Akira Suehiro, *Commercial Bankers and Industrial Elites in Thailand* (Tokyo: Institute of Developing Economies, 1986), pp. 6–7; and Bualek, *Wikhraw Naithun*, pp. 35–37, 53.

absolute monarchy.[9] By imposing restrictions on existing banks and establishing new ones, the new leaders attempted to reduce Chinese and Western economic influence and to build up their own economic base of support. As a result, all the local banks folded, except the SCB and the Wang Lee Bank. Efforts to reduce Western influence in banking, rice milling, tin mining, oil refining, and other areas generally succeeded.

The anti-Chinese effort in banking collapsed rapidly. By 1950 a total of eleven commercial banks were operating. Ten of these were Chinese-dominated and most had extensive involvement in commodity exports central to the country's economy. Taxes on these exports played a key role in financing state spending. Hence, state officials found themselves exceptionally dependent on the prosperity of the export industries. During the 1950s, Thai banks consolidated and formed the core of five large business groups led respectively by the Bangkok Bank, the Bangkok Metropolitan Bank, the Bank of Ayudhya, the Thai Farmers' Bank, and the Union Bank. The economic power of these groups lay not only in their control of credit and rice but also in a variety of other activities such as insurance, shipping, and light manufacturing.

The banks enjoyed increasing political leverage by virtue of their support for the competing factions that dominated Thai politics until 1957. After a series of coups from 1948 to 1951, the ruling oligarchy split into two cliques that shared political power. These cliques were without popular bases of support. In addition, Thailand had no natural resources that could be taxed to use for patronage demands. Perhaps most striking is the political elite's failure to capture rents from the country's large rice exports. The rice trade did pass through a government Rice Bureau until 1955. But as the international market became more competitive, the rice trade was turned over to the private sector and the potential for rent seeking by bureaucrats and politicians was cut sharply.

Under these conditions, the banks became important revenue sources for the competing cliques. Chinese merchants included top government officials on the boards of directors of banks and related firms. Some of the banks helped to finance the one hundred state enterprises that constituted another base of wealth for the political oligarchy. The most important case of this pattern concerned the Bank of Ayudhya's as-

[9]On the coup and the government financial crisis that led up to it, see Benjamin A. Batson, *The End of the Absolute Monarchy in Siam* (Singapore: Oxford University Press, 1984), chap. 7. The following discussion of the leverage and structure of commercial banks draws on Kraisak Choonhavan, "The Growth of Domestic Capital and Thai Industrialization," *Journal of Contemporary Asia* 14, no. 2 (1984): 140; and Silcock, "Money and Banking," pp. 178, 184.

sociation with the National Economic Development Corporation (NED-COL), a holding company for manufacturing firms run by the Phin-Phao clique. The relationship was helpful to the banks as well. Government officials rented out protection against their own ethnic nationalist threats. The Chinese were at times able to use discriminatory policies to obtain state resources in exchange for favors granted government officials. A case in point was the Bangkok Bank's success in convincing the Ministry of Finance to raise the government's share in the bank's registered capital to 60 percent in 1953.[10]

There were, in sum, few major pressures for preferential credit during the immediate postwar period. Central bank activities focused on controlling inflation and building up foreign exchange reserves. These efforts were facilitated by the BoT's own leverage within the bureaucracy and by the growth of an export-based commercial banking sector that itself constituted an important support for the political-military leadership.

III. Economic Expansion under Military Rule, 1957–1973

Two factors might have been expected to result in state enactment of mandated credit programs during the late 1950s and in the 1960s. First, the large number of state enterprises noted earlier required significant financial resources. Second, the authoritarian regime of Field Marshal Sarit Thanarat adopted an explicit strategy of import-substituting industrialization, creating new demands for industrial finance. The government promoted infant industries such as pharmaceuticals, textiles, and consumer durables with increased levels of protection, Board of Investment (BoI) incentives, and, from 1960 onward, an overvalued exchange rate.[11]

Yet there was no growth of preferential credit. Protection and fiscal incentives were not accompanied by financing for "promoted" areas. Targeted financial support was limited to a system of refinancing, first introduced in 1958 to support exports. The facilities were expanded in 1963 and 1964 to assist industry in obtaining raw materials and selling products on credit.[12] But these refinancing activities emphasized

---

[10] Suehiro, *Commercial Bankers,* table 3.

[11] Kevin Hewison, *Bankers and Bureaucrats: Capital and the Role of the State in Thailand* (New Haven: Yale University Southeast Asia Studies, 1989), pp. 118–19. See also Akira Suehiro, *Capital Accumulation in Thailand* (Tokyo: Center for East Asian Cultural Studies, 1989).

[12] This discussion draws on Silcock, "Money and Banking," pp. 193–202.

Table 4.1. Structure of BoT refinancing operations, 1976–1986 (percent)

Year	Export	Industrial	Agricultural
1976	72	26	3
1978	77	22	1
1980	75	13	12
1982	89	2	2
1984	96	4	1
1986	97	1	1

Source: Pakorn Vichayanond, Monetary Policies and Income Distribution (Bangkok: Thailand Development Research Institute, 1988), table 8.
Note: Does not include long-term credits to IFCT, BAAC, and finance companies.

agricultural exports, not industry. Four commodities—rice, tapioca, maize, and sugar—accounted for an annual average of 87 percent of all BoT rediscounts between 1959 and 1964 and over one-half of the total refinancing facilities devoted to exports from 1972 to 1985.[13] Exports, the dominant focus of refinancing operations (Table 4.1), were dominated by agriculture.

This emphasis reflected the central bank's overall concern with stability. But the BoT would probably not have been able to act on these preferences without increased centralization of the state financial apparatus and political support from the new Thai leader, Sarit. Also facilitating the central bank's approach were inflows of foreign funds and a thriving private sector dominated by strong commercial banks. These banks' own ties to agroexports and their ability to finance growing manufacturing activities helped to preclude the emergence of any significant import substitution coalition.

For the financial technocrats, avoiding speculative or dangerous investment of deposit funds was more important than stimulating bank lending to promote growth. Through selected rediscounting and its influence on the short-term money market, the central bank could supply adequate liquidity. By encouraging the banks' focus on more liquid types of business, such as trade, bank officials hoped to secure stability of the currency and the financial system overall.

The central bank's fiscal conservatism during this period obviously has its roots in Thailand's experience with external threats discussed earlier. But it also reflected the technocrats' deep-rooted antagonism toward patronage and profligacy growing out of a more contemporary event, that is, the NEDCOL disaster of the 1950s. Established by a group of state managers and local capitalists, NEDCOL became one of Thailand's largest companies, with interests in various manufacturing

[13] Silcock, "Money and Banking," table 8.3; and Pakorn Vichayanond, Monetary Policies and Income Distribution (Bangkok: Thailand Development Research Institute, 1988), table 9.

activities. The firm accumulated huge amounts of state-guaranteed debt. NEDCOL secured these loans, many from foreign sources, outside the Ministry of Finance's formal control. When the firm went bankrupt, thus threatening Thailand's credit worthiness, the government decided to honor the debts and, as Robert J. Muscat notes, effectively "mortgaged the development budget for several years."[14]

The ascension of an authoritarian regime under Sarit in 1957–1958 was critical to the pursuit of conservative macroeconomic policy by the central bank and Ministry of Finance. To begin with, the Sarit regime made private investment the centerpiece of its development strategy. The government shifted its role away from direct investment in state enterprises and into infrastructural development and the rationalization of macroeconomic policy. Although this did not involve the dismantling of state firms, it curtailed their overall role within the economy and helped to cut government deficits sharply. Meanwhile, new legal measures prohibited direct transactions between the BoT and private nonfinancial enterprises.

Sarit's shift away from direct state involvement in the economy reflected coalitional factors. The dozens of state companies in public utilities and import substitution and consumer goods that had been established in the 1950s constituted a major political base for the faction rivaling Sarit, who drew his support largely from other sources. Restrictions on the activities of state firms thus not only promoted the private sector but also destroyed the former ruling elite's economic base. By promoting his own backers in the military and placing civilians in top ministry posts, Sarit obtained funds mainly from the state lottery, illicit ventures (i.e., opium trafficking and extortion), and certain commercial banks. As a result, Sarit was relatively invulnerable to pressures from particular interests for selective credit. Consolidation of control over the military and repressive measures against dissent precluded political activity by popular sectors.

To regularize macroeconomic policy while guarding his own sources of income, Sarit centralized macroeconomic policy management. Consistent with the recommendations of a 1957–1958 World Bank mission, he created the BoI, the Budget Bureau, and the National Economic Development Board (a development planning agency), the latter two being within the Office of the Prime Minister. Sarit promoted young technocrats in these agencies as well as in the central bank and Ministry of Finance. The economists' ability to mobilize foreign pressures, especially from the IMF and the World Bank, furthered their leverage.

[14] Muscat, *Thailand and the United States,* p. 12. See also Silcock, "Money and Banking," p. 205.

Central bank chief Puey Ungpakorn, for example, reportedly sought World Bank loans, despite interest rates above commercial alternatives, because the former came with monitoring requirements that effectively constrained rent seeking.[15] Through their domination of the new agencies, these technocrats gained greater discipline over the line ministries.

The BoT's instruments for controlling aggregate money supply were relatively blunt. The economy's unequal monetization made control over inflation difficult. But these weaknesses were largely offset by financial officials' control over the budgetary process. The establishment of the Budget Bureau in 1959 centralized budgetary decisions and protected against political and bureaucratic pressures. In addition, new regulations prohibited government guarantees of private sector debt and, by the reorganizing of tax collection, increased state revenue.

State access to new sources of finance facilitated fiscal conservatism during this period. In addition to higher rates of sales and income tax collection, revenue from trade (especially rice export) taxes also grew, accounting for about one-half of total state revenue between 1959 and 1964.[16] External public loans and grants constituted an additional source of funds. From 1950 to 1975, U.S. military aid amounted to over one-half of state defense expenditures; between 1966 and 1971, U.S. military aid, along with World Bank loans, provided some one-third of public capital spending.[17] With foreign trade serving as an engine of growth and the state reliant on export taxes to finance imports, officials looked unfavorably on any import substitution policies that lowered the ratio of foreign trade to national income.

The central bank also tried to ensure financial system stability through greater supervision of commercial bank practices. Under the 1962 Commercial Banking Act, the BoT expanded its powers to vary cash and capital reserve ratios, to limit a bank's lending to any one borrower, to license and inspect banks, and to prescribe maximum loan and deposit interest rates. In fact, the central bank was often unable to exercise these powers. Enforcing rate structures on the more influential Thai banks was politically difficult. Where regulation was effective, it usually involved moral suasion by BoT officials.[18]

The BoT's inability to dominate the commercial banks was not a serious problem given the private sector's lack of demand for, and

---

[15] Interviews, Bangkok, Summer 1991.

[16] In 1963, rice constituted 36 percent of exports but accounted for 73 percent of revenue from export and similar taxes. Corden, "Exchange Rate System," pp. 167–68.

[17] Scott Christensen, "The Politics of Democratization in Thailand: State and Society since 1932," Unpublished background paper, Thailand Development Research Institute, Bangkok, 1991, p. 18.

[18] Silcock, "Money and Banking," pp. 199, 202; and Interviews, Bangkok, Summer 1991.

Table 4.2. Commercial bank credit by selected sectors, 1958–1990 (percent)

Sector	1958	1966	1974	1979	1983	1988	1990
Foreign trade	37.0	30.4	29.5	26.2	16.2	13.6	10.7
Domestic trade	16.8	15.5	21.1	22.4	24.6	18.9	17.6
Manufacturing	10.1	16.3	18.5	17.3	21.5	25.8	25.1
Construction and real estate	7.3	13.8	9.3	8.1	8.3	10.6	15.9
Agriculture	3.4	3.8	1.9	5.4	7.4	6.6	6.7

Source: Bangkok Bank, Ltd., *Commercial Banks in Thailand, 1991* (Bangkok: Bangkok Bank, Ltd., 1991).

indeed its ability to resist, a developmental state financial policy. Thailand's private sector during this period welcomed foreign capital and opposed state capital. These preferences grew out of the Sino-Thai private sector's experience with ethnic nationalism and politically risky collaboration with politicians. Foreign investment helped to regularize the market—privileges accorded foreign firms also applied to local capitalists, and links to foreign capital reduced the threat of nationalization or harassment.[19]

The import substitution strategy in force at the time might have been expected to give rise to protected sectors requesting more direct state financial support.[20] In fact, there is little evidence of any significant import substitution coalition. This may have reflected, in part, the predominance of agricultural exports in the portfolios of large banks. From the late 1950s until the mid-1970s, foreign trade accounted for roughly 30 percent of commercial bank credit (Table 4.2). Banks were directly involved in agriculture and related export activities. The Union Bank, for example, organized the cartels that controlled the export of sugar, maize, and rice. Rice exporters and at least three private financial institutions established linkages via interlocking directorates in the mid to late 1960s.

Manufacturing grew rapidly during the 1960s, led by entrepreneurs shifting from commerce to production of textiles, automobiles, glass, electrical appliances, consumer goods, and processed food for the domestic market. Although these firms sought protection, we do not find them calling for selective credit policies. The relative passivity of manufacturers with regard to selective credit probably reflected the availability of other financial sources, both foreign and domestic. Most new industrialists in larger operations were involved in joint ventures with

[19] Hewison, *Bankers and Bureaucrats*, p. 106.
[20] This paragraph draws on Silcock, "Money and Banking"; Suehiro, *Commercial Bankers*, p. 21; and information from Ministry of Commerce files in Bangkok gathered by Professor Nittaya Wongtada, American Graduate School of International Management, Thunderbird Campus.

Table 4.3. Commercial bank concentration, 1962–1990 (percent)

Bank	Assets					Deposits	Branches
	1962	1972	1980	1988	1990[a]	1990[a]	1990[a]
Bangkok Bank	21.5	29.5	34.5	28.3	26.5	26.6	15.4
Krung Thai Bank	18.7	14.6	13.4	14.2	13.4	14.7	15.7
Thai Farmers Bank	4.5	6.9	11.4	12.6	13.6	14.2	14.3
Siam Commercial Bank	5.6	4.9	5.5	8.3	9.4	9.8	9.9
Bank of Ayudhya	5.3	6.3	4.7	5.7	6.5	7.3	8.7
Thai Military Bank	2.5	3.3	2.8	5.6	5.3	5.6	7.9
Foreign banks	16.7	9.7	5.9	4.4	4.7	2.1	0.9[b]
3-bank concentration	44.7	51.0	59.3	58.1	53.5	55.5	45.4
4-bank concentration	50.3	55.9	64.8	63.4	62.9	65.3	55.3
5-bank concentration	55.6	62.2	69.5	69.1	69.4	72.6	64.0

Sources: World Bank, *Thailand Financial Sector Study*, vol. 2, p. 71; and Bangkok Bank Ltd., *Commercial Banks in Thailand, 1991* (Bangkok: Bangkok Bank, Ltd., 1991).
[a]Calculated from data in Bangkok Bank source.
[b]1988 data.

foreign (Japanese) capital. Although in no single year did foreign capital exceed 11 percent of gross fixed capital formation during the period, it provided over one-third of total financing to the Thai nonfinancial private sector from 1967–1973.[21]

Commercial banks functioned largely as merchant banks financing trade and domestic distribution of imported manufactured goods. Commercial bank credit to the manufacturing sector, however, rose from 10 percent to 18 percent from 1958 to 1974 (Table 4.2). By 1966, Bangkok Bank credits to the industrial sector were reportedly outstripping those to its traditional clients engaged in trade. Much of the domestic lending took the form of short-term instruments, especially overdrafts. Funds from the informal money market were also important, especially as sources of current operating capital.[22] In sum, ample private financial sources—not only foreign capital, but also commercial bank lending—probably obviated the need for selective credit on the part of the rising Thai manufacturer.

The lack of pressure for protection and selective credit also seems

[21] Choonhavan, "Growth of Domestic Capital," p. 142. For more on linkages with Japanese capital, see Suehiro, *Commercial Bankers*, p. 23.

[22] On Bangkok Bank loans, see *Bangkok Bank Monthly Review*, February 1982, as cited in Kevin Hewison, "The Financial Bourgeoisie in Thailand," *Journal of Contemporary Asia* 11, no. 4 (1981): 143. On the role of overdrafts, see Toshiya Kuramochi, "The Impact of Monetary Policy on Financial Development: A Case Study of Thailand," M.A. thesis, Faculty of Economics, Thammasat University, 1987, p. 82, figure 6.7. On the importance of noncommercial bank private finance for short-term needs, see Saeng Sanguanruang, Somsak Tambulertchai, and Nit Sammapan, *A Study of Small- and Medium-Scale Industries in Thailand* (Bangkok: National Institute of Development Administration and Faculty of Economics, Thammasat University, 1977), as cited in Saskatchewan Research Council, *Technology Adoption by Small and Medium-sized Enterprises (SMEs in Thailand)* (Bangkok: Thai Department of Industrial Promotion, 1991), p. 115.

Table 4.4. Financial system assets, 1970–1988 (percent)

	1970	1975	1980	1985	1988
Bank of Thailand	35.8	24.2	23.9	18	15.6
Private local commercial banks	35.8	39.6	40.1	47.3	47.7
Finance and security companies	–	9.9	10.8	10.5	10.1
Government savings bonds	8.1	6.1	4.7	5.2	6.4
Specialized financial institutions	3.9	6.0	7.5	6.9	6.8

Source: World Bank, *Thailand Financial Sector Study,* vol. 2 (Washington, D.C.: World Bank, 1990), p. 18/annex 12.

to have affected large commercial banks' varied sources of influence. Locally owned banks expanded their share of total financial assets while the market share of the four largest banks expanded (Table 4.3), and single families increased their control over each of the dominant banks. Four major banking families expanded their shares of total deposits from 32 percent in 1962 to 59 percent in 1972.[23] The new industrial groups that emerged during this period shared few of the sociological, political, or economic sources of leverage that characterized commercial bankers. Most industrialist elites were first-generation Chinese, whereas bankers typically were long-established, locally born Sino-Thai who had nurtured crucial political relationships with leading military figures.

The banks' leverage was also a function of their financial independence relative to the government itself. By 1970, assets of the BoT and the local banking sector were equal; by 1975 the commercial banks' assets, combined with those of finance and securities companies, began to overshadow those of the central bank (Table 4.4). Overseas banks sourced 68 percent of Thai commercial bank borrowing in 1973, whereas the BoT provided only 28 percent.[24] Finally, government or government-related shareholdings in three commercial banks declined sharply before or during this period. The most striking case was the decline of Ministry of Finance shares in the Bangkok Bank from 60 percent in 1953 to 15 percent in 1971.[25]

IV. Expansion of Political Participation and Financial Regulation, 1973–1980

The broad factors discouraging subsidized financing under Sarit and his successors underwent important changes during the 1970s. In-

[23] Suehiro, *Commercial Bankers,* pp. 13–15, 20.
[24] Noratana Saisanan, Na Ayudhya, "Credit Availability and Credit Rationing in Monetary Policy Transmission Mechanism of Thailand," M.A. thesis, Faculty of Economics, Thammasat University, 1991, p. 11, table 2.2. Figures for years before 1973 were not available.
[25] Suehiro, *Bankers Commercial,* pp. 4–71.

creasingly, mobilized popular sectors and assertive parties undermined the independence of state financial agencies. Pressures for selective credit grew, even as external revenue sources diminished. The resulting preferential credit program, however, was limited and directed to agriculture, not industry. New private financial institutions served industry relatively effectively but eventually generated new sets of problems for financial authorities.

In 1973, growing but discontented middle-class forces, with university students serving as their leading edge, ousted Sarit's military successors and ushered in three years of democratic rule. A broader range of business interests, themselves spawned by the economic stability and open investment regime of earlier years, now had access to political and economic resources. Support from particular political-military figures was less useful than before. During these years, the number of business leaders in parliament and holding ministerial portfolios increased sharply. Political parties became important vehicles for seizing control over ministerial resources, and politicians became more entrepreneurial in their efforts to enlarge electoral coalitions.

As the circle of significant political actors expanded, so did the range of demands on government. Pressures for expansionary policies from within the state, as well as without, grew during this period. Inflation increased rapidly, and a financial crisis developed. The broad technocratic policy consensus favoring conservative macroeconomic policies came under attack from some technocrats and academics, as well as politicians. More Thais began to see a need for an active state economic role to stimulate and anticipate future demand as well as to curb excessive concentrations of market power, particularly in the financial sector. Populist attacks on the economic and political power of private banks became more prominent.[26]

Simultaneously, foreign capital inflows slowed with the withdrawal of the U.S. military in 1975 and the shift of Japanese capital toward more resource-oriented investments abroad. The capital intensity of the country's growing emphasis on import substitution contributed to international payments imbalances that initially arose after the first oil shock. These deficits worsened as both public and private sectors borrowed abroad to counter a serious deterioration in foreign exchange earnings. The savings-investment gap jumped from 0.5 percent of GDP in 1974 to over 4.0 percent in 1975.[27] This gap was reflected in serious

---

[26] In 1978, the *Far Eastern Economic Review* quoted the U.S. Embassy in Thailand's estimate that five "Chinese" banking families controlled or "substantially influence[d]" over half of Thailand's private economy. Robert Girling, *Thailand: Society and Politics* (Ithaca: Cornell Univeristy Press, 1981), p. 78, n. 39.

[27] Thailand Development Research Institute, *Year End Conference on Financial Resources*

trade and current account deficits and eventually required borrowings from the IMF in 1976, 1979, and the early 1980s.

Political mobilization, increased demands on the state, increased party influence in the Ministry of Finance, and reduced external flows pushed the central bank toward a more expansionary and developmental set of economic strategies. To counteract the impact of the first oil shocks and external security concerns, public expenditures rose sharply, with rapid growth in outlays on defense and infrastructural investment. State officials kept prices of key inputs, including oil, below world market levels while raising tariffs. The outcomes were fiscal deficits and price distortions that began to create the conditions for serious macroeconomic imbalances that emerged only after the second round of oil price increases in the late 1970s. Revenue shortfalls also hampered efforts to implement a shift toward export-led growth, as the Ministry of Finance sustained, and even increased, tariffs in order to reduce those deficits. Minister of Finance Boonchu Roojanasathien implemented the country's first large-scale mandated credit allocation program. The program required that commercial banks extend a certain percentage of their total deposits as credits to farmers, either directly or through the Bank for Agriculture and Agricultural Cooperatives.

This focus on agricultural finance presents something of a puzzle. Increasingly powerful manufacturing interests, long dependent on foreign capital, faced a slowdown in direct foreign manufacturing investment in Thailand and did not yet enjoy access to foreign credit markets. We would expect, therefore, growing pressures for policies that directed credit to manufacturing. Indeed, some observers suggest that during the early to mid-1970s, ties between financial and industrial interests became stronger as the former moved to make up for industrialists' diminished access to foreign capital.[28] Yet, with some exceptions (as will be noted below), manufacturing's share of commercial bank credit actually shrank somewhat from 1974 to 1979 (Table 4.2).

Shifting demand factors help explain the apparent anomalous growth of rural financing in the face of problems in manufacturing. One factor has to do with the combined impact of increased party competition and popular concern with urban-rural disparities. Credit for agriculture reflected the politicians' desire to win rural votes as well as the support of mobilized urban voters expressing concerns about

---

Management (Bangkok: TDRI, 1986), pp. 10–11. On the sharp rise in commercial bank overseas borrowing compared with borrowings from the BoT between 1975–1978, see Peter Warr and Bhanupongse Nidhiprabha, *Macroeconomic Policies, Crisis and Growth in the Long Run: Thailand Country Study*, p. 2, revised (Bangkok: World Bank Research Project 673–99, 1988), p. 26.
[28] Choonhavan, "Growth of Domestic Capital."

income inequality. Legislators, students, and academics accused Thai commercial banks of profiteering, of lending only to friends in industry and commerce, and of generally ignoring the country's agricultural majority, which was the "backbone" of the country. In addition, financial interests were tied to these emerging industries. Unlike in earlier manufacturing ventures, links to foreign capital were not crucial in the development of new agroindustries. Thus, the largest such firm in Southeast Asia, Charoen Pokphand, was one of the major beneficiaries of the Bangkok Bank's support.[29]

Manufacturers, meanwhile, were more often concerned with access to credit than with receiving the benefits of subsidized interest rates. Although interest rate ceilings implied de facto credit rationing (in fact, during some periods market rates were below the ceilings), the larger and politically more influential manufacturing interests continued to have access to credit and, in some critical cases, that access increased. Indeed, commercial banks did expand their financing of certain key sectors. In these cases, local banks moved into niches vacated by foreign investors wary of domestic political turmoil and the region's instability.[30] For example, the Bangkok Bank supported efforts of one of Thailand's largest textile and apparel groups, Saha Union, to buy out Japanese joint venture partners who were prohibiting exports of Thai textiles.

Finally, and perhaps most important, industrialists benefited from a new source of credit—finance companies. Although the state did expand its rediscounting operations to provide access to working capital as well as to stimulate the economy during downturns, the major thrust of state industrial development efforts during this period lay in stimulating lending by private financial institutions. The licensing (but not regulation) of finance and securities companies was the key element in this effort. The number of these firms rose from 17 in 1971 to 113 in 1979.[31] State officials hoped to use these firms to meet the private sector's increasing financial needs by intensifying competitive pressures on commercial banks and by circumventing both interest rate ceilings and the moratorium on new banking licenses and on foreign branch banking. In 1980, manufacturing accounted for the largest component

[29] Victor Limlingan, *The Overseas Chinese in ASEAN: Business Strategies and Management Practices* (Manila: Vita Development, 1986), p. 118. Also see Suehiro, *Commercial Bankers.*

[30] The banking system increased loans to manufacturing from 16.5 billion baht in 1975 to 41.2 billion baht in 1980. In relative terms, however, manufacturing accounted for a slightly lower percentage of total loans in the latter year (18.4 percent versus 19.9 percent). The percentage of loans allocated to agriculture and the wholesale and retail sectors had expanded over the period. World Bank, *Thailand Financial Sector Study,* vol. 2 (Washington, D.C.: World Bank, 1990), p. 62. See also Choonhavan, "Growth of Domestic Capital," p. 145; and Suehiro, *Commercial Bankers,* p. 27.

[31] IMF, "Financial Reform in Thailand," Unpublished draft, Washington, D.C., May 1991, p. 2.

Table 4.5. Credit allocation of finance and securities companies by selected sectors, 1980–1988 (percent)

Sector	1980	1982	1984	1986	1988
Manufacturing	25.7	25.3	23.3	22.9	21.8
Construction and real estate	14.0	13.4	15.9	17.0	18.3
Trade	14.0	16.2	15.7	14.4	12.7
Finance	12.6	12.6	10.6	9.0	9.1
Total (Index 1980 = 100)	100	147	173	186	281
In billions of baht	55.0	79.5	95.0	102.2	154.4

Source: World Bank, *Financial Sector Study*, vol. 2 (Washington, D.C.: World Bank, 1990), p. 84/annex 43.

(26 percent) of these institutions' relatively well-diversified loan port-folios (Table 4.5).

Central bank autonomy, macroeconomic stability, and financial system stability became increasingly problematic as Thailand moved into the late 1970s. Responding to rural poverty, business concerns for expansion, and military demands for larger budgets, Boonchu pursued expansionary fiscal and monetary policies. Expansion was further encouraged by World Bank pressure to expand state enterprise borrowing for infrastructural purposes.[32] The BoT lost the leverage to counter Thailand's growing macroeconomic instability. Bank officials were not willing to depreciate the baht by delinking it from the dollar. Interest rates were significantly negative in 1973 and 1974, became somewhat positive in 1975 and 1976, and then hovered around zero in 1977 and 1978. Credit was increasing at roughly 20 percent a year, whereas deposits rose at only 11 percent. The central bank was also circumscribed in its ability to raise lending rates by the Thai civil and commercial code's anti-usury limits on nominal rates, which resulted in the danger of increased capital outflows as well as insufficient savings. Finally, with the rapid and unregulated growth of finance companies came increased manipulation, insider trading, and improper loans. These triggered the collapse of the Securities Exchange of Thailand in 1978 and the failure of a major finance company the following year.

Financial officials managed at the end of this period to initiate financial system reform. The 1979 Commercial Banking Act mandated the first formal controls on finance company operations. Under popular pressure, the act also included provisions requiring the banks to limit the scope of their investments in nonbanking businesses, channel more of their credit into priority development sectors, and compel banking

[32] Material on economic problems during this period is drawn from Richard Doner and Anek Laothamatas, "The Political Economy of Structural Adjustment in Thailand," Paper prepared for the World Bank project on the Political Economy of Structural Adjustment in New Democracies, Washington, D.C., 1992.

families to divest themselves of large direct holdings. Pressure from the Thai Bankers' Association, however, resulted in weaker divestiture provisions than originally planned. But taken as a whole, the reforms provided the BoT with additional instruments of monetary control through regulation of capital to asset ratios and minimum cash requirements. More broadly, they enabled stability-oriented officials to reassert regulatory authority and helped restore the influence of these officials over Thai macroeconomic policies. The increasingly assertive position of these officials was reflected in BoT governor Nukul Prachuabmol's 1979 success in convincing the legislature to revise the interest rate limits.

Indeed, after a number of years during which Thai officials followed an implicit strategy of emphasizing growth over stability, they came to recognize that emerging macroeconomic problems were threatening long-term growth prospects and a Philippines-like debt quagmire. They also recognized, the dynamism of the business class, and their belief in the need for private sector–led development intensified. But the number of claimants on state resources had grown, and the political struggle over the distribution of those resources had become more intense. With the emergence of a more democratic politics, the independence and flexibility of state financial officials had shrunk. Further, Thailand's macroeconomic stability—long sustained through openness to external markets—was now shaken by forces transmitted from abroad. Hence, even when it attempted to take necessary adjustment measures, the government was unable to do so. The limits of state power were reflected in broad opposition to Prime Minister Kriangsak Chomanan's 1979 raising of oil prices and his replacement by General Prem Tinsulanonda after a military coup in 1980.

V. Economic Crisis, Regime Change, and Stabilization, 1980–1985

Coalitional changes ushered in by the new Prem government effectively reduced the demand for preferential credit by severely narrowing the number of claimants on state resources. These same political shifts, combined with alarming external deficits and the weakness of import-competing interests in the private sector, bolstered the efforts of state financial officials to pursue stabilization and export promotion through macroeconomic measures. Weaknesses in the private financial sector impeded efforts at more interventionist support for exports; but these same problems strengthened the central bank's supervisory powers over commercial banks and finance companies.

Prime Minister Prem never ran for election. He remained in power from 1980 to 1988 as a compromise choice by balancing off the military against the political parties.[33] Labor, which had actively resisted austerity measures by the previous (Kriangsak) government, restrained itself under Prem. The unions were largely defenseless; they had only the most fragile links with the parties and feared that strike-induced instability would justify a return to harsh authoritarian rule under the military.

This balance allowed Prem to expand the political space within which the technocrats operated. Macroeconomic policy came under the control of a cohesive group of officials centered not only in the Bank of Thailand and the Ministry of Finance but also in the National Economic and Social Development Board, the Budget Bureau, and the Fiscal Policy Office. Economic posts in the cabinet were filled by appointed technocrats, not members of parliament. Technocratic leverage was further strengthened by the alarm with which many leaders perceived the country's external imbalances. Even with political parties vying for control over important ministerial portfolios, the technocrats contained politicians' influence over broad macroeconomic policy.

In addition to restraining public sector deficits through budgetary restraints and tax reforms, the technocrats focused on curbing the country's trade and balance-of-payments imbalances. In 1983, the BoT, having already raised reserve requirements and restricted letters of credit, imposed an 18 percent limit on commercial bank credit growth. The policy's effectiveness was limited by the commercial banks' failure to provide the central bank with the information necessary to regulate their compliance.[34] When a large number of smaller firms collapsed in early 1984, criticism of this policy intensified and led to the central bank governor's resignation.

In place of the limits, the government moved to address balance-of-payments shortfalls through a 14.8 percent devaluation of the baht in November 1984 and pegged the baht to a trade-weighted basket of currencies rather than to the U.S. dollar, which resulted in a de facto further devaluation of the baht. These steps proved crucial in getting the Thai economy back on its feet. The Prem government succeeded in implementing this (by Thai standards) sharp devaluation despite criticism of its earlier credit ceiling policy and the potential damage to banks with large open foreign exchange positions. Prem timed the devaluation so as to reduce its political costs.[35] The government also

[33] For background on coalitional shifts, economic conditions, and policy changes during this period, see Doner and Laothamatas, "Structural Adjustment in Thailand."

[34] Interviews, Bangkok, Summer 1990.

[35] Unlike the 1981 devaluation, the 1984 adjustment occurred when parliament was

Table 4.6. Domestic sources of manufacturing credit, 1981–1988 (percent)

	1981	1983	1985	1987	1988
Commercial banks	74.6	77.5	80.1	83.9	84.6
Finance companies	21.1	19.1	15.4	12.5	12.7
Industrial Finance Company Thailand	4.3	3.4	4.5	3.6	2.7

Source: World Bank, *Financial Sector Study*, vol. 1 (Washington, D.C.: World Bank, 1990), p. 112.

drew on broad fears of renewed military rule to overcome open op-position from parts of the military whose modernization plans and import-dependent clients were threatened by the increased costs of foreign goods. Prem's appeals to the national interest were combined with support from the king and funds to soften the impact of the devaluation on military purchases and labor's standard of living.

The cross-pressures of commercial bank interests facilitated accep-tance of the devaluation. Although the devaluation hurt the banks' import-substituting clients, it boosted the activities of their exporting customers. In addition, some banks, including the powerful Bangkok Bank, reduced their foreign exchange positions in anticipation of the devaluation. The weakness of an import-substituting coalition, reflected in part in the commercial banks' lack of a unified position, thus provided state authorities with the political space to initiate the devaluation. The emerging export-oriented enterprises in the early 1980s generally de-pended less on foreign capital and more on local financing.[36] Foreign investment in Thai manufacturing during these years remained stag-nant, except in the energy industry. With the collapse of several finance and security companies, industrialists' share of those institutions' loans began to drop. In their place, however, industrialists enjoyed a rising share of commercial bank loans (Table 4.2). Manufacturers, or the larger ones in any case, also benefited from excess liquidity and in-creasing competition among financial institutions for borrowers. Some indication of greater competition is suggested by the reversal of the Bangkok Bank's constantly growing market share during this period, although the market share of the top five banks remained constant (Tables 4.3 and 4.6).

In addition to stabilization and exchange rate shifts, Thailand's re-sponse to its external deficits included more activist efforts at export-

in recess and opposition parties were weak. The government thus had time to make its case to the public. The move was also timed to benefit farmers rather than middlemen. Warr and Nidhiprabha, *Macroeconomic Policies*, pp. 48–49; and Doner and Laothamatas, "Structural Adjustment in Thailand," from which the rest of this discussion is drawn.

[36] Suehiro, *Commercial Bankers*, p. 220.

promotion. These involved the dismantling of protection and the pro-vision of export incentives for several inefficient industries, including textiles, automobiles, and electrical goods. Some key proponents of liberalization assumed its implementation would also require an ex-plicitly interventionist credit allocation policy. The first step in this process was the establishment of a (public-private sector) national com-mittee for the development of the financial system. The committee would try to promote small firms, support manufactured exports, and exercise more discrimination based on products, markets, and perfor-mance criteria. The effort also called for a state-run Industrial Restruc-turing Fund to allow the Ministry of Finance to mobilize long-term funds from foreign and domestic sources for restructured industries.[37]

These plans never came anywhere near fruition. Trade liberalization encountered several fatal obstacles, including opposition from foreign and local industrialists in industries such as textiles and autos; conflicts among parts producers and assemblers in the same industries;[38] weak links between technocratic committees established to promote restruc-turing and the relevant industries; and opposition from the Ministry of Finance, which faced revenue losses during a period of chronic fiscal deficits.

Financial components of the export strategy were blocked by a series of massive finance company and bank failures. From April 1983 through 1986, the Ministry of Finance rescued thirty-two finance com-panies and three banks, which accounted for a quarter of total financial institution assets in Thailand. Fifteen other finance companies col-lapsed and had their licenses revoked by the BoT. Causes of the crises included weaknesses in the supervisory framework and poor manage-ment practices such as persistent lending to insiders.[39] As a result, plans for sector-specific credit and an Industrial Restructuring Fund were pushed aside in favor of a Fund for the Rehabilitation and Development of Financial Institutions. This fund, still in operation, receives man-dated interest-free contributions from all financial institutions.

Thus, although the financial crisis weakened modest state efforts to expand and rationalize credit allocation, it justified the BoT's imposi-tion on the commercial banks of new regulations concerning cash re-serves, the minimum holdings of government bonds necessary to open new branches, and the minimum percentages of deposits extended to

---

[37] Industrial Management Corporation, *Industrial Restructuring Study for the National Economic and Social Development Board: Summary* (Bangkok: IMC, 1985), p. 69.

[38] Chaipat Sahasakul, Nattapong Thongpakde, and Keokam Kraisoraphong, *Lessons from the World Bank's Experience of Structural Adjustment Loans (SALs): A Case Study of Thailand* (Bangkok: Thailand Development Research Institute, 1989), p. 60.

[39] Robinson, Byeon, and Teja, *Thailand: Adjusting to Success*, p. 22.

the rehabilitation fund.[40] To encourage more project lending, the BoT imposed a ceiling of fifty million baht on overdraft lines of credit per customer. And finally, 1985 amendments to the 1979 Commercial Banking Act empowered BoT officials to conduct on-site examinations, remove bank directors and officers, and restrict transactions between institutions and their directors. The amendments allow the central bank to bring suit against the shareholders of financial institutions, an important expansion of official regulatory powers.

Several participants in the Thai financial community suggest that the central bank's firm steps against fragile financial institutions helped lay the groundwork for closer cooperation between the bank and private financial firms. Central bank officials have made considerable use of these powers, as noted by the increase in the frequency and quality of BoT supervision since 1985. The emphasis of this supervision has been on promoting good management practices and ensuring system stability rather than on supporting sector-specific lending targets. Thailand's experience during the first half of the 1980s thus reinforces the impact of demand and supply factors on credit allocation policies. Unlike in the 1970s, demand for targeted funds was weakened by a political balance that neutralized parties advocating rural expenditures and the armed services pushing for higher military budgets. On the supply side, conservative technocrats were insulated by Prem from pressures both within and outside the state and encouraged by the country's external deficits to implement broader stabilization and exchange rate reforms.

VI. ECONOMIC BOOM AND FINANCIAL LIBERALIZATION, 1986–PRESENT

Beginning in the second half of the 1980s, the pace and scope of financial reform accelerated. These efforts involved only minimal emphasis on reversing selective credit policies as the latter were minimal to begin with. The main focus of reform was on increasing the efficiency of the financial and fiscal systems through measures to impose a value-added tax, deregulate capital flows, restructure the finance industry through approval of foreign bank operations, liberalize interest rates, and introduce new financial instruments.

Although not all these efforts were successful, many, in fact, did succeed, especially interest rate liberalization and capital market development. What is striking is that these measures were initiated during a

[40] These percentages are found in *Bangkok Bank Monthly Review*, September 1986, pp. 391–96.

period of political change. In 1988, the quasi-democratic regime under Prem was replaced by a fully elected coalition government under Chatichai Choonhavan. Following a coup in February 1991, the military installed a new government led by a former diplomat and respected businessman, Anand Panyarachun. This interim leadership was replaced by an elected government in April 1992, headed by a leader of the February 1992 military coup. Following massive opposition in May, Anand was reinstalled as an interim prime minister, until September 1992, when new elections installed a five-party civilian coalition government.

These regime changes influenced an important supply-side component of financial reform in altering the strength of the financial technocrats. Not surprisingly, we thus see an intensification of reform implementation during the two Anand periods, when technocrats enjoyed their greatest leverage. But the democratic periods of extensive party influence did not lead to rollbacks of reform. Even when officials in the BoT and the finance minister were less insulated, demand factors—resource surpluses and private sector openness—allowed the technocrats to continue on the reform path.

Although state officials recognized the need for significant fiscal and monetary policy changes in the early 1980s, they shunted aside the reform agenda and focused on limiting state spending growth and foreign borrowing. Other measures were still under consideration in 1988 when Prem resigned following a parliamentary vote of no confidence.

Chatichai Choonhavan, a leader of the Chart Thai political party, replaced Prem and quickly expanded party influence. Chatichai strengthenced a basic division of labor between the technocrats, who oversaw macroeconomic policy and politicians, who exercised considerable influence over the policies of the various ministries that had emerged during Prem's tenure. Despite the expanded role of party leaders, financial officials were able to initiate major reforms under Chatichai. Interest rate liberalization was the area of greatest success. Between June 1989 and June 1990, the BoT removed or raised ceilings on most commercial bank deposits and loans, as well as on promissory notes and loans by nonbank finance companies. Early in 1991, financial officials ended deposit rate ceilings and raised the limit on loans to 19 percent. Officials also deregulated capital flows and allowed commercial banks to approve the repatriation of investment funds, dividends, and profits as Thailand adopted IMF Article VIII in May 1990.[41]

[41] In June 1989, the ceiling on time deposits with a maturity of over one year was lifted to encourage long-term deposit taking and to allow commercial banks to adjust themselves to a more flexible interest rate system. In March 1990, ceilings on time deposits with a maturity of one year or less were abolished. Ceilings currently remain only on savings

The technocrats' ability to implement these reforms was in large part a function of relaxed revenue constraints. The policy reforms of the Prem years contributed to impressive growth rates led by a sharp expansion of manufactured exports.[42] This growth, combined with spending cuts, resulted in a rapidly diminishing external debt and rising fiscal surpluses. These, in turn, provided state officials with resources that emboldened them to undertake long-contemplated reforms. Bulging state coffers afforded political parties important spoils for which they competed as well as the means to finance the construction of badly needed transportation and telecommunications infrastructure. During the Chatichai years, political competition over access to the public trough increased rapidly but did not outstrip growth in the revenue pool.

The private sector's health and structure also encouraged the reform process. Private funds were available to finance the country's manufacturing export boom after 1985 and thus helped moderate any pressure for selective credit. Most of these funds were domestic; foreign investment is estimated to have accounted for only about 10 percent of manufactured export growth. Thus, at least through 1989, "the export and investment booms were overwhelmingly Thai supplied and financed."[43] Major local business groups made large investments, sometimes with foreign capital, in import-substituting sectors such as petrochemicals even as they initiated or expanded export and even overseas operations. Large firms' ratios of debt to equity fell as they enjoyed access to funds from among group-affiliated firms as well as to longer-term lending. The burgeoning securities market played a growing role. Foreign capital inflows, both direct and through the local equity market, provided firms new alternative sources of financing. The commercial banks themselves financed their expansion through large new issues on the local market. For the largest manufacturing firms, offshore loans became a realistic option, particularly when Finance Minister Pramual Sabhavasu slashed the withholding tax, as he did on two occasions. And as the impressive growth of small and medium-sized firms suggests, this financing was not limited to large firms.[44]

---

deposits and lending rates. In November 1990, ceilings on lending rates were raised from 15 percent to 19 percent. For reviews see Robinson Byeon, and Teja, *Thailand: Adjusting to Success*, pp. 24–26; and *Bangkok Post*, April 21, 1992, p. 20.

[42] Manufactured goods rose as a portion of total exports from 26 percent in 1976 to 49 percent in 1985, 55 percent in 1986, and 63 percent in 1987. See Phasuk Phongpaichit, "Thailand: Miss Universe 1988," in *Southeast Asian Affairs, 1989*, ed. Ng Chee Yuen (Singapore: Institute of Southeast Asian Studies, 1989), table 4.

[43] Narongchai Akrasanee, David Dapice, and Frank Flatters, *Thailand's Export-led Growth: Retrospect and Prospects* (Bangkok: Thailand Development Research Institute, 1991), p. 22.

[44] For information on internal financing, export activities, and diversification of Thailand's three largest industrial groups, see Paisal Sricharatchanya, "The Jewels of the

The balance of economic power between industry and finance thus seemed to be shifting in favor of the former. Yet any pressure for increased protection and preferential lending was offset by pressure to export and the availability of sufficient funding. In fact, the health of the real sector assisted BoT efforts to stabilize the financial system and provided officials with the opportunity to address problems evident during earlier periods of more sluggish growth. Reforms followed private interests, local and foreign, responding to the opportunities emerging during this period. More significant policy changes came only after enhanced access to foreign capital provided policymakers with the breathing room they felt they needed to implement reforms.

The structure of interests in the financial system also encouraged interest rate reform. State officials had long supported interest rate liberalization in order to reduce capital outflows, inflationary pressures, and current account deficits. Intensified competition among private financial institutions seems to have facilitated their ability to do so.[45] Although commercial banks spent much of 1987 pleading with the BoT to fix lending and borrowing rates as it had in the past, the Thai Bankers Association's efforts to reestablish the interest rate cartel had failed by 1988 in the face of competition from finance companies, foreign banks, and smaller banks. The top four commercial banks controlled two-thirds of all assets, yet smaller banks were becoming more attractive to investors because of their flexibility in industrial lending. Between 1986 and 1988, the top three banks lost some of their market share to the smaller banks. And, by 1991, the largest of the country's finance and securities firms' asset holdings rivaled those of the smaller banks.

An improved relationship between the BoT and commercial banks— largely a function of the BoT's successful stabilization of the financial system earlier in the decade—encouraged financial system stability. The BoT stabilized the financial system after external disturbances and criminal irresponsibility on the part of some financial institution managers threatened major disruption of the financial system as a whole. The central bank's management of some of these institutions and its success in stabilizing the system earned it the gratitude of private fi-

Crown," *Far Eastern Economic Review,* June 30, 1988, pp. 60–61; Jonathan Friedland, "Seeds of Empire," *Far Eastern Economic Review,* April 20, 1989, pp. 46–48; and Paul Handley, "Cuts from Different Cloth," *Far Eastern Economic Review,* October 27, 1988, pp. 88–89. On financial institutions and the equities market, see World Bank, *Thailand Financial Sector Study,* vol. 1, p. 148. On the export activities of small firms, see Phongpaichit, "Thailand: Miss Universe."

[45] The following draws on *Far Eastern Economic Review,* February 25, 1988, p. 80, March 26, 1988, p. 66, and April 4, 1991, pp. 38, 40. See also World Bank, *Thailand Financial Sector Study,* vol. 1, p. 29.

nancial interests and a greater willingness among all parties to cooperate. The result, according to one observer, was that the bank regulators "now are comfortable with their banks" and on many issues "are Japan-like."[46]

Although the reform effort generally succeeded, components of it failed or were implemented with some difficulty. Central bank reform efforts were neither smoothly accomplished nor universally successful. In an effort to cool off the overheated real estate market, the BoT asked financial institutions to provide reports estimating the sectoral allocation of their lending over the next six months. These measures failed to curb real estate loans. As one official put it, BoT window guidance is effective only when it is consistent with market trends. The central bank's efforts to raise interest rate ceilings were also blocked, at least initially, by Pramual, one of the rare politicians filling the post of minister of finance in Thailand. Pramual saw himself as representing the interests of put-upon smaller businesses, and his own experience of bankruptcy also may have inclined him to be antagonistic toward local financiers. As a result, his positions on liberalization were inconsistent, but his opposition to the broader financial community, public and private, was predictable. Pramual opposed financial officials' support for higher interest rate ceilings and retention of the withholding tax. But he supported a proposal to increase competition by granting foreign bank licenses, a move whose potential destabilizing impact worried career finance officials. Higher interest rate ceilings came only after the prime minister shunted Pramual aside in 1990.

General fear of politicization also weakened efforts to develop new financial instruments. Thailand traditionally lacked a well-developed debt instrument market, which reflected the commercial banks' disproportionate dependence on deposits with short-term maturities. This weakness threatened to check the growth of manufacturing expansion, and it has impeded the BoT's ability to sterilize capital inflows. In 1990, the central bank developed a three-year plan to develop primary and secondary issue markets. The plan included a greater variety of debt and equity instruments available to publicly listed and private companies; the establishment of a uniform tax rate on all investment vehicles; and the creation of a Securities and Exchange Commission to govern all existing and future markets for debt, equity, and derivative financial instruments. Because the commission was to be headed by the finance minister and was to be equal in status and responsibility with the BoT, the proposal stumbled on fears of political influence in the equities market.

[46] Interview, Bangkok, Summer 1991.

In February 1991, the military, responding to the Chatichai government's attempts to weaken the power base of senior military officials,
responded with a coup and installed Anand as prime minister. Anand's
thirteen-month interim government provided technocrats with perhaps
their greatest leverage ever and accelerated the reform process. In
April, the central bank initiated a new round of financial deregulation
and institutional development described as "a complete restructuring
of the relationship between capital and politics and an affirmation of
the rights of Thai capital groups."[47] New measures included the further
loosening of foreign exchange restrictions; the effective dismantling of
interest rate ceilings; the ending of requirements that commercial banks
hold government bonds; the implementation of a value-added tax; the
expansion of activities permitted to commercial banks and finance and
securities companies; the creation of secondary markets in various debt
instruments; and the creation of a Securities and Exchange Commission
responsible for overseeing most capital and debt market developments.

Political and institutional strength was critical to this wave of financial
reform. Some twenty bills were passed into law in a thirteen-month
period under the leadership of the Bank of Thailand in conjunction
with the Ministry of Finance, which was unhindered by political intervention. The central bank also used backing from the new regime to
increase its independence by, for example, divesting itself of credit
instruments that invited politicians seeking cheap loans to stabilize the
prices of agricultural and industrial products.[48] Yet if supply-side factors were important, they are insufficient explanations of the scope and
speed of change. Financial reform would have been impossible without
an increasingly competitive group of commercial banks and a broader
private sector capable of operating in increasingly open capital markets.

This chapter supports the "demand-and-supply" approach introduced at the outset. On the demand side, the Thai state did not perceive
itself to be under pressure to catch up with its neighbors, to satisfy
emerging industrialists, or to find new sources of revenue for itself.
The state generally had access to adequate levels of revenue through
a shifting combination of sin taxes on the Chinese, trade taxes, and
foreign military funds. When the major source of these funds, namely,
export taxes, declined in the early 1980s because of the slump in commodity prices, the government relied on macroeconomic policies to

---

[47] *Manager* (Bangkok), July 1992, p. 51. Also see *Bangkok Post*, April 26, 1991, p. 1, and
May 21, 1992, p. 20; and Paul Handley, "A Bridge Too Far," *Far Eastern Economic Review*,
July 9, 1992, p. 49.
[48] *Bangkok Post*, March 17, 1991, p. 17, and March 26, 1991, p. 1.

oachieve necessary adjustments while local firms initiated an export-based economic boom.

Two factors help explain the private sector's limited demand for preferential credit policies. One has to do with the structure of assets and the activities of powerful private actors. Agricultural export activities have been a large, albeit declining, portion of commercial bank portfolios. Commercial banks were politically and economically the dominant component of Thai capital well into the 1970s. And although commercial bank leverage vis-à-vis industrial capital clearly declined by the 1980s, the banks maintained significant influence through directorships, equity holdings, and the provision of finance. Moreover, Thailand's emerging industrialists had access to adequate supplies of private capital. Foreign investment was initially critical for larger investments, but local financing—whether through finance companies, internal capital markets, or commercial banks—has been increasingly important since the 1970s.

On the supply side, we have found that where even limited demands for preferential credit emerged, central bank mediation ensured that the demands were manifest in fiscal rather than financial policies. The lack of selective credit is thus in part attributable to the BoT's autonomy within the state, that is, its leverage over spending agencies such as the Ministries of Industry and Commerce. This leverage is, in turn, a function of both the central bank's clear preferences, cohesion, and expertise and the political arrangements through which the Finance Ministry has protected the BoT from the pressures of political parties.

Central bank autonomy from Thai business, however, is relatively weak and less important for the pursuit of open financial policies. Indeed, part of the BoT's strength derives from the congruence of its views with those of the commercial banks and other major business interests. The BoT has been successful at pursuing policies consistent with commercial bank preferences that is, low inflation, only limited mandated credit programs, and the maintenance of financial system stability through rescue operations and closer supervision of management and portfolio quality. But on issues requiring greater intervention, the BoT has either opted not to act or has seen its modest efforts rebuffed.

CHAPTER FIVE

The Politics of Finance in Indonesia: Command, Confusion, and Competition

ANDREW J. MACINTYRE

Indonesia earned a reputation during the 1980s for its willingness to make liberal economic reforms. Market-oriented trade and industrial policies introduced over the past decade have produced a more outward-looking economy. Moreover, deregulation has not been confined to the real sector of the economy as there have also been fundamental changes in financial policy that have spurred the process of financial deepening. Notwithstanding its recently earned liberal economic reputation, however, Indonesia has a long history of state intervention. This is particularly evident in the financial sector.

This chapter examines state intervention in credit markets and focuses on government attempts to allocate credit on the basis of preferential lending programs. It traces the evolution of intervention in credit markets from the immediate postindependence period to the present. The central concern here is to explain the political dynamics of intervention in credit markets and the subsequent move to draw back and liberalize the policy regime.

The state looms very large in Indonesia's political and economic life. For over thirty years, the country has been under authoritarian rule. In the period since the mid-1970s, systematic political exclusion has become institutionalized, with policy decisions being shaped by bureaucrats operating in a manner largely unconstrained by organized political action from societal groups. The state's domination of political life has been matched by its equally remarkable presence in the mar-

I thank Heinz Arndt, David Cole, Donald Emmerson, Stephen Grenville, Stephan Haggard, Laura Hastings, Hal Hill, Iyanatul Islam, David McKendrick, Jamie Mackie, Ross McLeod, and Richard Robison for helpful comments on an early draft.

ketplace.[1] This domination is especially clear in the banking sector, where state banks accounted for 80–90 percent of all loans extended over much of the period since the late 1960s. Until very recently, private (local) and foreign banks have played only a minor role in credit distribution. The weakness of the private and foreign banks, together with the fact that the state banks have lacked any real operational autonomy, has meant that bureaucrats have been able to tailor credit policy with little concern for the preferences of bankers.

Within this setting, there has been a high level of preferential lending. Central bank officials have drawn up elaborate lists ranking categories of borrowers and allocating subsidies on the basis of economic priority. Ultimately, however, it is not so much the extent of state intervention in credit markets that is remarkable but rather the ad hoc, uncoordinated, and largely inefficient manner in which it has taken place. Notwithstanding state domination of the financial sector and the relative autonomy of state officials in formulating policy, with some significant exceptions, preferential credit schemes do not appear to have been effective economic instruments.

To the extent that any sector has been systematically favored by preferential credit programs, it is agriculture and particularly rice farmers that stand out. The manufacturing sector has not received a large share of preferential credit, which sets the Indonesian experience apart from that of a number of other developing countries. Against this, however, it is widely acknowledged that credit diversion has been a common phenomenon in Indonesia: subsidized finance officially earmarked for particular categories of borrowers has frequently been appropriated by nonpriority borrowers. One important factor contributing to the diversion of preferential finance has been the need of senior government officials for discrete economic benefits and favors that could be distributed to supporters and associates. Patrimonial politics, together with sheer bureaucratic incapacity, undermined the possibility of preferential credit functioning as an effective economic policy instrument. Viewed from a purely political perspective, however, preferential credit has been of enduring value. Subsidized finance has aided Indonesia's political leaders in the crucial task of winning friends among the elite and preserving mass support in the countryside. It is for this reason that preferential lending has continued (even if on a much

[1] State-owned enterprises play a large role in the Indonesian economy. One study found that as late as 1988, the public sector still accounted for as much 30 percent of GNP and 40 percent of nonagricultural GNP. See Hal Hill, "Ownership in Indonesia: Who Owns What and Does It Matter?" in *Indonesia Assessment: 1990*, Political and Social Change Monograph, no. 11, R.S.Pac.S., ed. Hal Hill and Terry Hull (Canberra: Australian National University, 1990), p. 54; and Andrew MacIntyre, *Business and Politics in Indonesia* (Sydney: Allen and Unwin, 1991), pp. 251–52.

reduced basis) in the wake of the swing toward market-oriented economic policies in the 1980s.

To date, research on finance and credit in Indonesia has been almost exclusively the realm of economists. The attraction of Indonesia for economists is not hard to understand; its recent history seems in many respects to confirm the canons of neoclassical economics. When he came to power in 1966, General Suharto was confronted with a divided polity and an economy in utter disarray after a calamitous experiment with state-led industrialization. A quarter of a century later, he presides over a country that has notched up an average annual growth rate of around 7 percent.

Although the oil boom obviously played a crucial role in Indonesia's economic turnaround, the consensus among economists is that the cornerstone of the country's economic performance is the sound policy advice promoted by a group of liberal economists within the government. Broadly speaking, the Indonesian government has earned the praise of economists for its moves to deregulate the economy and allow market forces to shape allocational decisions.[2] In the area of finance, emphasis has been on prudent management of the money supply, the mobilization of domestic savings, and the overall efficiency of the banking sector.[3] When the system of credit allocation has been considered, it has usually been in relation to these variables. Not surprisingly perhaps, there is little enthusiasm in the economics literature for government efforts to harness credit and use it as an instrument to steer resources to particular sectors of the economy. Particularly during the oil boom years of 1974–1982, the government employed a range of direct and indirect measures to guide credit allocation. Most economists see this period as one in which the country's financial development was retarded. A series of reforms deregulating the financial sector over the

[2] See, for example, World Bank, *World Development Report, 1987* (New York: Oxford University Press, 1987), pp. 24–25.

[3] Among the major studies are Heinz Arndt, "Banking in Hyperinflation and Stabilization," in *The Economy of Indonesia,* ed. Bruce Glassburner (Ithaca: Cornell University Press, 1971), and "Monetary Policy Instruments in Indonesia," *Bulletin of Indonesian Economic Studies* 15, no. 3 (1979): 107–22; David Cole and Betty Slade, *Financial Development in Indonesia,* Development Discussion Paper no. 336 (Cambridge: Harvard Institute for International Development, Harvard University, 1990); Stephen Grenville, "Monetary Policy and the Formal Financial Sector," in *The Indonesian Economy during the Soeharto Era,* ed. Anne Booth and Peter McCawley (Kuala Lumpur: Oxford University Press, 1981); Benjamin Higgins and William Hollinger, "Central Banking in Indonesia," in *Central Banking in Southeast Asia,* ed. S. G. Davies (Hong Kong: Hong Kong University Press, 1960); Ross McLeod, "Finance and Entrepreneurship in the Small Business Sector in Indonesia," Ph.D. diss., Canberra; Australian National University, 1980; Anwar Nasution, *Financial Institutions and Policies in Indonesia* (Singapore: Institute of Southeast Asian Studies, 1983); and Douglas Paauw, *Financing Economic Development: The Indonesian Case* (Glencoe: Free Press, 1960).

course of the 1980s, however, is seen as stimulating a surge of financial deepening by promoting competition and industrial diversification.

The politics of finance in Indonesia is very largely an untold story. Before Richard Robison's important work in 1986,[4] political economy writings were scant indeed. Two decades earlier, Jamie A. C. Mackie had examined political variables underpinning Indonesia's fight with inflation in the 1950s and 1960s, as well as the beginnings of the country's state-owned enterprise complex.[5] In a study of the role of the army in Indonesian politics, Harold Crouch threw light on military efforts to raise revenue through formal and informal commercial activities.[6] But it was Robison's work that really lodged political economy questions firmly on the research agenda. Writing from a structuralist perspective, Robison was basically concerned with demonstrating that a local capitalist class had developed in Indonesia. In this, he focused on the role of the state in nurturing the budding bourgeoisie. Inevitably, therefore, he addressed the state's provision of financial support to facilitate local industrial development. Robison was not concerned primarily with the politics of finance, but he did draw attention to a number of preferential credit schemes and underscored the significance of several variables, including the importance of ethnicity in the allocation of credit, the state's domination of the financial sector, and the prevalence of corruption and administrative "leakage" in preferential credit schemes.

Yoshihara Kunio's comparative study of the emergence of an industrial bourgeoisie in Southeast Asia also points to the importance of political connections and patronage in the creation of an "ersatz" capitalist class.[7] Yoon Hwan Shin and Yahya A. Muhaimin have also examined the significance of patrimonial interests in the state's sponsorship of Indonesia's nascent capitalist class.[8] Industry studies of automobiles by Ian Chalmers, of banking and aerospace by David McKendrick, and my work on insurance touched similar themes.[9] The

[4] Richard Robison, *Indonesia: The Rise of Capital* (Sydney: Allen and Unwin, 1986).

[5] Jamie A. C. Mackie, *Problems of the Indonesian Inflation* (Ithaca: Cornell University, 1967), and "Indonesia's Government Estates and Their Masters," *Pacific Affairs* 34, no. 4 (1961).

[6] Harold Crouch, *The Army and Politics in Indonesia* (Ithaca: Cornell University Press, 1978).

[7] Yoshihara Kunio, *The Rise of Ersatz Capitalism in Southeast Asia* (Singapore: Oxford University Press, 1988).

[8] Yoon Hwan Shin, "Demystifying the Capitalist State: Political Patronage, Bureaucratic Interests and Capitalists-in-Formation in Soeharto's Indonesia," Ph.D. diss., Yale University, 1989; and Yahya A. Muhaimin, *Bisnis dan Politik: Kebijaksanaan Ekonomi Indonesia, 1950–1980* (Jakarta: Lembaga Penelitian, Pendidikan, Penerangan Ekonomi dan Sosial, 1990).

[9] Ian Chalmers, "Economic Nationalism and the Third World State: The Political Economy of the Indonesian Automotive Industry, 1950–1984," Ph.D. diss., Australian National University, 1988; David McKendrick, "Acquiring Technological Capabilities: Aircraft and Commercial Banking," Ph.D. diss., University of California, 1989; and MacIntyre, *Business and Politics in Indonesia*.

study that probably comes closest to the concerns of this essay is an important article by M. Hadi Soesastro exploring the politics and economics of deregulation in the 1980s.[10] Soesastro highlights the internal struggles within the bureaucracy and the impact of the collapse of oil prices as key variables in the liberal reorientation of economic policy over the last decade, but the financial sector does not figure prominently.

Apart from this small body of political economy writings, most work on Indonesia by political scientists deals with questions about the nature of the regime and patterns of bureaucratic politics. The two principal themes that emerge from the existing literature are the dominant role of the state in both politics and economics and the permeation of the state by patrimonial networks of allegiance and corruption. The general point, however, is that we know very little about the politics of finance in Indonesia.

I. THE EVOLUTION OF STATE INTERVENTION IN CREDIT MARKETS

It is tempting to divide Indonesia's economic and political history into two basic periods: the Sukarno years (1949–1965) and the Suharto years (1966 onward). The country has had only two presidents, and their approaches to economic policy differed radically. But this division of Indonesian history is too crude. On one hand, there are important subdivisions to be drawn within each period; on the other, there are some significant continuities that run throughout Indonesia's postindependence history.

Indonesia's economic history can be usefully separated into five periods: (1) the early postindependence years of 1949–1957, (2) the Guided Economy period of 1957–1965, (3) the period of economic stabilization and rehabilitation in the first years of the Suharto regime (1966–1973), (4) the oil boom years of 1973–1982, and (5) the period of economic slowdown and liberal reform in the 1980s. In each of these periods, we can see important developments emerging in financial policy and, in particular, the distribution of credit.

The Early Years, 1949–1957

Despite the cessation of hostilities and the political withdrawal of the Dutch in 1949, Indonesia's financial system remained little changed

---

[10] M. Hadi Soesastro, "The Political Economy of Deregulation in Indonesia," *Asian Survey* 29, no. 9 (1989): 853–69.

from the colonial period. The limited number of existing foreign exchange banks were primarily concerned with facilitating trade with the Netherlands by providing short-term finance. The Dutch semipublic Javasche Bank approximated a central bank to the extent that it held a monopoly on issuing notes. In 1951 the Javasche Bank was nationalized, and in 1953 it officially became the new central bank, the Bank Indonesia. Significantly, however, Bank Indonesia retained some commercial banking functions and continued lending directly to private borrowers. As one might expect in a newly independent country, the central bank did not enjoy great independence from the government. Bank Indonesia was under the authority of the Monetary Board, which was chaired by the finance minister rather than the bank's governor. As a result, the bank tended to operate as the implementing agency of the government's monetary and credit policies.[11]

One of the priorities of successive cabinets in these early years was the promotion of local industry. As already noted, the financial system inherited from the Dutch was oriented mainly toward financing import and export activity and was thus little suited to this task. Moreover, the seven foreign banks (three Dutch, two British, and two Chinese) operating in Indonesia at this stage had little enthusiasm for extending credit to local firms and not surprisingly preferred to concentrate on lending to lower-risk foreign enterprises. To overcome these obstacles and in keeping with the emphasis on the promotion of local industry, several fledgling state-owned banks were developed. There was a rough differentiation of function among the state banks. Bank Industri Negara was established as a development bank, with responsibility for providing long-term credit to industry, plantations, and mining. Among the industries it supplied with preferential loans were textiles, cement, and automobile assembly.[12] A second state bank, Bank Negara Indonesia 1946, specialized in providing export and import credit to Indonesian traders and was used to finance the so-called Benteng Program, which was designed to foster locally owned import companies through the granting of special licensing and preferential credit. The third of the state-owned banks was Bank Rakyat Indonesia, which concentrated on providing credit to small and medium-sized industries.[13]

Table 5.1 shows the distribution of credit from the state and foreign banks among sectors and industries. The import sector emerges clearly as the recipient of the largest single slice of credit, followed by sugar plantations and various state-owned and semi-state-owned enterprises. It must be emphasized, however, that credit to commercial enterprises

---

[11] Nasution, *Financial Institutions and Policies in Indonesia*, p. 59.
[12] Robison, *Indonesia*, p. 40.
[13] Paauw, *Financing Economic Development*, pp. 134–35.

Table 5.1. Allocation of credit by sector and industry, state banks and foreign banks, 1953–1957 (millions Rp)

	1953	1954	1955	1956	1957
State and semistate firms	162	321	407	455	526
Private firms	2,096	2,339	3,393	3,470	3,007
Banks and credit institutions	50	60	186	55	70
Insurance and savings institutions	7	4	8	16	19
Rice mills	7	8	6	4	10
Domestic trade	55	103	84	83	105
Exporters	257	359	394	375	434
Importers	516	457	859	1,367	996
Sugar plantations	490	444	504	318	218
Other plantations	219	156	245	241	130
Industry	239	366	548	354	383
Storage and transport	111	127	85	69	45
Other firms	130	239	433	463	499
Individuals	15	16	44	125	118
Total	2,258	2,660	3,800	3,925	3,533

Sources: Bank Indonesia, *Report for the Financial Year, 1954/55, 1955/56*, and *1957/58* issues (Jakarta: Bank Indonesia, various years).

Note: Figures are for the month of December each year. They include commercial credits from Bank Indonesia, but not Bank Rakyat Indonesia.

was dwarfed by Bank Indonesia funding to the government. In 1956, for example, credit from the state and foreign banks to commercial enterprises (public and private) amounted to Rp 3.9 billion, whereas Bank Indonesia credits to the government totaled Rp 10.3 billion.[14]

The state banks (including Bank Indonesia), together with the seven foreign banks, dominated the formal financial sector during this period. Nevertheless, there was a rapid expansion in the number of local private banks between 1950 and 1957. In 1951 there were 15 private Indonesian banks, and by 1957 there were 104.[15] This proliferation of banks was initially encouraged by the government as part of the overall drive to foster local industry, with many of the private banks depending on state handouts rather than on a depositor base to finance their lending activities. Of the one-hundred-odd local private banks, however, most were very small and many were not, in fact, operational. The twenty largest local private banks accounted for roughly 90 percent of the total business of all local private banks, and of this twenty, only four were permitted to conduct foreign exchange operations.[16] Statistical data on the size of the various categories of banks during this period are problematic. Nevertheless, it is clear that local private banks played only a very small role in the formal credit market. Table 5.2 provides a com-

[14] Ibid., p. 139.
[15] Bank Indonesia, *Report for the Financial Year 1951/52* (Jakarta: Bank Indonesia, 1952), and *Report for the Financial Year 1957/58* (Jakarta: Bank Indonesia, 1958).
[16] Higgins and Hollinger, "Central Banking in Indonesia," p. 55.

Table 5.2. Distribution of commercial credit by bank type, 1953–1957 (millions Rp)

	1953	1954	1955	1956	1957
State and foreign banks	2,258	2,660	3,800	3,925	3,533
Twenty largest local private banks	102	199	185	462	660

Sources: Bank Indonesia, *Reports for the Financial Year, 1954/55, 1955/56,* and *1957/58* issues (Jakarta: Bank Indonesia, various years).
Note: Figures are for the month of December each year.

parison of the value of credit extended by the twenty largest local private banks to the value of credit extended to commercial enterprises by the state and foreign banks. Again, however, if central bank lending to the government is included, the proportion of total credit extended by local private banks becomes minute.

State subsidization of the expansion of local private banks was part of a wider endeavor to promote the development of local industry. The state and private banks were used to channel credit to various sectors. Right from the outset, though, this policy had dual objectives. In addition to the usual postindependence economic nationalist goal of financing local industrial development, the government was anxious to direct credit toward indigenous Indonesians, as opposed to those of Chinese descent.[17] Although amounting to only about 3 percent of the population, Chinese Indonesians have played a dominant role in the economy. The economic jealousy of indigenous Indonesians (who had been little involved in commercial activity under the Dutch) and concerns about national commitment have stimulated deep-seated resentments that have seen Chinese Indonesians subjected to sometimes violent outbursts of racial prejudice. This has been an enduring and fundamental variable in economic policy in Indonesia. To this day the government is concerned with this issue and favors indigenous Indonesians to promote greater economic equality between the two racial groups. Racial sensitivities have been an important factor encouraging state intervention in the allocation of credit; policymakers in Indonesia have long understood that if market considerations alone were permitted to determine allocational decisions, indigenous Indonesians would lose out very badly to Chinese Indonesians. In the banking industry itself, the great majority of local private banks were controlled by Chinese Indonesians. Those banks that were controlled by indigenous interests were typically associated with influential groups within the state elite such as the major political parties and the military.

[17] See, for example, John Sutter, *Indonesianisasi: Politics in a Changing Economy,* Data Paper no. 36-I, Southeast Asia Program (Ithaca: Cornell University, 1959); and Frank H. Golay, "Indonesia," in Frank H. Golay et al., *Underdevelopment and Economic Nationalism in Southeast Asia* (Ithaca: Cornell University Press, 1969).

Attempts during this period to stimulate the development of a local industrial base through the use of preferential credit schemes, as well as other measures such as the selective allocation of import licenses, met with only very limited success. In part, this lack of success was due to a glaring shortage of indigenous Indonesians with entrepreneurial skills and training. Equally, however, it reflected the highly unstable and factionalized nature of the government in these early years. The multiparty system of parliamentary government was crippled by shifting party coalitions, with cabinets rising and falling in rapid succession.[18] In this situation the pattern of credit allocation was typically quite politicized. Successive finance ministers ensured that the state banks channeled credit in the direction of firms and individuals associated with their party or faction.

In such a fluid political environment, attempts by the central bank to impose credit controls on the banking industry were of doubtful value. In 1955 and 1957, regulations were introduced empowering the central bank to assert new controls over the banking industry. One of the aims was to contain the unchecked expansion of the small private banks by imposing capital adequacy requirements. These efforts were constantly frustrated by the political immunity some banks enjoyed as a result of being closely allied with powerful ministries. Moreover, a number of ministries established specialized nonbank agencies to grant or guarantee credit to local firms experiencing difficulties in raising credit.[19] Ministries such as Economic Affairs, Agriculture, Internal Affairs and Labor all ran small credit agencies channeling funds directly to particular segments of the market, with an emphasis on indigenous Indonesians being a common theme. Typically, these were autonomous organizations, accountable only to the ministry concerned or, more particular, to the individual or party currently controlling the ministry.

The level of state intervention in credit markets during this period was quite extensive but lacked central control or direction. Bureaucratic fragmentation and the capture on a rotating basis of specific agencies by leaders of the numerous political parties served to hinder central bank attempts to contain the growth of the money supply (through credit ceilings) and manage balance-of-payments pressures (principally through attempts to limit import-financing credits). Although there is relatively little detailed data about credit allocation available for this period, the general picture that emerges is one of nascent economic nationalism. The state banks and the small credit agencies attached to

[18] For a classic study of this period, see Herbert Feith, *The Decline of Constitutional Democracy in Indonesia* (Ithaca: Cornell University Press, 1962).
[19] Arndt, "Banking in Hyperinflation and Stabilization," pp. 362–63; and Paauw, *Financing Economic Development*, pp. 135–37.

various ministries were used for directing credit to encourage the development of local and, particularly, indigenous business. The scope for a coherent effort to foster the development of indigenous industry was, however, severely limited by the highly fluid and patrimonial nature of the political system. As will be seen, despite various subsequent regulatory and institutional changes, this pattern was to prove an enduring one.

The Guided Economy Years, 1957–1965

The character of financial policy and, indeed generally, economic and political life in Indonesia underwent important changes beginning in 1957. The catalyst for change was the breakdown in the system of parliamentary government and the outbreak of regional rebellions. With the support of the military, Sukarno declared martial law, returned the country to an earlier constitution that provided for a much stronger presidency, and pushed the political system steadily in the direction of authoritarianism. Sukarno's leadership was marked by strident nationalism and a vigorous drive for economic and political autonomy from the West.

Although the state had been actively involved in economic life since independence, this involvement became much more extensive during the Guided Economy years. The first step in this direction came in 1957–1958 with the nationalization of all remaining Dutch firms. Rather than transferring former colonial enterprises to local entrepreneurs as happened, for example, in South Korea, however, it was decided that these enterprises should be owned and controlled by the state itself. In part this was because transferring the former Dutch assets to local entrepreneurs would in most cases mean handing them to Chinese Indonesians, something quite unthinkable for indigenous Indonesians. In general, however, this decision reflected an ideological preference for state enterprise as opposed to private enterprise, which became a hallmark of the Sukarno years. Unimpressed by the failure of earlier attempts to stimulate significant levels of private sector industrialization, Sukarno set off on an intensified drive for state-led industrialization.

Control of the banking system was part of Sukarno's push for state-led industrialization. We have already seen that before 1957, the central bank enjoyed little operational autonomy from the government. Under Sukarno's leadership, however, the central bank became little more than a rubber stamp. Most important, it was powerless to resist government pressure for increasingly open-ended financing of budget deficits. In 1957 and 1958, legal restrictions on both the level of central

Table 5.3. Allocation of bank credit by sector (advances from foreign exchange banks, percentage)

Year	Public sector	Private sector
1955	18	82
1956	12	88
1957	15	85
1958	29	71
1959	57	43

Source: Heinz Arndt, "Banking in Hyperinflation and Stabilization," in *The Economy of Indonesia*, ed. Bruce Glassburner (Ithaca: Cornell University Press, 1971), p. 370.
Note: Central bank funding of government budgets is not included.

bank finance to the Treasury and note issue reserve requirements were discarded. The standing of the central bank was further eroded when its conservative governor, Sjafruddin Prawiranegara, resigned to lead the rebel government that had been declared in Sumatra in 1958. Any lingering illusions of central bank autonomy from the government disappeared in 1961, when Sukarno appointed one man, Jusuf Musa Dalam, to serve as both governor of Bank Indonesia and minister for central bank affairs.[20]

The government's ability to control the distribution of credit increased markedly with the elimination of the foreign banks. The three remaining Dutch banks were nationalized in 1958, and the other four foreign banks either had their licenses revoked or simply ceased operating between 1963–1964. This left only the state banks (and specialized credit agencies) together with the few medium-sized and numerous small local private banks.[21] Control over the distribution of credit was achieved by way of the central bank's own direct credit operations as well as its authority to regulate liquidity ratios, interest rates, and credit levels of the various state and private banks. By these means, the government was able to bring about a reorientation in the allocation of credit away from the private sector toward the state sector. Whereas the aim in the early postindependence period had been to facilitate the development of local entrepreneurs, during the Guided Economy years, the emphasis was on promoting state-owned enterprises. In this situation, access to credit by private entrepreneurs became increasingly difficult in the absence of influential political connections. Table 5.3 illustrates the near reversal in proportional terms of the distribution of credit between the public and private sectors.

As time went on, the state and private commercial banks became

[20] Arndt, "Banking in Hyperinflation and Stabilization," p. 363.
[21] In 1959 further private entry to the banking industry was stopped. This regulation was relaxed slightly in 1964.

increasingly dependent on Bank Indonesia for credit. The central bank advanced direct loans to the commercial banks, which were supposedly lent to approved categories of borrowers. But this central bank financing of the commercial banks (and, more important, the government budget) was made possible only by the tireless efforts of printing presses churning out new bank notes. As the rate of growth in the money supply began to escalate rapidly, the government's ability to channel credit to preferred sectors of the economy quickly eroded. In 1964 the government attempted to strengthen its control of credit distribution and boost flagging local production by introducing regulations requiring all commercial banks to allocate 60 percent of credit to the productive sector (principally agriculture), 20 percent to the export sector, and 20 percent for other purposes (such as imports). These regulations proved all but meaningless, however. Those able to get their hands on bank credit not surprisingly poured it into speculative activity, such as hoarding rice.[22] The allocation of credit during this period became utterly politicized. Sukarno sought to harness the central bank, and through it the rest of the banking system, as part of his grand spending plans.[23] In addition to funding the government budget and state enterprises, Bank Indonesia became a source for discretionary finance to support Sukarno's ambitious nation-building projects, including a huge mosque (the largest in the world), monuments, international hotels, and diplomatic escapades.

In May 1965, a massive restructuring of the banking sector was planned under which the various state banks (including Bank Indonesia) would be amalgamated into one giant entity to be known as the State Bank of Indonesia (Bank Negara Indonesia). There was even talk that the private banks might be incorporated into this proposed new institution. The new megabank, or "fighting bank" as its architect Jusuf Musa Dalam sometimes described it, was conceived as a means of strengthening the government's capacity to turn the financial system to its grand developmental designs. In practice, however, little came of the scheme; the names of the state banks were changed, but institutional integration did not proceed very far.[24]

Sukarno's extreme statist economic adventures were leading to spectacular disaster. Mismanagement and corruption in many of the new state enterprises saw industrial output and export earnings slide. This was especially clear in the plantation sector, where official export earnings fell from US $442.5 million in 1958 to US $330 million in 1966.[25]

---

[22] Arndt, "Banking in Hyperinflation and Stabilization," pp. 372–83.
[23] Nasution, *Financial Institutions and Policies in Indonesia,* p. 61.
[24] Arndt, "Banking in Hyperinflation and Stabilization," pp. 380–81.
[25] Robison, *Indonesia,* p. 74.

Despite its significant investment in state industries, the government had been unable to develop them as viable export alternatives. As a result, the country slipped into an increasingly acute balance-of-payments crisis as export revenue fell while foreign borrowings and imports increased.

Manipulation of the banking system and the distribution of credit enabled Sukarno to sponsor a program of state-led industrialization, but it came at a price of uncontrolled growth in the money supply and a condition of hyperinflation by 1965. Notwithstanding heightened state domination of the banking industry, preferential credit plans lacked coherence and were subject to extensive diversion to patronage networks.

The New Order and Economic Rehabilitation, 1966–1973

The rapidly escalating crisis on the economic front in Indonesia during 1965 was overtaken by political developments. A coup attempt in September, allegedly supported by the Indonesian Communist party, triggered a fundamental realignment of political forces in the country that saw Sukarno disgraced and gradually eased from office and the military take hold of the reins of power under the leadership of General Suharto. The coup attempt resulted in profound national trauma, with a wave of violence and political retribution sweeping the country in the ensuing months. Estimates of the number of casualties range from one hundred thousand to one million. The immediate consequence of the wave of killings was the obliteration of the Indonesian Communist party. Emerging from the chaos was the so-called New Order regime, which has seen Suharto in the presidency for a quarter of a century. The twin themes of the New Order period have been a commitment to rapid economic development and political stability (maintained by authoritarian rule).

When Suharto assumed power in 1966, the immediate economic priority was to reach an agreement with the country's international creditors and to rein in inflation which was running at around 600 percent. Suharto and the military advisers surrounding him were not well versed in economics and so came to rely on a small team of Western-trained economists from the University of Indonesia to devise a strategy for economic rehabilitation. This group of liberal economists, the so-called technocrats, worked in conjunction with the IMF to develop a stabilization plan. Suharto's evident anti-Communist credentials and his willingness to accept much of the advice of the technocrats were important ingredients in winning cooperation and emergency relief from international creditors. This was a watershed period in Indonesia's history, for it represented a turning away from the highly statist economic orientation of the Sukarno period and an increased readiness to allow the market mechanism to play a greater role in allocational decisions.

As a first step toward economic stabilization, very tight fiscal and monetary policies were adopted. Government spending was slashed and a budget was drawn up for the first time in several years. In a bid to reimpose discipline on the money supply, Bank Indonesia was directed to implement tight new selective restrictions on bank credit. With active IMF involvement, strict credit ceilings were imposed on all banks. Tough deflationary policies, together with the IMF's standby arrangements, served to stabilize the economy; within two years the economy moved from a position of hyperinflation to virtual price stability. The emphasis of economic policy shifted from stabilization to rehabilitation. Having been starved of credit by both Sukarno and the emergency measures adopted by Suharto, the private sector was in disarray. In 1967, credit restrictions were eased, development expenditure was increased, and, most important, a new foreign investment code was introduced in a bid to attract foreign capital. This last measure was indicative of the extent of the reorientation of economic policy under Suharto. Only a few years earlier, Sukarno had confiscated Dutch enterprises and driven most other foreign investors out of the country. Now they were being wooed back, and many of the businesses previously nationalized were returned to their owners as a gesture of good faith.[26]

Another key component of the drive to resuscitate the economy was the reform of the banking system and changes in the system of credit allocation. As we have seen, under Sukarno the banking system had been totally dominated by the state and used not just to channel credit to particular social and economic sectors but also to finance government budget deficits. One of the most crucial features of the new financial regime was the rejection of deficit financing on the basis of money creation. The experience of hyperinflation had left a deep political scar, and the new government was determined to pursue a balanced-budget strategy, with expenditure not to exceed domestic revenue plus foreign loans. In 1967 and 1968, a series of new banking laws was introduced to overhaul the structure of the banking industry. The most immediate effect was to overturn the attempt to forge a single gigantic banking conglomerate initiated by Jusuf Musa Dalam near the end of the Sukarno period. Bank Indonesia was separated out and returned to a more traditional central bank role, with its own direct commercial loan

---

[26] Arndt, "Banking in Hyperinflation and Stabilization," pp. 383–87.

activities being reduced. To the disappointment of some, however, Bank Indonesia was not granted a significantly higher level of operational autonomy and remained closely tied to the government. As a result, although it began to focus more closely on prudent management of the financial system, it did not become a politically independent institution in its own right.

The reversal of Sukarno's attempt to create a monolithic state banking structure meant that the five former state-owned commercial banks were once again given independent identities, as were a state savings bank and a state development bank. Each of the state banks was to specialize in providing services to particular sectors of the economy. Of the five commercial banks, Bank Rakyat Indonesia was to focus on rural development and small-holder agriculture, Bank Bumi Daya on estate agriculture and forestry, Bank Negara Indonesia 1946 on manufacturing, Bank Dagang Negara on mining, and Bank Ekspor-Impor on the export sector. These functional divisions were not rigid, and indeed the whole thrust of the banking reforms was to reintroduce competition in the financial sector by providing borrowers and investors with a choice of institutions once again. At the same time, however, the government retained a firm grip on the operation of the state banks via Bank Indonesia. To build the state banks up to play a larger developmental role as mobilizers of domestic savings and distributors of credit, the government directed them to dramatically increase the interest rates they offered on term deposits. (The rates on twelve-month deposits rose from 30 percent to over 70 percent per annum.) The move was extremely successful, with the high interest rates attracting investors from overseas and local depositors once again beginning to place trust in the banking system. The effect of this move was, of course, to greatly increase the deposit base of the state banks and thereby lift the volume of credit available for development investment.

Under Sukarno the development of the banking sector had been retarded, with the real level of bank lending and deposits actually falling between 1960–1966.[27] Following the effective stabilization of the economy and the move to rehabilitate the state banks, beginning in 1968 the banking sector experienced a major growth spurt.[28] Foreign banks were once again welcomed back into the country and there were still, nominally, one-hundred-odd local private banks in existence. Overwhelmingly, however, the growth in the banking sector was concentrated in the state banks. By comparison with the state banks, the foreign and local private banks handled only a very small percentage

[27] David Cole, "New Directions for the Banking System," *Bulletin of Indonesian Economic Studies* 5, no. 2 (1969).
[28] Cole and Slade, *Financial Development in Indonesia*, p. 6.

Table 5.4. Distribution of credit by bank type, 1968–1990 (percentage of total outstanding bank credit)

Year	Central bank [1]	State banks [2]	Total [1 + 2]	Private banks	Foreign banks
1968	49	44	93	6	1
1969	36	56	92	7	1
1970	27	64	91	7	2
1971	21	69	90	7	3
1971	19	70	89	7	4
1973	15	70	85	6	9
1974	15	72	87	6	8
1975	33	58	91	4	4
1976	34	56	90	5	4
1977	31	58	89	5	5
1978	36	53	88	6	5
1979	35	52	87	6	5
1980	31	55	86	7	5
1981	26	58	84	8	5
1982	21	62	83	9	5
1983	15	64	79	12	6
1984	5	71	76	16	6
1985	4	69	73	19	5
1986	4	67	71	21	5
1987	4	66	70	23	4
1988	4	65	69	24	4
1989	1	62	63	29	5
1990	1	55	56	36	6

Sources: Bank Indonesia, *Monthly Report*, various issues.

Note: Includes direct central bank credit only; liquidity credits (rediscounting) are not included. Does not include regional development banks, which have distributed between 1 and 3 percent of total credit.

of the total credit extended. In 1968 the direct lending activities of Bank Indonesia, together with that of the commercial state banks, accounted for 93 percent of outstanding credit. Local private banks were responsible for 6 percent of the total, and newly returned foreign banks were responsible for a mere 1 percent (see Table 5.4).

The central bank viewed local private banks with some reserve (twenty-four of them were temporarily suspended from operations in 1967) and actively encouraged the smaller ones to merge and form larger concerns. The development of private and foreign banks was not a priority for the government at this stage. The preferred distributional conduit remained the state banks, as was made clear by the government's refusal to allow private or foreign banks access to the substantial credits and rediscount facilities from Bank Indonesia.

An important feature of the 1967–1968 banking reforms was that state intervention in credit markets (via Bank Indonesia) remained extensive, if somewhat less direct. There were three basic mechanisms by which Bank Indonesia influenced the distribution of credit during this period.[29] One mechanism was through the direct provision of preferential loans to priority borrowers such as the major state enterprises and Bulog, the government agency responsible for stabilizing rice prices. A second mechanism for state intervention was through central bank control of the deposit and loan rates offered by the state banks. The state banks had no say in this fundamental issue. The central bank set differing interest rates for borrowers according to economic priority. For example, in early 1969, credit for importing and distributing fertilizer was set at 1 percent per month, whereas the rate for lending to the tourist industry was set at 3 percent per month.[30] As already mentioned, state bank term deposit rates had been raised dramatically (to increase domestic savings mobilization). To enable the state banks to offer relatively low lending rates while maintaining high deposit rates, the central bank provided substantial subsidies.

The third mechanism for intervening in credit allocation was through a system of central bank preferential refinancing known as liquidity credits. State banks were encouraged to lend to designated priority areas on the basis of substantial rediscounting facilities offered by Bank Indonesia. The higher the priority attached to the target sector, the higher the proportion of the loan that was eligible for rediscounting and the lower the rate of interest charged by Bank Indonesia. Top-priority categories such as the Bimas rice intensification program and other related forms of farmer credit were eligible for 100 percent refinancing with Bank Indonesia. Central bank rediscounting funded a number of preferential credit programs at this stage. The most wide-ranging was the medium-term investment credit program (*Kredit Investasi*) introduced in 1969 under the auspices of the first of the Five-Year Development Plans (*Repelita I*). The aim of the program was to provide cheap and longer-term finance to priority sectors as part of a wider effort to encourage productive investment in key areas. All preferential credit programs subsidized by rediscounting facilities were financed from central bank reserves and an injection of supplementary funds from the state budget. In sum, the government, via the central bank, had a number of instruments at its disposal for guiding credit allocation as it moved to rehabilitate the economy and promote productive investment.

In 1971, Indonesia took a very unusual move for a developing coun-

[29] Cole and Slade, *Financial Development in Indonesia;* and Thomas A. Layman, "The Development of Indonesia's Financial Sector: Past, Present and Future," Paper presented to the Yayasan Padi and Kapas/Asia Foundation Conference on Economic Policy Making Processes in Indonesia, Bali, September 6–9, 1990, p. 12.

[30] Bank Indonesia, *Report for the Financial Year 1969/1970* (Jakarta: Bank Indonesia, 1970), p. 16.

try with such an erratic economic record when it decided to remove controls on foreign exchange and maintain an open capital account. Although the government retained some controls over international borrowing by state enterprises, the private sector was free to import or export capital as it pleased. There appear to have been dual motives involved in the move. On one hand, the decision was taken out of recognition that any attempt to regulate international capital movements was doomed given the proximity of Singapore as a major financial center. On the other hand, the move was also in keeping with other reforms to the investment regime at this time that sought to woo foreign investors and, equally important, to encourage local investors to bring their funds back on shore, safe in the knowledge that they were free to leave again at will. Although it is clear that the economists within the government were cognizant of the extraordinary discipline this would impose on economic policy-making, it is possible that not all sections of the state elite fully appreciated the magnitude of the decision. This move was to be of long-term importance for economic policy, as capital flight became a ready option if investors became nervous. More to the point, as will be seen, it mitigated government attempts to control the allocation of credit.

The early years of the New Order were a period of extraordinary economic transformation; the country was pulled back from the abyss, and with far-reaching policy reforms, it began moving down the road to rehabilitation. Many of the economic policy reforms introduced were of a liberal nature, having the effect of reducing state intervention and freeing up the flow of domestic and international capital. But the government's abandonment of dirigisme and its embrace of the market was by no means complete, as the record in the area of credit policy attests. Although the state ceased to be the main consumer of credit, it remained actively, if somewhat more indirectly, involved in the allocation of credit. The government maintained a firm grip on the central bank, the central bank remained deeply involved in determining state bank lending policies, and the state banks were the dominant mobilizers of domestic savings and distributors of credit. Private banks, both local and foreign, played only a minor role, distributing 15 percent of total credits in 1973 (see Table 5.4).

Economic policy generally and financial policy in particular were largely shaped by the economists within the government. Neither the state banks nor any private sector actors had a significant voice in the policy process. With regard to external actors, the IMF played a crucial role at the height of the economic crisis (1966–1967), but after this, its involvement and presence diminished, and the IMF came to assume what is best described as a supportive role to the economists within the government. The influence of the economists was very high during these early years of the New Order regime; in a period of economic turmoil, they were seen as the only group within the government capable of producing solutions. Moreover, the upheaval surrounding the traumatic political events of 1965–1966 served to dislodge and temporarily diminish the web of patronage networks. As a result, during these early years, the economists were at the height of their power, and the scope for relatively coherent and coordinated policy action was greater than ever before. Before long, however, the picture would change markedly.

The Boom Years, 1974–1982

Following the period of economic stabilization and rehabilitation in the first years of the New Order, Indonesia underwent a prolonged economic boom lasting throughout the early 1980s. The key to the country's strong economic performance during this period was the sharp rise in the price of oil. Oil and liquid gas exports came to account for as much as three-quarters of total export earnings and two-thirds of government revenue. As a result of the oil bonanza, the government found itself awash with funds for the first time. One of the consequences of this was a resurgence of nationalist economic thinking in policy circles. In the pressing circumstances of the late 1960s, the market-oriented policy prescriptions of the economists carried greater weight. In the situation that prevailed after 1974 as funds became plentiful, however, arguments in favor of a more interventionist economic approach gained ground rapidly. In particular, there was support within the government for making greater use of credit as an instrument to promote industrial development and as a distributional mechanism to reduce economic disparities within the community.

That this should have been the case is not particularly surprising, for as Peter Gourevitch has argued, "hard times" and "good times" tend to breed quite different policy dispositions.[31] But oil was not the only factor causing the swing in the policy pendulum away from more market-oriented policies. Although the market-oriented policies of the technocrats had succeeded in rehabilitating the economy and restoring investor confidence, they had also generated a resurgence of nationalist ideology. The early 1970s saw mounting concern that liberal economic policies were simply benefiting Chinese Indonesians and foreign investors, with the economic interests of indigenous Indonesians being overlooked. This resentment came to a head in the so-called Malari Affair in January 1974, when student demonstrations targeted against visiting

[31] Peter Gourevitch, *Politics in Hard Times* (Ithaca: Cornell University Press, 1986).

Japanese prime minister Tanaka spread to become anti-Chinese and antigovernment riots.[32]

The boom in oil prices and the revival of governmental enthusiasm for extensive economic intervention combined to bring about intensified state involvement in credit allocation. In response to mounting unrest about the pattern of income distribution and, in particular, the economic position of indigenous Indonesians, the government announced a series of reforms to credit policy. It introduced a new program of subsidized short- and longer-term credits for small indigenous business people (KIK/KMKP). In addition, in February 1974 it was determined that the wide-ranging, medium-term investment credit program (Kredit Investasi) would be reserved exclusively for firms in which indigenous Indonesians held majority ownership.[33] State banks were to implement these new programs and subsidize them through generous rediscounting with the central bank. In short, instead of simply seeking to allocate credit on the basis of economic priorities, officially at least, the government was now emphasizing more explicitly political variables, namely, race and firm size.

The other major change to credit policy at this stage stemmed from the influx of oil revenue, which gave rise to excess liquidity in the financial system and thereby generated serious inflationary pressures. Inflationary pressure had, in fact, been mounting before the 1973–1974 oil price increases. Having been as low as 2 percent in 1971, the inflation rate moved up to 26 percent in 1972 and 33 percent in 1974. In attempting to contain the upsurge in inflation, monetary authorities found their existing policy instruments inadequate for the task. The government had shifted toward more indirect means of controlling bank credit and the money supply, principally, selective rediscount facilities (liquidity credits) and interest rate controls applied to state banks.[34] These instruments declined in effectiveness as state banks were no longer so dependent on central bank funds.[35]

Confronted with rapidly rising inflation and inadequate monetary instruments, the government decided to revert to direct central bank controls on credit expansion in April 1974 through a system of credit ceilings.[36] Under the new arrangement, Bank Indonesia determined a

[32] For a more detailed discussion of the incident and the political and economic tensions behind it, see Robison, *Indonesia*, pp. 147–68.

[33] Bank Indonesia, *Report for the Financial Year 1973/74* (Jakarta: Bank Indonesia, 1974), pp. 18–19.

[34] Layman, "Indonesia's Financial Sector," p. 17; and Arndt, "Monetary Policy Instruments in Indonesia," pp. 110–13.

[35] Note, however, that the rediscount facilities increased again as an important source of funding for state banks shortly after this period. Stephen Grenville, "Survey of Recent Developments," *Bulletin of Indonesian Economic Studies* 10, no. 1 (1974), pp. 25–26.

[36] Increasing the value of the rupiah was rejected as a policy option because of the impact this would have had on export and import-competing industries.

credit ceiling for each state, private, and foreign bank on the basis of its performance during the previous year. In addition, the central bank drew up credit ceilings for particular economic sectors and subsectors on the basis of economic and social priorities. It was assumed that tight restrictions on the nonpriority sectors would encourage the banks to channel credit to priority groups such as rice farmers. Though introduced as a mechanism for controlling the growth in overall bank credit, the system of credit ceilings became blurred with allocational considerations.

The combination of the direct credit controls introduced in 1974 and the preexisting controls produced a financial system in which the market mechanism played a smaller role in the allocation of credit than at any time other than at the height of state interventionism in the Guided Economy years. Further entry to the industry by new private or foreign banks was blocked, and the state intervened in credit allocation directly and indirectly to limit the price, volume, and direction of credit flows. To recapitulate, there were now four main mechanisms by which the banking system and the allocation of credit were manipulated.

(1) *Credit Ceilings.* Introduced in 1974, credit ceilings were initially intended as a monetary policy instrument to control credit expansion, but government lists of sectoral and subsectoral ceilings favored some sectors over others.

(2) *Interest Rate Controls.* Private and foreign banks were free to set their own levels, but the lending rates of the state banks were substantially lower than market rates.

(3) *Rediscounting.* State banks (and, after 1978, occasionally private banks) were encouraged to provide loans to designated priority sectors because such loans were eligible for rediscounting (liquidity credits) at subsidized rates. This system of preferential credit became increasingly elaborate during the 1970s, as the central bank compiled ever more lengthy and detailed lists prioritizing loan categories. These ranged from various farmer credit programs and the KIK/KMKP program for small borrowers to items as detailed as a special loan category for subsidized credit to assist schoolteachers to purchase motorbikes.

(4) *Direct Central Bank Loans.* Bank Indonesia continued to provide direct credits at subsidized rates to support priority borrowers. These direct loans were used primarily to fund Bulog (the national rice stock authority) farmer credit, and struggling state enterprises. As seen in Table 5.4, these direct credit transfers from the central bank became increasingly important during the 1970s. In particular, they increased very rapidly in 1975 as part of the financial rescue operation to aid Pertamina, the stricken state oil company.

The oil boom years from 1974 to 1982 were marked by a persistently high level of state intervention in credit markets. By 1982, not only did state banks handle 83 percent of all outstanding loans but the total value of central bank credit subsidies also amounted to 50 percent of outstanding credit. Using a variety of instruments, the government attempted to divert credit on the basis of an elaborate hierarchy of social and economic priorities. But such achievements as did flow from state intervention came, as Heinz Arndt has noted, "at the price of almost complete subordination of the commercial banks [state, private, and foreign] to central bank control which deprived the commercial banks of any incentive to compete with one another for business and limited their opportunities to exercise skills or initiative in the allocation of credit."[37]

Economic Hardship and Liberal Reform, 1983–1990

The excess liquidity generated by the oil boom in the 1970s had driven monetary authorities to turn to direct credit controls in a bid to contain inflationary pressures. This macroeconomic motive was re-inforced by political pressure to use the credit system as a distributional mechanism to channel resources to particular sectors of the economy in order to ease or contain social resentment. In the boom years of the 1970s, when one of the problems confronting the government was the task of disbursing oil and aid revenues, the economic costs of subop-timal resource allocation were less apparent. This situation changed rapidly in the 1980s.

The catalyst for change was the collapse in the price of commodities and, in particular, the price of oil and gas. In 1981–1982, earnings from oil and gas had reached a peak of almost US $19 billion. In the following year this figure dropped to US $14.7 billion and then fell all the way to US $6.9 billion in 1986–1987. These following prices created acute economic problems, given the country's heavy dependence on oil and gas exports. As a sense of urgency mounted, the authority of the liberal economists within the government grew in policy debates.

One of a series of key adjustment measures introduced in 1983 was a set of deregulatory reforms to the financial sector, which marked an important turning point in the country's financial history. The inspi-ration for the 1983 reforms was the need to mobilize private savings more effectively in order to replace the oil-funded system of subsidized credit. By revitalizing the banking industry and making it more com-petitive, the government hoped that new sources of credit could be

[37] Arndt, "Monetary Policy Instruments in Indonesia," p. 115.

tapped and that financial resources would be allocated on a more economically efficient basis. There were four key elements to the reform package: (1) the abolition of the system of credit ceilings introduced in 1974, (2) the deregulation of state bank deposit and loan rates, (3) the reform and the curtailing of central bank refinancing (liquidity credits) of preferential lending by the state banks, and (4) the reduction of subsidized direct commercial lending by the central bank.

An important consequence of the reforms was a diminished role for the central bank in the allocation of credit with much greater autonomy and discretion being ceded to the commercial banks. As a result of the abandonment of direct credit controls, the central bank was deprived of a key instrument for overall monetary control. Consequently, new indirect money market instruments were developed during 1984–1985. Further reforms to the financial sector that had a crucial bearing on credit allocation arrangements followed several years later in 1988–1990. Again the thrust of the reforms was to promote a more competitive and mature financial market. The major consequences of the series of reforms in 1988–1990 were increased industry competitiveness with the mushrooming of new private and foreign banks following the lowering of entry barriers, a further reduction of central bank rediscounting, legal lending limits to prevent private banks from extensive "internal lending" to ownership groups, and the diversification of the financial sector, especially through the promotion of the stock exchange.

The first two reforms were of particular importance in terms of state intervention in credit markets. By 1989–1990, private banks were at last starting to become a significant force in the banking industry, accounting for one-third of all outstanding credit. Although state banks still dominated the banking industry, their market share had receded considerably. State involvement in credit markets was further cut back by the January 1990 decision to greatly reduce the scope and scale of preferential lending funded by central bank rediscounting. Overall, the effect of the reforms introduced during the 1980s was to promote the development of private financial institutions and a more diversified and competitive financial sector. The allocation of credit became increasingly tied to judgments about commercial risk rather than national priorities. Using a variety of measures, several studies have concluded that reforms during this period contributed directly to accelerated financial development. Financial deepening as measured by M2/GDP rose from 19 percent in 1983 to over 30 percent by the end of 1988 (see Table 5.5).[38]

---

[38] Cole and Slade, *Financial Development in Indonesia*, pp. 6–13. See also Yoon-Je Cho and Deena Khatkhate, *Lessons of Financial Liberalization in Asia: A Comparative Study*, World

Table 5.5. Key economic indicators, 1965–1989

Year	Real GDP (% change)	M1/GDP (%)	M2/GDP (%)	CPI (% change)
1965	n.a.	10.8	11.3	n.a.
1966	2.8	7.0	7.1	1,000.0
1967	6.7	6.1	6.3	170.5
1968	10.9	5.4	6.0	125.4
1969	6.8	6.7	8.6	17.9
1970	7.6	7.5	9.9	12.4
1971	6.7	8.7	12.8	4.0
1972	9.4	10.4	15.2	6.7
1973	11.3	9.9	14.6	30.6
1974	7.6	8.8	13.6	41.0
1975	5.0	9.9	15.6	18.8
1976	6.9	10.4	17.0	20.0
1977	8.8	10.6	16.5	11.0
1978	6.9	10.9	16.7	8.2
1979	4.9	10.5	16.0	20.6
1980	6.9	11.0	17.0	20.0
1981	7.4	12.0	18.0	12.2
1982	5.0	11.9	18.6	9.5
1983	3.3	10.0	19.3	11.8
1984	6.0	9.6	20.0	10.5
1985	2.5	10.5	23.9	4.7
1986	5.9	11.3	26.9	5.8
1987	4.8	10.2	27.2	9.3
1988	5.7	10.3	30.1	8.0
1989	6.5	13.0	37.0	6.5

Sources: David Cole and Betty Slade, *Financial Development in Indonesia*, Development Discussion Paper no. 336 (Cambridge: Harvard Institute for International Development, Harvard University, 1990); and Thomas A. Layman, "The Development of Indonesia's Financial Sector: Past, Present, and Future," Paper presented to the Yayasan Padi and Kapas/Asia Foundation Conference on Economic Policy Making Processes in Indonesia, Bali, September 6–9, 1990.

II. The Political Dynamics of State Intervention in Credit Markets

As seen in Section I, Indonesia has a long history of intervention in credit markets. The final section of this essay concentrates on the period since Suharto took control of the country and focuses on a number of issues relating to the politics of financial policy-making and the consequences of intervention in credit markets. It concludes by addressing the question of whether the more liberal policy regime adopted during the 1980s can be sustained.

Bank Discussion Papers (Washington. D.C.: World Bank, 1989), p. 30; and Layman, "Indonesia's Financial Sector," p. 26.

The Impact of Intervention

To make an assessment of the impact of state intervention in credit markets in Indonesia, it is necessary to begin by recognizing that there have been multiple and indeed competing objectives driving government actions. Simplifying things, it is possible to distinguish three broad types of objectives: macroeconomic, developmental, and distributional. Although all three are interrelated, for analytical purposes, it is helpful to disentangle them to some extent. The macroeconomic concerns are relatively straightforward; the principal purpose of the credit ceilings introduced in 1974 was to impose direct controls on money supply growth in a bid to contain the inflationary pressures created by the oil boom. The developmental category is somewhat broader, covering all attempts to promote particular industries. This can be loosely thought of as embracing all industrial policy concerns, which range from attempts to promote a local manufacturing base to programs aimed at increasing agricultural productivity. The third broad set of objectives for state intervention in credit markets comprises distributional concerns. Under this heading we can list various credit programs aimed at transferring resources to low-income groups such as rice farmers and indigenous entrepreneurs, as well as unofficial schemes to distribute rent-taking opportunities within the political elite. Plainly, there can be no sharp distinction between the second and third categories; developmental policies inevitably also favor some sectors over others and thus have distributional implications, and policies with distributional objectives can also have developmental spin-offs. Real though this ambiguity is, it will be helpful to think of some policy actions as being conceived of primarily in developmental terms and of others as essentially distributional exercises.

The macroeconomic objective of fighting inflation can be dealt with briefly. Although there were plainly major costs associated with the system of aggregate ceilings on bank lending, it seems clear that it did at least succeed in helping to contain inflation. After rising rapidly as a result of the influx of oil revenue, between 1974 and 1978 the rate of increase in the consumer price index was lowered from 41 percent to 8 percent (Table 5.5). As Heinz Arndt put it, "To this success, the system of direct central bank control of bank credit undoubtedly made an effective contribution."[39]

Assessing the impact of state intervention in credit markets in terms of developmental and distributional objectives is more complex and centers around preferential credit programs. Available financial statis-

[39] Arndt, "Banking in Hyperinflation and Stabilization," p. 115.

Figure 5.1. Direct and indirect Bank Indonesia credit subsidies, 1965–1990 (percentage of total outstanding bank credit)

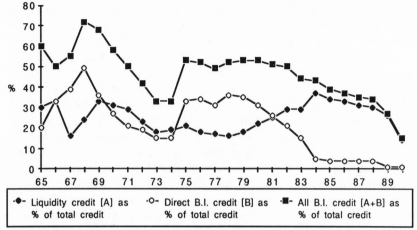

Source: Bank Indonesia, *Monthly Report*, various issues.

tics point to a consistently high level of state intervention in credit allocation throughout the period of Suharto's New Order government. Figure 5.1 charts the development of Bank Indonesia liquidity credits (refinancing available to commercial banks on loans to priority sectors) as well as direct subsidized credits from Bank Indonesia to priority borrowers. The sum of these two forms of central bank financing is a rough indication of the extent of preferential lending. This figure ranges from a peak of 72 percent of total outstanding bank credit in 1968 to a low of 15 percent of total bank credit in 1990.[40] On average, however, central bank subsidies for preferential credit programs amounted to some 48 percent of total credit.

That there has been a consistently high level of intervention in credit markets is clear. The more interesting question is, Who have been the principal beneficiaries? This is a vexed issue. Table 5.6 sets out consolidated data indicating the major official target groups of preferential credit. These figures combine both liquidity credits (rediscounting) and direct Bank Indonesia credits. The two categories that stand out are credits to support Bulog's rice price stabilization scheme and the fi-

[40] The high figure for 1968 reflects the commencement of direct state bank funding of the rice stabilization scheme managed by Bulog. The sharp rise in 1975 represents the beginning of special direct Bank Indonesia credits to Pertamina, the state oil company, to assist it in repaying the massive debt it had built up. The marked rise of liquidity credits in 1984 and the simultaneous decline in direct credits reflect the transfer of subsidies to Bulog from the latter to the former.

nancial rescue operation for the debt-stricken Pertamina.[41] Bulog's rice stabilization scheme has been a remarkable success, playing a major role in the achievement of rice self-sufficiency (in what had been the world's biggest rice importer) and also helping to bring about stable prices for consumers as well as an improvement in income for rice farmers.[42] The next two most significant categories are farmer credits and the medium-term investment credit program. The former category covers various specific programs designed to provide cheap finance to farmers such as special credits for fertilizer and the Bimas rice intensification program. The medium-term investment credit program (Kredit Investasi) is a broad category spread across the industrial, agricultural, and service sectors and includes many specific programs such as the KIK plan for small businesses. Credits under this category were officially earmarked for indigenous Indonesians. Preferential credit for the manufacturing sector existed throughout this period but only became significant (as a percentage of total credit) in 1975, when special subsidies were provided for the large and chronically inefficient state-owned steel mill Krakatau Steel.[43] Export finance has also received preferential status throughout this period, but it became a significant category only in the mid-1980s. A variety of other categories are specified in Bank Indonesia statistics as targets for subsidized credit; when expressed as a percentage of total outstanding bank credit, however, they are very small.

The data on the distribution of preferential credit are interesting as they suggest that farmers have received consistently favorable treatment; medium-term investment credits were also available for agriculture, and some portion of the rice stabilization financing must be considered as constituting a benefit to farmers as well. Conversely, the fact that the manufacturing sector has not been a big winner (particularly once we discount for special financing to the ailing Krakatau Steel) is also a distinctive feature.[44] The absence of a major sustained

[41] For details of the extraordinary story surrounding the near bankruptcy of the country's largest company, see Peter McCawley, "Some Consequences of the Pertamina Crisis in Indonesia," *Journal of Southeast Asian Studies* 9, no. 1 (1978).

[42] For an overview of this remarkable success story, see Leon Mears, "Rice and Food Self-Sufficiency in Indonesia," *Bulletin of Indonesian Economic Studies* 20, no. 2 (1984); C. Peter Timmer, "The Political Economy of Rice in Asia: Indonesia," *Food Research Institute Studies* 14, no. 3 (1975), as well as Timmer's excellent recent piece "Food Price Stabilization: The Indonesian Experience with Rice," Unpublished paper, Harvard Institute for International Development, Harvard University, January 1990.

[43] A portion of subsidized credit allocated under the medium-term investment credit program went to the manufacturing sector, which, once accounted for, pushes up the overall level of subsidized credit to manufacturing. But note that this is true of other sectors as well, as the medium-term investment credit program was widely spread.

[44] Some qualification is needed here, however. In addition to the preferential lending activities of the state banks, Pertamina also undertook lending operations between 1973

Table 5.6. Principal targets of central bank credit subsidies, 1968–1990 (percentage share of total outstanding bank credit)

Year	Rice stabilization	Farmer credits	Pertamina repayments	Medium-term inv. credits[a]	Industry credits	Export credits
1968	29	13				
1969	30	11		2		
1970	17	12		7		
1971	12	10		11		
1971	14	7		11		
1973	12	7		7		
1974	13	8		5		
1975	5	8	26	3	4	
1976	5	7	29	3	3	
1977	4	5	26	5	3	
1978	4	4	31	3	3	
1979	4	3	30	4	4	
1980	6	3	23	5	6	
1981	8	3	16	8	6	
1982	8	4	11	9	5	1
1983	7	3	5	11	5	2
1984	9	3		12	4	3
1985	8	2		11	4	3
1986	6	1		10	3	5
1987	5	1		9	3	6
1988	3	1		9	1	7
1989	3			8		4
1990	2			5		

Sources: Bank Indonesia, *Monthly Report*, various issues.

Note: Combines Bank Indonesia direct credits and liquidity credits (or rediscounting facilities) to state commercial banks. For years with no entry, subsidies are either nonexistent or insignificant as a percentage of total credit.

[a] Figures for 1989 and 1990 are informal Bank Indonesia estimates.

and coherent attempt to use preferential credit for the purposes of subsidizing the development of the manufacturing sector marks an important difference between Indonesia and countries such as South Korea. Indeed, on the basis of official statistics, preferential credits channeled to the manufacturing sector have tended to take the form of financial first aid rather than industrial seed money. Certainly, there is no sign of the state attempting to "discipline" corporate recipients of preferential credit along the lines Alice Amsden has described in South Korea.[45]

Beyond broad conclusions such as these, statements about the distribution of preferential credit in Indonesia are inherently problematic. In a number of important respects, the available statistics are ques-

---

and 1975. One of its activities was to run a de facto investment bank arm, which channeled funds to various state-owned industries, most notably the Krakatau Steel plant, but the extent and significance of these activities is uncertain.

[45] Alice Amsden, *Asia's Next Giant: South Korea and Late Industrialization* (New York: Oxford University Press, 1990).

tionable. As Bank Indonesia and Ministry of Finance officials themselves acknowledge, there is a significant degree of uncertainty as to whether the nominal target groups were, in fact, the actual recipients of the preferential credit and, if so, the purposes to which the funds were put.

There are at least four strong reasons for doubting that the operations of the preferential credit system coincided with official policy. First, notwithstanding the centralization and rationalization of the state bureaucracy that has taken place under Suharto, Indonesia has lacked the bureaucratic capacity to monitor and enforce the elaborate system of preferential credit that developed. Although the state banks were indeed subject to a whole range of regulatory controls by the central bank, its capacity to enforce some of these was questionable. For example, commercial banks were required to provide detailed information regarding the allocation of many types of preferential credit, but in practice, Bank Indonesia had no real way of confirming where the funds went. It simply lacked the administrative resources to monitor the situation closely.

Second, in addition to problems of bureaucratic capacity, the entire system of preferential credit, by its very nature, was an invitation for malpractice and corruption. The difference in price between a subsidized loan and the market rate was essentially a rent to be shared between the loan officer and the borrower. Bank officials therefore had a material interest in lending to customers *not* falling within a priority category if such customers were prepared to allow them a generous slice of the rent arising from the interest differential. The benefit of subsidies was either dissipated or not received at all by the nominal target groups. Not infrequently, rent sharing or rent diversion of this sort was initiated not simply by bank officers, but also by senior figures within the government who would "command" banks to make finance available on favorable terms to supporters, relatives, or assorted cronies. In short, the patrimonial needs of political leaders often took precedence over the official hierarchy of priority borrowers, a pattern similar to that in the Philippines.

A third factor undermining the elaborate preferential credit scheme was the very high transaction costs involved with small-scale subsidized lending. Moreover, among both small and large borrowers, there was a high level of nonrepayment. One estimate in 1978 suggested that as much as one-third of outstanding bank credit was either overdue or uncollectable.[46] If banks had in fact reserved all preferential credits under the medium-term investment credit program for indigenous

[46] David Jenkins, "Indonesia Adds Up after 10 Years of Bad Debts," *Far Eastern Economic Review*, August 18, 1978.

Indonesians as nominally required by government policy, their books would have been even more littered with nonperforming loans. Not surprisingly, then, much of the credit earmarked for indigenous Indonesians in fact went to nonindigenous Indonesians; credit earmarked for small borrowers in fact went to larger borrowers.[47] Quality corporate clients have been so scarce that the major commercial banks have been more than willing to provide significantly discounted finance in order to retain blue-chip corporate customers.[48]

Finally, the effort to concentrate credit on priority borrowers was weakened by the fact that since 1971 Indonesia has had an open capital account. To the extent that large domestic and foreign firms could not gain access to "leaking" earmarked funds, they simply went offshore to raise capital.[49] Credit fungibility was increased by the fact that for much of the period of extensive credit controls from 1974 to 1983, the economy was highly liquid because of oil and aid inflows.

Taken together, these factors suggest that there are strong grounds for suspecting that the actual recipients of loans subsidized under preferential credit plans and the price paid for them may well have differed appreciably from the stipulated guidelines. It is widely accepted, for example, that much of the credit nominally intended for indigenous Indonesians did not reach its destination. But this same administrative leakage suggests that unofficial distributional objectives, namely, the patrimonially based granting of access to subsidized credit by government leaders, may well have operated smoothly and to their political satisfaction. One crude indicator of this is the fact that it was during the 1970s that business people who were associated with key government figures—most important, the president—were able to increase the scale of their business activities dramatically. Among the most prominent were Liem Sioe Liong, Probosutedjo, Bob Hassan, and William Soeriadjaya.[50]

---

[47] Stories are legion in Jakarta banking circles of entrepreneurs arranging for their chauffeurs to act as front men in order to access subsidized credit for small indigenous borrowers. See McLeod, "Finance and Entrepreneurship in the Small Business Sector in Indonesia." Another recent study suggests that although programs for small business achieved some significant successes, their impact varied greatly across sectors. Bruce Bolnick and Eric Nelson, "Evaluating the Economic Impact of a Special Credit Programme: KIK/KMKP in Indonesia," *Journal of Development Studies* 26, no. 2 (1990).

[48] Interestingly, this pattern has continued even in the seller's market created by the government's current tight monetary policy.

[49] International borrowing was made still easier for prime firms by the fact that they maintained sizable deposits in offshore banks because of the higher interest rates obtainable in Singapore, Hong Kong, and elsewhere. These deposits thus served readily as collateral to support loans from the offshore banks.

[50] For detailed accounts of the rise of business groups linked by patrimonial ties to government figures see Yoon Hwan Shin, "Demystifying the Capitalist State"; and Robison, *Indonesia.*

To summarize, credit policy has been an instrument that has been employed in the service of several different objectives. On one hand, direct quantitative controls on credit were used to some effect in the mid-1970s to contain inflationary pressures within acceptable limits. On the other hand, attempts to allocate credit on a preferential basis in pursuit of developmental and distributional objectives have achieved mixed results. With a few notable exceptions, credit does not appear to have been allocated efficiently to official target groups. The picture that emerges is one of bureaucratic weakness and patrimonially based allocation of rent-taking opportunities within the state elite.

It must be remembered, however, that a government's intentions are not always identical with officially declared objectives. There can be little doubt, for instance, that in addition to official developmental and distributional objectives, it was well understood by senior government figures that subsidized credit was an economic benefit that lent itself to convenient and discrete diversion. In a political system in which patrimonial loyalties overshadow institutional affiliations, the distribution of selective economic rewards is a vital instrument for political leaders. The difficulty here is that we have no way of knowing the extent to which subsidized credit was in fact diverted, who the major beneficiaries were, and, moreover, what political significance such activities carried. Nevertheless, it seems reasonable to assume that the patrimonial allocation of cheap finance has, to some extent at least, enhanced the stability of the web of personal and factional coalitions that underpin the New Order. Although preferential credit programs may have had only limited impact in terms of their declared developmental and distributional objectives, if judged on the basis of the unofficial political agenda of senior figures within the government, the verdict is likely to be more positive. To explore this further, it is necessary to examine the political dynamics of state intervention in credit markets.

The Institutional Setting: Actors and Interests

Since Suharto's military-based regime came to power in the late 1960s, there has been a striking trend toward political centralization and exclusion, with effective control of the policy-making process becoming increasingly concentrated in the hands of a narrow state elite. This is in stark contrast to the Guided Democracy period under Sukarno, when the Communist party in particular had been very successful in mobilizing mass public support. Having overseen the annihilation of the Communists in the wake of Sukarno's fall, Suharto and the military leaders around him were determined to prevent a

ANDREW J. MACINTYRE

return to the politics of mass participation. To this end, they moved
gradually, but systematically, to reduce the scope for political involvement by societal groups during the 1970s. The political parties were
neutered, and nascent interest groups were co-opted within an exclu-
sionary corporatist framework. The backbone of this wide-ranging
campaign of political restructuring was a chain of military command
reaching down to every district and small town.

This strategy for political demobilization and control was remarkably
successful, so much so that by the early 1980s, the state elite enjoyed
a considerable degree of autonomy from societal forces in the shaping
of policy. Peasant groups, labor unions, and business associations were
all co-opted and were thus in no position to challenge or bargain with
bureaucrats over policy decisions. Although business was not repressed
coercively in the manner of labor, the racial barrier, together with the
unresponsive representational arrangements imposed by the state, certainly constrained collective demand making. In such a situation, clien-
tal links have been the most rewarding mode of interest representation.
This state-dominated system has been sustained by a combination of
the government's oil-given capacity to deliver strong economic growth
and selective patrimonial inducements, together with the willingness
of the armed forces to enforce Suharto's will if need be.[51]

In this environment, policy-making has very largely been in the hands
of the bureaucrats, who have been able to operate with relative immunity from collective societal demands. With the important exception
of particular patrimonial links between individual officials and businesspeople, the prevailing picture is that economic policy-making is
mainly a story of bargaining and alliance building within the state elite.
As will be seen, notwithstanding recent studies[52] that suggest that collective business interests began to make some political impact in the
1980s, the story of credit policy in Indonesia indeed appears to be very
much a statist one.

Who have been the principal players determining the nature of state
intervention in credit markets? In broad terms there have been two
opposing policy camps within the state elite: the economists and a
diverse grouping committed to interventionism. Of the two camps, that
of the economists has been the most coherent. It comprises a small
group of senior officials steeped in liberal economics and concentrated

[51] For further discussion of this subject, see Andrew MacIntyre, "Corporatism, Control,
and Political Change in 'New Order' Indonesia," in *Observing Political Change in Asia:
Essays in Honour of J. A. C. Mackie*, ed. R. J. May and W. J. O'Malley (Bathurst: Crawford
House Press, 1989).
[52] MacIntyre, *Business and Politics in Indonesia;* and Chalmers, "Economic Nationalism
and the Third World State."

in the Ministry of Finance and the Economic Planning Board. Among the most prominent have been Widjoyo Nitisastro, Ali Wardhana, Radius Prawiro, and J. B. Sumarlin. The economists have mainly been interested in credit controls as an instrument for containing inflation. Although they have generally had little enthusiasm for preferential credit policies, they have supported subsidized financing of the rice stabilization scheme, both on orthodox comparative advantage grounds and in terms of food security arguments. The economists have traditionally lacked a solid domestic power base, and their influence within the government has been linked in no small part to the perception that acceptance of their policy prescriptions is a necessary condition for the continued financial support of international creditors such as the World Bank and the Inter Governmental Group on Indonesia (IGGI) consortium of donors as well as for the maintenance of investor confidence. It is for this reason that the influence of the economists has been inversely correlated with oil prices; in times of oil-generated prosperity, the approval of foreign donors and investors has been less critical.

The second group, the interventionists, is somewhat nebulous. It is made up of officials who are linked by their rejection of the faith placed in the marked mechanism by the economists. Some members of this cluster have been committed to the idea of the state accelerating the development of a strong local industrial base, in short, what we have labeled here as developmental objectives. Others have favored state intervention in credit markets for primarily distributional reasons. Interventionists have been based in an array of institutions, most notably, the central bank, the Ministry of Industry, the Investment Board, the Ministry of Science and Technology, and prominent state-owned enterprises such as Pertamina and the aeronautics company Nurtanio. As the allocator of credit, the central bank has been in a different position to that of spending or sponsoring agencies such as the Ministry of Science and Technology or the Ministry of Industry. Particularly under the activist leadership of Rachmat Saleh (who was governor during the 1970s and early 1980s), the central bank developed a strong institutional commitment to the maintenance of preferential credit arrangements. In addition to those various bureaucratic agencies and state-owned enterprises that have been institutionally committed to interventionist economic policies, key power brokers within the government have also been interested in preferential credit to the extent that it facilitated the allocation of patrimonial rewards.

The central bank has had primary responsibility for managing the system of preferential credits. It has drawn up the list of priority sectors and target groups, ranking them all and determining the levels at which they will be subsidized. This process involved extensive bargaining with the departments and agencies concerned, which would invariably seek the highest possible level of subsidization for the projects of interest to them. Bank Indonesia was thus the keeper guarding the gate to subsidized finance. But its commitment to intervention in credit markets was not simply a philosophical one; Bank Indonesia had a considerable political interest in preserving this function, in terms of both bureaucratic empire building and rent allocation. This was evidenced by its opposition to the deregulatory reforms of the credit system that began in 1983 and its rearguard action resisting the elimination of central bank rediscounting through the liquidity credits.

These, then, have been the major players shaping financial policy in Indonesia. Two groups are notable by their absence from the list and deserve special mention: the military and the banks themselves. Despite the fact that the military has stood at the very center of Indonesian politics for over thirty years now, it has had remarkably little involvement in economic policy issues. The core interests of the military have been the maintenance of political stability and the preservation of its pivotal position in national politics. As a result, army leaders have principally focused on security issues, and credit policy has certainly not been a major concern. Before the mid-1970s, the military had been actively involved in seeking informal sources of finance to supplement the limited resources received through the budget.[53] But this declined once the effects of the oil boom began to work their way through the economy. Senior army officers have appreciated the political importance of maintaining strong economic growth, recognizing that economic success has been the foundation on which the New Order regime has been built. As a result, in the tougher economic climate of the 1980s, they have generally been prepared to accept the policy reform agenda of the economists. Although the military has no doubt exploited opportunities for gaining access to concessional finance through "command loans" (along with other sections of the state elite), they have not opposed the moves by economists to narrow the scope for rent-taking opportunities through the scaling down of preferential credit arrangements. Indeed, signs indicate that senior army leaders have concluded that pervasive corruption has the potential to be regime-threatening.[54]

But what of the commercial banks? The small part played in it by commercial banks is one of the striking features of financial policymaking in Indonesia. It is not hard to see why. The commercial banking sector is divided among three quite different sets of institutions—state banks, local private banks, and foreign banks. Their

[53] The best account of this is provided by Crouch, *Army and Politics in Indonesia*.

[54] In the late 1980s, there were many rumors of rumblings within the military leadership about the rapacious business activities of members of the president's family.

interests are in many respects divergent, and they have seldom acted cooperatively. For example, the banking industry association, Perbanas, is made up of only the national private banks. More important, until very recently, the state banks completely overshadowed the rest of the industry. They have shown very little autonomy, however, functioning more as implementing agencies of government policy than as independent financial institutions. An important factor in the passive behavior of the state banks is that bank presidents have been beholden to the government for their positions. The heads of the state banks have had no independent power base from which to bargain with government ministers. As a result, they have tended simply to respond to government directives and make the most of the perquisites associated with their office.

As for private banks, until very recently they have simply accounted for too small a share of banking activity to carry any weight. Unlike in Japan or even in Thailand, commercial banking has not been a core activity for the major business conglomerates in Indonesia. Corporate empires have not been built around an in-house bank. This applies even to the largest of the private banks (BCA) which is controlled by Liem Sioe Liong, who heads what is easily the largest business conglomerate in Indonesia. Although BCA has become an important source of finance for other firms in the Liem empire, it does not constitute his core business. Typically, banking is an industry the conglomerates have entered *after* achieving a critical mass in other sectors.

The point is that one looks in vain for strategic alliances linking state and business actors in the shaping of credit policy in Indonesia. It has been state-based actors who have controlled the agenda in this policy arena. This is true of both the maintenance of the interventionist policy regime during the 1970s and early 1980s and, important, of the period of change during the latter 1980s, when economists in the Ministry of Finance began to push through liberalizing policy reforms.

The Politics of Deregulation

In view of the long record of state intervention in credit markets in Indonesia and the weighty array of individuals and institutions with an interest in the maintenance of the status quo, how are we to explain the swing toward a more liberal credit policy regime beginning in 1983? Plainly, the economists in the Ministry of Finance and their supporters in the World Bank and various other international advisory bodies in Jakarta were behind the policy reorientation. But why did change not come until 1983, and why does it take the form it does?

The issue of timing is relatively straightforward; there is little doubt that the external shock delivered by the drop in oil prices in 1983 was the catalyst for change. The marked decline in oil revenue placed the government's developmental plans under mounting strain and threw into sharp focus the need for reform of the financial system to enable more efficient mobilization of domestic savings. The external shock thus created a window of political opportunity for the economists.

The question of the nature or substance of the reforms is more involved. Here it must be understood that although the reforms introduced in 1983 mark a crucial turning point in Indonesia's financial development, in political terms the only potential loser was the central bank. The 1983 financial reforms did not involve a fundamental political showdown between the economists and the interventionists. Most of the changes introduced directly affected only Bank Indonesia; the elimination of credit ceilings, the winding down of direct central bank lending operations, and the deregulation of state bank deposit and lending rates were not of major concern to other government departments. Moreover, other elements of the reform package introduced at this stage (principally, the decision to freeze a number of very large upstream industrial development projects[55]) were of much greater concern to the interventionists than were the proposed changes to the financial sector.

In terms of Bank Indonesia's core institutional interests, the only reform that represented a potentially serious attack was the decision to scale down the level of preferential lending subsidized through rediscounting arrangements. This, of course, was one of the central bank's chief rent-generating activities. Previously, there had been an elaborate system of preferential lending involving dozens of different categories of priority borrowers. Following the 1983 reforms, this number was reduced to a mere twenty categories of priority borrowers who were eligible for preferential finance. As Figure 5.1 shows, however, far from declining as prescribed by the 1983 reforms, liquidity credits in fact came to constitute a *larger* share of total lending.[56] Part of this increase was due to the switching of funding for Bulog's rice stockpile from direct central bank lending to indirect subsidization via liquidity credits channeled through one of the state banks. For a time at least, Bank Indonesia was thus able to salvage its core interests, preserving its prized system of preferential credits.

---

[55] For details, see Susumu Awanohara, "Tomorrow Is Postponed," *Far Eastern Economic Review*, May 26, 1983; and Heinz Arndt, "Survey of Recent Developments," *Bulletin of Indonesian Economic Studies* 19, no. 2 (1983).

[56] This lending was in line with the move to reduce Bank Indonesia's direct commercial lending and to confine it to the more traditional role of a central bank, namely, being a banker's bank.

The overall level of subsidized lending did decline in the wake of the 1983 reforms, but it did so only gradually. It was not until a further wave of reforms to the financial sector in 1988–1990 that central bank intervention in credit markets and the system of preferential lending declined markedly (see Figure 5.1). In January 1990, it was announced that rediscounting would henceforth be available for only four priority programs: the Bulog rice stockpile, farmer credit, cooperatives, and the now much-reduced, medium-term investment credit scheme.

The politics of financial reform shifted markedly in the latter 1980s. Whereas in 1983 the principal institutional opponent of the economists in the Ministry of Finance had been the central bank, by the late 1980s, Bank Indonesia had undergone a marked "cultural" transformation and had taken on much of the market-oriented outlook of the economists. Following the departure of Rachmat Saleh as governor of the central bank in 1983, the philosophical commitment to interventionism began to wane. In 1988, Adrianus Mooy was appointed central bank governor. Mooy was the first governor to be appointed from outside Bank Indonesia. He came to the position from the Economic Planning Board, an institution known as a base for economists within the bureaucracy. Although Mooy, and indeed Bank Indonesia as a whole, had particular institutional interests to guard, communication and cooperation with other economics-oriented agencies became much easier following his appointment. With the shifting policy orientation of the central bank, the principal obstacle remaining to economic liberalization became the patrimonial needs of power brokers within the government and, most important, the president himself. If credit markets were liberalized entirely, the government would lose an important pool of rents that could be discreetly drawn on and allocated to favored individuals. Rather than seek to eliminate preferential credit and the scope for rent seeking altogether, the compromise strategy of the economists has been to narrow the parameters steadily, while still leaving a margin of opportunity for perquisite-seeking members of the government.[57]

Credit Allocation: In Search of a Pattern

As noted earlier, one of the distinctive features of credit allocation in Indonesia since the late 1960s is the lack of any systematic attempt to use preferential credit schemes to subsidize the development of local

---

[57] Since the central bank's direct lending operations have been reduced, the second largest single line item appearing in published statistics is for "other" (or miscellaneous) lending. This appears to be the category under which preferential loans requested by senior government figures are now listed.

industry. To the extent that there has been a sector that has been routinely favored, it is the rural sector and, specifically, rice farmers. As indicated in Table 5.6, various farmer credit programs have consumed a consistently significant share of total outstanding credit. In addition, a portion of preferential credits under the medium-term investment program has been consumed by farmers, and even though they themselves have not received the credit directly, farmers have plainly derived a substantial dividend from Bulog's stabilization scheme for rice prices. How is this persistent subsidy to rice farmers to be explained?

Elementary public choice logic would suggest that rice farmers would be unlikely to secure such a consistently significant benefit. Effective mobilization for collective action by rice farmers is likely to be inherently difficult as they are extremely numerous and highly dispersed. Moreover, one of the defining political features of Suharto's New Order has been the sustained campaign to demobilize the rural population and prevent it from becoming an active participant in political life. The explanation for this puzzle is twofold. Supporting rice growers was an economically rational course of action in terms of both comparative advantage and food security arguments. To this extent it was a policy choice acceptable to the economists and the interventionists alike. Moreover, although the techniques employed varied considerably, there has been a long policy tradition of state intervention in rice markets to limit price fluctuations, one that stretches back to the seventeenth century.[58] On their own, however, arguments about economic rationality are an inadequate explanation.

The second and more powerful logic at work is explicitly political. Since 1966, security planners have been concerned with demobilizing the rural population in order to guard against the possibility of mass political action. The image of widespread rural support for the Communist party has continued to exercise a powerful hold on the thinking of the armed forces long after all organized political radicalism has been eliminated. As a consequence, the government has been keen to discriminate in favor of the rural sector, even though the prospects for mass action appear remote. Channeling preferential credit to rice farmers has thus been one form of preemptive compensation.[59]

[58] Timmer, "Political Economy of Rice in Asia," pp. 206–12.

[59] Liddle has developed a wider version of this argument, suggesting that anticipatory action by Suharto's government has been an important means of preempting political unrest. See William Liddle, "The Politics of Shared Growth: Some Indonesian Cases," *Comparative Politics* 19, no. 2 (1987). Woo and Nasution have argued that the bias toward the rural sector results from the government's concern to prevent a resurgence of rural radicalism. Wing Thye Woo and Anwar Nasution, "Indonesian Economic Policies and Their Relation to External Debt," in *Developing Country Debt and Economic Performance:*

One conclusion to be drawn from the pattern of credit allocation since the late 1960s is that rice farmers appear to be the only group that has been subsidized to a significant degree and on a long-term basis. But there is a more basic point: what is most striking in view of the degree of state intervention in credit markets is that at least in terms of official or declared policy, no group or sector has received anything approaching a large slice of the preferential credit pie. As argued earlier, there seems to have been no coherent attempt to use preferential credit for developmental purposes. The overall picture that emerges is of an ad hoc approach to preferential credit. In drawing up its priority lists, the central bank responded to demands from a wide variety of bureaucratic constituencies without apparently having a concerted strategy. This conclusion is further strengthened once we take into account the fact that such formal plans and priorities as were drawn up by the central bank were routinely circumvented by the patrimonial harvesting of the rents that were on offer.

In Indonesia the normal processes of intramural bureaucratic politics are overlaid with a web of patrimonial loyalties that binds the political elite. To sustain this web, the president and other key political figures surrounding him have needed to allocate economic rewards to a diverse range of supporters. To the extent that dispensing cheap finance was a convenient instrument of patronage, power brokers within the government had a regular, if ad-hoc, interest in diverting preferential credit away from official target groups and toward their personal associates and supporters.

In sum, something of an irony emerges, for the seemingly strong state of Suharto's New Order—a state that is remarkably insulated from organized societal pressures—reveals itself to be surprisingly weak in terms of developing and implementing coherent strategies in this policy arena.[60] Patrimonial imperatives and sheer bureaucratic incapacity have been the principal stumbling blocks. In short, the obstacles to decisive state action have not been the countervailing actions of societal groups but have been in the nature of the state itself. Preferential credit may have been an effective developmental instrument in countries such as South Korea that had more disciplined bureaucracies where credit diversion was less common. In Indonesia, however, once the years of

---

Indonesia, Korea, the Philippines, and Turkey, vol. 3, ed. Jeffrey Sachs and Susan Collins (Chicago: University of Chicago Press, National Bureau of Economic Research, 1989).

[60] Although concerned with advanced industrial countries and their responses to the oil shocks, Ikenberry has developed an analogous argument as part of a critique of the "weak state–strong state" literature. See G. John Ikenberry, "The Irony of State Strength: Comparative Responses to the Oil Shocks in the 1970s," *International Organization* 40, no. 1 (1986).

oil-given wealth ended and the economic climate became inclement, the need for greater efficiency drove the government to abandon many of its interventionist practices and rely more heavily on the market mechanism to determine credit allocation.

Controls or Competition?

Given Indonesia's long history of state intervention in financial markets, the question of whether the swing toward deregulation that began in the early 1980s is likely to be sustained is of particular interest. The issue becomes all the more pertinent in view of disquiet in Indonesia about some of the consequences of liberalization.

Liberalization of the financial sector has indeed led to a markedly increased rate of financial growth.[61] In the highly regulated environment of the 1970s, the ratio of broad money (M2) to GNP increased only slightly, from 14.6 percent in 1973 to 19.3 percent in 1983. By 1989, however, the figure had increased to 37 percent (see Table 5.5). Another indicator of the impact of deregulation is that following the lowering of entry barriers to the banking industry in October 1988, the number of local private and foreign banks operating increased dramatically. In 1988, there were 63 local private banks and 11 foreign banks trading in Indonesia. By 1990 these figures had grown to 106 and 28, respectively.[62] Almost inevitably, however, this rapid expansion of the banking sector has given rise to a number of problems. These have centered around two main issues: the possibility of a shake-out of the industry resulting in the collapse of some of the new banks and the vexed matter of bank ownership and economic concentration.

The flood of new entrants into the banking industry after 1988 gave rise to intense competition as banks struggled to attract depositors and borrowers. Competition for market share is thought to have led a number of banks to overextend themselves and to have assembled loan portfolios of dubious quality. Concerns about the stability of the banking industry were accentuated by the discovery in 1990 that a leading private bank had suffered massive losses through foreign exchange dealings and mismanagement.[63] In these circumstances, a shake-out of the industry seems quite possible.

Although Bank Indonesia has declared that it will not bail out strug-

[61] Cole and Slade, *Financial Development in Indonesia*, pp. 6–9.

[62] The pattern is similar in terms of branching. In 1988, local private banks had 559 branches among themselves, whereas the figure for foreign banks was 21. By 1990 the respective totals were 2,052 and 48. Bank Indonesia, *Monthly Report* (April 1991).

[63] For a discussion of some of the problems produced by the rapid deregulation of the banking sector, see Adam Schwarz, "Free and Uneasy," *Far Eastern Economic Review,* December 20, 1990.

gling banks, the prospect of bank failure and the inevitable protests of aggrieved depositors is certainly a worrying one for the government. Concerns of this sort are heightened by the fact that the major winners of financial deregulation are seen to have been the large Chinese Indonesian business groups who own the great majority of the private banks. Deregulation of the banking sector and of the Jakarta Stock Exchange has had the effect of bringing the perennial and ever politically sensitive issue of Chinese economic domination into sharp focus again. Since 1988 there has been a marked upsurge in public comment and critical debate about the concentration of wealth in big (Chinese) business.[64]

The worrying prospect of bank failure, together with public disquiet about the increasingly conspicuous economic dominance of the large Chinese Indonesian business groupings, has led to concern in some quarters that there may be a reversion to heavy state regulation of the financial sector, but real though these concerns are, it seems unlikely. To be sure, there may well be some adjustment and refinement of the new regulatory framework, but barring a major crisis in the industry, a return to extensive state intervention seems improbable. There are two major reasons for this conclusion.

First, financial deregulation, along with liberal reforms in other sectors of the economy, has been a vital factor underpinning the upsurge of foreign investment in recent years. Any abandonment of the market-oriented reform strategy of the 1980s would likely damage investor confidence and for this reason must be judged an unlikely development. Second, the political matrix within the financial sector is beginning to change. One of the central themes of this chapter has been the way in which financial policy-making has been very closely controlled by bureaucrats in the Ministry of Finance and the central bank, with state and private banks having little voice in policy debates. As such, the liberal economic reforms of the 1980s were introduced not at the bidding of any private sector interests but at the initiative of the Ministry of Finance. By virtue of their own success, however, the reform measures have created a new and potentially potent constituency, namely, the local private banks. By the end of 1990, local private banks accounted for 36 percent of outstanding credits. (If foreign banks are included, the share rises to 42 percent.) Although still overshadowed by state banks, private banks are clearly emerging as a major force within the industry. This is of considerable political importance because it is the private banks that have been the principal beneficiaries of

---

[64] This phenomenon is examined by a number of contributors in Hill and Hull, *Indonesia Assessment*.

deregulation. They have a direct interest in the maintenance of the new competitive environment, as a return to intervention would only favor their major competitors, the state banks.

The increasing commercial clout of private banks, together with recent moves to upgrade the Private Bankers Association, Perbannas, into a more credible and professional organization, may signal the beginnings of long-term political change. The emergence of private banks as independent actors suggests that the political economy of finance in Indonesia is likely to change significantly in the years ahead and cease to be such a state-centered story.

CHAPTER SIX

Selective Squander: The Politics of Preferential Credit Allocation in the Philippines

PAUL D. HUTCHCROFT

The Philippines has long had an extensive system of preferential credit, but the allocation of this credit has done little to promote larger goals of economic development. Economists have labeled the system arbitrary and haphazard, rife with favoritism, and lacking in objective criteria. Multilateral institutions have been troubled by both the "fragmentation" and the "inconsistency" of government credit programs; recently, the World Bank declared that the Philippine government "has no overall view of its various credit programs."[1] Although the government has repeatedly published lists of economic activities to be targeted by selective credit programs, these lists commonly become so all-

Research for this chapter was supported by a grant from the U.S. Department of Education Fulbright-Hays Doctoral Dissertation Research Abroad Program, as well as by a grant from the Social Science Research Council and the American Council of Learned Societies, with funds provided by the William and Flora Hewlett Foundation. Additional support was provided by the University of the Philippines School of Economics, where I was based in 1990–1991, and the Harvard Academy for International and Area Studies.

In addition, I thank all those who offered suggestions and comments for this chapter, most especially Stephan Haggard and Manuel Montes. Thanks also go to Rick Doner, Jeff Frieden, Laura Hastings, Chung Lee, Sylvia Maxfield, Andrew MacIntyre, Jim Scott, and David Timberman.

[1] Edita A. Tan, "Development Finance and State Banking: A Survey of Experience," Philippine Institute for Development Studies, Staff Paper Series no. 84–04 (Makati, Metro Manila, 1984), p. 58; Hugh Patrick and Honorata A. Moreno, "Philippine Private Domestic Commercial Banking, 1946–80, in the Light of Japanese Experience," in *Japan and the Developing Countries: A Comparative Analysis*, ed. Kazushi Ohkawa and Gustav Ranis (New York: Basil Blackwell, 1985), pp. 311–65, 322; World Bank, *Philippines Financial Sector Study*, Report no. 7177–PH, vol. 1 (Washington, D.C.: World Bank, 1988), p. 135 (all citations are to vol. 1 unless otherwise specified); and World Bank/IMF, *The Philippines: Aspects of the Financial Sector* (Washington, D.C.: World Bank, 1980), p. 58.

encompassing as to lose their ability to achieve specific developmental goals.

The Philippine system of selective credit makes important selections, to be sure, but the political logic of these selections is generally far more apparent than any economic rationale. As we shall see, the allocation of preferential credit displays much greater coherence in terms of particularistic criteria (i.e., allocation to particular banks and particular individuals) than in terms of developmental goals (i.e., allocation to specific industries and specific investment priorities). The selection of beneficiaries has more to do with particularistic plunder of the state apparatus—and favoritism shown by those who oversee that apparatus—than with targeting by cohesive government agencies or lobbying pressure from coherent sectoral groups.

This chapter explores the political logic that underlies the system of preferential credit allocation in the Philippines; I argue that one cannot understand these programs without examining the broader nature of interactions between the state and dominant economic interests. In other words, it is important to analyze the state apparatus that provides cheap credit and the oligarchic forces that raid the state for the private gains that such credit provides. In the course of this comparative research project, it has become clear that selective credit programs in the Philippines are more deeply and consistently plagued by rent-seeking behavior than are similar programs in any of the other countries analyzed in this volume. To explain why rent-seeking behavior is both more prevalent and more persistent in the Philippines than in other settings, it is necessary to turn our attention to large structural variables. In particular, I argue that only by examining the nature of the state and the relative strengths of the state apparatus and business interests can we begin to explain cross-national differences in the prevalence and endurance of rent-seeking behavior.[2]

---

[2] Buchanan uses the term *rent seeking* "to describe behavior in institutional settings where individual efforts to maximize value generate social waste rather then social surplus." He, as well as other rent-seeking theorists, tends to presume that the degree of rent seeking is dependent on the degree of government intervention in an economy: "Rent-seeking activity is directly related to the scope and range of governmental activity in the economy, and to the relative size of the public sector." The case studies in this volume, however, demonstrate that the relationship is far more complicated than Buchanan would lead us to believe. See James M. Buchanan, "Rent Seeking and Profit Seeking," in *Toward Theory of the Rent-Seeking Society*, ed. James M. Buchanan, Robert D. Tollison, and Gordon Tullock (College Station: Texas A&M Press, 1980), pp. 3–15.

A trenchant structuralist critique of "neo-utilitarian" political economy is found in Peter Evans, "The State as Problem and Solution: Predation, Embedded Autonomy, and Structural Change," in *The Politics of Economic Adjustment*, ed. Stephan Haggard and Robert R. Kaufman (Princeton: Princeton University Press, 1992), pp. 139–81. Evans shows that one cannot understand variation in state structures or in relations between state and capital by focusing only on the microlevel behavior of individual maximizers

First, the state apparatus is weakly institutionalized. Although all states possess patrimonial features to some degree, there is a particularly large gap between the Philippine state and the archetypal bureaucratic state. In fact, to paraphrase Max Weber, "the conceptual separation of the 'state'... from all personal authority of individuals" is often remote from Philippine "structures of authority."[3]

Second, unlike certain other states with strong patrimonial features, the Philippine state is more often plundered than plunderer; we find not a predatory state but rather a predatory oligarchy. The primary direction of rent extraction is not toward a bureaucratic elite based inside the state but rather toward oligarchic forces with a firm independent economic base outside the state.[4] Even with their economic base outside the state apparatus, however, the major oligarchic families

---

within a state apparatus. If one seeks to address these larger questions, it is useful to begin with the "classic institutional perspectives" of Max Weber and others (p. 142). As we shall see, the case of the Philippines demonstrates that it is entirely appropriate to presume the existence of rational actors, but it is a big mistake to presume the existence of a rational legal state.

[3] Max Weber, *Economy and Society,* ed. Guenther Roth and Claus Wittich (Berkeley and Los Angeles: University of California Press, 1978), vol. 2, p. 998. "The patrimonial office," writes Weber, "lacks above all the bureaucratic separation of the 'private' and the 'official' sphere" (p. 1,028). Several scholars have noted the weak distinction between the public and the private spheres in the Marcos years. See Emmanuel S. de Dios, "The Erosion of the Dictatorship," in Aurora Javate-de Dios et al., *Dictatorship and Revolution: Roots of People's Power* (Metro Manila: Conspectus, 1988), p. 94; Stephan Haggard, "The Political Economy of the Philippine Debt Crisis," in *Economic Crisis and Policy Choice: The Politics of Adjustment in the Third World,* ed. Joan Nelson (Princeton: Princeton University Press, 1990), p. 217, and "The Philippines: Picking Up after Marcos," in *The Promise of Privatization,* ed. Raymond Vernon (New York: Council on Foreign Relations, 1988), p. 95; and David Wurfel, *Filipino Politics: Development and Decay* (Ithaca: Cornell University Press, 1988), pp. 137–38. In my analysis, the weak separation of private and public spheres is a characteristic of the Philippine political economy that transcends political regime (and can be found before, during, and after the 1972–1986 martial law regime of Ferdinand Marcos). See Paul D. Hutchcroft, "Oligarchs and Cronies in the Philippine State: The Politics of Patrimonial Plunder," *World Politics* 43, no. 3 (1991): 414–50.

[4] In another work, I develop the contrast between the patrimonial administrative state, where a bureaucratic elite is the major beneficiary of patrimonial largesse and exercises power over a weak business class, and the patrimonial oligarchic state, where a powerful business class extracts privilege from a largely incoherent bureaucracy. By analyzing such variation in patrimonial polities (and the types of rent-seeking capitalisms that they engender), we can better account for the evolution of patrimonial features in certain settings (such as Thailand, formerly a patrimonial administrative state) and their persistence in other settings (such as the Philippines, which remains a patrimonial oligarchic state). A patrimonial administrative state may contain the seeds of its own destruction, because the process of economic growth can create a new social force—an autonomous business class—that is likely to begin to challenge the patrimonial basis of power. In the patrimonial oligarchic state, on the other hand, the major impact of the process of economic growth is merely to strengthen the oligarchic social force that has already been the major beneficiary of patrimonial largesse. See Paul D. Hutchcroft, "Patrimonial State, Predatory Oligarchy: The Politics of Private Commercial Banking in the Philippines," Ph.D. diss., Yale University, 1993, chaps. 1 and 2.

rely heavily on their access to the political machinery to promote private accumulation. This access is largely particularistic and commonly determined on the basis of personalistic criteria. The Philippine state is so swamped by the demands of these powerful oligarchic forces that it is incapable of playing a coherent role in guiding economic development.

Although a thorough analysis is beyond the scope of this chapter, one cannot ignore the role of external forces in shaping basic features of the Philippine political economy. The country's particular colonial experience produced far more "oligarchy building" than state building; external factors are central to understanding the historical development of the patrimonial state and the predatory oligarchy. Moreover, the state that emerged in the postcolonial era has depended on external resources for its sustenance. Throughout the postwar era, clientalist relations with the United States have created a hothouse within which patrimonial features have flourished. No matter how flagrant the oligarchy's plunder of the state, the country's role as host of U.S. military bases has ensured repeated rescue from the balance-of-payments crises that have plagued the postwar economy. It is not coincidental that the agency most influential in economic policy-making, the Central Bank, is also the agency with the greatest responsibility in external economic relations. The Philippine state derives its power, in large part, from its role in handling the country's external economic relations: it disburses aid and loans received from abroad and sets policies on foreign exchange, trade, and investment. Further, external forces have been a major obstacle to change in the prevailing domestic social imbalance, propping up unproductive social forces and protecting oligarchic plunderers from revolutionary upheaval. The withdrawal of U.S. military bases confronts the Philippines with a greatly altered international environment. Over the long term, I conclude, it will likely serve as a major impetus for fundamental change in the nature of relations between the state and the oligarchy.[5]

I. THE PHILIPPINE FINANCIAL SYSTEM: AN OVERVIEW

Before proceeding to a more detailed examination of selective credit programs in the Philippines, it is important to examine briefly the political contours of the larger financial system in which these programs are set. There are two overarching characteristics of this system. The

[5] The complex interaction of external forces with the state and social structures of the Philippines is discussed in greater detail in Hutchcroft, "Patrimonial State, Predatory Oligarchy," chaps. 1 and 2.

first is rampant favoritism, which reflects the patrimonial character of the state. The favor or disfavor of the oligarchs currently holding state office is a major determinant of the relative success or failure of particular banks. The Central Bank's allocation of valuable privileges—whether they be bank licenses, government deposits, or loans—is rarely made on the basis of clear-cut, objective rules that apply to all players. Although the type of favors extracted from the state may have changed through the years, one can note parallels between how sugar interests raided the newly formed Philippine National Bank after World War I, how foreign exchange licenses were obtained in the 1950s, how banks bribed officials for government deposits in the 1960s, how the Marcos regime raided state financial institutions for "behest loans" during the martial law years (1972–1986), and how the large banks harvested windfall profits by investing government deposits in government securities in the late 1980s.[6]

The second overarching characteristic is the largely ineffectual state regulation of the banking sector, which reflects both the patrimonial nature of the state and the weakness of the state apparatus in relation to the powerful social forces that are concentrated in the banking sector. Despite three major financial reform efforts—two of which specifically targeted problems of bank supervision—the Central Bank remains largely incapable of systematically disciplining banks that violate its own regulations, even those related to abuse of loan portfolios, which has contributed to four major episodes of bank instability in a twenty-five-year period. This weakness becomes especially apparent in examining legal actions lodged against Central Bank personnel; in the Philippines, Central Bank officials are more likely to be intimidated than to intimidate. A 1988 World Bank report notes that Central Bank staff "feel personally vulnerable to suits brought against them for their official acts." Even when the Central Bank has acted against those who milk their banks, former bank owners have been known to use personal connections, all the way up to the Supreme Court, to confound Central Bank discipline. Former governor Jaime Laya noted that even martial law "didn't seem to stop the lawsuits against Central Bank personnel." He actually laughed when explaining that the Central Bank legal office has "never won a case." But the former head of the bank supervision sector, who was herself sued, doesn't find it a laughing matter. "Why

---

[6] Favored treatment, it should be noted, is not imperative to the success of a commercial bank; certain institutions, by adopting a conservative lending policy and striving for steady growth, seem to have done reasonably well without any obvious special treatment by Central Bank officials or the palace. But in instances where banks have enjoyed mercurial growth, one is nearly sure to find special favors, granted through special relations with prominent officials.

only in this country," she exclaimed, "do the regulators go to jail and the bankers go scot-free?"[7]

If the system genuinely worked for the greater good, perhaps rampant favoritism and weak state regulation could be overlooked. But there are four major areas in which the Philippine financial system performs poorly and hampers larger developmental objectives. First, a review of the commercial banking system (which overwhelmingly dominates the financial system as a whole) shows that political factors discourage the efficient allocation of credit. There are three major types of commercial banks: patronage-infested government banks (most important, the Philippine National Bank, but formerly two smaller banks as well); a large number of private banks, most of which are family dominated; and four highly profitable branches of foreign banks, all of which have been in operation since at least the late 1940s. First priority in loan allocation by government banks generally goes to those with greatest proximity to the political machinery. Within private domestic banks, first priority on loans commonly goes to related enterprises of the extended oligarchic family (or families) owning the bank. The basic building blocks of the Philippine business community are the diversified family conglomerates, and the surest means for these conglomerates to secure credit is through ownership (or partial ownership) of a commercial bank.[8]

Second, the banking system has a weak record of mobilizing savings. In part because real savings deposit rates have generally been negative over the past two decades, the Philippines has by far the worst record of promoting financial intermediation of all countries in the Association of Southeast Asian Nations (ASEAN). Rates of financial intermediation have been very weak—the ratio of M3/GNP, for example, was 0.20 in 1970, peaked at 0.31 in 1983, and fell to 0.23 in 1988.[9] This has led to considerable reliance on foreign savings, which may have been allocated even more inefficiently than domestic savings.

Third, the banking system has created a high degree of financial instability, the root cause of which is the regulators' inability to curb

---

[7] World Bank, *Philippines Financial Sector Study*, pp. viii, x.; and from interviews with Jaime C. Laya, former governor of the Central Bank (1981–1984), May 21, 1990, and Carlota P. Valenzuela, former deputy governor, Supervision and Examination Section, Central Bank of the Philippines, March 22, 1990.

[8] In chapter 2 of "Patrimonial State, Predatory Oligarchy," I explore how the high degree of arbitrariness in the political sphere helps to explain the continuing weak separation of the household and the enterprise in the Philippines. Because the success of the enterprise depends to such a large extent on the political connections of the household, it would be foolish for Philippine entrepreneurs to force a clear separation between the two.

[9] Edita A. Tan, "Bank Concentration and the Structure of Interest," Discussion Paper no. 8915, School of Economics, University of the Philippines, Quezon City, 1989, p. 3.

the milking of loan portfolios by bank owners, directors, and officers for related family enterprises. As early as 1970, Robert F. Emery noted that the Philippines "has probably had more financial scandals or financial institutions in distress than any other Southeast Asian country."[10] Since then, the problems have intensified, with major episodes of bank failure in the mid-1970s, the early 1980s, and again in the mid-1980s. Banking reforms have been largely unsuccessful either in curbing loan abuses or in altering the ownership patterns that encourage them.

Finally, the banking system provides enormous profits to those banks that are primarily in the business of banking for the sake of banking profits and not for the sake of financing related family enterprises. According to a World Bank study, pretax profit margins in the Philippines are roughly 300 percent higher than the average of such margins in eight other countries. As a 1988 World Bank Study indicates, "The high profit margin in the Philippines [as compared with margins in the other sample countries] was the result of continued tolerance of small and weak banks with high operating costs in the system; the more efficient banks priced their products and services with reference to the cost structure of the smaller banks, a practice which effectively enabled them to capture higher profits."[11] Bankers enjoy oligopolistic power that is unchallenged by the Central Bank. Large spreads between interest rates for loans and deposits—initially enforced by regulation but more recently maintained, it seems, by a bank cartel—guarantee high levels of profitability for those banks whose loan portfolios are less flagrantly milked by their directors, officers, and stockholders. As a result, the four foreign banks find profits from their Philippine branches to be among the highest in their entire international branch network.[12] In short, the banking system produces enormous particularistic advantage amidst rampant wastage of domestic savings and the squandering of foreign resources.

II. PREFERENTIAL CREDIT: A TYPOLOGY

Subsequent sections of this chapter provide a historical analysis of the origins, effectiveness, and attempted reform of the preferential credit system. As a foundation for that analysis, it is useful to provide

[10] Robert F. Emery, *The Financial Institutions of Southeast Asia: A Country-by-Country Study* (New York: Praeger, 1970), p. 482.
[11] World Bank, *Philippines Financial Sector Study*, pp. iii, 73 (quote from p. iii).
[12] World Bank, *Philippines Financial Sector Study*, p. 73; and information obtained from an anonymous interview, May 1990.

a brief typology of the major types of preferential credit found in the Philippines.

(1) *State Financial Institutions.* The two major state banks are the Philippine National Bank (PNB), which was a commercial bank formed in 1916, and the Development Bank of the Philippines (DBP), which was first established as the Rehabilitation Finance Corporation in 1947 and later transformed into the better-capitalized DBP in 1958. Both these state banks were established to promote the allocation of subsidized credit, and their presence in financial markets has been substantial. From the 1970s until the mid-1980s, their combined share of assets of the total financial system averaged 20–25 percent.

(2) *Foreign Exchange Allocation.* The licensing of imports and foreign exchange began in response to the 1949 balance-of-payments crisis but later became an important (yet often "haphazard") means of shaping the course of Philippine industrialization in the 1950s.[13]

(3) *Rediscounting.* Across time, there has been no Central Bank program of selective credit more important than the rediscounting window. Although primarily designed as a tool of selective credit, variance in the availability of selective rediscounting has at the same time been a very important mechanism for controlling the money supply. In a country with a very poorly developed tax system, rediscounting has been much easier to implement than fiscal techniques of financing favored sectors.[14] As will be shown, however, there has been a high degree of favoritism in institutions' access to the window.

(4) *Forward Exchange Cover or "Swaps."* A swap occurs when "a commercial bank obtains a foreign currency loan or deposit, converts the currency (typically dollars) into pesos, and purchases forward dollars at a favorable rate from the Central Bank."[15] These transactions began in 1972 but were particularly important in the late 1970s and early 1980s. Swaps were extremely profitable and were disbursed on a highly discretionary basis.

(5) *Consolidated Foreign Borrowing Program.* This program, also known as the "jumbo loan" program, ran from 1978 to 1983. The Central Bank obtained favorable terms on external loans, assumed the currency risk, and then disbursed them to domestic borrowers at low rates and liberal terms. The vast bulk of the $2.3 billion in loans went to the DBP, the PNB, and the national government.

(6) *Government-managed Credit Programs.* Dwarfed in size by the rediscounting window, these programs are often financed by external agen-

[13] Frank H. Golay, *The Philippines: Public Policy and National Economic Development* (Ithaca: Cornell University Press, 1961), p. 239.

[14] Edita A. Tan, "Central Banking and Credit Policies in the Philippines," Institute of Economic Development and Research, School of Economics, University of the Philippines, Quezon City, 1972, pp. I.3, III.3.

[15] Patrick and Moreno, "Philippine Private Domestic Commercial Banking." p. 322.

cies and often have a technical assistance component. They tend to be longer-term and oriented more toward smaller lenders than are rediscounting facilities.[16]

(7) *Controls on Lending Portfolios.* There are several ways in which the Central Bank attempts to impose controls on the lending activities of commercial banks, but legal loopholes and inadequate regulation often enable banks to evade the rules. Most important are the regulations on loans to "directors, officers, stockholders, and related interests," or DOSRI loans. Although these regulations date from 1948, their enforcement has been a highly intractable problem for the Philippine banking system.

In addition to these programs and measures, which are explicitly intended to influence patterns of credit allocation, there are other "preferential" government actions that also have a powerful influence on the shape of the banking industry and the allocation of credit. The allocation of branch licenses is a process in which certain banks have often benefited greatly from connections with high Central Bank officials. By having more branches, these banks enjoy better access to sources of funds. In addition, the allocation of government deposits has been important in three periods: in the early 1960s, the 1970s, and the late 1980s. Finally, the allocation of bank licenses and the ownership structure of the commercial banking system is, ultimately, among the most important factors determining the allocation of credit, precisely because first priority on the allocation of loans by private banks generally goes to the enterprises of families who own the bank. Given the importance of bank licenses, it is not surprising that their allocation has often been a controversial process in the history of Philippine banking.

III. THE HISTORICAL ORIGINS OF SELECTIVE CREDIT, 1916–1960

State intervention in the modern Philippine financial sector has its roots in the early years of the American colonial regime, a regime that was, ironically, noted for its minimalist approach to government.[17] During the tenure of the Democratic governor-general, Francis Burton Harrison (1913–1921), various state enterprises were created. At the same time, Filipinos began to control both houses of Congress (in 1916), and the bureaucracy was substantially Filipinized. Simultaneous to the

---

[16] World Bank, *Philippines Financial Sector Study*, p. 131.
[17] See Benedict Anderson, "Cacique Democracy in the Philippines: Origins and Dreams," *New Left Review*, May/June, 1988, p. 11.

expansion in the role of the state was an expansion in the oligarchy's control over that state.

By far the largest of the new state enterprises—and the richest new source of booty for the emerging national oligarchy—was the PNB, established in 1916. The government provided $5 million in capitalization and was required to deposit all its funds in the bank. When these resources proved inadequate, the bank began printing money and made a "systematic raid" on the currency reserve fund in New York, snatching $41.5 million to lend out in the Philippines. Within five years, the newly empowered landed oligarchs had plundered the bank so thoroughly that not only the bank but also the government and its currency system were threatened by "utter breakdown." By 1921, an accounting firm had determined that PNB had squandered the entire capital stock contributed by the government, as well as half of all government deposits in the bank. It declared the bank "hopelessly insolvent" and accused it of violating "every principle which prudence, intelligence, or even honesty, dictate." Although the bank operated on a greatly reduced scale after it was reorganized in 1924, its loan portfolio continued to be used for private gain. Under Manuel L. Quezon (the first president of the Philippine Commonwealth, created in 1935), the bank was an especially effective instrument of patronage.[18]

The second major government financial institution, the Rehabilitation Finance Corporation (RFC), was created by President Manuel Roxas in 1947, six months after the country became independent. The RFC absorbed the Agricultural and Industrial Bank, a government-owned bank established by Quezon in 1938, and was given the specific mandate of assisting with postwar rehabilitation. From the start, however, it suffered from a shortage of funds. Most of its initial paid-in capital was committed within its first five months, largely to residential loans.[19]

The most important government economic institution formed in the early years of independence was the Central Bank of the Philippines. The Central Bank opened its doors in 1949 during a momentous balance-of-payments crisis and soon found itself consumed with the task

[18] Peter W. Stanley, *A Nation in the Making: The Philippines and the United States, 1899–1921* (Cambridge: Harvard University Press, 1974), pp. 246–47; George F. Luthringer, *The Gold-Exchange Standard in the Philippines* (Princeton: Princeton University Press, 1934), pp. 67–214, 121n, 155; and Claro M. Recto, "The Political Philosophy of Manuel L. Quezon," in *Quezon: Paladin of Philippine Freedom*, ed. Carlos Quirino (Manila: Filipiniana Book Guild, 1971), p. 394.
[19] Ronald King Edgerton, "The Politics of Reconstruction in the Philippines, 1945–1948," Ph.D. diss., University of Michigan, 1975, pp. 378–82; and Joint Philippine-American Finance Commission, *Report and Recommendations of the Joint Philippine-American Finance Commission* (Washington, D.C.: Government Printing Office, 1947), pp. 57–58.

of helping to administer import and exchange controls. Initially instituted as an ad hoc means of overcoming the crisis, these controls soon became an important impetus both for industrialization and for the diversification of family conglomerates into industrial ventures. They remained in force throughout the 1950s and became the dominant tool in both regulating the money supply and allocating selective credit. In an economy dominated by the system of controls, Frank H. Golay explains, Filipino entrepreneurs preferred to take their loans in foreign exchange, and the "capacity of banks to expand earning assets [was] not essentially a function of excess reserves but of the availability of foreign exchange."[20]

Filipino importers and producers were given increasing priority in the allocation of foreign exchange, but Filipino-Chinese entrepreneurs and foreign firms also benefited greatly.[21] On the whole, however, the power to allocate foreign exchange licenses was used haphazardly, and many opportunities were squandered. When efforts at more coherent industrial planning did begin in 1958, they were hampered by intra-agency squabbles and inadequate Central Bank capacity to audit firms.[22]

[20] Golay, *Philippines*, pp. 163, 237. The Central Bank's arsenal of other selective credit measures was dwarfed in potency by the exchange controls. These measures are discussed in Miguel Cuaderno, "The Central Bank and Economic Planning," in *Planning for Progress: The Administration of Economic Planning in the Philippines*, ed. R. S. Milne (Manila: Institute of Public Administration and Institute of Economic Development and Research, 1960), pp. 92–108, 104–5.

[21] For more on the favoring of Filipino over Filipino-Chinese entrepreneurs, see Miguel Cuaderno, *Problems of Economic Development* (n.p., 1964), p. 83. Filipino-Chinese firms nonetheless constitute a very large chunk of the local manufacturing sector; the vast majority of these firms can be traced to the 1950s and 1960s. See Temerio Campos Rivera, "Class, the State, and Foreign Capital: The Politics of Philippine Industrialization, 1950–1986," Ph.D. diss., University of Wisconsin-Madison, 1991, p. 131. Among Filipino entrepreneurs, the old landed families did especially well in the competition for licenses, although there were many new faces as well (Rivera, "Class, the State, and Foreign Capital," pp. 101–6). Because of widespread diversification of oligarchic familial interests, allegiance to particular economic sectors became increasingly weak. In fact, it is in the 1950s and 1960s that the diversified family conglomerates emerged as *the* dominant segment of capital. Even today, these conglomerates typically combine a range of enterprises (in such diverse areas as agriculture, manufacturing, finance, commerce, urban real estate, and services) under one roof, and cohesive sectoral interests remain weak. See Hutchcroft, "Patrimonial State, Predatory Oligarchy," chap. 3.

Joint ventures with foreign capital were widespread. For a persuasive analysis of U.S. sponsorship of ISI in the Philippines, see Sylvia Maxfield and James H. Nolt, "Protectionism and the Internationalization of Capital: U.S. Sponsorship of Import Substitution Industrialization in the Philippines, Turkey, and Argentina," *International Studies Quarterly* 34 (March 1990): 49–81.

[22] Golay describes the criteria used to award licenses as "economically irrational" and explains that the most successful industries were highly dependent on imported raw materials. See Golay, *Philippines*, pp. 141, 239. On squandered opportunities for industrial planning, see Laurence Davis Stifel, *The Textile Industry: A Case Study of Industrial Development in the Philippines*, Southeast Asia Program, Cornell University, Data Paper no. 49 (1963), pp. 70, 74, 80.

Most important, the allocation of licenses was rife with corruption. The controls were first administered by a separate Import Control Board (on which the Central Bank was represented), but anomalies in the operation of controls became a scandal, and in 1953 the Central Bank took over the administration of the controls. In subsequent years, the Central Bank was itself accused of corruption in its allocation of foreign exchange. Because exchange licenses were such a windfall to recipients, there was great competition over their allocation. Manufacturers, in fact, considered effort at the Central Bank as important as at their plants. In one (perhaps apocryphal) incident from the late 1950s, Congressman Ferdinand Marcos "burst into [the] office" of a Central Bank official who had refused to license the imports of "a well-heeled Chinese businessman" and pointed a revolver at the head of the official until "the documents were signed and turned over to him."[23]

The controls were initially successful in augmenting international reserves, but as the decade progressed, foreign exchange earnings were unable to keep up with demands for foreign exchange. Cuaderno was, at the same time, confronted by powerful officials linked to the "sugar bloc," who were pressuring for dismantling of the controls and devaluation. The Central Bank governor and his foes engaged in a major debate over monetary policy, which was temporarily resolved in 1956, when Cuaderno returned from the United States with $85 million in official and private credits. He was able to reassert his dominance over the economic policy-making process and reestablish a greater degree of monetary stability.[24] As long as Cuaderno was successful in bringing in external funds, it seems he could fend off pressures from agroexporters for decontrol and devaluation. But by 1960, the seemingly unavoidable decontrol process had finally begun, and two years later the peso was devalued by roughly 50 percent.[25]

---

[23] Golay, *Philippines*, pp. 163–68, 85n, 92, 95; and Stifel, *Textile Industry*, p. 104. The Marcos anecdote comes from Sterling Seagrave, *The Marcos Dynasty* (New York: Harper and Row, 1988), p. 162. See also Frank H. Golay, "The Philippine Monetary Policy Debate," *Pacific Affairs* 29, no. 3 (1956): 261–62; Carlos Quirino, *Apo Lakay: The Biography of President Elpidio Quirino of the Philippines* (Makati, Metro Manila: Total Book World, 1987), p. 112; and Jorge R. Coquia, *The Presidential Election of 1953* (Manila: University Publishing, 1955), pp. 102–3. Coquia reports that "with the aid of . . . influential officials, import licenses were easily procured at 10% commission."

[24] On the overall monetary policy debate, see Cuaderno, *Problems of Economic Development*, pp. 55, 134–36; and Golay, *Philippines*, pp. 229–30, and "Philippine Monetary Policy Debate," pp. 253–64. U.S. support was a central element of Cuaderno's influence. See Maxfield and Nolt, "Protectionism and the Internationalization of Capital," p. 67; and Golay, *Philippines*, p. 412. Many in the Philippines felt that the United States and the American Chamber of Commerce were siding with Cuaderno and rewarding the Philippines for adopting Cuaderno's policy advice.

[25] Golay, *Philippines*, p. 240. The most comprehensive account of the decontrol process is found in Robert Baldwin, *Foreign Trade Regimes and Economic Development: The Philippines*

Although Cuaderno's Central Bank was largely preoccupied with maintaining the international reserve and heading off the impact of government deficit financing, the 1950s also saw several important changes in the institutional development of the financial sector. The issue of government bonds in 1954 (against Cuaderno's advice) induced a marked growth of total assets of the banking sector. Moreover, in 1955, Congress increased the authorized capital of the PNB, the first such increase since 1924. In addition, the RFC, which had long suffered from a shortage of funds, was transformed into the better-capitalized DBP in 1958. It enjoyed fresh infusions of funds from both Japanese reparations and the government insurance systems. Finally, rural banks were nurtured through generous government incentives beginning in 1952.[26]

There was also significant growth within the private domestic commercial banking sector. In 1949, the banking system was dominated by the PNB, foreign banks, and locally chartered banks owned by the Manila archdiocese, Americans, Chinese, and Filipino-Chinese; there was only one private Filipino bank. But during the course of Cuaderno's twelve-year tenure as Central Bank governor (1949–1960), nine new private domestic commercial banks were established, seven by families that would popularly be labeled Filipino.[27] Because some of these banks had ownership links to the country's new industrial ventures, the percentage of credit allocated by private commercial banks to industry increased from 9.5 percent in 1954 to 26 percent in 1959. By 1958, the combined total assets of private domestic banks for the first time exceeded the total assets of the PNB. At the same time, the proportion of total assets held by the four foreign banks declined from roughly

(New York: Columbia University Press for the National Bureau of Economic Research, 1975), pp. 50–64. See also Cuaderno, *Problems of Economic Development,* pp. 71–77; and Cheryl Payer, *The Debt Trap: The International Monetary Fund and the Third World* (New York: Monthly Review Press, 1974), pp. 60–61.

[26] On the impact and controversy surrounding the 1954 government bond issue, see Cuaderno, *Problems of Economic Development,* p. 120; and Andres K. Roxas, "The Commercial Banking System: Past and Future," in "Top 100 Corporations," a special report in the *Manila Chronicle,* September 22, 1969, p. 20. The increase in the PNB's capitalization is discussed in PNB, *Philippine National Bank, 60th Anniversary: July 22, 1916–1976* (n.p., n.d. [Manila, 1976?]), p. 14; Cuaderno, *Problems of Economic Development,* p. 41; and Golay, *Philippines,* pp. 56, 86, 246. On the DBP, see Golay, *Philippines,* p. 246; and Gregorio S. Licaros, "The Banking System and Economic Planning," in Milne, *Planning for Progress,* pp. 109–22, 113–17. The assets of the rural banks were, and continue to be, a minor element of the overall financial system; yet they are lucrative "milking cows" for many of their owners.

[27] Just as the system of import and exchange controls was an effective instrument in promoting the Filipinization of retail and import trade and manufacturing, there were complementary efforts to promote Filipino banks at the expense of Filipino-Chinese banks. See Frank H. Golay et al., *Underdevelopment and Economic Nationalism in Southeast Asia* (Ithaca: Cornell University Press, 1969), pp. 47–49, 89, 90–91.

Table 6.1. Total assets, Philippine commercial banking system

Year-end	All KBs (million pesos)	Domestic KBs (%)	Government KBs (%)	Private Dom. KBs (%)	Foreign KBs (%)
1900	40	29.4	n.a.	n.a.	70.6
1925	264	74.6	n.a.	n.a.	25.4
1950	1,079	69.7	n.a.	n.a.	30.3
1955	1,413	85.8	48.9	36.9	14.1
1960	2,337	85.1	36.0	49.1	14.9
1965	6,786	92.8	36.3	56.5	7.2
1970	13,841	91.1	34.0	57.1	8.9
1975	49,980	89.7	36.8	52.9	10.3
1980	146,026	87.2	28.4	58.8	12.8
1985	285,578	84.6	26.7	57.9	15.4
1990	497,489	87.1	13.6	73.5	12.9

Sources: Nicanor Tomas, "Banking in the Philippines from 1925–1950," in *The Fookien Times Yearbook, 1951* (Manila: Foobien Times, 1951), pp. 71, 173; Sycip, Gorres, Velayo, & Co., *A Study of Commercial Banks in the Philippines* (Manila, various annual issues), Philippine National Bank, Division of Economics and Research, *The Philippine Commercial Banking System* (Manila, 1990).
Note: KB = commercial bank.

30 percent in 1950 to 15 percent in 1955 and 1960[28] (see Tables 6.1 and 6.2).

IV. DECONTROL AND THE RISE OF NEW BANKS, 1960–1972

The rate of expansion of the private domestic banking sector under Cuaderno, however, was dwarfed by the mushrooming of new commercial banks under the governorship of his successor, Andres V. Castillo. By 1965, nearly every major family had diversified into commercial banking, and the number of private domestic commercial banks ballooned from thirteen at year-end 1960 to thirty-three at year-end 1965. The Central Bank provided three important incentives to private bank development: government deposits, rediscounting, and continued low minimum capitalization requirements. Government deposits began to be placed in private banks in late 1960 and remained an important source of funds for several banks until the mid-1960s. The rediscount-

[28] Edita A. Tan, "Philippine Monetary Policy and Aspects of the Financial Market: A Review of the Literature," in *PIDS Survey of Development Research I* (Manila: Philippine Institute for Development Studies, 1980), p. 181; Nicanor Tomas, "Banking in the Philippines from 1925–1950," in *The Fookien Times Yearbook, 1951* (Manila: Fookien Times, 1951), p. 73; and Sycip, Gorres, and Velayo & Co., *A Study of Commercial Banks in the Philippines, 1960* (Manila, 1961). The 1948 General Banking Act effectively froze the number of branches of foreign banks at four, and in fact, no other foreign banks have been able to establish wholly owned branches in the Philippines thus far.

Table 6.2. Total assets, Philippine commercial banks (by rank and by percentage of total assets of all commercial banks)

Bank	Years of operation	1955		1960		1965		1970		1975		1980		1985		1988	
		Rank	% All KBs	Rank	% All KBs	Rank	% All KBs	Rank	% All KBs	Rank	% All KBs	Rank	% All KBs	Rank	% All KBs	Rank	% All KBs
Allied (formerly General, relicensed 1977)	1977–present					25	0.8	26	1.0	20	1.5	4	5.0	9	3.2	9	3.1
Associated (formerly Associated-Citizens, renamed 1981)	1975–present									19	1.5	26	1.1	27	0.9	27	0.8
Citizens	1962–75					23	0.9	23	1.1								
Associated	1965–75					33	0.5	35	0.7								
BPI	1851–present	3	5.3	4	4.4	5	3.3	5	3.7	3	4.2	3	6.1	5	5.7	4	8.5
Peoples	1926–74	8	2.7	12	2.2	11	2.1	20	1.7								
Comtrust	1954–80	12	0.9	11	2.8	9	2.4	9	3	16	2.3						
Family	1981–present													29	0.7	28	0.7
Boston (formerly Combank, renamed 1988)	1981–present																
Overseas	1964–68					17	1.5										
China	1920–present	2	7.8	2	7.5	4	4.2	3	4.1	7	3.1	13	2.4	19	1.6	17	1.9
CityTrust (formerly Feati, renamed 1977)	1961–present					29	0.7	36	0.6	28	0.7	27	1.0	16	1.8	13	2.6
Equitable	1950–present	5	3.2	3	5.7	2	4.6	4	3.9	8	2.9	17	2.0	20	1.4	12	2.6
FEBTC	1960–present			16	1.3	15	1.6	13	2.0	4	3.5	5	4.0	7	4.4	3	9.1
Pacific	1955–85					13	1.9	10	2.8	12	2.5	15	2.3				
Progressive	1977–present																
Interbank	1963–74					34	0.5	38	0.4								
Continental	1961–present					30	0.7	33	0.8	35	0.2	24	1.1	14	1.9	16	2.3
Manila	1962–present					18	1.5	14	1.9	10	2.7	14	2.3	10	2.8		
Metrobank	1939–present	4	4.7	6	3.7	22	0.9	22	1.6	5	3.2	6	3.8	4	5.7	5	8.3
PBCommunications	1957–present	14	1.8	14	1.8	8	2.7	11	2.2	22	1.3	19	1.9	23	1.1	19	1.6
Philbanking	1957–present					14	1.7	19	1.7	15	2.3	22	1.5	24	0.9	23	1.2

Table 6.2. (cont.)

Bank	Years of operation	1955 Rank	1955 % All KBs	1960 Rank	1960 % All KBs	1965 Rank	1965 % All KBs	1970 Rank	1970 % All KBs	1975 Rank	1975 % All KBs	1980 Rank	1980 % All KBs	1985 Rank	1985 % All KBs	1988 Rank	1988 % All KBs
PCIB	1960–present			9	3.0	3	4.4	6	3.6	9	2.7	8	3.3	3	5.8	6	6.3
PBCommerce	1938–76	7	3.1	7	3.4	10	2.3	17	1.8	25	1.0						
Merchants	1963–76					32	0.5	32	0.8	31	0.7						
IBAA	1974–85									13	2.4	20	1.9				
First Insular	1961–74					28	0.7	25	1.0								
Asia	1963–74					27	0.8	30	0.8								
Philtrust	1916–present	6	3.1	8	3.0	16	1.5	27	1.0	30	0.7	30	0.6	28	0.8	21	1.3
Pilipinas	1976–present											29	0.7	30	0.6	29	0.5
(formerly Filman, renamed 1980)																	
Manufacturers	1957–76			15	1.4	19	1.3	28	0.9	34	0.3						
Filipinas	1964–76					36	0.3	37	0.5	33	0.5						
Producers	1971–present									29	0.7	28	1.0	25	0.9	26	1.0
Prudential	1952–present	9	2.4	5	4.0	7	3.1	8	3.1	14	2.4	23	1.5	17	1.7	14	2.5
RPB	1961–present					6	3.2	16	1.8	32	0.6	7	3.3	12	2.1	15	2.5
(formerly Republic, renamed 1977)																	
RCBC	1963–present					26	0.8	21	1.7	6	3.1	11	2.5	13	1.9	8	3.6
Security	1951–present	10	2.3	10	3.0	12	2.1	12	2.1	24	1.0	21	1.8	11	2.1	20	1.5
Solidbank	1963–present					20	1.2	7	3.3	11	2.5	16	2.0	15	1.9	11	2.9
Traders Royal	1963–present					24	0.9	34	0.7	26	1.0	10	2.6	18	1.7	22	1.2
(formerly Traders, renamed 1974)																	
Union	1982–present													21	1.4	24	1.2
UCPB	1963–present					21	1.1	29	0.9	21	1.3	9	3.2	6	4.9	7	5.2
(formerly First United, renamed 1976)																	
Total, PDKBs			36.9		49.3		56.5		57.1		52.9		58.8		58.0		72.4
PNB	1916–present	1	48.9	1	35.8	1	35.2	1	32.1	1	34.5	1	26.5	1	26.7	1	12.5
PNCB	1960–72	n.a.	n.a.	n.a.	n.a.	31	0.6	39	0.2								
Veterans	1964–85					35	0.5	18	1.7	17	2.2	18	1.9				
Total, Govt. KBs			48.9		35.8		36.3		34.0		36.8		28.3		26.7		12.5

Bank	Years											
BA	1947–present	n.a.	n.a.	15	1.9	18	2.1	12	2.5	8	4.0	10	2.9
Chartered	1873–present	n.a.	n.a.	31.0	0.8	23.0	1.3	31.0	0.6	26.0	0.9	25.0	1.0
Citibank (formerly FNCB)	1915–present	n.a.	n.a.	2.0	5.1	2.0	6.1	2.0	8.7	2.0	9.2	2.0	9.4
HSBC	1875–present	n.a.	n.a.	24.0	1.1	27.0	0.8	25.0	1.1	22.0	1.2	18.0	1.8
Total, Foreign branches		14.2	14.9	7.2	8.9		10.3		12.8		15.4		15.1
Total, All KBs		100.0	100.0	100.0	100.0		100.0		100.0		100.0		100.0

Source: Sycip, Gerra, Velago & Co., *A Study of Commercial Banks in the Philippines* (Manila: SGU & Co, various annual issues).

Abbreviations: BPI = Bank of the Philippine Islands; Comtrust = Commercial Bank and Trust Co.; Combank = Commercial Bank of Manila; FEBTC = Far East Bank and Trust Co.; PBCommunications = Philippine Bank of Communications; PCIB = Philippine Commercial and Industrial Bank (after 1983, Philippine Commercial International Bank); PBCommerce = Philippine Bank of Commerce; IBAA = Insular Bank of Asia and America; RPB = Republic Planters Bank; RCBC = Rizal Commercial Banking Corp.; UCPB = United Coconut Planters Bank; PNB = Philippine National Bank; PNCB = Philippine National Cooperative Bank; BA = Bank of America; FNCB = First National City Bank; HSBC = Hongkong and Shanghai Banking Corp; KB = commercial bank

ing window, which had been monopolized by the PNB before 1957, was increasingly used by private banks beginning in the early 1960s. As loan rates increased relative to the rediscount rates (creating a substantial profit margin), it was in the interests of banks to borrow as much as they could from the Central Bank. There were no minimum capitalization requirements from 1949 to 1966, except for an implicit rule that each new bank licensee must exceed the initial capitalization of the previous licensee.[29]

Many family conglomerates were facing a major credit crunch arising from the 1960–1962 lifting of exchange controls and the accompanying devaluation. As discussed above, banks lent primarily to those entrepreneurs fortunate enough to obtain foreign exchange licenses. When the period of decontrol began, however, many businesses (especially those most dependent on imports) were scrambling for credit. Because the best way to satisfy the credit needs of the family enterprises was to diversfy into banking, most prominent families set out to obtain bank licenses, if they had not already done so. These families included both those of old landed wealth and those families (of old and new wealth) that had been involved in the import substitution industries of the 1950s.

By the mid-1960s, one could begin to see a major evolution in the structure of the financial system. Private domestic commercial banks were increasing their dominance within the system as a whole, although the PNB and the four foreign banks remained very influential actors. A host of new entrants—representative of powerful social forces—had flocked to the banking industry. But from 1966 on, the doors were nearly shut on additional entrants: new banking licenses were not dispersed (with the exception of one new license granted in 1971), and the locus of institutional development shifted from expanding the number of banks to pushing banks to higher levels of capitalization.

In addition, it is in the mid-1960s that market interest rates began to reach ceilings imposed by the usury laws. This encouraged the formation of an unregulated money market, which provided investors with an easy means of evading the ceilings.[30] The money market was

[29] Central Bank of the Philippines, *Central Bank Annual Report* (Manila: Central Bank of the Philippines, 1960), p. 122, and interview with Carlota P. Valenzuela, March 22, 1990. See also other later issues of the *Central Bank Annual Report;* Central Bank circulars; Tan, "Philippine Monetary Policy," p. 177, and "Conduct of Monetary Policy and Quantitative Control of Credit," Discussion Paper no. 73–8, School of Economics, University of the Philippines (Quezon City, 1973), p. 14.

[30] See Jaime C. Laya, "Floating Interest Rates in the Eighties: A New Dimension in the Philippine Financial System," in *Fookien Times Philippines Yearbook, 1981–82* (Manila: Fookien Times, 1982), p. 147; and Tan, "Philippine Monetary Policy," p. 177. Statutory ceilings were evaded not only through the use of unregulated money market instruments but also through service fees and other charges that banks required of their lenders.

pioneered by investment houses, whose earnings depended overwhelmingly on short-term financial instruments (and very little on traditional merchant bank dealings in securities and equities). Because investment houses were able to skirt interest rate ceilings and offer higher rates, investors flocked to their doors.[31]

With the demise of exchange controls, other means of selective credit came to the fore. Of particular significance are changes in the rediscounting window. In 1959 and 1960, the Central Bank of the Philippines (CBP) created four broad agricultural and industrial categories that were to enjoy preferential rediscounting rates; additional broad categories were added in 1962. Not until June 1966 did the Central Bank make its first effort to outline priorities more comprehensively—so comprehensively, in fact, that (at least on paper) nearly every entrepreneur in the Philippines was a potential recipient of Central Bank largesse. "Priority I" classification, for example, was given to extremely broad categories, such as agricultural or industrial products, with "Priority II" picking up pretty much everything else, including "other nonproductive and speculative activities."[32] Given the utter absence of selectivity in the guidelines, one can surmise that other noneconomic criteria provided the true basis for "selectivity."

The placement of government deposits in private banks also supplied a rich opportunity for those able to develop the right connections. Republic Bank claimed a large chunk of government funds and lent them out liberally to related interests and government officials.[33] In 1964, the bank's financial position had become so grave that the Central Bank asked the PNB to assume its management. The owner of Overseas Bank of Manila, Emerito M. Ramos, Sr., admits to "campaigning" for deposits by paying interest rates of 24 percent, up front, to government officials who would put their agencies' funds in his bank (a deposit of P 1 million would thus yield P 240,000, or roughly $60,000, "under the table"). In addition to strong demand for loans from other sectors,

---

Because of these added charges, effective rates of interest commonly exceeded nominal statutory rates. See National Economic Council et al., *Report of the Inter-Agency Committee on the Study of Interest Rates* (Manila: National Economic Council, 1971), pp. 2, 56–62.

[31] The money market is estimated to have grown 34 percent per year between 1966 and 1973. See Victoria S. Licuanan, *An Analysis of the Institutional Framework of the Philippine Short-Term Financial Markets* (Manila: Philippine Institute for Development Studies, 1986), p. 6.

[32] Tan, "Central Banking," chap. 3, p. 26, and "Philippine Monetary Policy," p. 176; Central Bank Circular No. 223, June 25, 1966; Central Bank Circular no. 227, August 15, 1966; and R.A. (Republic Act) 265 (The Central Bank Act), Section 87.

[33] *Manila Times*, February 13 and March 3, 1963. These allegations were confirmed by a ranking Central Bank official (interview, mid-1990). In addition, there were charges that relatives of the superintendent of banks (of the Central Bank) were given positions in the bank.

his own companies borrowed much more than he had put up as initial capital for the Overseas Bank of Manila.[34] By 1968, after a bank run that spread to certain savings banks as well, the Central Bank was trying to close down Ramos's bank (albeit with great difficulty, as he had friends on the Supreme Court).

Finally, it was during 1960–1972 that the Central Bank first attempted to provide stronger sanctions against DOSRI loans. But as the cases of Republic Bank and Overseas Bank reveal, the Central Bank was far from capable of enforcing its own rules.[35] The mushrooming of banks in the early 1960s was accompanied and followed by a high degree of bank instability. The roots of bank instability are found, first of all, in the purposes for which the banks were initially formed. Loyalty is rarely to banking per se but rather to the family conglomerate that the bank is meant to serve. As Governor Gregorio Licaros remarked in 1978, "The average Filipino banker is in banking not for banking profits; he uses his bank for allied businesses." Loan portfolios are often milked by insiders, and the most abused banks soon encounter serious liquidity problems. DOSRI loan abuses were at the center of bank failures not only in the 1960s but also in the 1970s and 1980s: according to one official, there was "not a single case where the Central Bank moved [against a bank] where it didn't find signs of family operations involved."[36] Moreover, although regulations on DOSRI loans have continually been promulgated, the Central Bank is still unable to regulate the powerful family groups that diversified into banking a generation ago.

Bank Reform and Crony Abuses, 1972–1980

Given the profound weakness of regulators vis-à-vis the regulated, one might surmise that the only period in the postwar Philippines when the state may have been able to effect serious reforms in the banking industry was after the declaration of martial law by President Ferdinand Marcos in September 1972. The Joint IMF-CBP Banking Survey Commission had just completed the first comprehensive effort to address

[34] Interviews with Emerito M. Ramos, Sr., February 24 and March 17, 1990.

[35] Central Bank Circular no. 183, September 4, 1964; and Central Bank Circular no. 199, May 27, 1965. On January 13, 1971, the Central Bank promulgated particularly tough regulations against DOSRI loans. For some reason, however, the circular was weakened and revised on April 30, just three months later, perhaps in recognition of its inability to enforce it. See Central Bank Circular no. 318; and Central Bank Circular no. 318 (revised).

[36] *Far Eastern Economic Review*, April 7, 1978; and interview with Armand Fabella, June 8, 1990. Fabella was cochairman of the Joint IMF-CBP Banking Survey Commission, 1971–1972, and ranking consultant at the Central Bank from 1969 to 1989.

the problems of weak family-owned banks, and with a few modifications, its recommendations were promulgated by decree in November. Yet, as the history of "crony capitalism" shows, Marcos had personal interests that took clear precedence over the rationalization of the Philippine political economy. Developmentalist rhetoric notwithstanding, reform was not his major priority; rather, martial law merely facilitated the monopolization of state resources and privileges by Marcos and his cronies.

The reform episode of the 1970s is nonetheless worthy of careful examination. The package had three major elements. First, it led to the clear separation of functions among different types of financial institutions and extended the supervisory reach of the Central Bank to nearly the entire financial system (including the investment houses). Second, the decree introduced a major reform agenda to try to strengthen weak family-based private banks through increased capitalization requirements (to P 100 million), mergers, infusions of foreign equity, and diffusion of ownership within banks. Third, there was a formal cap on new bank licenses. According to Armand Fabella, who headed the Philippine side of the panel, there was a clear effort to reform those banks that were dominated by familial interests: "We wanted to make sure [they] would have a fighting chance to improve. We were concerned that [these banks] were being used as part of a conglomerate and used to support the projects the family were involved in. . . . The family banks just wanted to be a big frog in a small pond— they didn't want to be disturbed." After the reforms were promulgated, a Central Bank advisory group headed by Fabella oversaw banking reform efforts throughout the 1970s. The group achieved moderate success in effecting mergers (the number of private commercial banks declined from thirty-three to twenty-six between 1972 and 1977), but the ultimate problem of weak family-controlled banks remained unresolved. The regulations seeking to restrict the holdings of a particular family were easily ignored or circumvented, and in any case the Central Bank was afraid to enforce them.[37] The greatest concern, Fabella said, was economic destabilization. If families thought they were going to lose control of their banks, they would siphon off funds from their bank and perhaps trigger a bank run, the fear of which "has always been paramount" within the Central Bank because of the persistence of bank instability in the mid-1970s.[38]

---

[37] Interviews with Armand Fabella, June 8 and 12, 1990; and Memorandum of Arnulfo B. Aurellano, special assistant to Governor Licaros, October 8, 1979, p. 6. My thanks go to Robin Broad for generously sharing the Aurellano memo and certain other documents from this period.

[38] Interview with Armand Fabella, June 12, 1990. The particular instance of bank

The martial law regime's impact on the banking industry goes far beyond these halting efforts at reform. "Crony capitalism" brought unprecedented changes to the ownership structure of the banking system, as seven banks—all in a weak position—ended up in the hands of Marcos associates. Moreover, with the state machinery firmly under the control of a much smaller segment of the elite, the allocation of credit to regime favorites could proceed in a particularly unhampered fashion. The state financial institutions became "personal piggy bank[s]," flush with new funds that were then loaned out at the behest of the palace.[39] Meanwhile, certain private banks were highly favored by the Central Bank and the palace in the granting of rediscounting privileges, foreign loans, foreign swaps, and government deposits.

One of Marcos's earliest presidential decrees in September 1972 provided for a fivefold increase in the authorized capital level of the PNB, the first since 1955. In the following three years, assets nearly tripled. The DBP was given unprecedented access to Central Bank loans and advances, as its borrowings grew nearly sixfold between 1970 and 1980. Beginning later in the decade, an especially important source of funds for the two institutions was the Central Bank's Consolidated Foreign Borrowing Program, or "the jumbo loans" program.[40]

The PNB has long had a reputation as an institution from which it is "difficult to borrow . . . unless you have phone calls" from influential persons. As discussed above, both its loan portfolio and that of the DBP were raided from the time of their inception. Even given this history, however, it can be said that Marcos managed an attack of unprecedented proportions. "Both banks became insolvent," the World Bank notes dryly, "largely due to problem loans granted on political rather than economic grounds." "Behest loans" (i.e., loans made at the behest of the palace) bloated the size of their nonperforming assets to such an extent that when rehabilitation did take place in 1986, it involved the reduction of DBP assets by 86 percent and of PNB assets by 67 percent.[41]

---

instability to which he was referring was the 1974 failure of Continental Bank, which was the worst shock yet to the postwar financial system. It was followed in 1976 by the failure of General Bank and Trust Company. In each case, the banks were not only weakened by DOSRI loan abuse but had also become overextended in the poorly collateralized and unstable money market.

[39] Details of changes in bank ownership can be found in Hutchcroft, "Patrimonial State, Predatory Oligarchy," chap. 6 and 7. The term "personal piggy bank" was used by U.S. prosecutors in the 1990 racketeering trial of Imelda Marcos and refers to the PNB. *Philippines Daily Globe*, April 5, 1990.

[40] *Philippine National Bank, 60th Anniversary*, pp. 17, 22; Emmanuel S. de Dios, ed., *An Analysis of the Philippine Economic Crisis* (Quezon city: University of the Philippines Press, 1984), p. 37. Perhaps 43 percent and 29 percent of total jumbo loans went to the DBP and the PNB, respectively. These figures are extrapolated from CBP, *Central Bank Statistical Bulletin* (Manila: CBP, 1987 and 1988 vols.).

[41] Interview with Armand Fabella, June 8, 1990; World Bank, *Philippines Financial Sector*

Priorities for the rediscounting window were once again adjusted in 1974. This was the first major adjustment since 1967, when export production was added to the voluminous list. But despite appearances of rationalization, the list remained nearly all-encompassing. The PNB, not surprisingly, was consistently able to finance a large portion of its assets with rediscounts. Among private banks, the most clear-cut cases of favoritism began in 1977 and continued into the early 1980s. In these years, three banks that were controlled by Marcos cronies (Allied Bank, International Corporate Bank, and Republic Planters Bank) financed 28–52 percent of their assets from subsidized credit, a level that far exceeds the average of all private domestic commercial banks.[42]

Allied Bank provides an especially dramatic illustration of the dynamics of the allocation process. From their initial purchase of a bank that failed in 1976 (Genbank, renamed Allied Bank), tobacco magnate Lucio Tan and his partner, Willy Co (from the textiles industry), adroitly used political connections to effect mercurial growth in the bank's total assets; Allied was the thirteenth-largest bank at year-end 1977 and the third largest bank by year-end 1979 (exceeded in size only by the PNB and Citibank).

After Genbank failed in late 1976, five business groups expressed their interest in the bank. Tan and Co not only won out over other interested parties but also struck an exceptional deal. According to charges made in a recent court case, Tan allegedly conspired with Central Bank governor Licaros to buy Genbank for less than 1 percent of its actual value. Marcos himself is thought to have been cut into the deal with a 60 percent equity stake.[43] After acquiring the bank, Allied officials enjoyed particularly favored access to the Central Bank. Not coincidentally, it seems, Allied was among the most favored commercial banks in its access not only to the rediscounting window

Study, p. 16. Reflecting on the history of the PNB, a pillar of the banking industry said that "PNB was some kind of a milking cow . . . with low interest rates and low credit standards." Interview with Jose B. Fernandez, Jr., former governor of the Central Bank (1984–1990), April 6, 1990.

[42] On rediscounting priorities, see Winifrida V. Mejia, "Financial Policies and Industrial Promotion," in *Industrial Promotion Policies in the Philippines*, ed. Romeo M. Bautista, John H. Power, and Associates (Manila: Philippine Institute for Development Studies, 1979), pp. 409–28. Quantitative rediscounting data are from Sycip, Gorres, Velayo & Co. annual studies of commercial banks; Philippine National Bank Division of Economics and Research, *The Philippine Commercial Banking System* (Manila: PNB, various annual issues); and Patrick and Moreno, "Philippine Private Domestic Commercial Banking," pp. 348–49.

[43] *Far Eastern Economic Review*, January 14, 1977, pp. 55–56, and February 11, 1977, p. 104; *Manila Chronicle*, August 28, 1990; *Newsday*, August 28, 1990; and anonymous interviews, mid-1990. On Marcos's ownership stake, see *Manila Chronicle*, July 28, 1989. See also *Far Eastern Economic Review*, December 15, 1988, pp. 112–16.

(which financed an average of 18.4 percent of assets between 1977 and 1980) but also to swap privileges (which financed the equivalent of 18.1 percent of assets in the same period).[44] Moreover, Allied had privileged access to government-guaranteed foreign loans, including "jumbo loans."[45]

There are many other cases of private banks receiving special favors from the Central Bank and the presidential palace. Government deposits were central to the success of Marcos's crony Eduardo Cojuangco, who acquired an enormous manufacturing and financial empire over the course of martial law. Beginning in the mid-1970s, enormous sums of money from the (publicly decreed) coconut levy were deposited interest-free in the privately held United Coconut Planters Bank, enabling it to rise from the nineteenth-largest bank at year-end 1976 to the fourth-largest bank at year-end 1983. (The rise and decline of banks is charted in Table 6.2.) It was the controversy over the allocation of selective credit that led to the resignation of Governor Licaros in early 1981. As a former high-ranking official remarked, "He got caught with his hand in the till."[46] The multilateral institutions, long at odds with Licaros, likely expected that under his successor, Jaime Laya, the way would be clear for thoroughgoing reforms.

V. FURTHER REFORM, FURTHER FAILURE, 1980–1983

In the midst of the morass of crony abuse afflicting the Central Bank, a textbook-style liberalizing reform effort began in 1980. Supported by the World Bank, the IMF, and Finance Minister Cesar Virata (but largely opposed by Licaros and the Central Bank), its aim was to reorient the financial system toward longer-term intermediation. This goal was to be accomplished by (1) formally liberalizing interest rates, and (2) breaking down the functional specialization of different elements of the financial system (imposed in the 1972 reforms) and creating "expanded commercial banks" or universal banks that are able to underwrite securities and take equity positions in "nonallied" enterprises.[47]

---

[44] Interview with Leo Gonzaga, former business correspondent of the *Far Eastern Economic Review*, February 6, 1990. Sycip, Gorres, Velayo & Co., *Study of Commercial Banks*, various annual issues. Former senior Central Bank officials have confirmed that the Licaros–Willy Co relationship was central to these favored allocations, particularly in the case of the swaps.

[45] CBP, *Total Foreign Exchange Liabilities as of December 31, 1986*, vol. 4 (Manila: CBP, 1986); *CB Review*, August/September 1982, p. 23; and CBP, *Central Bank Statistical Bulletin*, various issues.

[46] Anonymous interview, mid-1990.

[47] Though interest rate ceilings began to be adjusted after 1973 to better reflect market

The interest rate ceilings had long been blamed for skewing credit allocation. As Hugh Patrick and Honovata A. Moreno write, "The ceilings have distorted incentives and biased lending toward the most creditworthy—large firms, those with excellent collateral—and away from the more risky; toward large and against small transactions, where administrative costs are relatively higher; toward known, established borrowers and against those where costs of evaluation are greater; and toward the short term." The 1974 International Labour Office study had termed the ceilings a "regulated monopoly," with high spreads "producing windfall profits for the banking system."[48] But judged by its initial goals of promoting longer-term lending, encouraging equity investments by banks, and permitting "free-market" determination of interest rates, the end results of the 1980 reform package were largely unsuccessful. The formal lifting of interest rate ceilings produced few results, as bankers have been able to use their oligopolistic power to set a range of prices within the banking industry. The Central Bank did not want competition to "run out of control" and has not challenged collusive practices among the banks.[49]

Larger economic and political crises were afflicting the martial law regime during this period. In the end these crises not only ensured the demise of the reform effort but also did far more to reshape the financial system than did the reform package itself. In 1981, the country experienced a major financial crisis, triggered when a Filipino-Chinese industrialist-banker by the name of Dewey Dee fled the country without paying nearly $85 million in debt, much of it in short-term commercial paper. All investment houses and banks with loans to Dee or his associates experienced a major run, and two major investment houses collapsed. The money market never fully recovered, as investors shunned commercial paper for the more secure time deposits of commercial banks. Several commercial banks were badly shaken by the

---

conditions, effective loan interest rates usually exceeded formal ceilings. See World Bank/IMF, *Philippines*, p. ii.

[48] Patrick and Moreno, "Philippine Private Domestic Commercial Banking," p. 351; and international Labour Office, *Sharing in Development: A Programme of Employment, Equity, and Growth for the Philippines* (Geneva: International Labour Office, 1974), pp. 240, 242.

[49] Governor Jaime Laya said that the Central Bank welcomes a "certain degree of competition" but does not want rates to "run out of control." *Far Eastern Economic Review*, March 19, 1982, p. 75. It is ironic to note that the bankers' oligopolistic power did not come to full fruition until 1981; before "liberalization," there was less need for collusion because the ceilings effectively set the deposit rate. Since "liberalization," however, the Bankers Association of the Philippines (BAP) and particularly the largest of its member banks seem to have enjoyed the full cooperation of the Central Bank as they set a range of prices within the banking industry. Interview with Armand Fabella, June 8, 1990; interview with Jaime C. Laya, May 21, 1990; anonymous interview, May 1990; and interview with Edgardo J. Carvajal, executive officer, BAP, May 14, 1990.

crisis and were saved only when the Central Bank provided the funds for equity infusions by key government entities, thereby greatly increasing the government's stake in the banking industry.

The triumph of cronyism over reform is especially well illustrated by the failure of efforts to transform the system of selective credit. In their 1979 report, the IMF and the World Bank observed that "the Central Bank's lending policy is a major source of uncertainty in the financial sector," both because of frequent "rearrangements of credit priorities" and because rediscount windows were "often partly closed for the purpose of monetary management." They suggested that the Central Bank move toward a "non-allocative rediscounting policy of the 'lender-of-last-resort' type" and thus provide greater predictability to the banks.[50]

Governor Laya claimed that "the number of areas given preferential rates has been reduced and properly defined" and declared the Central Bank's intention "to discourage dependence of financial institutions on cheap Central Bank funds and instead make the rediscount window operate more as a lender of last resort." Despite such declarations, the Central Bank proceeded to move in nearly the opposite direction. Rather than a consolidation of priority areas, one finds instead a mushrooming of new rediscounting windows in the years 1981–1983, covering everything from tobacco trading to the trading of blue-chip stocks to coconut milling.[51] As Eli M. Remolona and Mario B. Lamberte note, "Instead of being the 'lender of last resort' as spelled out in the 1980 financial reforms, the Central Bank... continued to be the 'lender of first resort.' "[52] There are seemingly two reasons for this: (1) the government's countercyclical response to the 1980–1982 world recession, and (2) the Central Bank's reluctance to give up its discretionary power over allocation of credit.

At the same time as the World Bank and the IMF were pushing for a "nonallocative (i.e., nontargeted) rediscounting policy," the World Bank was applauding increases in targeted credit for nontraditional exports; between 1977 and 1980, this category steadily increased its share of total loans from 5 percent to 30 percent. In effect, the mul-

[50] World Bank/IMF, *Philippines*, pp. 57–58.
[51] Laya, "Floating Interest Rates in the Eighties," p. 149. Somehow oblivious of the morass of cronyism around him, Finance Minister Cesar Virata assured the World Bank that the "preferential rediscounting policy shall constantly be reviewed in order to ensure that only sectors justified by *rigorous economic analysis* will receive preferential treatment." Letter from Cesar Virata to the World Bank, March 13, 1981 (emphasis added). See also Armida S. San Jose, "Central Bank Rediscounting Operations," *CB Review*, September 1983, pp. 12–28, 16–17.
[52] Eli M. Remolona and Mario B. Lamberte, "Financial Reforms and the Balance-of-Payments Crisis: The Case of the Philippines, 1980–83," *Philippine Review of Economics and Business* 23, nos. 1 and 2 (1986): 101–41.

tilateral institutions seem to have been willing temporarily to sacrifice one goal (a nonallocative rediscounting policy) for another (the promotion of nontraditional exports). The relative success of the second goal must be counted as one of the few cases in which the multilateral institutions were relatively successful in achieving their goals of policy reform. But as a later World Bank study reveals, even this success had major limitations. The shift to financing of nontraditional exports has benefited a relatively few large enterprises (most likely those controlled by the already established oligarchic families). The World Bank concedes that it is "highly likely that most new and smaller exporters are denied access"; only two-hundred to three-hundred export firms, out of about three-thousand had access to the window. Moreover, the nontraditional exports are highly import-dependent and have done little to ease the country's recurring balance-of-payments difficulties.[53]

In the midst of these halting efforts at reform, cronyism continued to dominate the allocation of selective credit. A few banks continued to enjoy especially favorable access to the rediscounting window, notably the Republic Planters Bank, which was controlled by Roberto S. Benedicto, the crony in charge of the sugar industry.[54] At the same time, a few banks grabbed especially large quantities of foreign exchange swaps. Security Bank, the bank that Marcos used for laundering money, financed more than 100 percent of its assets from swaps between 1982 and 1984. Other banks, such as the Traders Royal Bank (also controlled by Benedicto), grabbed major allocations as well.[55] In summary, despite certain shifts that took place in the

---

[53] *CB Review*, July 29, 1980, p. 4, and May 1987, pp. 24–25; and World Bank, "Philippines Staff Approach Report on the Industrial Finance Project," Report no. 3331-PH (Washington D.C., World Bank, 1981), p. 7, and *Philippines Financial Sector Study*, p. 143. As the World Bank explains, "Export expansion has been concentrated on a few items and backward linkages with the rest of the economy have been limited." World Bank, "Philippines Staff Approach," p. 1. The obstacles to this export expansion actually go much deeper: entrepreneurs of small and medium-sized firms who might be wholeheartedly oriented toward exports have very little political clout. See Emmanuel S. de Dios, "A Political Economy of Philippine Policy-Making," in *Economic Policy-Making in the Asia-Pacific Region*, ed. John W. Langford and K. Lorne Brownsey (Halifax, Nova Scotia: Institute for Research on Public Policy, 1990), pp. 109–47.

[54] Between 1979 and 1982, Republic Planters Bank financed 44–52 percent of its total assets through rediscounts. See Sycip, Gorres, and Velayo annual studies of commercial banks; PNB, *Philippine Commercial Banking System*, annual issues; and Patrick and Moreno, "Philippine Private Domestic Commercial Banking," pp. 348–49. As de Dios discusses, the sugar industry's heavy use of the rediscounting window was an important issue in the mounting tensions between "technocrats" and "cronies" in 1982. See de Dios, "Erosion of the Dictatorship," pp. 107–8.

[55] Security Bank's link to Marcos is discussed in *Malaya*, March 4, 1986; *Manila Chronicle*, October 1, 1989; and *Far Eastern Economic Review*, May 23, 1991, p. 65. Marcos's financial adviser, Rolando C. Gapud, was president of the bank. Data on swaps come from various annual issues of CBP, *Fact Book: Philippine Financial System* (Manila: CBP), and Sycip, Gorres, Velayo, & Co., *Study of Commercial Banks*, various annual issues.

sectoral allocation of credit during this period, political logics continued to overwhelm economic rationale in the allocation of Central
Bank largesse. Efforts at reform largely failed and "selective squander"
endured.

VI. Cleaning Up: The Fernandez Years, 1984–1990

In the aftermath of the assassination of Benigno Aquino, the Philippines faced its worst balance-of-payments crisis since 1949. When it
became apparent in late 1983 that the Central Bank had been over-
stating its international reserves for two years, Governor Laya was
forced to step down, thus making him the second governor in a row
to resign under a cloud of controversy. Jose B. "Jobo" Fernandez, a
veteran banker, became governor of a tarnished Central Bank just as
the economy was going into a free fall and the Marcos regime was
facing unprecedented popular opposition. Under these conditions, crisis management supplanted the 1980 reform agenda, and the Central
Bank's work became, according to Fabella, "basically a fire engine job."[56]
Fernandez proved more than ready to adopt draconian measures to
control the money supply, which had ballooned to particularly awesome
proportions in the wake of the May 1984 elections. The economy nearly
ground to a halt, but the impact of the crisis on the banking sector was
twofold. Three commercial banks (and a large savings bank) failed,
and efforts to keep the PNB and the DBP afloat drained 20 percent of
the national budget in 1985.[57] At the same time, other banks enjoyed
lucrative income from the high-interest "Jobo bills" that were floated as
part of Fernandez's stabilization program.

In this latest round of bank instability, the Central Bank did not
coordinate a rescue of banks by government firms. Fernandez rejected
the post–Dewey Dee strategy of shoring up the weak banks and displayed a readiness to let certain banks fail. Nonetheless, there was a
marked rise in emergency loans, which reflected the gravity of the crisis.
The World Bank complained that "procedures governing...emer-
gency advances to banks in difficulty appear to be ad hoc in nature
and lacking consistent application." Fernandez's many critics, in fact,
accused him of using personalistic criteria in deciding which banks to
close and which banks to support.[58]

[56] Interview with Armand Fabella, June 8, 1980.

[57] *Far Eastern Economic Review*, June 4, 1987, p. 75.

[58] Jose B. Fernandez, "The Momentum of Economic Recovery," Speech delivered to
the Management Association of the Philippines, June 29, 1987; World Bank, *Philippines
Financial Sector Study*, pp. 133, 159; and CBP, *Central Bank Annual Report*, various issues.
See also Hutchcroft, "Patrimonial State, Predatory Oligarchy," chap. 8.

Other selective credit programs were slashed, both as part of the Fernandez stabilization program and because of governmental budget constraints. Total rediscounts were cut in half between 1983 and 1984 and reduced by more than half again in the following year. Rediscounts also began to finance a much smaller portion of total commercial bank assets.[59] In a historic shift, the Central Bank in November 1985 reduced the subsidy element of its rediscounting program: it adjusted rediscounting rates to market rates, removed the fixed spreads that had long brought windfall profits to financial institutions, eliminated the ceilings on lending rates, and established a single rate for all categories of rediscounting. Despite the Central Bank's claim that rediscounting had been transformed from a tool of credit allocation into a "liquidity mechanism," it in fact continued to play some role in selective credit allocation: in the face of scarcity, the rediscounting window concentrated its resources on providing working capital for exporters. But although rediscounts for nontraditional exports increased as a proportion of total rediscounts, they actually decreased in absolute terms.[60] By 1987, Governor Fernandez was declaring, with some exaggeration, that the Central Bank's "developmental function" is now "a thing of the past."[61]

Yet although programs proclaiming benefits for economic development were being reduced in scale, developmental efforts on behalf of the large banks were more plentiful than ever. At the heart of Fernandez's stabilization program was a scheme that ensured big profits for the banks: the floating of "Jobo bills," as well as treasury bills, which provided the banks with large quantities of low-risk, high-yielding investments. As the *Asian Wall Street Journal* reported in 1986, "Local banks snapped up the profitable bills, and their customers went without credit." At the suggestion of the BAP (of which Fernandez had formerly been president), the minimum lot available to savers was

[59] World Bank, *Philippines Financial Sector Study*, p. 133; Sycip, Gorres, and Velayo & Co., *Study of Commercial Banks*, various annual issues; and PNB, *Philippine Commercial Banking System*, annual issues.

[60] Other factors for the decline in rediscounts are (1) "the reduction of CBP's role as a credit allocator"; (2) the high liquidity of the banking system, due to slack demand; and (3) "the increasing number of banks (notably rural banks) disqualified . . . because of their high arrearages." See World Bank, *Philippines Financial Sector Study*, pp. 133, 143; and *CB Review*, November 1985, p. 1. In the midst of these reforms, Central Bank officials became more forthcoming in discussing past limitations of the rediscounting window. There was also acknowledgment of major problems of credit fungibility, which, in turn, calls into question all Central Bank data on how credit is allocated among various economic sectors. See Purita F. Neri, "Current Policy Considerations on Credit Allocation," *CB Review*, March 1985, p. 9.

[61] *Business World*, November 16, 1987. By 1991, the major government-managed credit programs had been withdrawn from the Central Bank at World Bank insistence, and only the export rediscount facility remained. *Newsday*, April 19, 1991.

set at a high level "so that the traditional market segment of banks, which consists of small and medium-sized investors, can be retained by them."[62] As severe austerity measures were being imposed on the general population, many bankers and others with large sums of liquid assets cleaned up.

As the decade progressed, there was an important shift in the direction of lending between commercial banks and the government. With the reduction in rediscounting, commercial banks had less opportunity to borrow from the government; rather, they became major lenders to the government through their purchases of government securities. In terms of bank profits, gains from holding high-yielding government securities compensated for the loss of subsidized credit. By 1990, the value of outstanding government securities actually exceeded the value of all bank deposits. Moreover, many banks enjoyed enormous profits from their role as dealers within what was a restricted market.[63]

Another policy that was of particular benefit to the largest of the private banks was the 1987 transfer of large quantities of government deposits from government institutions to five private banks, including the bank that Fernandez had headed before his entry into the government, Far East Bank and Trust Company. Initially, the banks were not required to pay any interest on these deposits, but in 1988 the government asked for 5 percent interest on its money. Using these low-cost (or no-cost) funds, the banks could turn around and invest in government securities yielding 20 percent interest and more. Funds

---

[62] *Asian Wall Street Journal,* June 13, 1986; and *Times Journal,* October 16, 1984, quoting a BAP document. At the same time, the BAP sought to use interest rate differentials to "shield the banking system from a massive shift of deposits into CB[P]/Treasury Bills." The Central Bank acknowledges that their bills "are aimed at the upper bracket of the market" and that the minimum placement "excludes most savers or the general public which the banks depend upon for much of their business." *CB Review,* June 1984, p. 23.

[63] In August 1990, outstanding government debt instruments totaled P 256 million ($9.9 billion), whereas deposits in the banking system were P 220 million. *Far Eastern Economic Review,* November 8, 1990, p. 48. "The government's recurring budget deficits have been a boon for the banks. They purchased and resold at least 70 percent of the P 408 billion in treasury bills and other government securities issued [in 1990]. At a conservatively estimated margin of 1 percent on the sales, commercial banks' income from these risk-free instruments would have been at least P 2.8 billion." *Far Eastern Economic Review,* January 24, 1991, p. 48.

Tan explains that the auction for government securities (GS) is limited to eighteen financial institutions, fourteen of which are banks. "The features of closed dealership and large denominations have turned the market for GS into a protected one for banks, conceding them a degree of monopoly power over GS trading. The restricted dealership has disallowed fair auction or competitive bidding. . . . An open dealership combined with smaller denomination issues would definitely increase the market for GS and lower their interest rates." Edita Tan, "How to Bring Down the Interest Rate on Loans," *Issues and Letters,* vol. 1, no. 10 (1991), pp. 3–4.

borrowed from the government were re-lent to the government at much higher rates![64] This arrangement gave a fat advantage to these five banks and was a significant factor in the increasingly dominant position that they enjoyed by the decade's end.

The PNB, meanwhile, was rehabilitated from rags to riches, as its financial woes were transferred to the government, just as had happened after the fiasco that followed the establishment of the bank in 1916. In 1986, P 47 million (over \$2 billion) in assets was transferred to the Asset Privatization Trust, and P 55 billion in liabilities was transferred to the central government. A similar process occurred at the DBP. Shorn of its burdens, the PNB invested heavily in government securities and began to post hefty profits by the late 1980s.[65]

After the bank failures of the mid-1980s, Fernandez devoted significant attention to the problems of weak banks and DOSRI loan abuse.[66] When the Aquino government came to power in 1986, the Central Bank hoped that the new administration would use its emergency powers to decree important reforms in the supervisory structure of the banking system. Nineteen proposed amendments were submitted to the presidential palace, most of which focused on curbing DOSRI abuse. But only two of the amendments were acted upon, and the task of bank reform was left to the newly convened Congress.[67]

To bolster his position perhaps, Fernandez invited a World Bank mission to examine problems in the banking sector. Its 1988 report discusses three major issues: (1) frequent lawsuits against Central Bank personnel and weak laws and regulations dealing with bank supervision, for which it proposed a major strengthening of the regulators vis-à-vis the regulated; (2) too many small weak banks, for which it proposed consolidation of the banking sector; and (3) high profit rates for the

[64] The other four banks were Bank of the Philippine Islands, Metropolitan Bank, United Coconut Planters Bank, and Philippine Commercial International Bank. After deposits were withdrawn from private banks in 1989 (primarily to control excess liquidity in the monetary system), government financial institutions again became the government depository banks. See *Manila Chronicle*, June 2, August 3, and December 27, 1989, and January 5, January 15, and January 22, 1990.

[65] World Bank, *Philippines Financial Sector Study*, p. 16; and *Far Eastern Economic Review*, June 1, 1989, p. 68.

[66] As Fernandez admitted in 1986: "I spend an inordinate amount of time looking at reports on individual [banking] institutions. The system has got to be purified." *Asian Wall Street Journal*, June 13, 1986. More recently, Fernandez remarked that although his closing of banks in the mid-1980s had heightened the "fear of being caught" for DOSRI abuses, the Central Bank's ability to prevent such abuses is "still not adequate." Interview with Jose B. Fernandez, April 6, 1990.

[67] The proposed amendments would have added requirements for the processing of loans, given the Monetary Board more power to curb DOSRI loans, increased penalties for violations of the General Banking Act, and given "cease-and-desist" powers to the Central Bank.

large banks, for which it proposed increased levels of competition through the licensing of new banks and other means. As with earlier reform efforts, however, there have been far more pronouncements than concrete results. World Bank conditionality notwithstanding, Congress has displayed little enthusiasm to strengthen the hand of the Central Bank. Regulators remain largely ineffectual and the problem of weak banks endures.[68] Meanwhile, the large banks continue to thrive in an environment of languid competition.

In effect, the stronger and the weaker banks exist in substantial harmony, despite their contrasting approaches to banking. The stronger banks are indeed more profitable in terms of bank profits. But it is also important to remember that the weaker banks are playing a critical role in profit making for the family conglomerate even when their bank profits may be relatively low. The Philippine banking system, therefore, offers two routes to success. If bankers are in business for the sake of bank profits, it is probably difficult to find profit margins much more lucrative than those available in the Philippines. If, on the other hand, banks are established primarily to support the family conglomerate, the loose regulatory environment provides enormous possibilities for milking the loan portfolio to promote high profits in one's related enterprises. In short, as long as an oligarchic family has a stake in a bank, the possibilities for further enrichment are legion.

Throughout the extensive history of preferential credit programs in the Philippines, one finds far more "selective squander" than developmental success; political logics have swamped economic rationale in determining the allocation of selective credit. First, state financial institutions might have played a central role in development, given their influential position in the larger financial system. But the PNB and the DBP have been repeatedly milked and have been restored to health only at great cost to the public treasury. Second, foreign exchange allocations in the 1950s could have been a potent tool of industrial planning, but the Central Bank dispensed licenses to political favorites with little regard for larger developmental goals. Third, the rediscounting window might have given the Central Bank great power to promote the development of specific industries, but its allocation was all too rarely determined by economic criteria. Fourth, the allocation of swaps and foreign loans in the 1970s and 1980s would seemingly have given the Central Bank powerful leverage over commercial banks. But cronyism, not reform, determined the agenda. In summary, al-

---

[68] In the wake of recent legal actions ta'.en against the Central Bank, one Central Bank official was quoted in mid-1991 as saying that "we're helpless now" if any new crises hit the banking sector. *Far Eastern Economic Review*, July 18, 1991, p. 54.

though there is a great deal of selectivity in the system of preferential credit in the Philippines, favoritism and particularistic plunder are a larger part of the story than are sectoral pressure or careful government targeting. The system of "selective squander" provides a rich trough from which Philippine oligarchs can feed, yet it inhibits the country as a whole from enjoying the feast of sustained economic growth.

Even in the midst of change, one can see persistence in certain basic patterns of how private banks raid the public trough for particularistic benefits. Budget constraints forced a shrinking of the rediscount window in the mid-1980s, thus depriving commercial banks of an easy source of subsidized credit. But another windfall came their way in the form of high-interest government securities. The type of privileges available from the state may change across time, but there is great continuity in how these privileges are disproportionately allocated among particular banks and particular individuals. At one point, certain institutions will benefit more than others in their access to rediscounts and swaps; at another point, certain banks will benefit disproportionately in the allocation of government deposits and branch licenses. The Central Bank's power to dispense privilege has been squandered for particularistic gain, and the Central Bank itself has failed to acquire the institutional leverage necessary for promoting important reforms in the commercial banking sector. In fact, the Central Bank is now severely hobbled by the enormous financial losses it suffered in the massive give-away programs of both the Marcos and the Aquino regimes.[69]

Why does one find such prevalent and persistent rent seeking in Philippine preferential credit allocation? As argued at the outset, one cannot understand the political logic of this system of "selective squander" outside of a larger examination of the patrimonial nature of the state and the extent to which a predatory oligarchy plunders that state for particularistic gain. There is a weak distinction between the "official" sphere and the "private" sphere and a high degree of arbitrariness in the operations of the state. Indeed, the administrative and legal apparatus is unable to promote the "political and procedural predictability" necessary for nurturing more advanced forms of capitalism.[70] In addition, the Philippine state is continually plundered by an oligarchy which relies on the state apparatus for wealth accumulation but which at the same time enjoys an independent economic base outside the state itself. Because of the state's captivity to particularistic interests, it is incapable of playing a more coherent role in guiding economic development.

[69] See *Far Eastern Economic Review*, July 23, 1992, pp. 44–46.
[70] Weber, *Economy and Society*, vol. 2, p. 1095.

Prevailing patterns of state-oligarchy relations—those which shaped the system of selective squander—clearly stunt the development of the Philippine economy. Indeed, until the oligarchy's control over the state is dismantled and there is greater development of the state apparatus, attempts at genuine reform will continue to be hampered by a highly uncongenial political environment. In other words, until there are changes at the level of the state, short-term agendas will predominate in economic policy-making, and the country will remain unable to move coherently along either of two major paths of economic development: the model of a high degree of state involvement in economic trans-formation, as found in the East Asian newly industrializing countries; or the laissez-faire model peddled by the multilateral institutions.

What, then, might induce such a major transformation within the Philippine political economy? In examining potential sources of change, it is important to turn our attention, once again, to a brief examination of the international context within which patrimonial fea-tures have flourished. Now that the U.S. military bases have departed the country, the Philippines and its entire political economy are clearly at a crossroads. For the first time in modern history, clientalist relations with the United States will no longer insulate it from external economic pressures and shield the country from potential external threats. These new imperatives in the international environment may hopefully en-courage a long-term process of change in the relationship between the state and dominant economic interests.[71]

Throughout most of this century, the Philippine oligarchy has dis-played tremendous talent in exploiting the opportunities provided by the international dole. Its major external concern has been how to secure sufficient external funds to keep the economy moving and how to ensure continued U.S. sponsorship for its domestic hegemony. With the removal of the bases, however, external resources are likely to decline; new talents—and, in all likelihood, the emergence of new social forces—will be necessary to guarantee national economic survival. In the future, the country will be under growing pressure to institute major economic reforms and to reorient government, business, and finance toward internationally competitive modes of operation. If goals of economic development are to be reached, thoroughgoing reform of the financial sector will be necessary. The banks must finally be har-nessed as a positive rather than an obstructive force in achieving larger developmental objectives.

[71] For a more detailed discussion of the potential dynamics of change, see Hutchcroft, "Patrimonial State, Predatory Oligarchy," chap. 2.

PART III

LATIN AMERICA

CHAPTER SEVEN

Regulatory Revenge: The Politics of Free-Market Financial Reforms in Chile

LAURA A. HASTINGS

In 1974, after four decades of state-led policies of credit allocation, Chile's newly installed military regime embarked on a sweeping reform of the country's financial markets. Banks were authorized to set their own bank deposit and lending rates and to disburse credit according to market, rather than government, imperatives. The policy was initially successful, and observers began to refer to Chile's performance as the "economic miracle."

In 1982, Chile underwent a severe economic downturn, and by 1983, the banking system had collapsed; the "magic of the marketplace" had turned malevolent. To head off widespread bank failures, the central bank intervened in eight financial institutions, giving the government control of 70 percent of the domestic banking sector. By 1985, Chile began to recover, recording strong growth, low inflation, and a more diversified export structure. But through the end of the decade, the central bank continued to hold over 25 percent of the total bank loan portfolio. Chile's radical free-market experiment resulted in a changed, but nevertheless substantial, government role in the allocation of credit. What explains this pattern?

This chapter argues that before the military coup in 1973, most socioeconomic sectors in Chile had developed strong vested interests in government subsidies. Under a democratic regime, private sector groups exercised substantial influence, even veto power, over the country's economic decision-making. The *grupos económicos*, or extended family enterprises, ran their fiefdoms with support from state credit agencies. From 1930 to 1973, credit policy shifted somewhat in response to changing political coalitions, but government intervention in credit allocation was a constant.

The military takeover in September 1973 ended this close public-private collaboration in economic policy-making. Under a neoliberal banner, an insulated economic team crafted policies that favored financial over industrial concerns. The liberalization drive itself created new interests and new political coalitions. In 1983, the widespread collapse of private financial firms revealed that the mix of financial liberalization and inadequate supervision could be extremely costly. The crisis brought the state firmly back into the business of allocating credit. The Chilean government used new policy instruments—central bank bailouts, the reissuing of bank shares to the public, and private pension funds—to restructure the financial sector. Bankers found themselves with very few institutional or political grounds for taking part in these decisions.

A centralized, insulated style of financial decision making continues today under a democratically elected government; the central bank and regulatory agencies continue to guide the operation of Chile's financial sector. Many of the grupo conglomerates have been disbanded, and although several of the same powerful families continue to own and operate banks, the face of the Chilean private sector has changed; new international players have emerged, and bankers have developed a more arms-length relationship with the state.

Section I describes the historical development of the system of state-led credit allocation in Chile, highlighting the characteristics of the Chilean economic organization, the economics group, and the increasing political tensions over economic decision making. Section II analyzes the 1975 financial reform, and the last two sections explore the consequences of sweeping liberalization on the political economy of the financial sector.

I. The Origin and Development of State-subsidized Financing

Historically, the Chilean financial system was driven largely by the needs of primary goods exporters. Beginning in the early nineteenth century, British trading companies worked with private merchant banks and state officials to handle the financing, transport, and marketing of Chile's agricultural and mining exports. By 1891, twenty-seven banks operated in Chile, of which seven were wholly foreign-owned. Government intervention was limited to the state mortgage bank, founded in 1855, which supplied capital (by purchasing the land-owners' mortgages) to upgrade irrigation facilities.[1]

[1] By 1914, the two British-owned banks alone controlled approximately one-quarter

In 1925, the U.S.-led Kemmerer Commission arrived to put Chile on the gold standard and to set up a central bank and bank-monitoring agency. Chile's fifteen domestic and ten foreign (mainly British) commercial banks welcomed these developments to stabilize financial markets. The central bank was organized as a semi-public institution (with joint ownership by the government, commercial banks, and the general public) and was granted the sole right to print currency. The supervisory agency, a separate institution, was charged with examining banks and regulating their operations.[2]

State-led Industrial Credit: CORFO

The collapse of trade associated with the Great Depression justified to Chile's economic elite increased state participation in credit allocation. After a few years of orthodox monetary policies, the central bank began in 1935 to control interest rates on bank deposits. For most years until 1974, the maximum legal interest rate to depositors was less than the rate of inflation; in some years, it was sharply so. Low bank deposit rates financed low interest rates to favored borrowers. Chile's state banks increased their share of total loans, primarily to the agricultural sector.

The Alessandri administration (1934–1938) enhanced the system of preferential credits to landowners and nitrite exporters through commercial bank legislation. By classifying the type of assets that could be counted toward the reserve requirement, the government was able to exercise direct controls on particular kinds of credit expansion. In 1935, a preferential loan rate was applied to wheat credits, and in 1937, this policy was extended to all agricultural loans.

Industry did not receive preferential financial treatment until the Popular Front administration—which united Radicals, Communists, and Socialists—came to power in 1939.[3] Representing new groups in Chile, the administration under Pedro Aguirre Cerda set out to speed up Chile's industrialization process. The state mortgage bank and its

---

of all deposits of the banking system in Chile. See David Joslin, *A Century of Banking in Latin America* (London: Oxford University Press, 1963), pp. 110, 182–83.

[2] Out of a total of fifteen members on the central bank's board of directors, four were appointed by the state, four were selected from Congress, three were nominated by private national and foreign banks, and four by other business and labor groups, thus corresponding to a formula proposed by the Kemmerer Commission. See Paul W. Drake, *The Money Doctor in the Andes: The Kemmerer Missions, 1923–1933* (Durham: Duke University Press, 1989), pp. 76–124.

[3] An Institute of Industrial Credit was created in 1928, but its resources were small. See World Bank, *Chile: A Country in Transition* (Washington, D.C.: World Bank, 1979), p. 46.

export bank were not equipped to embark on new lending, nor was Chile's private financial system organized to finance an industrialization drive. The major intermediary, commercial banks, offered mostly short-term loans, steering clear of riskier, longer-term industrial projects. The privately run Santiago stock market, a venerable institution established in 1893, raised funds mostly for its select members. In 1939, the Popular Front government established a state development agency to provide longer-term financing to the emerging Chilean industrial sector. Over the course of the next thirty years, the state development company (Corporación de Fomento de la Producción or CORFO) functioned as financier, investor, and entrepreneur, extending credit at reduced interest rates, making direct investments, and guaranteeing outside loans to both public and private enterprises.[4]

At the outset, CORFO simply extended long-term credit to industry. In its original mandate, CORFO was to draw its capital base from state contributions, receiving an average of about 5 to 6 percent of the national budget. When copper (and government) revenues dropped, however, the central bank began to extend credit to CORFO. As CORFO expanded and as international support for government development agencies grew, foreign credit supplemented its funds. Between 1950 and 1964, credit from foreign sources averaged one-fourth of CORFO's total disbursements.

CORFO emerged as the central state mechanism to implement preferential loans to industry. Its investment decisions were based on a general import substitution criterion; products were ranked according to the value of their imports and to the potential foreign exchange savings. Representatives from each ministry, the central bank, the state banks, and the private sector sat on its board of directors. By 1957, CORFO was supplying at least 30 percent of aggregate investment in machinery and equipment, more than one-quarter of public investment, and 15 percent of gross domestic investment.[5] With CORFO assistance, domestic-oriented industry became the most important growth sector.

Expanding State-led Financing Arrangements, 1952–1973

During the postwar period, each Chilean government contributed to enlarging the system of state-led credit allocation. Under the dem-

---

[4] See Markos J. Mamalakis, "An Analysis of the Financial and Investment Activities of the Chilean Development Corporation: 1939–1964," *Journal of Development Studies* 5, no. 2 (1969): 118–37.

[5] Markos J. Mamalakis, *The Growth and Structure of the Chilean Economy: From Independence to Allende* (New Haven: Yale University Press, 1976), pp. 293–314. Agriculture received less support, although after 1955, CORFO regional assistance programs included some agrarian financing.

ocratically elected administrations of Carlos Ibañez (1952–1958), the conservative Jorge Alessandri (1958–1964), the U.S. government's "Alliance for Progress" favorite, Eduardo Frei (1964–1970), and the socialist Salvador Allende (1970–1973), state banks and state agencies grew, regardless of the political party in office. Although new political coalitions shifted the criteria of credit policy, its volume only increased.[6]

The state Banco del Estado, which had been established in 1953 by the merger of the three separately administered state banks, acted as both a commercial and a state bank, offering credit to areas the government sought to foster. It gave preferential credit lines for industry and agriculture and shared with the national savings and loan system (SINAP) a monopoly over medium-term indexed deposits. In 1966, the Banco del Estado activity accounted for some 40 percent of commercial banking loans to industry. State agencies such as CORFO, the housing corporation (Corporación de la Vivienda or CORVI), the agricultural development institute (Instituto de Desarrollo Agropecuario or INDAP), and the National Mining Company (Empresa Nacional de Mineria or ENAMI) increasingly granted medium- and long-term credits to targeted sectors.[7]

Meanwhile, by the 1960s, CORFO had grown into a relatively autonomous public agency, both from the executive branch and from the private sector. It extended credit for working and investment capital, setting its own subsidized interest rates for industry clients. CORFO had also become an investor; it was a majority owner of forty-six firms and held interest in ninety other concerns across a range of sectors. Many of these direct equity investments resulted from CORFO's acquisition of bankrupt firms that had formerly received state financing.[8]

A "politics of accommodation" in Chile's electoral system contributed to the growth of these state preferential credit arrangements. The diversity of positions represented by the political parties meant that no single party was able to win more than 25 percent of the Chilean vote in a presidential election. Between 1938 and 1973, presidents came to office on coalition platforms and, in order to pass legislation, were forced to build alliances (mostly short-lived) with opposing parties. Such arrangements often led to back-room bargaining that blocked passage

[6] Barbara Stallings points to the similarities in the economic policies of the Alessandri, Frei, and Allende administrations. Stallings, *Class Conflict and Economic Development in Chile, 1958–1973* (Stanford: Stanford University Press, 1978), pp. 181–205.
[7] CORFO, CORVI, INDAP, and ENAMI credits were rarely included in data on aggregate credit, although they were major suppliers. The Banco del Estado shared with CORFO the responsibilities of long-term industrial financing; the two small mortgage credit banks offered long-term indexed credit directed toward agricultural or real estate loans; and SINAP (created in 1960) financed construction and housing purchases on long-term credit.
[8] In 1940, CORFO undertook major direct investments in energy and heavy industries, including steel, coal, sugar refining, and copper processing.

of economic policies of potential harm to different groups. The divisions impeded the emergence of an overall policy vision for state-directed credit allocation; instead, interest groups sought particularistic economic gains through lobbying.[9]

Bank owners and business leaders, particularly those of the private sector groups, exercised influence over government credit policy. These economic groups were organized as family-run conglomerates that operated several productive and financial enterprises under one roof. Economic groups shaped public policy through participation on public credit institutions' boards, such as those of the central bank, CORFO, and the state banks. Half of the central bank's board of directors were appointed from the private sector; CORFO and the Banco del Estado also had private sector representation. Moreover, as shareholders of Chile's banks also had controlling interests in the country's industrial, commercial, and agricultural operations, banking representatives served on numerous company boards as directors. These economic groups did not necessarily oppose state allocation of credit as government regulation of financing had the effect of limiting competition and minimizing the risks in banking.[10]

Grupo leaders were also members of the powerful agricultural, mining, or business lobby groups, the Sociedad Nacional de Agrícola (SNA), Sociedad Nacional de Minería (SNM), and Sociedad de Fomento y Fabril (SOFOFA), which were influential in government policy-making. Established in the nineteenth century, these associations used their voting membership in the central bank and in other state boards and their influence in Congress to call for more government loans to agriculture or industry or for state incentives to increase foreign capital.

By 1960, these "finance capitalists" belonged to a handful of extended families.[11] By 1970, out of the twenty economic groups that had emerged in Chile, three groups dominated in terms of the number and size of the enterprises that they controlled: the Agustín Edwards group,

[9] For accounts of this political stalemate, see Peter S. Cleaves, *Bureaucratic Politics and Administration in Chile* (Berkeley: University of California Press, 1974); and Arturo Valenzuela, "Political Constraints to the Establishment of Socialism in Chile," in *Chile: Politics and Society*, ed. Arturo Valenzuela and J. Samuel Valenzuela (New Brunswick, N.J.: Transaction Books, 1976), pp. 19–24.

[10] In 1922, 77 percent of the proprietors of large enterprises owned businesses in areas outside their main line of business. See Henry W. Kirsch, *Industrial Development in a Traditional Society* (Miami: University Presses of Florida, 1977), pp. 73, 129–33.

[11] Out of twenty-four domestic private commercial banks, the six largest banks held 77.6 percent of the deposits and provided more than four-fifths of private commercial banking credit. See Maurice Zeitlin and Richard Earl Ratcliff, *Landlord and Capitalist: The Dominant Class of Chile* (Princeton: Princeton University Press, 1988), pp. 119–21, 138–39; and Philip J. O'Brien, *Chile, The Pinochet Decade: The Rise and Fall of the Chicago Boys* (London: Latin American Bureau, 1983), p. 72.

which ran the daily newspaper and controlled Banco Edwards; the Eliodoro Matte group, which owned the Banco Industrial y de Comercio Exterior (BICE); and a newer group led by Javier Vial, Fernando Larrain, and Ricardo Claro, who called themselves the Piranhas and who owned the Banco Hipotecario y Fomento de Chile (BHC). Grupo banks were Chile's largest; their banking assets were highly concentrated, and foreign competition was effectively curbed by government regulations.

In the early 1960s, a new centrist political movement, the Christian Democratic (CD) party, emerged. CD president Eduardo Frei introduced ambitious constitutional laws to reform economic policy-making without systemic (or socialist) change. Legislation to reorganize the central bank and the state bank was proposed. A newly created Office of National Planning of the Presidency (ODEPLAN) and an informal Economic Committee were set up to orchestrate economic policy, excluding, for the first time in Chile's history, the formal participation of private sector groups. At the same time, the government openly appealed to U.S. and European governments and private corporations for their help in expediting this reform effort.[12]

Until the introduction of the Frei administration reforms, privileged sectors had been assured inside access to public sector decision-making centers. The private economic groups had favored the expansion of the state credit programs, as long as the ability to control the state apparatus was preserved. The Frei administration, however, moved to disengage the central bank from both executive branch and private sector influences, which had regularly pressured the institution toward credit expansions. In 1965, all central bank direct credits to the public were eliminated. Legislation to remove all representatives of private industry from the board of directors was submitted, although the proposal never passed.[13]

The central bank narrowed the interest rate differentials among types of loans and geographic destinations. As in previous administrations, however, preferential interest rates continued to be fixed for a range of priority uses, now for loans to newly established firms or for export credits. Banks were specifically instructed to increase the proportion of their total loan portfolio to small enterprises with a goal to

---

[12] The private sector also received foreign credit. Between 1960 and 1965, foreign financing of private sector expenditures rose from US $63 million to US $219 million, and by 1970, it reached US $436 million. See World Bank, Chile. In other areas, the Frei administration passed legislation to increase Chilean ownership and control of the copper industry and to redistribute arable land among farmers.

[13] See Ricardo Ffrench-Davis, *Políticas económicas en Chile, 1952–1970* (Santiago: Ediciones Nueva Universidad, 1973), p. 59; and Banco Central de Chile, *Estudios monetarios* (Santiago, various issues).

develop small businesses and "democratize" the availability of credit. Thus, as the Frei presidency drew to a close in 1970, public sector institutions (i.e., the central bank, Banco del Estado, the savings and loan associations, and agencies such as CORFO, CORVI, ENAMI, and INDAP) were responsible for almost all medium- and long-term credits. In the short-term credit markets, the Banco del Estado dominated, granting over 50 percent of credits.[14]

Despite the Frei administration reforms, the distribution of state funds was eclipsed by the increasing volume of financial transactions in the informal sector, which grew primarily because of interest rate controls.[15] Since 1940, a parallel financial system comprised of loans among firms, between producers and suppliers, and from private finance companies and unregulated brokers had grown sharply, particularly during periods of high inflation when real rates could turn sharply negative. By 1971, almost one-half of all loans to the private sector were originating in nonbank institutions, informal activities, or supplier credits. Moreover, a substantial share of corporate savings never passed through the banking system, moving through interconglomerate financing. Grupo firms could rely on funds from affiliated firms and banks. Partly as a result of this structure, funds allocated by state agencies rarely reached their mark.[16] Funds borrowed under subsidized credit programs were frequently diverted by the original borrowers to other (unregulated) uses, such as private credit to companies' suppliers or consumer loans. This meant, however, that state credit facilities became increasingly dispensable.

Late in his administration, Frei announced his intention to bring private financial transactions back into the legal market. The central bank raised the interest rate ceilings to positive real levels for the first time in years to encourage the growth of savings and the movement of funds into the formal market. The informal market continued to thrive, however, as the reforms had little time to take effect before the 1970 elections.

Although the Frei crusade had threatened the historical agreements between private capitalists and state authorities, Salvador Allende's Un-

[14] By the end of 1969, the IMF calculated that about 90 percent of bank credit operations were subject to quantitative guidelines. World Bank, *Chile*, p. 48. See also Banco Central de Chile, *Boletín Mensuel*, September 1971.

[15] In 1960, informal sector transactions comprised 34 percent of all loans to the private sector, compared with 21 percent in 1950 and 3 percent in 1940. See Jorge Gregoire Cerda and Hugo Ovando Zeballo, "El mercado de capitales en Chile," in *Estudios monetarios*, vol. 3 (Banco Central de Chile, 1974).

[16] See Gregoire and Ovando "Mercado de capitales"; Javier Fuenzalida and Sergio Undurraga, *El crédito y su distribución en Chile* (Santiago: Lambda, 1968); and World Bank, *Chile*.

idad Popular platform went much further, socializing the very means of production. Many industrial firms were taken over by CORFO, agrarian reform was sped up, and the remaining foreign-run copper mines were expropriated.

In December 1970, the Allende administration announced that it would nationalize Chile's banking sector with the aim of breaking the large property owners' control over production and credit. CORFO was authorized to buy shares from private bank stockholders (usually comprising only a handful of affiliated business partners) to gain majority ownership of the financial institutions. The development agency also took control over banks where "infractions" could be proved. CORFO then designated new members for the banks' boards of directors. Foreign bank branch offices operating in Chile, which by this time accounted for only a small percentage of total banking activity, were also bought out, as were savings and loan associations. By 1972, the state controlled the majority of the twenty-one commercial banks.[17]

The bank expropriations themselves created surprisingly little stir among capitalists. By 1970, many economic groups retained access to sources of private international capital and to informal channels of finance. Although the specter of declining foreign investment and the prospect of a longer-term weakening of the economic groups' power were real, the Allende bank appropriations no longer necessarily affected their operations; under the previous two administrations, bankers had already become accustomed to state-led financial arrangements.

The banks nationalized under the Allende government continued to lend funds to the grupo businesses, often at terms that were more favorable than in previous administrations. Interest rate ceilings were lowered, and the rate structure became more differentiated by sector and types of loans. Selective credit policies (already a complex network of regulations under the Frei administration) continued as a major tool for directing resource allocation. No set limits, however, were established on the expansion of either sectoral or overall credit. Allende's economic team was preoccupied with administering structural reforms, and few paid attention to the task of coordinating credit authorizations that emerged independently out of the central bank, the Ministry of Finance, CORFO, and the Banco del Estado. The Banco del Estado even began to distribute merchandise, tractors, and seeds directly to its customers. Although state-directed subsidized credit did help the

[17] See Alfonso Inostroza, "Nationalization of the Banking System in Chile," in *Chile 1970–73: Economic Development and Its International Setting: Self-Criticism of the Unidad-Popular Government's Policies*, S. Sideri (The Hague: Martinus Nijhoff, 1979), pp. 275–312. CORFO paid the stockholders well, and in some cases payment was made in dollars. Only one bank owner refused to sell his shares.

small Chilean firm to prosper, the increase in lending and loss of control over monetary policy also contributed to high inflation and a general economic crisis.[18]

Opposition to Allende administration policies came from both the political Left and Right. Infighting within the Unidad Popular coalition and sabotage from the large industrialists frustrated many government initiatives. By 1973, the growth of the Chilean economy had stalled. Worker strikes had closed down much of Santiago. The rate of inflation was nearing 600 percent annually, thus destroying any normal functioning of the financial system.

II. TRANSITIONS UNDER MILITARY RULE: THE BIG SHIFT

Financial Reform and Financial Boom, 1975–1981

The sweeping economic reforms under the military-authoritarian regime that came to power on September 11, 1973, fundamentally changed the relationship between the Chilean state and banker in policy-making. Banking practices, however, took longer to change. Chilean bankers initially understood little about evaluating risks. State agencies, through the preferential sale of banks and the absence of banking oversight, sanctioned highly speculative behavior. By 1983, policymakers were forced to salvage the banking system and put in place a new regulatory structure. Although preferential credit favoring specific economic sectors was not reimposed, the selective bailout of banks and state-led refinancing settlements directed the private sector toward particular kinds of lending and borrowing arrangements.

By the time of the military coup in 1973, "free-market" ideas had been well marketed in Chile. In 1955, an academic exchange program between the departments of economics at the University of Chicago and Santiago's Universidad Católica was launched to train a generation of Chilean economists. Originally, Chilean business associations generally viewed the Chicago School economic theories with suspicion. Nonetheless, by 1970, the Universidad Católica had emerged as an influential institution promulgating liberal theories.[19]

In 1973, most bankers and industry groups were not in favor of a radical policy switch to open up financial markets; government controls

<hr>

[18] Interview with Julio Barriga, former general manager of the Banco del Estado, spring 1990, Santiago, Chile. Monetary authorities assumed that inflation would disappear with the structural reforms. See Stephany Griffith-Jones, *The Role of Finance in the Transition to Socialism* (Totawa, N.J.: Allanheld, Osman 1981), p. 151.

[19] For an excellent study of the spread of the neomonetarist ideology in Chile, see Juan Gabriel Valdes, *La Escuela de Chicago: Operacíon Chile* (Buenos Aires: Zeta, 1989), pp. 196, 294, 304.

provided adequate profits in a risk-free environment. The right wing "alessandrista" business group in particular was opposed to the project of financial market liberalization. Once the free-market policies were introduced, however, most business organizations accepted them. There were some advantages. Explained a business leader, "We accepted liberalization, not for university reasons, but because we were sick of the *trámites* [red-tape procedures] of government meddling." Moreover, bankers viewed increasingly centralized credit controls and the recent bank nationalizations under Allende as political and economic failures. As one banker recalled, because of the memory of the 1970–1973 socialist experiment, "it was natural to want to do everything opposite from what Allende represented."[20]

The decision, however, to adopt sweeping free-market policies rested primarily with Army General and Commander-in-Chief Augusto Pinochet. Until 1973, a relatively cloistered Chilean armed forces had stayed out of electoral politics and governmental decision-making. Ironically, the military's historical obedience to elected civilian rule and its constitutionalist ideology resulted in an insulated and hierarchical structure that gave Pinochet the institutional basis for his personal authority. President Pinochet most likely chose the "Chicago Boy" economists to run the country's economic policy because of the transformative nature of their economic project. The opportunity to change old structures, namely, to smash the traditional powers of business and labor unions, absent the meddling of political parties—was appealing.[21]

After this initial decision, economists (rather than the military leadership) formulated and implemented policy in Chile's new authoritarian regime. The number of civilians in Pinochet's cabinet was high and remained high throughout his tenure: in 1980, civilians comprised all the economic ministries, ODEPLAN, and the ministers of interior, agriculture, mining, labor, and education. The economic team included no former politicians; most who took positions in economic ministries were economists and advisers (or members) of the leading economic

[20] Interviews with Hernan F. Errazuriz, banker, and Ernesto Ayala and Rodolfo May, businessmen, spring 1990, Santiago. Genaro Arriagada, *Pinochet: The Politics of Power* (Winchester, Mass.: Unwin Hyman, 1988), p. 30, suggests that this "class" perception might have been due to an excellent publicity job by the economic team of technocrats. Attempts to protest the dismantling of the state were also subject to military repression.

[21] Adolfo Canitrot has written persuasively on the political advantages of a similar neoliberal project in Argentina, in "La disciplina como objetivo de la política económica: Un ensayo sobre el programa económico del gobierno argentino desde 1976," *Estudios CEDES*, vol. 2, no. 6 (Buenos Aires, 1979). On the military doctrine, see Augusto Varas and Felipe Aguero, "El desarrollo doctrinario de la fuerzas chilenas," in *Documento de Trabajo* (Santiago: FLACSO, 1978). For a theoretical discussion of the development of military-civilian links, see Manuel Antonio Garreton, *The Chilean Political Process* (Boston: Unwin Hyman, 1989), p. 92.

groups, and over the years, these government officials retired to jobs in banks and grupo businesses.

By April 1975, these university economists and bankers were directing economic policy, ready to impose the first "economic shock" measure. The package of banking reforms was part of an ambitious Programa de Recuperación Económica to address a severe foreign exchange and fiscal crisis. The blueprint laws set few explicit restrictions on bank activities, letting the market determine the allocation of funds. A few months later, interest rates were freed for commercial banks. Commercial banks were authorized to extend one- to three-year credits (three-month term loans had been the standard); later even this restriction was eliminated. Export and import transactions, which had required central bank paperwork, could now be carried out without state approval.[22]

The complicated web of regulations concerning geographic and sector lending was dismantled. By late 1975, state-targeted credit lines had been removed, and in May 1976, quantitative credit controls were lifted. In the place of regulation, commercial banks operated on a fractional reserve system. In 1979, international capital flows were freed, and commercial banks were authorized to accept foreign deposits. The government also rescinded its guarantee on bank deposits, a standard insurance in most liberal capitalist economies, promising that banks would go bankrupt if they mismanaged their affairs.

The central bank underwent radical reorganization. Its board of directors, formerly comprised of representatives from banks and business groups, was disbanded. Central bank functionaries who had been hired in the Allende administration were summarily fired. Although central bank ties to the private sector were dissolved, the institution's conduct and policy were still governed by the Finance Ministry and executive branch. The Banco del Estado, the only remaining publicly owned commercial and development banking institution, lost its monopoly access to government accounts in 1978, and its participation in the overall financial system declined. It continued to offer longer-term loans to large companies or state-targeted projects, although it could no longer grant blanket credits to state-owned firms. SINAP announced its bankruptcy in early 1977.[23]

---

[22] See José Pablo Arellano, "De la liberalización a la intervención: El mercado de capitales en Chile, 1974–83," *Colección Estudios CIEPLAN* no. 11 (Santiago, December 1983): 5–49. For a description of the other programs, such as the reforms in the fiscal sector, prices, and tariff reductions, see Patricio Meller, *Los Chicago Boys y el modelo económico chileano: 1973–1983*, Apuntes CIEPLAN, no. 43 (Santiago, January 1984).

[23] Interviews with former central bank functionaries; interviews with J.B., former general manager, Banco del Estado, summer 1989 and spring 1990. See also Superinten-

Free-Market Financial Reforms in Chile

The sweeping financial reform led to a rapid redistribution of economic power in Chile. Beginning in late 1975, before the financial liberalization measures had taken hold, CORFO, now under military command, was charged with reselling the stock of the recently nationalized banks through "public bidding." Few persons or firms, however, had the capital to participate. Banks were selectively sold to interested buyers with financing provided by the government. Participants were selected based on criteria of previous business experience, reputation, and social connections. Most banks not only were sold on credit but also were sold well below their asset value.[24]

CORFO officials also indirectly sanctioned the increased concentration in bank ownership. The original privatization decree stipulated that only 1.5 percent of the total shares could be sold to an individual and 3 percent per firm. Interested owners soon accumulated controlling shares through holding companies, brothers and housekeepers and even through credit extended by the purchased banks themselves. The newly established financiers, comprising new economic groups, were the most aggressive seekers of bank shares.[25]

Before the reform, finance houses, or *financieras*, were also authorized to operate in the formal market. They were permitted to lend money without any interest rate restrictions and to maintain low capital requirements. Twenty-one new finance houses sprang up in under a year. These agencies could operate with little risk capital from owners, who prospered in the new environment. They had foreign contacts, were comfortable with the new financial instruments, and were willing to take risks. Between 1974 and 1977, this market flourished, until higher minimum capital requirements were set for these private finance companies. As the conditions for their operations tightened, however, owners used their collateral to buy majority shares in auctioned-off banks.[26]

This short-lived experiment in free banking, together with the bank

---

dencia de Banco e Institucíones Financieras (SBIF), *Información Financiera* (Santiago, March 1979).

[24] Interview with Lieutenant Colonel (Rt.) Luis Danus Covian, former CORFO official. Most buyers took five to eight years to pay off the credit. See also Fernando Dahse, *Mapa de la extrema riqueza: Los grupos económicos y el proceso de concentracíon de capitales* (Santiago: Aconcagua, 1980), pp. 175–79. *Fortune* magazine estimated that in 1981, assets that Javier Vial's economic group acquired from CORFO in 1975 were worth eight times what he originally paid (November 2, 1981, 142).

[25] See Rolf Luders, "Commentary on Recent Experience in the Southern Cone," in *Economic Liberalization and Stabilization Policies in Argentina, Chile, and Uruguay*, ed. Nicolás Ardito Barletta, Mario I. Bleyer, and Luis Landan (Washington, D.C.: World Bank, 1983), pp. 66–69.

[26] Existing banks also opened up finance agency branches to take advantage of the favorable operating conditions and to raise cash. See Ricardo Lagos, "La burguesía emergente," in *Chile-America*, nos. 72–73 (July-September 1981): 86–88.

privatizations, created the foundation for newcomers into the commercial banking system. The origins of the Banco de Santiago exemplified this trend. In 1968, financier Manuel Cruzat, who held a degree in administration from Harvard University, joined as consultant to the group of Ricardo Claro, Fernando Larrain, and Javier Vial. After the 1974 policy shift, his economic group, now jointly owned with Fernando Larrain, his brother-in-law, started up a finance agency. In 1978, the finance house was converted to the Banco de Santiago, and by 1983, the bank had become the second largest private national bank in Chile.

As these reform measures took hold, the volume of financial business skyrocketed.[27] New economic groups established a handful of national banks out of former regional banks and converted finance agencies, thus raising the number of private banks from eighteen in 1973 to twenty-seven in 1981. Foreign banks converged on the Chilean market after 1980; by 1981, sixteen new banks had opened branches in Santiago (see Table 7.1). By 1982, private domestic banks controlled 68 percent of the market, finance companies about 1 percent, and the Banco del Estado about 18 percent (see Table 7.2).

Revolutionary changes in international finance and continued high domestic rates provided new opportunities for foreign borrowing that, in the short run, further strengthened the position of Chile's financial sector. Between the end of 1979 and the end of 1981, Chile's private external debt tripled. Bankers now solicited these international funds directly, channeling them toward the economic groups.[28]

These new economic groups were distinctive from their prereform forerunners. Groups of entrepreneurs, rather than families, formed their nuclei. Manuel Cruzat Infante and Javier Vial Castillo led the two largest economic groups. Vial, heading the BHC group (thus called for its ownership of the Banco Hipotecario de Chile), owned almost 30 percent of the shares in the Banco de Chile and exercised controlling

---

[27] See Sebastian Edwards and Alejandra Cox Edwards, *Monetarism and Liberalization: The Chilean Experience* (Cambridge, Mass.: Ballinger, 1987), p. 56. According to SBIF head Mauricio Larrain, the ratio of M2 over GDP rose from 9.3 percent in 1974 to 25.7 percent in 1982. World Bank, "How the 1981–83 Chilean Banking Crisis Was Handled," *Policy, Planning, and Research Working Papers* (Washington, D.C.: World Bank, 1989), p. 5. See also the excellent work by Pilar Vergara, *Auge y caída del neoliberalismo en Chile* (Santiago: Ainavillo, 1985).

[28] In 1979, the financial sector received 42–45 percent of foreign credits. See Raul Green, *Finances internationales et groupes nationaux en amérique latine* (Paris: Institut National de la Recherche Agronomique, 1982), p. 23; Gustavo Marín and Patricio Rozas, "El endeudamiento bancario de los grupos económicos: Su incidencia en la crisis de pagos y en las políticas del estado de Chile, 1982–1987," in *El endeudamiento externo y los grupos económicos en el Cono Sur: Argentina, Brasil, Chile, Uruguay,* Documento de Trabajo no. 14, Programa Regional de Investigaciones Económicas y Sociales del Cono Sur, Buenos Aires (February 1988); and SBIF, *Información Financiera* (February 1980).

Table 7.1. Structure of the Chilean financial system: Number of establishments, 1970–1988

	1970	1974	1978	1980	1981	1982	1983	1984	1988
Banks									
State banks									
Central bank	1	1	1	1	1	1	1	1	1
State bank	1	1	1	1	1	1	1	1	1
Private banks									
National	22	19[a]	21	24	26	19	17	17	15
Foreign	5	1	5	13	17	19	19	19	21
Nonbanking institutions									
Public									
Housing mortgage			3	0	0	0	0	0	0
Private									
Finance agencies "formal"[b]	0	0	21	17	16	9	7	7	4[c]
Savings and loan	19	21	1	1	1	1	1	1	1
Pension funds	0	0	0	0	7	10	12	12	14

Sources: Asociación de Bancos, *Memoria*, "Síntesis de Actividades" (Santiago, 1980); Juan Carlos Casas, ed., *Saneamiento de bancos: Estudios de crisis financieras en la Argentina, Colombia, Chile, España, EE.UU., Italia, y Uruguay* (Buenos Aires: Cronista Comercial, 1989), p. 171; Superintendencia de Bancos e Instituciones Financieras (SBIF), *Información Financiera* (Santiago, 1988).

Note: This table excludes CORFO, a public institution that grants credit.

[a]Fifteen of these banks had been purchased by CORFO.

[b]Finance agencies (whose liabilities are primarily short-term time deposits) under the supervision of the supervisory agency.

[c]After 1987, one of these finance agencies was foreign-owned.

215

Table 7.2. Structure of the Chilean financial system: Assets and liabilities, 1974–1988 (percent)

	Total liabilities				Total assets			
	1974	1978	1981	1988[a]	1974	1978	1981	1988[a]
Banks								
State bank	34.6	20.0	15.0	12.9	36.5	23.0	17.8	19.0
Private banks								
National	45.3	68.9	71.9	72.3	51.3	66.3	68.0	61.8
Foreign	0.4	0.7	4.3	10.5	0.4	0.8	4.7	15.2
Nonbanking institutions								
Private finance agencies	0	4.0	3.3	1.5	0	4.4	3.1	1.2
Savings and loan pension funds	19.3	6.3	5.5	3.0	11.7	5.6	6.3	2.8

Sources: Superintendencia de Bancos e Instituciones Financieras, *Información Financiera*, (Santiago, various issues); and Banco Central de Chile, *Boletín Mensual* (Santiago, various issues).

[a]Includes liabilities that the central bank controls and letters of credit (*ventas de cartera*) owed to the central bank.

ownership in seven other banks, finance agencies, and assorted industries.

Manuel Cruzat, together with Fernando Larrain, owned the Banco de Santiago, twenty-six investment and real estate companies, and five other finance and insurance companies, as well as forestry, construction, industrial, and trade companies. The Banco de Santiago entered into an arrangement with New York's Citibank to receive bank training courses and new, computerized equipment, and it was the first Chilean bank to offer separate banking services according to loan type and special personal credit services along the Citibank model. The consumer loan also made its debut in these banks. By 1979, Chilean economic groups controlled 80 percent of banking sector equity, compared with 40 percent in 1970. Five financial conglomerates controlled 53 percent of the capital of the largest 250 Chilean enterprises.[29]

Traditional banking practices did not disappear, however. Instead, a juxtaposition of old and new operated together. Alongside international practices, the familiar "name-lending" banking persisted. Initially, the average banker understood little of how "market signals" worked. One central banker recounted receiving a call in the early years of the reform from a local private banker, who, unable to grasp the concept of free interest rates, asked him at what percentage the "free interest rate" would be set. Bankers rarely assessed the quality of

[29] Fernando Dahse, *Mapa de la extrema riqueza*. This figure may overstate the relative importance of the economic group, however; because of its pyramidal structure, grupo assets and equities might have been counted twice.

216

debtors through credit analyses of loans, nor did they review the state of their own portfolios. Most commercial banks continued to offer short-term credits, and investment banking departments remained small.[30]

Traditional financing arrangements also persisted among the economic groups under the liberal economic climate. In the past, in an environment of restricted but cheap credit, it had made sense to shift funds within an economic group. Under new conditions of free and expensive credit, there were even greater incentives to intragroup lending, and managers of these banks came under strong pressure to extend loans to affiliated businesses.[31]

Moreover, most bankers considered such "incestuous" loans to be a smart business strategy under the new financial regime. Extending loans to a firm that was legally connected to that lending institution appeared to reduce transaction costs and risks. The bank enjoyed access to financial and production figures of an affiliated company and could count on personal experience with the credibility of the borrower. The grupo enterprises were often in better economic health than were their free-standing industrial counterparts as banker and economist Juan Andres Fontaine noted: "Today, the economic group is treated as the problem. But at the time, to be a grupo was considered an advantage. While the spirit of the law might not have permitted portfolios of 'related' loans, lending to these firms was a better business decision; they simply were the better clients."[32]

Despite its perceived merits, these financing arrangements proved unstable. By 1981, Chilean economic groups had become highly leveraged, relying extensively on funds from the banks or finance companies that the conglomerate controlled, and their subsequent expansion strategies rested on the grupo-controlled bank extending more credit. Moreover, particularly after 1979, when the capital account was liberalized, banks took advantage of the large interest rate differentials between the domestic and foreign markets; they contracted substantial external debt and speculated against the increasingly overvalued peso rather than investing in the real sector of the economy.[33]

[30] Interviews with Ernesto Illanes, banker; Leon Dobry, banker; an anonymous former central banker, spring 1990, Santiago. Mauricio Larrain also makes this point in "World Bank, 1981–1983 Chilean Banking Crisis," p. 4.

[31] Bank loans within the group often went to speculative activities, including construction, real estate, and personal loans. Chilean banks operated two separate divisions for local and foreign businesses, which obscured the full extent of indebtedness of a particular firm or client. See SBIF, *Información Financiera*, 1979 issues; and interviews with Oscar González and Ernesto Illanes.

[32] Interview with Juan Andrés Fontaine, banker and economist, spring 1990, Santiago.

[33] Beginning in 1978, Chilean monetary authorities preannounced the path of the exchange rate as a stabilization device and opened the capital market on the assumption

In addition, this activity was permitted by the Chilean government, which freed up banking regulations without furnishing appropriate banking oversight. The supervisory agency, (the Superintendencia de Bancos e Institucíones SBIF), failed to monitor the share of loans outstanding to one company or client, nor did it check the existence of these loans or of the companies. The lax regulatory policies resulted in high-risk and overly leveraged loan portfolios. Bank practices became highly irregular. Young managerial technocrats devised elaborate schemes to transfer funds through a triangle of three banks, a technical record-keeping transaction that covered up "incestuous" loans. Another legal trick was the fabrication of "paper" companies, or fictitious firms, that borrowed funds for other uses. Grupo leaders also deposited the savings accounts from their affiliated mutual funds and insurance companies in grupo banks to finance speculative projects.

When distress occurred, banks were reluctant to call in overdue loans and register losses. Rather, they rolled over loans, attracting additional deposits (including those from abroad) to finance their new commitments. By December 1982, private banks run by economic groups had taken out more than 80 percent of foreign loans. The top five banks had extended more than 26 percent of total loans to "related parties."

The Financial Bust, 1982

The year 1980 marked the height of the banking boom and of Pinochet's authoritarian political rule. In September, a plebiscite approved a new constitution. The charter extended Pinochet's power until 1990, demonstrating his firm hold on society and the ruling military junta. The financial boom began to lose its strength by mid-1981, however. In May of that year, one of the oldest, largest, and most internationally exposed conglomerates—the Compañía Refinería de Azucar de Viña del Mar (CRAV)—announced that it would go bankrupt as a result of the fall in the price of sugar on international markets; the conglomerate comprised insurance companies, mutual funds, sugar plants and other businesses. From that moment, the business environment changed. A banker recalled thinking, "If the established CRAV could go under, perhaps 'name lending' to large companies wasn't such a good idea."[34]

---

that domestic inflation and interest rates would converge with world rates. Instead, the currency became overvalued and domestic interest rates remained high. See Ricardo Ffrench-Davis, "El experimento monetarista en Chile: Una síntesis crítica," *Colección Estudios CIEPLAN* 9 (Santiago December 1982); and Sebastian Edwards, "Stabilization with Liberalization: An Evaluation of Ten Years of Chile's Experiment with Free Market Policies, 1973–83," *Economic Development and Cultural Change* 33, no. 2 (1985): 237.

[34] Interview with Oscar González, banker. The CRAV conglomerate was no innocent international player. In the nineteenth century, CRAV operated on a pounds sterling

Table 7.3. External debt of the banking sector, December 31, 1982

Bank	External debt (US $ millions)	Share of total company debt (percent)	Controlling groups
Domestic banks			
Private banks			
Chile	$2,047.4	28.19%	Vial, Soza, Hirmas, Guilisasti
Santiago	879.4	12.11	Cruzat-Larrain
Sud Americano	462.0	6.36	Luksic, Borda, Schiess
Credito	354.7	4.88	Yarur
Concepción	316.4	4.36	Cueto-Martinez, Giner, Saenz
BHC	259.9	3.58	Vial
Edwards	243.4	3.35	Edwards
O'Higgins	242.7	3.34	Luksic (and foreign groups)
Trabajo	208.0	2.86	Foreign group, Said
Osorno	143.1	1.87	Many different groups
BHIF	137.4	1.89	Cruzat-Larrain, Soza
BUF	134.8	1.86	Foreign group, Abalos-Gonzalez
Nacional	108.0	1.49	Errazuriz
Colocadora	107.7	1.48	Cruzat-Larrain
BICE	104.0	1.43	Matte
Morgan Finansa	102.2	1.41	Vial and foreign groups
Other banks	141.5	1.95	
All private banks	5,992.6	82.52	
State bank			
Banco del Estado	779.2	10.73	
Foreign banks			
19 institutions	490.6	6.75	
Total	**$7,262.4**	**100.00%**	

Source: Superintendencia de Bancos e Instituciones Financieras, *Información Financiera* (Santiago, various issues), interviews.

Note: Figures do not indicate the percentage of debt in comparison with capital, that is, if debt represented a burden to the bank activities.

During the early years of the reform, the government economic team regarded the deterioration of most of Chile's industrial base with indifference. They remained convinced that industry had inappropriately benefited from government support before 1973. As industry began to feel the adverse influences of the program, effective political lobbying by industry interests was blunted by its own representatives' support for the overall government project. Despite huge losses for many producing firms, SOFOFA, the powerful association of industrialists, kept silent.

⚡ In part, SOFOFA members could present no alternative policy other than a return to government intervention. Many were skeptical that

capital base. See Kirsch, *Industrial Development*, p. 118. Through the 1970s, CRAV profited from foreign exchange operations. CRAV itself did not own a bank; rather, company failures affected the bank balance sheets.

the application of the policy would endure. Moreover, many on the SOFOFA board of directors were themselves prospering from government policies. As owners and directors of grupo organizations, the activities of the SOFOFA leadership were linked increasingly to the thriving financial sector. As the economic groups were composed of both financial and industrial holdings, grupo leaders simply shifted activities to the financial side of their operations. Thus the SOFOFA lobby group presented little opposition to policies that hurt industry. The conglomerates wrote off the losses in industry in exchange for gains in finance, as well as in the importing business.[35]

The world economic recession hit Chile in 1982. The situation of industrialists (and of the bankers who had lent to them) worsened. The liberalization of capital flows in 1979, together with Chile's high interest rates, had resulted in substantial foreign borrowing, fueling high growth. But speculative capital movements could just as easily be reversed. As the real exchange rate appreciated, the fixed nominal rate began to lose its credibility, and funds headed for more secure investments in dollar-denominated assets. When foreign lending ceased, many banks were caught both with substantial external debt and with nonperforming domestic assets.[36]

State takeovers of private banks increased. In late 1981, Finance Minister Sergio de Castro assumed public management of four private banks and four finance houses. Over the course of the next year, another three financial institutions were taken over. In all instances, depositors were compensated, and losses were taken by the banks' shareholders and ultimately by the government. In August 1982, Rolf Luders, an economist who sat on the boards of grupo companies, replaced Finance Minister de la Cuadra. Luders instructed the largest banks to renew the loans that Chilean industries had taken out, but commercial banks dragged their feet on these operations.

On January 13, 1983, Luders instructed the SBIF, the bank regulatory agency to take control of seven banks and one finance company and to liquidate three outright. The Banco de Santiago and the Banco de Chile, the first and second most important commercial banking

[35] Although economic groups Matte and CRAV were active on SOFOFA, the Cruzat and Vial economic groups were not. Industry, with the backing of key military officials, did succeed in forcing the resignation of the powerful finance minister Sergio de Castro in April 1982. He was replaced, however, by his close associate and president of the central bank, Sergio de la Cuadra, who maintained much the same policy stance. See *El Mercurio*, various issues; and *Latin American Economic Review* 25, no. 1 (1977): 98.

[36] The shift in exchange-rate policy was forced by the loss of export (and import substitution) competitiveness, the drop in world copper prices, and the rise in international interest rates. See Juan Pablo Arellano, "La difícil salida al problema del endeudamiento," *Colección Estudios CIEPLAN* 13 (Santiago, June 1984).

institutions in Chile, were included in this takeover and were subsequently assigned to new management.

The speculative behavior and the subsequent collapse of banks were largely the result of the lax regulatory environment prevailing in the 1970s. At the outset of the reform, Ministry of Finance and central bank authorities had announced that banks would be left to go bankrupt, rescinding the government insurance on deposits. As the pace of changes in bank rules accelerated, neither central bank authorities nor the Finance Ministry gave financial regulation serious consideration. Those who did argue for revamping state supervision of bank activity had few institutional resources. The watchdog agency, the SBIF, was a low-prestige institution. Few funds were allocated to carry out oversight activities such as visits to banks or audits of bank records, and the agency had neither the resources nor the knowledge to keep track of rapidly changing and expanding private financial activities. The changes in international banking rendered many of Chile's regulations ineffective, and new instruments quickly superseded the jurisdiction of existing rules.

Chilean monetary authorities did not hesitate, however, to get back into the business of bank management at the first instance of financial difficulty. Already in November 1976, the state bailed out a private bank and reimbursed its depositors, fearing that a publicized bankruptcy would put a damper on Chile's internationally acclaimed experiment at a moment of enthusiastic foreign interest. With increasing regularity, the central bank assisted more failing banks: in November 1981 and again in January 1983. Despite the official abdication of responsibility—60 percent of all bank debt was still not officially backed by state guarantees by late 1982—the SBIF and the central bank ultimately found themselves assuming both external and domestic obligations of the failing banks.[37]

Shortly before the first massive bank interventions in late 1981, the economic team switched course and began to implement and enforce regulatory measures. In 1979, regulations prohibiting loans to related companies were passed. A maximum ceiling of 10 percent of a bank's loan portfolio could be extended to one client or company, and banks were prohibited from investing in stockholder companies. In 1982, the central bank began to publish volumes of instructions on compliance, and the SBIF's new research team, identifying "related loans" as the culprit responsible for the country's financial morass, distributed a monthly newsletter disclosing financial data on individual banks. As-

[37] Interviews with Leon Dobry, banker; Sergio de la Cuadra, former central bank head and finance minister; and Ernesto Illanes, banker and "interventor" of the bank, spring 1990, Santiago. After 1976, some deposit insurance was offered.

sessing the quality of the portfolios, however, was a difficult task. The SBIF could do little more than calculate liquidity and levels of indebtedness. There was no centralized data base or standard measure to evaluate bank balance sheets.[38]

In response to these new decrees and as the health of the productive companies deteriorated, grupo owners and managers searched for new bank loopholes and expanded the use of others already in practice before 1981. When the central bank decreed that the asset value of "related" portfolios could not exceed the capital base of the bank, Banco de Santiago owners simply transferred their personal deposits to official bank capital. Not until 1983 could the SBIF actually document illegal practices.[39]

II. THE STATE MOVES IN

The massive SBIF takeover of selected banks marked the end of the liberalization experiment. In January 1983, the supervisory agency intervened in eight financial institutions, named outside inspectors for several of the banks, and chose the new management of the intervened banks, who were mostly former central bank, SBIF, or Banco del Estado functionaries. After one day's work, the Chilean state controlled 70 percent of the domestic banking sector. The Chilean government bought up the bad debt of the banks and absorbed other nonperforming loans, promising state guarantees on deposits. It selectively liquidated commercial banks and subsequently took over management, putting some bank presidents and managers in jail and leaving others to rebuild their fortunes. By 1984, state-appointed regulators were reorganizing these banks and reissuing bank stock to the public, and government regulations were requiring all Chilean employees to deposit 12 percent of their salaries in privately run pension funds.

What was the politics behind this new round of interventions? States typically intervene in financial markets to stem crises of confidence. Yet the manner and the extent of the interventions that occur are political. After the takeovers, Chilean monetary officials used innovative policy instruments to ensure that its private sector partners would survive. By reshaping the agreement concerning its role in financial interme-

[38] See SBIF, "Algunos aspectos relacionados con el riesgo en la intermediación financiera. El caso Chileno," *Información Financiera* (September 1982): 5–12; and Carlos Urenda Zegers, "Evolución reciente de la legislación financiera," in *La revolución financiera: Manifestaciones y perspectivas en Chile,* ed. Leon Cohen Delpiano (Santiago: Algarrobo, 1989).
[39] Interviews with bankers and SBIF officials. See also Manuel Delano and Hugo Translavina, *La herencia de los Chicago Boys* (Santiago: Ornitorrinco, 1989), p. 113.

Table 7.4. Chilean financial institutions that were intervened or liquidated subject to intervention or liquidation, 1981–1983

	November 1981	1982	January 1983
Banks	4[a]	2[a]	7[b]
Finance companies	4[a]	1[a]	1[a]
Total	8	3	8
Loans of institutions	13.0%	1.5%	45.0%

[a]First intervened, subsequently liquidated.

[b]Two banks liquidated, one intervened and subsequently merged; four intervened, subsequently privatized.

diation, the state successfully shored up its coalition of support by appealing to new participants, particularly international bankers. At the same time, it retained control over banking resources to prevent the private sector—foreign and domestic—from becoming truly autonomous.

Keeping International Allies

The Chilean monetary authorities did not initially plan to bail out the entire banking sector. Neither domestic nor foreign creditors had received any explicit guarantees from the Chilean state. Five days before the interventions, the central bank offered to purchase credits of failing banks at 70 percent of their face value. According to the new economic team, the costs of absorbing all of the accumulated debt was unimaginable. The international creditors to the intervened banks would also be reimbursed the same 70 percent.[40]

Domestic depositors agreed to these conditions and sold their credits at the discount. Foreign creditors, however, refused Luders's demands and "exerted severe pressure to get full compensation, in several cases conditioning their foreign trade credit lines and participation in possible external debt rescheduling to full repayment." Chilean authorities, regarding their weakened, nearly bankrupt financial sector and decimated industrial sector, had few options. After three days, Finance Minister Luders reversed the declaration. The central bank would extend guarantees to all foreign liabilities in the context of an overall restructuring of external debt.[41]

[40]Interviews with Claudio Skarmeta and Guillermo Ramirez, SBIF functionaries.

[41]Quoted from Mauricio Larrain, "1981–1983 Chilean Banking Crisis," p. 14. Foreign banks argued that they had granted loans on the basis of official SBIF reports about the solvency of banks, which had misled them; they did, however, then grant special terms to restructure their Chilean loans. See Rolf Luders, "La razón de ser de la intervención del 13 de enero," *Economía y Sociedad* 4 (1985).

The Bank Interventions

After the decision was reached to prop up the banks, the choice of banks that fell under the state hatchet and the extent of state arbitration after the takeovers revealed the role of political factors in determining financial market outcomes. Although the government officially intervened in banks carrying losses of more than 100 percent of capital and liquidated those with losses of over three times capital, inadequate data often led government officials to consider other factors, including the standing of the bank owner or controlling shareholder in society, the bank's history, and its ties to international banking centers.

The fate of banks was handled on a case-by-case basis. Politically, the object of the government crackdown was the economic groups.[42] The concentration of loan portfolios in affiliated companies (a grupo characteristic) does not itself explain why the state intervened in certain banks, however. The amount of "related loans" in such banks varied between 12 percent and 45.8 percent of total loan portfolios.

The owners of the two largest private banks, the Banco de Santiago and the Banco de Chile, met different fates. Manuel Cruzat, having lost ownership of the Banco de Santiago, successfully negotiated with the government to keep some of his companies. Javier Vial, however, was sent to jail after the state intervened in both his Banco de Chile and Banco Hipotecario de Chile. The Cruzat and the BHC economic groups (which owned majority shares of the banks) were liquidated; the banks sold off those companies that the economic groups had indebted to the banks as collateral. The banks themselves were too important to liquidate. They were instead "rehabilitated" and their depositors reimbursed.[43]

The Banco Unido de Fomento, with few loans outstanding to affiliated companies, was experiencing temporary liquidity difficulties. The bank was intervened and subsequently liquidated, and its owners were left with few resources. In this case, the central bank received political pressure from the bank's foreign creditors to "get rid of the problem." But the government did not intervene in the Banco Edwards and the Banco de Crédito e Inversiones, largely because they still had a positive capital flow and partly because their portfolios of "related" loans was small. An SBIF official also explained that the Edwards family had a

[42] For example, Finance Minister Luders became one grupo "offering." He was forced to resign soon after the interventions, accused of "conflict of interest" because of his commanding position on the board of directors of Javier Vial's economic group.

[43] Out of 180 firms listed as creditors of the Banco de Santiago, only 20 were "chimney," or producing, companies. The rest were "shells," that is, either investment companies or merely fictitious firms. Interviews with Julio Barriga, intendente. See also Larrain, "1981–1983 Chilean Banking Crisis," p. 14.

Table 7.5. Concentration in the Chile banking sector, 1982–1983

Bank	June 1982	Dec. 1982	Dec. 1983
Banco de Chile (Vial and others)	16.1%	18.6%	17.9%
Banco Hipotecario y de Fomento de Chile (Vial group)	17.1	na	na
Banco de Santiago (Cruzat-Larrain)	44.1	42.3	49.3
Banco Hipotecario de Fomento Nacional (Cruzat-Larrain)	28.2	27.4	21.4
Banco Colocadora Nacional de Valores (Cruzat-Larrain)	23.4	23.8	27.2
Banco de A. Edwards (Edwards group)	15.9		
Banco de Crédito e Inversiones (Yarur group)	8.6	11.9	9.3
Banco Nacional (Errazuriz)	29.1	25.7	24.0
Banco Industrial y de Comercio Exterior (Matte group)	4.0		
Banco O'Higgins	8.0	9.1	8.7
Banco Internacional	20.1	22.8	3.4
Banco Sud Americano	13.0	14.8	16.3
Finance houses			
Ciga[a]	26.3	24.1	
Corfinsa	19.3	20.8	18.0
Fusa	21.0	22.5	12.0
Interés Social[b]	14.9	15.4	

Sources: Superintendencia de Banco e Instituciones Financieras, *Información Financiera* (Santiago, December 1982 and February 1984).

Note: Concentration is defined as the percentage of bank credit loaned out to "related" ownership or management. "Related" persons or firms are those linked directly or through a third party to the ownership or management of the institution. Loans between banks are excluded.

[a]Liquidated in December 1983.

[b]Interés Social was transformed into a bank in December 1983.

"long tradition of good banking" behavior and that the Banco de Crédito's owner, Jorge Yarur, "was a gentleman." As Table 7.5 shows, at the time of the massive 1983 state interventions, Banco Nacional records showed a bank with a highly leveraged portfolio and high percentages of loans to related companies. The bank was not taken over, nor did its owner, Francisco Javier Errazuriz, receive any penalties.

Some banks won, others lost. A former Banco de Santiago manager opined: "We thought that our bank had sufficient international contacts to negotiate our own capital increases. But people had to find martyrs, to make statements."[44]

[44] Interviews with bankers and economists, spring 1990, Santiago; and SBIF, *Información Financiera*, February 1983. Errazuriz was a public figure and an old school classmate with several high military commanders. His investments in forestry were important for the state's targeted export plans. The Banco Nacional was intervened in 1987. It is questionable whether, given tight international financial conditions, banks could have negotiated their own deals with foreign bankers.

State Initiatives

Over the next two years, the central bank subsidized operations and used elaborate mechanisms to keep selected banks afloat. Under the flourishing command of SBIF head Hernán Buchi, three strategies were devised: debt-relief programs for borrowers, central bank purchases of loans, and recapitalization and sale of banks. Debt "reprogramming" granted lines of credit at subsidized interest rates to indebted companies to roll over their more "expensive" loans, and schemes to refinance mortgage and consumer loans kept other sectors from collapsing. CORFO also moved to inject new resources into the system, establishing new credit lines to priority sectors. The central bank program of the "preferential dollar" helped borrowers to pay back international loans. Debtors paid the debts to banks at the official rate and received a central bank cash subsidy. In exchange for these subsidies, the SBIF demanded compliance from the banks in providing information on bank activities.[45]

In August 1982, the central bank purchased selected nonperforming loans, and banks were given an indefinite time to buy back the letters (up to one hundred years). In February 1984, the central bank began to buy risky loans from those banks in which the state had not intervened.[46] A few months later, the two rehabilitated banks, the Banco de Santiago and the Banco de Chile, joined the program. Nonperforming loans were taken off the bank books and replaced with bonds bearing low interest rates. Banks were required to use the income from operations to repay loans before distributing dividends. Chilean banks now became indebted to the state.

In early 1985, the government offered yet another initiative to infuse capital into the banking system. Banks under state management (in particular, the Banco de Santiago and Banco de Chile) offered new stock to existing shareholders and to the public, a program called "popular capitalism." To facilitate these purchases and guarantee their success, the central bank provided generous subsidies to small investors.[47]

Monetary authorities also devised new instruments to promote sav-

---

[45] Eliminated in 1987, this program resulted in the largest drain to the central bank. See Ricardo de Tezanos Pinto Domínguez and Arsenio Molina Alcalde, "Evolución reciente de la regulación financiera," in *La revolución financiera*, pp. 48–77.

[46] For details, see "Avances en la superación de la crisis financiera," SBIF, *Información Financiera*, vol. 1 (December 1983): 5–14.

[47] The credit conditions for this popular capitalism program were liberal: a 5 percent down payment, zero percent interest rate (in real terms), and tax-free dividends. This recapitalization was completed by 1987. Dividends were expected to be low, given that banks had to use most of their profits to repay bad loans. A state guarantee on all bank deposits was granted until December 1984.

ings and boost confidence in the credit markets. Leasing companies, mutual funds, and stock brokerages were introduced. The privately run pension system, set up in May 1981 to replace the existing social security system, was expanded, requiring employees to deposit 12 percent of their income with private Pension Fund Administrators (AFP). Originally these agencies were set up as legally independent companies, and before 1983 the most important were controlled by the leading economic groups. Two or three of the largest pension funds, which among several investment instruments acquired stock of privatized companies, were in turn increasingly controlled by large multinational holding groups. By 1989, pension funds savings amounted to 60 percent of domestic savings in Chile.

III. MODIFIED STATE-BANKER ARRANGEMENTS

In 1985, the country was recording strong growth, and Chile's banking sector was pronounced stable. The campaign against the economic group had been completed. Responsibility for the crisis was put squarely on the "incestuous" industry links to banks, although the culprit was ultimately poor supervision of financial institutions and their high indebtedness rather than the grupo structure itself. As a result of this drive, Chile's conglomerates were no longer organized around banks; industries were sold off, and their structures were reconstituted.[48]

In 1989, Augusto Pinochet held a second referendum to affirm his authoritarian rule. This time, his mandate to govern was soundly rejected, and a transition to democracy was set in motion. In September 1989, a coalition government under the leadership of veteran Christian Democrat Patricio Aylwin was elected. This new administration took pains not to dislodge (or even modify) the financial reforms that had been implemented over the last six years. Legislation to create a central bank more independent of the executive was completed briefly before the end of military rule. The terms of office of the central bank president were set to alternate with those of the executive branch. The 1983 banking crisis appeared a distant bad dream.

Chile's devastating financial crisis of 1983, however, bore longer-term consequences than the elimination of the grupo structure. The economic team's lax monitoring of banking practices revealed that the mix of free-market ideology, together with little institutional experience in

[48] Dhase's *Mapa de la extrema riqueza*, condemning Chile's economic groups, had a profound impact. Even those who opposed his perspective accepted the analysis and conclusions. See also Oscar Muñoz, "Chile: El colapso de un experimento económico y sus efectos políticos," *Colección Estudios CIEPLAN* 16 (June 1985).

regulation, can be fatal. Moreover, subsequent state interventions re-affirmed Chile's use of traditional instruments of statecraft. The government was forced to resort to preferential lending to the banks by the magnitude of the crisis. The "popular capitalism" stock offering was, in effect, dispensing government funds to particular sectors of the banking community, as were the central bank purchases of nonperforming loans. The pension system similarly acted as a forced savings scheme that ultimately assisted the financial sector. Monetary authorities used the country's politically authoritarian structure not to liberalize but to continue to intervene in financial markets.

The lessons of the Alessandri, Frei, and Allende administrations, however, had not been forgotten. The prudential oversight of financial institutions that the state eventually implemented was a far cry from the selective credit controls of the past. Although the Chilean state acted firmly to reregulate the country's financial institutions, it maintained an officially distanced relationship with private sector groups. The era of bankers as the "benevolent dispensers of state largesse" had passed.

The episode cemented new dynamics in the state's relationship with private sector bankers: an arms-length—but, by no means impartial—support for market-oriented, outward-looking activities. The state has stayed away from direct sectoral financing. State participation in finance dropped from its 1975 figure of 46.0 percent of loans and 54.8 percent of deposits to 16.8 percent and 20.9 percent, respectively in 1988. Chile's central bank no longer directly allocates credit or determines its cost. The notion of a centralized financial clearinghouse has been abandoned.

Perhaps more striking than the character of state policy and power was the acquiescence from the Chilean economic group leaders. Armed with a tradition of keen political deal making, these finance capitalists nonetheless appeared to yield at every step to government initiatives. Chile's bankers could well have challenged the legal propriety of the state liquidation of banks or the selection of officials to manage those banks in which the state intervened. In the midst of major social upheaval—in which a May 1983 "National Day of Protest" demonstrated a profound disapproval of the regime—the financial class nonetheless submitted to all government demands.[49]

In 1983, Chile's finance capitalists had no institutional venue to lobby for alternative strategies. The private banker lobby group, the Asocía-

---

[49] The case of Argentina suggests that not all bankers permit their governments to carry out such "housecleaning." See Laura A. Hastings, "The Politics of Financial Policy in Argentina and Chile: Liberalization, Crisis, and Re-regulation," Ph.D. diss., Massachusetts Institute of Technology, 1993.

cion de Bancos e Instituciones Financieras, which had only recently become active under the leadership of grupo head Javier Vial, was discredited. No private sector representatives sat on government policy-making boards. As Manuel Cruzat and Javier Vial had been identified as the largely responsible for the financial bust, few such leaders from the heady days of the financial boom wielded credibility.

It could well have been in the interest of bankers to remain docile. By all indications, the central bank and the SBIF were making every effort to revive the country's financial base, and there was no need to resist.[50] But this explanation is unconvincing. Although in retrospect, central bank policies did rejuvenate the banking sector, grupo leaders could not have foreseen this particular outcome, nor could they have been certain that, as individual capitalists, they would survive.

The financial sector's passive response to the central bank's interventions documents a key institutional shift in the relationship between the public sector and the private banker in Chile. The military coup and regime change in 1973 established radical new economic and political contracts between the state and its constituents that effectively insulated the administration's economic team from traditional and direct private sector participation.

As champions of a free-market doctrine, monetary authorities under the Pinochet regime proclaimed that the state had abdicated direct control over key economic decisions, including the allocation of financial resources. They induced private sector groups to act as individual profit maximizers. Yet, as the banking sector faced a systemic crisis in 1982, the state retained substantial power and was itself subject to international pressures. The crisis weakened the economic power of the economic groups. The empires of key grupo leaders, which rose under the short-lived period of liberalization without regulation, were then dismantled relatively easily by the authoritarian regime, which was able to dictate both the pace of the restructuring and the nature of the new regulatory apparatus.

[50] By the end of 1983, the net losses of the banks in which the government intervened amounted to 250 percent of their capital and reserves. That the capitalist state would ensure the long-run survival of capitalism is a classic tenet of Marxist analysis.

CHAPTER EIGHT

The Politics of
Mexican Financial Policy

SYLVIA MAXFIELD

The study of the politics of financial regulation in developing countries cannot be separated from study of the politics of macroeconomic
management. This is particularly true for the period before the 1980s,
when selective credit policies, whether tied to reserve requirements,
rediscounting or portfolio restrictions, were a key instrument of monetary policy. In his study of Taiwan, Tun-jen Cheng stresses that a
perennial obsession with macroeconomic stability was among the factors
that conditioned credit policy. From the 1940s through the 1960s,
central banks in many developing countries saw selective credit policies
as a way to control inflation by "discouraging inflationary 'unproductive'
commercial credits and encouraging supposedly noninflationary production credits for agriculture and certain 'essential' industries."[1]

From a more orthodox viewpoint, selective credit controls were also
perceived as a way to prevent the inflationary expansion of bank credit
in times of growing deficit spending by the government.[2] Targeted
exemptions to monetary restraint applied through selective credit policy took the sting out of macroeconomic policies that were otherwise

I extend profound thanks to Regina Cortina, Denise Dresser, Yemile Mizrahi, Jesús
Reyes Heroles, Eduardo Suárez, and the staff of Grupo de Economistas y Asociados for
facilitating my research. I benefited greatly from comments on earlier drafts by Gerardo
Bueno, Jeffry Frieden, Stephan Haggard, Nathaniel Leff, and participants at a seminar
at the Center for U.S.-Mexican Studies, University of California–San Diego. Unless
otherwise noted, translations are my own.

[1] J. Ahrensdorf, "Central Bank Policies and Inflation: A Case Study of Four LDCs,
1949–1957," in *Money and Monetary Policy in Less Developed Countries*, ed. Warren L. Coats,
Jr., and Deena R. Khatkhate (New York: Pergamon, 1980), p. 437.

[2] I. G. Patel, "Selective Credit Controls in Underdeveloped Areas," in Coats and Khatkhate, *Money and Monetary Policy*, p. 563.

politically unpalatable to influential industry or agricultural groups.[3] Although econometric research has failed to prove that there is any link between financial regulatory policies and monetary stability or instability, central bankers perceived such a relationship, and as a result, the politics of financial regulation and the politics of macroeconomic policy are generally intertwined.

In Mexico, large-scale changes in financial regulation and monetary policy occurred together. The Cárdenas era (1934–1940) was one of growing state intervention in financial markets and loose monetary policy. The policy of selective credit controls was consolidated in the 1942–1954 period. The year 1954 is usually taken as the beginning of the predominantly orthodox policy era of "stabilizing development." In this period, the central bank used selective credit controls extensively, but other forms of state intervention in financial markets were minimal, and monetary policy was relatively tight. In the next period, beginning in 1970, state intervention in financial markets grew through the creation of hundreds of special-purpose government trust funds (*fideicomisos*) and the takeover of at least one private bank. Monetary policy also became extremely expansive. This period involved two devaluations and culminated with the nationalization of virtually all of Mexico's banks in 1982. Since then, greater monetary stringency has accompanied financial liberalization.

In short, there were four major shifts in financial and monetary policy after the Mexican revolution: (1) Cárdenas's shift away from the relative orthodoxy of the 1920s; (2) the gradual shift back to orthodoxy, but with the emergence of selective credit controls as an instrument of macroeconomic policy; (3) the reversion to expansionary monetary and fiscal policy and the creation of new state credit institutions under Echeverría; and finally, (4) the shift toward liberalization in the 1990s.

What were the politics behind these changes in financial and monetary policy? What explanatory factors appear important? I explore two types of political variables. The first set which draws on recent studies of U.S. and European monetary and financial policy, is institutional and focuses on the power and interests of the central bank.[4]

---

[3] Yung Chul Park, "The Ability of the Monetary Authorities to Control the Stock of Money in LDCs," in Coats and Khatkhate, *Money and Monetary Policy*, p. 333.

[4] See John B. Goodman, *Monetary Sovereignty: The Politics of Central Banking in Western Europe* (Ithaca: Cornell University Press, 1992); Vittorio Grilli, Donato Masciandaro, and Guido Tabellini, "The Political and Monetary Institutions and Public Financial Policies in the Industrial Countries," Paper prepared for the Economic Policy Panel Meeting in London, October 18–19, 1990; Paulette Kurzer, "The Politics of Central Banks: Austerity and Unemployment in Europe," *Journal of Public Policy* 7, no. 1 (1988): 21–48; Nathaniel Beck, "Politics and Monetary Policy," in *Political Business Cycles,* ed. Thomas D. Willett (Durham: Duke University Press, 1988); and John T. Woolley, "Central Banks and

The second cluster of variables concerns the power and interests of social actors, particularly the financial community and industrialists.

The core of the argument concerning the central bank can be stated simply: the more powerful and traditional the central bank, the more likely monetary policy will be passively neutral or actively restrictive and the more likely state intervention in financial markets will be limited. The central bank may tolerate comparatively limited state intervention in financial markets in the name of macroeconomic stability. Although a central bank that is able to dominate other government agencies in policy debates may be a proximate explanation of relatively orthodox policies, this contention leaves one wondering about the ultimate sources of central bank power.

Two factors are important in this regard. The first consideration is the perceived need of government leaders for credibility in the eyes of creditors. The greater the perceived need, the more power and autonomy accorded the central bank.[5] As I have argued elsewhere in more detail, the power of orthodox central bankers and their allies in the financial sector varied over time in Mexico with the president's desire to attract foreign capital or resolve outstanding creditor-debtor disputes.[6] In most cases financial crisis will lead government leaders to accord greater power to state financiers, who are presumed to have the capacity to mobilize rescue financing. Although this relationship is highly probable, it is not certain. Financial crisis most frequently produces a desire to increase credibility with potential creditors, but it can also engender an anticreditor backlash, depending on the strategic concerns of political leaders. In a balance-of-payments crisis, the former strategy might lead to the central bank's having more power over macroeconomic policy, whereas the latter could result in increased controls or even bank nationalizations, as occurred in Mexico and Peru in the 1980s.[7] To predict with certainty, we need more information on the domestic political pressures that shape the responses of government leaders to financial crisis.

The second important motivation for central bank behavior and strength lies in the historical relationship between the central bank and

---

Inflation," in *The Politics of Inflation and Economic Stabilization,* ed. Leon N. Lindberg and Charles S. Maier (Washington, D.C.: Brookings Institution, 1985).

[5] For a similar argument with reference to the creation of the Bank of England, see Douglass C. North and Barry R. Weingast, "Constitutions and Commitment: The Evolution of Institutions Governing Public Choice in Seventeenth-Century England," *Journal of Economic History* 49, no. 4 (1989): 803–32.

[6] Sylvia Maxfield, *Governing Capital: International Finance and Mexican Politics* (Ithaca: Cornell University Press, 1990).

[7] Sylvia Maxfield, "The International Political Economy of Bank Nationalization: Mexico in Comparative Perspective," *Latin American Research Review* 27, no. 1 (1992).

the private banking community. Where a central bank grows out of a strong private banking community, perhaps at the behest of private bankers who are major state creditors as was the case in England, the central bank will have a greater desire and capacity to pursue orthodox policies than if founded under different circumstances. When central banks are founded in the absence of a strong private financial community, it is typically by a government seeking financing. These circumstances of central bank founding are important in understanding monetary and financial policy patterns because they establish a lasting set of norms and expectations about central bank priorities. These "structural" considerations are most valuable in efforts to explain recurrent patterns in one country and differences in historical policy patterns across countries; they are of less value in understanding the types of policy changes that have taken place over time in Mexico. But the changing interests of the private financial sector do help explain policy shifts. The more financially sound private banks are, independent of central bank resources, the greater their preference for tight monetary policy and little state regulation of financial markets. Conversely, the more private banks depend on central bank loans, the greater their preference for loose monetary policy and relatively greater state intervention in financial markets.

Commercial banks could come to depend on state support in a variety of situations. Where there is little tradition of public deposit in commercial banks—because there are alternatives such as informal credit societies, lack of trust in banks, or low interest rates—banks could find themselves unable to raise sufficient funds to cover lending activity without borrowing heavily from the central bank. Similarly, if banks lend at relatively long terms or for unsound purposes, they may develop a gap between liabilities and assets that must be covered through borrowing from the central bank. In cases where commerical banks are financially weak by this definition, they will support more expansionary monetary policy than might be expected typically.

In addition to their importance for an examination of the central bank and its relationship to government politicians and commercial bankers' interests and policy preferences, industrialists' policy preferences are also important for an understanding of the domestic politics of monetary and financial policy. Industrialists' policy preferences and political weight can play an important role in determining how political leaders will react to financial crises. A politician's desire for credit and credibility can be counterbalanced by industrialists' demands for expansionary monetary policy and state favors in the form of subsidized, directed bank credit. This is especially true when a politician perceives that his or her tenure in office depends on industrialists' support or the support of an industrial coalition that might include labor as well.

Sources of industry financing are an important determinant of industrialists' monetary and financial policy preferences. Where industrial entrepreneurs depend heavily on commercial bank credit, they will be more likely to support easy-money policies and state intervention to subsidize and guide credit toward their enterprises. This argument is occasionally found in the literature on the financial politics of advanced industrial countries but is not well explored in the context of a developing country. Michael Loriaux, for example, refers to the dependence of French firms on credit as an "overdraft" economy and argues that this situation explains French policies of state intervention in financial markets and expansionary monetary policy.[8] As industry financing patterns change, we would expect industrialists' financial and monetary policy preferences to change; changes in industry financing are therefore an important factor to consider in searching for explanations of shifts in financial and monetary policy.

The following sections outline how shifts in the Mexican government's intervention in financial markets can be understood by examining three factors: (1) the central bank and its relationship to the government, with particular emphasis on how politicians' desire to establish creditworthiness shapes the relationship; (2) the ties between the central bank and the private banking sector, particularly in terms of how the private banks' financial health shapes both their and the central banks' policy preferences; and (3) how the financial situation of industrialists shapes their policy preferences and influences government action.

I. Central Bank Founding

The private banking community was quite strong at the time the Banco de México was founded in 1925. The Mexican revolution virtually wiped out the wealth of Porfirian-era agricultural elites but left private banking intact. The central bank was founded as a new institution created "from scratch" with guidance from private bankers and careful provision to include bankers among the owners and directors. Although the Banco de México did not evolve out of an existing bank, as did the Bank of England, the idea that creating a central bank would help increase Mexico's credibility with international creditors was never

---

[8] Michael Loriaux, "States and Markets: French Interventionism in the Seventies," *Comparative Politics* 20, no. 2 (1988): 175–95.

far from the minds of the technocrats who designed it. Manuel Gómez Morín, one of three men who wrote the central bank statute in 1924, spent two years in New York City in the early 1920s as Mexico's financial agent trying to resolve disputes between Mexico and international banks and oil companies. During these negotiations, Gómez became convinced that Mexico should establish a central bank to prove Mexico's financial strength and organizational capacity.[9]

Although Mexico's 1917 constitution established the principle of a public central bank with a right to monopolize the issue of money, no specific guidelines or timetable for establishing a central bank were included. In the early 1920s, several proposals for establishing a central bank were debated in the Mexican legislature. The political context of these debates included tremendous popular animosity toward private banking, which was seen to embody all the defects of the Porfirian dictatorship that the revolutionaries had shed so much blood to overthrow. The proposals ranged from postponing creation of a public single-issue bank and granting issue privileges to eight established private banks on one extreme to creating a 100 percent government-owned bank with a monopoly of note issue on the other. All three proposals were buried in the chaos of presidential succession in 1923–1924.

Plutares Calles, who succeeded Ávaro Obregón as president of Mexico in 1924, appointed Alberto J. Pani as finance minister. Pani and his advisers, including Gómez Morín and Miguel S. Macedo, had worked closely with Porfirio Díaz's last finance minister, José Limantour, to develop plans for financial modernization. Pani convoked the first national banking convention within one month of Calles's inauguration in 1924 with the goal of bringing together private bankers and government officials to devise guidelines for the financial system generally and central banking in particular. Congress, pressured by Calles, gave Pani extraordinary decree powers in order to circumvent congressional debate, which had hindered passage of earlier financial legislation. Miguel S. Macedo authored the overarching General Law of Credit, which went into effect in January 1925. Pani charged the National Banking Commission, established by decree in December 1924, with enforcing this legislation. The "three musketeers"—Manuel Gómez Morín, an economist; Fernando de la Fuente, a laywer; and Elías de Lima, a private banker—authored the central bank statute.

Private banks were not initially required by law to register with the central bank, nor did the central bank have a monopoly of money issue in the first half of the decade after its founding. In this period, the

[9] This material is taken from Maxfield, *Governing Capital*.

bank functioned most successfully as a profit-making commercial bank. It competed in limited fashion with the nation's two largest private banks, the Banco Nacional de México and the Banco de Comercio, but did not threaten their profitability as either a competitor or a regulator. In its infancy, the Banco de México's operations were circumscribed by a powerful private financial community. Although government stockholders held a scant majority of Banco de México stock, the interests of private stockholders, among them many bankers, were guaranteed a powerful voice on the board of directors. With little juridical basis for the central bank to establish authority over the financial system, Pani suggested in 1928 that private bankers organize themselves into a bankers association to facilitate public-private financial collaboration and perhaps establish a basis for the central bank to increase its authority through the informal mechanism of "moral suasion."[10] This foreshadowed a system of "reciprocal consent" between the central bank and private bankers which blossomed during the stabilizing development era.

Although the Banco de México's regulatory functions were restricted, so was its capacity to serve as a source of government financing. The central bank charter provided for substantial central bank autonomy from government, including a legal limit on the extent of central bank financing to government.

It is difficult to draw firm conclusions about the political implications of the way in which the Mexican central bank was founded without delving much more deeply into the comparative historical record than is possible here. Schematically, we have a semipublic, semiprivate institution with heavy private bank involvement and, probably not coincidentally, great de jure autonomy from government. The institution was created at a time when Mexican presidents were trying to resolve disputes with international creditors. It was not initially conceived of or designed to perform development functions or support growth-oriented policies, as were central banks in many other late industrializing countries. The Banco de México's close ties to a relatively strong private banking community would have been a recipe for orthodox financial and monetary policy had it not been for Cárdenas-era decisions to create noncentral bank institutions capable of intervening in financial markets and to limit the autonomy of the Banco de México, purposefully paving the way to increase central bank financing of government deficits.

[10] Thanks to exchange of personnel between public and private financial institutions and close informal ties between private bankers and the government, the Mexican Bankers Association (ABM) developed the reputation of enjoying a more direct channel of communication to the highest levels of the Mexican government than did any other business organization.

II. THE CARDENAS ERA, 1934–1940

In the early 1930s, as the Calles era drew to a close, several revisions of the banking and credit laws added to the Banco de México's regulatory capacity. But two decisions taken under Cárdenas had a more significant impact on financial and monetary policy.

The first was the decision to create a series of state development banks to help the government finance agriculture and industry. Of these, the largest and eventually the most well-known bank was Nafinsa. This decision was motivated by frustration with private bank lending behavior. In the pattern of private bank credit allocation in the 1930s, older manufacturing companies borrowing for the short term—often for speculation—took the place of large landowners as preferred bank customers. Agriculture was sorely neglected.[11] This allocation of private bank credit led to a squeeze on peasants and the newer industrialists soon to be organized in Canacintra, the association of manufacturing industries.[12]

During the 1934 bankers' convention, Minister of Finance Marte R. Gómez lectured the private banking community on their responsibility in Mexico's development effort: "The Mexican government has done more than one could expect; bankers!... Do the part which corresponds to you: work solidly... staying away from anything that is or seems to be of a merely speculative nature."[13] Members of the Cárdenas administration accused private bankers of fomenting speculation, especially during the foreign exchange crisis following the oil nationalization in 1938. Data showing that short-term financing accounted for three-quarters of total financial resources in the 1930s lend credence to this charge.[14]

Admonishments aimed to encourage private finance of development were relatively unsuccessful. Private bank credit relative to GNP expanded only sluggishly, much to the frustration of Finance Minister Eduardo Suárez.[15] Between 1925 and 1940, although the number of private bank offices grew, their resources fell from 12 percent of GNP

---

[11] In the 1940s, the earliest period for which data are available, the value of banks' deposits from the agricultural sector was greater than loans to that sector. For a bibliographic survey of the history of agricultural credit in Mexico, see Philip P. Boucher, "El crédito agrícola en México," *Historia Mexicana* 24, no. 3 (1975): 442–70.

[12] Sanford A. Mosk, *Industrial Revolution in Mexico* (Berkeley: University of California Press, 1954); and Robert Jones Shafer, *Mexican Business Organizations: History and Analysis* (Syracuse: Syracuse University Press, 1967), pp. 109–11.

[13] Miguel Angel Calderón, *El impacto de la crisis de 1929 en México* (Mexico City, SEP/80, 1982), p. 64.

[14] Raymond Goldsmith, *The Financial Development of Mexico* (Paris: OECD, 1966), p. 29.

[15] David Shelton, "The Banking System: Money and the Goal of Growth," in *Public Policy and Private Enterprise in Mexico*, ed. Raymond Vernon (Cambridge: Harvard University Press, 1964), p. 145.

to 10 percent.[16] Capital flight amounted to 900 million pesos between 1935 and 1939, more than double the value of total investment in that period.[17]

This financial weakness gives a hint of the financial and political context in which Nafinsa and six other national credit institutions were created by the Cárdenas administration to help finance public investment in roads, irrigation, and energy production to improve agricultural output and spur industrialization.[18] These institutions, which became the major channels through which the government channeled credit to preferred uses, were essentially administrative arms of the Finance Ministry and the central bank, though they were also subject to the authority of the ministry specifically concerned with their area of lending. Banjidal, set up to provide lending to the *ejidos* (agricultural cooperatives), for instance, answered to both the Finance Ministry and the Ministry of Agriculture.[19]

Bankers had survived the revolution better than any other segment of the Porfirian-era elite. They played a relatively large role in shaping postrevolutionary financial interests and policy. This role left private bankers vulnerable to a continuation of the popular animosity toward bankers, which had reached a fever pitch under the revolutionary leadership of Venustiano Carranza. Given this popular animus, Cárdenas's decision to create a parallel set of state credit institutions, rather than nationalize existing private banks, reflected a relatively moderate political strategy.

By this logic, one could also interpret Cárdenas-era changes in the de jure and de facto autonomy of the central bank as relatively moderate for a populist government. A direct role for the Banco de México in financing the government through emission of new paper money

[16] Goldsmith, *Financial Development of Mexico*, p. 29.

[17] Enrique Fernandez Hurtado, *Cincuenta años de banca central* (Mexico City: Fondo de Cultura Económica, 1967), p. 55; and Juan M. Martínez Nava, *Conflicto Estado-empresarios* (Mexico City: Nueva Imagen, 1984), p. 104.

[18] These included for public works, Banobras (1933); for rural finance, Banjidal (1935); for foreign trade, Bancomext (1937); and for unionized laborers' personal credit needs, Banco Obrero (1939). See Calvin P. Blair, "Nacional Financiera: Entrepreneurship in a Mixed Economy," in Vernon, *Public Policy and Private Enterprise;* Shelton, "Banking System," pp. 116–20; Octavio Campos Salas, "Las instituciones nacionales de crédito," in Hurtado, *Cincuenta años de banca central;* Robert L. Bennet, *The Financial Sector and Economic Development* (Baltimore: Johns Hopkins University Press, 1965), pp. 54–60; José Hernández Delgado, *Nacional financiera como coadyudante de la industrialización* (Mexico City: Nafinsa, 1961); Joséph S. La Cascia, *Capital Formation and Economic Development in Mexico* (New York: Praeger, 1969), pp. 39–42; and Mosk, *Industrial Revolution in Mexico,* pp. 242–49.

[19] Although much has been written on the economic role of Nafinsa, there is no analysis of the political history of the institution that is similar to the excellent work on the Brazilian development bank by Eliza Jane Willis, "The Politicized Bureaucracy: Regimes, Presidents, and Economic Policy in Brazil," unpublished manuscript, 1990.

was not considered until 1935 during discussions leading up to the revision of the central bank charter in 1936. The changes limited the central bank's statutory autonomy from government and ushered in an era of growing state intervention in financial markets and deficit financing of government by the central bank. Where there had previously been a strict limit on the amount of money printed by the Banco de México, rules were changed so that money could be printed with government paper backing.[20]

Even before the 1936 statutory change, it was clear that Cárdenas wanted the central bank institutionally subordinated to the presidency, through the Ministry of Finance and its head, Eduardo Suárez. This is evident in an anecdote recounted in Suárez's autobiography. In 1934, President Cárdenas was considering appointing Luis Montes de Oca (formerly finance minister from 1927 to 1932) to head the central bank. Cárdenas first consulted Finance Minister Suárez as he feared that Montes de Oca might find it difficult "to subordinate himself."[21] Suárez recalls that he suggested to Cárdenas that "to maintain the necessary discipline and coordination between superior and subordinate, it was indispensable that all agreements the president wished to recommend to me or directives for the Banco de México be communicated directly to me to transmit to Mr. Montes de Oca ...that to ensure the progress of Finance Ministry business...I [Suárez] should be present at any meeting the president should have with Montes de Oca."[22]

During the two terms he served as minister of finance during presidencies of the Cárdenas and Manuel Ávila Camacho (1934–1946), Suárez was a champion of state intervention in financial markets and expansionary monetary policy in the name of economic development. Suárez is reported to have said, "New debts I turn into old, and the old ones I don't pay."[23] When World War II began to put strong inflationary pressure on the Mexican economy, Suárez—working closely with Banco de México director Villaseñor and his promising young

[20] The 1936 legislation also gave the central bank the legal authority to collect mandatory reserve requirements from all commercial banks operating in Mexico. This legislation caused most foreign banks in Mexico to close their offices. Later, legislation prohibited foreign banks from operating in Mexico, although maintenance of "representative offices" was permitted. The legislation also finally made Banco de México notes the only legal tender in the country.

[21] Eduardo Suárez, *Comentarios y recuerdos* (Mexico City: Porrua, 1976), p. 163.

[22] Suárez, *Comentarios*, pp. 163–64.

[23] Interview with Eduardo Turrent Díaz, Mexico City, August 22, 1991. Suárez tended to justify his policies on Keynesian grounds. Turrent, one of Mexico's leading financial historians, emphasizes that Suárez didn't start out as a Keynesian. Parodying Keynes's own phraseology, Turrent notes, "The way the Inquisition conquered Spain, Keynes conquered Suárez."

assistant, Rodrigo Gómez—chose a system of reserve requirements to help control credit expansion.

There was considerable opposition from private bankers to Cárdenas and Suárez's expansionary monetary policies and later to the reserve requirements, but there was relatively little opposition to the high state share of total financial activity (Table 8.1). This was primarily because the state credit institutions operated strictly in long-term financial instruments that private banks considered too risky and because the state institutions did not compete with private institutions for deposits as they received funds through the Banco de México.

III. Selective Credit Controls and Stabilizing Development

The politics behind Mexico's system of selective credit controls, first introduced in 1942, provide an excellent window into the politics of Mexican financial policy in general. Perhaps the most important point to note from the outset is that from 1940 through 1970, the primary motivating factor for the credit control program in the central bank's eyes was minimizing the inflationary impact of World War II on the Mexican economy. This goal conflicted to some extent with those of government agencies such as the Ministry of Agriculture or Ministry of National Patrimony, which pushed the program for more heterodox reasons. They wanted a tool of intervention to support specific geographic or sectoral activities and to increase their ability to respond to "populist" political pressures. Under Presidents Adolfo Ruiz Cortines, Adolfo López Mateos, and Gustavo Díaz Ordaz, however, the primary goal of the selective credit program, which was administered by the central bank, was to preserve monetary stability. In this sense, the credit control program was not as great a deviation from liberalism as it might otherwise appear. Compared with exchange controls or state ownership of commercial banks, it was a relatively mild form of government intervention in financial markets.

The central bank and sector–oriented approach suggests that we look at the relationship between the central bank and the rest of the government, the relationship between the central bank and the private banking community and the latter's policy preferences, and the financial situation of industrialists in order to understand the politics of Mexico's selective credit control program. In the realm of government–central bank relations, there are two key points. First, Cárdenas's heterodox financial and monetary policy approach, like the rest of his economic policy, reflected a choice to eschew international

Table 8.1. Shares of financial system resources, 1940–1991 (percent)

Year	Banco de México	National development banks	Total public institutions	Total private institutions
1940	0.48	0.16	0.64	0.36
1941	0.46	0.17	0.63	0.37
1942	0.45	0.14	0.60	0.40
1943	0.46	0.13	0.59	0.41
1944	0.46	0.11	0.57	0.43
1945	0.42	0.12	0.54	0.46
1946	0.38	0.16	0.54	0.46
1947	0.41	0.20	0.61	0.39
1948	0.36	0.20	0.56	0.44
1949	0.36	0.23	0.59	0.41
1950	0.36	0.21	0.57	0.43
1951	0.33	0.24	0.57	0.43
1952	0.32	0.25	0.57	0.43
1953	0.31	0.28	0.59	0.41
1954	0.31	0.31	0.62	0.38
1955	0.30	0.27	0.57	0.43
1956	0.28	0.30	0.58	0.42
1957	0.27	0.28	0.55	0.45
1958	0.26	0.29	0.55	0.45
1959	0.25	0.29	0.54	0.46
1960	0.22	0.33	0.55	0.45
1961	0.21	0.34	0.55	0.45
1962	0.21	0.33	0.54	0.46
1963	0.20	0.33	0.53	0.47
1964	0.18	0.32	0.50	0.50
1965	0.17	0.32	0.49	0.51
1966	0.17	0.31	0.47	0.53
1967	0.16	0.31	0.47	0.53
1968	0.16	0.30	0.46	0.54
1969	0.15	0.29	0.44	0.56
1970	0.14	0.28	0.42	0.58
1971	0.14	0.29	0.43	0.57
1972	0.19	0.27	0.46	0.54
1973	0.21	0.28	0.49	0.51
1974	0.24	0.28	0.52	0.48
1975	0.24	0.30	0.53	0.47
1976	0.21	0.37	0.59	0.41
1977	0.27	0.35	0.61	0.39
1978	0.27	0.31	0.58	0.42
1979	0.27	0.28	0.55	0.45
1980	0.26	0.27	0.53	0.47
1981	0.25	0.29	0.54	0.46
1982	0.25	0.35	0.60	0.40
1983	0.27	0.33	0.60	0.40
1984	0.28	0.31	0.58	0.42
1985	0.24	0.35	0.60	0.40
1986	0.21	0.39	0.61	0.39
1987	0.22	0.41	0.63	0.37
1988	0.21	0.38	0.59	0.41
1989	0.20	0.33	0.53	0.47
1990	0.20	0.24	0.44	0.56
1991	0.17	0.21	0.37	0.63

Source: Banco de México, *Informe Anual*, various years.

financial support and concentrate on building a national populist political party to support his presidency. Building up or protecting the strength and autonomy of the central bank and its international credibility, was not of great concern to Cárdenas for this reason. Mexico's rapprochement with foreign capital began in the 1950s with the Ávila Camacho administration. Establishing international creditworthiness became a strong concern as it became evident that Mexico's foreign exchange reserve problems were severe. In contrast to Cárdenas-era financial and monetary policy, the selective credit program was developed in the context of growing concern for Mexico's international creditworthiness which dictated a change in status of the central bank vis-à-vis other government economic policy-making agencies. The selective credit program was consistent with an increasingly strong and internationally credible central bank because it was aimed at achieving orthodox macroeconomic goals rather than the more heterodox industrial planning ends that selective credit programs were designed to accomplish in other developing countries. In some ways, it was a second-best tool for the central bank and was chosen because the aspects of the relationship between the central bank and the industrial development bank, Nafinsa, and with the private banks ruled out the best policies.

The relationship between Nafinsa and the Banco de México in the 1940s is an aspect of intragovernment politics important to understanding the credit control program, including selective credit controls. As indicated, the central bank's overriding concern was how to mitigate the inflationary impact of World War II on the Mexican economy. Its first choice would have been to develop the central bank's capacity for open market operations. Nafinsa insisted that the stock market was under its jurisdiction and that any issues, such as its own *certificados de participación,* needed to carry a repurchase guarantee. The Banco de México was not willing to make such a guarantee on government issues, and Nafinsa's staunch commitment to its guarantee policy virtually closed off the option of open-market operations.

Let us turn next to constraints stemming from the central bank's relationship with private banks. Nafinsa policy aside, the Banco de México knew from earlier experience that the private banks were extremely reluctant to hold government paper. The central bank could also not count on effectively using the rediscounting tool to regulate credit expansion and the money supply because the major banks were relatively liquid. The Banco de México had few options other than to turn to credit control instruments linked to reserve and portfolio requirements. On May 31, 1942, the central bank for the first time imposed what it called "qualitative controls on credit" (referring to selective credit controls) requiring all associated banks to maintain 60 percent of their assets in activities the Banco de México defined as "productive" as an eligibility condition for central bank rediscounted credits.[24]

In the same year, the central bank also raised reserve requirements selectively; it raised the requirement less for provincial than for Mexico City banks because the former supposedly extended more credit for productive activity than the latter. The Banco de México's annual report for the year states that the selective credit controls were not effective because the banks had little need for the central bank's rediscounted credit.[25]

The relative ineffectiveness of the selective credit control program in its early stages led to heightened controversy within the government, this time between Minister of Finance Suárez and central bank director Villaseñor. As the problems of the Mexican economy worsened, Suárez's Keynesian predilections led him to stress what later came to be called a "structuralist" interpretation, whereas Villaseñor clung to a more orthodox analysis. At the annual national banking convention in 1945, Suárez chastised private banks for not authorizing sufficient credit to the nation's agricultural ejidos. Villaseñor, in contrast, suggested that problems in Mexican agriculture were due to lack of investment, not lack of credit. Lack of investment, he went on, followed from the uncertainty created by social reforms such as land redistribution and state support for workers. Pointing to the Soviet Union's move away from a program of total economic nationalization with its New Economic Policy, he called for an end to social reform "to save Mexicans from hunger."[26]

From the time the central bank was founded, Mexican private bankers had four main channels through which to communicate their policy preferences: (1) representation on the Banco de México board; (2) the annual bankers' convention, typically attended on the government side by the minister of finance, the director of the central bank, and often the president himself; (3) relatively formal consultations with a large group of private bankers initiated by the Banco de México; and (4) informal meetings with top government officials initiated by the largest banks.

The private bankers were most successful in extracting policy concessions in these informal meetings. The initial 1942 policy of selective

---

[24] Banco de México, *Informe Anual, 1942* (Mexico City: 1943), p. 27; and "Banking Program for Industrial and Agricultural Promotion," *Mexico News,* March 31, 1942, p. 3.

[25] Banco de México, *Informe Anual,* p. 27.

[26] Luis Medina, *Historia de la revolución mexicana: Del cardenismo al avilacamachismo* (Mexico City: Colegio de México, 1978), p. 266.

credit controls was discussed with private bankers in a private meeting between the head of the Banco de México, other central bank officials, and many private bankers. During this meeting, various initiatives were discussed in a "cordial atmosphere" that private bankers said reflected the "good disposition of Banco de México officials to reconcile interests."[27] Nevertheless, the private bankers were not pleased with any program of controls, and they vehemently protested in informal meetings with high-level technocrats and politicians. Their protests of Villaseñor's incipient credit control program led to Miguel Alemán's choice of a private banker to replace Villaseñor at the central bank.

Under Carlos Novoa's directorship, the credit control program—in both its aggregate and selective respects—initially languished, and credit expanded relatively rapidly. Yet by late 1950, it had become increasingly difficult to ignore the contribution to rising inflation of this de facto policy of easy credit. As a result, on January 12, 1951, the central bank ordered banks to abstain from loans for luxury items or any goods not destined for production.[28] This marked the beginning of a renewed effort to control inflation through selective credit controls.

The credit control program was revitalized at the beginning of the Ruiz Cortines sexenio (1952–1958). Ruiz Cortines had campaigned on an austerity platform, basing his policy proposals on a preliminary draft of what was later published as the 1954 report of the International Bank for Reconstruction and Development (IBRD) on the Mexican economy. In 1954, accompanying a major devaluation, the Banco de México strengthened selective credit controls to avoid speculative activity and inflation and to stimulate production.[29] Beginning on January 9, 1955, with the intention of channeling credit selectively to limit money supply growth, the central bank again changed the requirements for Mexico City and provincial banks.[30] The selective credit control program remained in force throughout the 1954–1970 period of stabilizing development.[31]

Given the private bankers' earlier protests and the sometimes public controversy between the central bank and the Ministry of Finance, one must ask what made this selective credit control program possible. On the intragovernment side, the answer lies in the tremendous strength gained by the Ministry of Finance from the 1954 devaluation and the

[27] "Otorgamiento de créditos para la producción," *Excelsior,* May 16, 1942, p. 1.

[28] Hurtado, *Cincuenta años de banca central,* p. 100; and "Todo aumento en los depósitos desde hoy, al Banco de México," *Excelsior,* January 12, 1951, p. 1.

[29] Hurtado, *Cincuenta años de banca central,* pp. 104–5.

[30] Hurtado, *Cincuenta años de banca central,* p. 109.

[31] Some put the start and end of stabilizing development two years later, dating it from 1956 to 1972.

very close relationship between the Ministry of Finance and the central bank, which dates to Carillo Flores's nomination as minister of finance in 1954. Both of these events are related to the importance of establishing credibility with international creditors such as the IMF and the IBRD. On their side, the private banks agreed to the program in an implicit bargain through which they gained a variety of compensating benefits.

The 1954 devaluation was worked out by the newly appointed finance minister, Carillo Flores, and the IMF. It was announced to Ruiz Cortines as a virtual fait accompli.[32] This was a highly unusual departure from Mexican presidentialism. By not firing Carillo Flores, Ruiz Cortines significantly strengthened the Ministry of Finance's position in the policy-making process. Also in 1954, on Carillo Flores's recommendation, Rodrigo Gómez became director of the Banco de México. Carillo Flores had groomed Rodrigo Gómez for the position, and the two enjoyed a close working relationship. Rodrigo Gómez had a similar relationship with Carillo Flores's succesor, Ortiz Mena.

Rodrigo Gómez's success in developing a selective credit control program stemmed from the backing of a forceful minister of finance—first Carillo Flores and later Ortiz Mena—and from an implicit bargain struck with the private bankers. Although not pleased, the bankers agreed to selective reserve and portfolio requirements in return for freedom to oligopolize the unregulated portion of the market that involved charging very high fee-inclusive interest rates of 30 percent in the commercial bank loan market, which was not government-controlled; freedom to own investment banks (*financieras*), which were unregulated and highly profitable despite the fact that the banking system was supposed to be specialized; and largesse to partially comply with sectoral lending requirements by lending to industries to which the banks were linked through ownership or management. The bankers also agreed not to make the benefits of this arrangement too obvious; Rodrigo Gómez kept close personal watch over the bank owners, and if they began to display their wealth ostentatiously, he would remind them of the need for discretion.[33]

The selective credit control program was tremendously effective in achieving the macroeconomic goal of noninflationary government finance. The high reserve requirements with selective exemptions provided resources that could be employed by the government without great risk of inflation. The program was not effective as a subsidy to small-scale agriculture or industry. But during the period of stabilizing

---

[32] Interview with Victor Urquidi, Mexico City, August 27, 1991.
[33] Confidential interview, Mexico City, August 22, 1991.

development, the former goal was more important to the central bank than was the latter. The Banco de México was willing to tolerate only limited compliance with sectoral lending requirements in return for acceptance of what were on average very high reserve requirements. Nonetheless, because the program could be presented in a populist light, it was easier to gain broad political support than it might otherwise have been for a program with relatively orthodox goals. The populist rationale for the credit control program reflected the same beliefs and goals that lay behind financial regulations during the Cárdenas administration. Agricultural, industrial, and social credit needs would not be met under an unregulated market allocation system.

Questions of intention aside, the Banco de México did not attain significant control over the quality, as opposed to the quantity, of credit distribution. Data from the Banco de México show a continued bias in private bank credit allocation away from industry and agriculture in favor of services including short-term financial arbitrage from 1940 through 1970. Private financing of industry and agriculture as a percentage of total system resources grew only modestly from 1942 to 1958. After that, financing to industry rose slightly, whereas financing to agriculture fell. Within industry, lending was biased toward production and sale of consumer durables, commerce, and construction. Manufacturing received a declining share of private sector financing between 1957 and 1970; 34 percent of total private sector loans went to manufacturing in 1957 and only 19 percent in 1970. Small and medium-sized producers continued to suffer from restricted access to private bank credit.[34]

The Mexican government did not achieve significant control over credit allocation because selective credit controls have the most impact on investment in systems where the price of money is fixed, growth in the money supply is restricted, private banks depend heavily on state financing, and enterprises rely heavily on domestic financing external to the firm.[35] The latter two conditions were not met in Mexico largely because of the organization of Mexican capital, which

[34] Maxfield, *Governing Capital*, p. 67.

[35] A system of government-set interest rates and control of the money supply is a requisite for effective selective credit controls because it allows the government to create a situation in which demand for money exceeds supply at the administratively controlled prices. Some nonmarket rationing criteria have to be adopted. As Zysman points out, the resulting set of privileges and administrative decisions implies that the government must make explicit choices about credit allocation and financing. "Intervention is a necessity, which gives government leverage on the allocation decisions of all actors in the system." John Zysman, *Governments, Markets, and Growth: Financial Systems and the Politics of Industrial Change* (Ithaca: Cornell University Press, 1983) p. 130. This is the essence of the type of financial structure that Zysman argues will facilitate state-led industrial development.

was dominated by a small number of large financial-industrial-commercial conglomerates.[36] Selective credit controls did not achieve the desired goal of stimulating investment in strategic areas because the existence and growth of financial-industrial conglomerates gave industrial concerns a source of finance internal to the group, that is, credits from their groups' bank.[37] From the private bank side, the grupos hindered the effectiveness of the government's selective credit controls because a financial institution belonging to a grupo could comply by lending within its circle of associated companies. Although this is not what is usually meant by "internal financing," it may have been considered so by the industrial firms and banks involved, which may help account for the relatively high rates of internal financing reported in Mexico in the 1960s. Estimates of internal industry financing in the 1950s and 1960s place it between 68 and 90 percent. The only time series data available show that external industry financing shrank from 29 percent in 1950 to 14 percent in 1965, reaching a low of 10 percent in 1960.[38]

Whatever the explanation for these relatively high rates of internal financing in industry, this financing pattern helps explain the politics of financial and monetary policy during the stabilizing development era. Where industry relies relatively heavily on competitive commercial loan markets, its opposition to tight monetary policy or support for investment-oriented credit control programs will be high. We would also expect the reverse to hold true; little industry dependence on commercial bank credits would mute their potential opposition to tight

[36] Camp's survey of major corporate boards in the 1980s confirms that there was a high degree of interlocking between the boards of banks and major holding companies. Members of the Garza-Sada family, which controlled two major industrial groups, Alfa and Visa, also sat on the board of Banca Serfin. Representatives of a large industrial group (Desc), one of country's two leading retailing chains (Aurrera), and of another banking group (Cremi) sat on the board of Bancomer. Members of the Legoretta family, which controlled Banamex, sat on eight top company boards, and in many cases representatives from those companies, in turn, sat on Banamex's board. Camp's data provide numerous other examples of the connections through board representation of banks and leading nonbank firms. Another set of data from Camp's study suggests the centrality of bankers among Mexico's leading entrepreneurial families. He finds that these families were better represented in the ABM than in any other business organization. Roderic A. Camp, *Entrepreneurs in Politics in Twentieth-Century Mexico* (Oxford: Oxford University Press, 1989).

[37] Growth of existing grupos and formation of new ones became "an important barrier to achievement of greater rationality in the application of available investable resources." Shelton, "Banking System," p. 161.

[38] Flavia Derossi, *The Mexican Entrepreneur* (Paris: OECD, 1971), p. 113; Goldsmith, *Financial Development of Mexico*, p. 46; Dwight S. Brothers and Leopoldo Solís, *Mexican Financial Development* (Austin: University of Texas Press, 1966), p. 101; and John K. Thompson, *Financial Markets and Economic Development: The Experience of Mexico* (Greenwich, Conn.: JAI Press, l979), p. 150.

money and limit their support for selective credit programs. Had Mexican industry relied more heavily on "external" bank loans, it would have had the financial motivation to pressure for different policies. In this sense, the pattern of industry finance was a necessary condition for the orientation of Mexico's credit control program toward macroeconomic rather than industrial policy objectives.

IV. ECHEVERRIA, LOPEZ PORTILLO, AND THE BANK NATIONALIZATION

After 1970 the tenor of both financial regulation and monetary policy changed dramatically. The portion of the selective credit control system directed at private banks was overshadowed by the creation of a plethora of state special-purpose trust funds (fideicomisos) to liberally sprinkle subsidized credit where needed. Monetary policy became extremely expansionary to accommodate rising state expenditure. A sorely needed devaluation was delayed for the entire sexenio.

There were several important factors behind this shift. The first factor was the rise of an era of easy money internationally and the growing awareness that Mexico's oil reserves would ultimately bring a huge foreign exchange windfall. This financial context greatly facilitated Luis Echeverría's decision to pursue a political strategy involving heavy state spending. Moreover, Echeverría shifted control over economic policy away from the Ministry of Finance-central bank alliance by replacing personnel, creating new institutions, and changing consultation hierarchies. Finally, inflation and overextension weakened private banks, which also lost traditional communication channels to government with Echeverría's changes in government personnel and structure.

The importance of securing international credit had been crucial to Mexican presidents after the foreign exchange crises of the late 1940s and early 1950s, which partly explains how the Ministry of Finance and Banco de México came to play such a powerful role in economic policy formulation. Echeverría, in contrast, governed Mexico in an era in which international bankers were beginning to push loans on Third World borrowers with ever greater fervor and new information about the size of Mexico's oil reserves promised incalculable revenues. The problem for Echeverría was not gaining credibility with international creditors but restoring the ruling party's political legitimacy as a populist party.

Echeverría came to the Mexican presidency at a time of particularly acute concern over the future legitimacy of the ruling Institutional

Revolutionary Party (PRI). Among other economic problems, the stabilizing development program had led to growing income inequality; this engendered rising political opposition to the PRI among intellectuals and students. The PRI's legitimacy was especially affected by the regime's exceptionally authoritarian response to 1968 student demonstrations, in which people were killed by police and for which President Díaz Ordaz and the PRI were held accountable.

Echeverría turned to populist economic rhetoric and increased state involvement in the economy to try to renew the PRI's populist credentials. He proclaimed a shift from stabilizing development to "shared development." The basic objectives of this new strategy were growth with equitable distribution of income, strengthening public finances and state-owned enterprises, reorganizing Mexico's international economic relations and reducing foreign debt, modernizing agriculture, increasing employment, and the rationalization of industry.

As part of the effort to strengthen public finances, Echeverría followed a fairly orthodox fiscal and monetary course for the first year of his administration. But when the consequent recession in 1971–1972 proved deeper than anticipated, Echeverría turned to a policy of using government spending to stimulate growth. The role of government trust funds (fideicomisos) in providing preferential credit grew along with the overall growth of public spending during the Echeverría sexenio. Some of these fideicomisos dated to the stabilizing development era, during which they formed a part, along with selective credit controls on private banks, of the overall preferential credit program. Fideicomisos were created under the jurisdiction of the Banco de México and occasionally Nafinsa or the government trade bank, the Banco de Comercio Exterior. Although difficult to quantify, the amount of the subsidy involved in the preferential credits distributed through fideicomisos in the stabilizing development era was slight, and the opportunity for diversion was slight. Preferential credit channeled through these institutions was overseen by experts who monitored credit use. Again, the idea behind the creation of the original fideicomisos was to increase the control of central monetary authorities over the use of preferential credit and also to be able to combine foreign loans, government budget contributions, and funds from the reserve requirements in single specific-purpose credit institutions. As it was with the selective credit controls on private banks, the economic ideology behind the fideicomiso program in the stabilizing development era was relatively orthodox.[39]

[39] Confidential interview, Mexico City, August 20, 1991. Among these early fideicomisos were the Fondo de Garantía y Fomento a la Industria Mediana y Pequeña (to support small and medium-sized industry) under Nafinsa jurisdiction; the Fondo de Guarantía

This orthodoxy changed in the Echeverría years. The extent of the subsidy and the quantity of credits from existing fideicomisos grew, and new ones were created. Between 1970 and 1973, the amount of money distributed by the fideicomisos almost tripled, growing by roughly 25 percent annually. The number of special funds mushroomed and is much too long to list, but examples are instructive of the scope of state action. In 1970, the Fideicomiso para el Estudio y Fomento de Conjuntos, Parques, Ciudades Industriales y Centros Comerciales was created to facilitate appropriate industrial location, promote industrial decentralization, and finance and provide technical assistance for industrial parks. The Fondo de Equipamiento Industrial (for improvement of industrial equipment) and the Fideicomiso de Equipo Marítimo y Portuario (for improvement of port and maritime equipment) were created in 1971. An impressive list of new funds was created in 1972, including funds to facilitate borrowing for farming and municipal development, improve facilities for training in the fishing industry, increase education in farming and forestry, promote industrial decentralization, create industrial employment, promote exports, and assist in correcting the balance-of-payments deficit by supporting import substitution and developing appropriate technology for Mexican industry. The trend continued in 1973 with the creation of even more specialized fideicomisos, which were established to build housing for the workers of the Lázaro Cárdenas-Las Truchas steel complex on Mexico's Pacific coast, to improve the handicrafts derived from palm, and to regulate landholding and distribution in one of Mexico City's slum areas. Other funds created later in the Echeverría administration included the Fondo Nacional de Turismo and INFONAVIT (to promote development of low-cost urban housing) as well as funds to upgrade the technological capacity of industry and channel credit to farmers in irrigated areas.

Not surprisingly, the proliferation of fideicomisos became the source of many political jokes. One suggestion was for a fideicomiso to create a penguin sanctuary in Antarctica to which meddlesome former politicians could be exiled.

Although reserve requirements on private banks were raised and increasingly large foreign loans contracted, part of the credit distrib-

y Fomento para la Agricultura, Ganadería y Avicultura (to promote agriculture and cattle and bird breeding); the Fondo de Operación y Descuento Bancario a la Vivienda (to finance housing); and the Fondo Especial para Financiamiento Agropecuario (to finance agriculture and animal breeding), all of which were under the jurisdiction of the Banco de México; and the Fondo para el Fomento de las Exportaciones de Productos Manufacturados (to finance export of manufactured products), under the jurisdiction of the Banco de Comercio Exterior. See Gustavo Petricioli Iturbide, "Política e instrumentos de orientación selectiva del crédito en México," in Hurtado, *Cincuenta años de banca central.*

uted by the fideicomisos was financed through deficit creation and loose monetary policy. Devaluation, already overdue in 1970, was delayed for the entire sexenio. To implement these policies, Echeverría had to purge officials in the Finance Ministry and the central bank who opposed his effort to expand the state's role in the economy. Even before his inauguration, Echeverría called in Minister of Finance Ortiz Mena and requested that the minister resign. In this way, Ortiz Mena's replacement, Hugo Margain, became minister of finance even before the Díaz Ordaz administration formally came to an end.

Yet Margain did not stay in this position for long. When he protested to Echeverría in 1971 that certain spending could not be authorized because revenues were insufficient, he was dismissed. Echeverría declared that "economic policy is made at Los Pinos" (the presidential mansion) and turned the Office of the Presidency into a shadow economic cabinet that persistently fought other economic policy-making instititutions. Ernesto Fernandez Hurtado, director of the central bank, found the Banco de México's policy preferences subordinated to the president's spending plans. He tried to resign several times but was talked into staying on in the chief central bank position. In some respects, Fernández Hurtado was "used and manipulated" by Echeverría.[40] Fernández Hurtado disagreed frequently with José López Portillo, Margain's replacement as finance minister, and finally did leave the Banco de México when the latter became president. When several government economic consultants independently urged Echeverría to devalue, which would have implied considerable monetary restriction, he had them ostracized, calling them "traitors of the fatherland."[41]

Channels of communication about financial and monetary policy within the government changed with Echeverría's administration as well. Echeverría broke the pattern of reciprocal consultation on financial and monetary policy between the presidency, the central bank, and the Finance Ministry. He consulted in a haphazard and unpredictable way, establishing the presidency alone as the key economic decision-making office.

Private banks also perceived themselves to be cut out of communication circles during the Echeverría years. Many bankers felt that when Margain was fired, an important channel of communication had been closed. Furthermore, they were increasingly squeezed by inflation. As the nominal lending subsidy called for in the selective credit program rose, banks had to raise lending rates in the free market to compensate.

---

[40] Confidential interview, Mexico City, August 22, 1991. According to Eduardo Turrent's interview sources, Echeverría refused Fernández Hurtado's resignation on one occasion, saying, "Eres mi gato, me sirves" (You are my cat, you serve my purposes).

[41] Interview with Victor Urquidi, August 27, 1991, Mexico City.

The increase in these rates met with resistance from borrowers who now had access to much larger pools of state funding through the fideicomisos and, in some cases, directly from international sources. At least one bank had to be taken over by the government and reorganized into the Banco Somex. Hoping to strengthen private banks, the government began negotiating with the bankers over a plan to switch from a system of specialized banking to multiple banking, which would include mergers of several smaller banks.

Under Echeverría's successor, López Portillo (1976–1982), erosion of the Ministry of Finance's previously dominant position in economic policy-making continued. López Portillo created a new Ministry of Budget and Planning (SPP) in 1976 with many of the functions of the Office of the Presidency and the expenditure budgeting function of the Finance Ministry. From the beginning of the SPP's institutional life, disputes with the Finance Ministry frequently involved competition for supremacy in the "Economic Cabinet." The three most prominent battles were between Carlos Tello in the SPP and Moctezuma Cid in the Finance Ministry in 1977, Miguel de la Madrid in the SPP and David Ibarra in the Finance Ministry from 1979 to 1982, and between Carlos Salinas in the SPP and Jésus Silva Herzog in the Finance Ministry from 1982 to 1986.

Ironically, remote institutional origins of the Finance Ministry's downfall lie in the formation in 1954 of a Commission of Investment in the office of the nation's president. In 1958, President-elect López Mateos (1958–1964) pushed the idea of one of his advisers that the commission be reformed and given budget and planning functions. Minister of Finance Ortiz Mena strongly opposed the idea. As a compromise, López Mateos transformed the commission into the Secretaría de la Presidencia (Office of the Presidency), giving it an ambiguous role in economic policy-making and no authority over current spending or global planning as initially suggested for the commission. At the same time, López Mateos created the Ministry of National Patrimony to supervise state-owned enterprises. There were occasional fights between Finance, National Patrimony, and the Office of the Presidency, with the Finance Ministry almost always prevailing, until the Echeverría years.

López Portillo continued expansionary monetary policy and delayed devaluation as Echeverría had done. The 1982 bank nationalization can be seen as the culmination of a trend of increasing centralization of economic policy-making power in the presidency and of growing government intervention in financial markets that began with Echeverría's efforts to use easy access to foreign exchange to support programs aimed at increasing the ruling party's national populist profile.

The specific motivations for bank nationalization are less important than is the fact that the boom-bust cycle of the Echeverría and López Portillo years left private banks so weak that to avoid bank failures would have required significant government intervention, if not take-overs, in any case. The bankers were certainly not pleased with the expropriation of their property, nor does the devaluation's negative impact on their financial health fully explain the timing of the decision. Nonetheless, the weak financial position of the banks as a consequence of boom-era lending and the devaluation is an important part of the context of policy change. Both banks and their industrial clients were caught holding large dollar-denominated loans that became a much larger burden in peso terms after the devaluation. An increase in government intervention, although not necessarily outright nationalization, would have had to occur sometime in the aftermath of the Mexican boom-turned-bust because of its impact on the financial health of the banking sector.[42]

V. FINANCIAL LIBERALIZATION IN THE 1980s

After the period of nonorthodox financial and monetary policy culminating in the bank nationalization, Mexico began returning to a policy of relative monetary austerity and retreat from state intervention and ownership in financial markets. This policy shift was driven by the need to reestablish credibility with international and domestic creditors and was accompanied by renewed respect for central bank power and autonomy within the government. Under government tutelage, the private banks regained financial strength, an important precondition for their reprivatization.[43]

The trend toward financial liberalization began with the partial reprivatization of the commerical banks shortly after their nationalization in 1982 and the reduction in provision of preferential credit through public development banks beginning in 1986.[44] The period of extensive

[42] For more on the politics of the bank nationalization, see Maxfield, *Governing Capital*, chap. 6.

[43] The leftist press in Mexico has suggested that financial liberalization and bank reprivatization are responses to World Bank conditionality. Although some pressure existed, this is not a primary explanation for the current policy pattern. The government has carried financial liberalization further and faster than World Bank advisers have suggested.

[44] Between 1982 and 1986, preferential credit distributed through public development banks and fideicomisos amounted to 4 percent of GDP on average. This was down to 1.7 percent in 1987, according to Dwight S. Brothers, "Financial Sector Planning and Mexico's New Development Strategy," paper for presentation at the conference on Mexico's Search for a New Development Strategy, sponsored by the Economic Growth Center

liberalization—which included freeing interest rates, lifting credit controls and reserve requirements on private banks, shrinking the size of public development banks, and fully reprivatizing the commercial banks—dates to early 1989.

In March 1989, Undersecretary of Finance Guillermo Ortiz announced the government's intention to liberalize interest rates and stop financing public debt through reserve requirements on the commercial banks. Reserve requirements were reduced from 90 percent to 30 percent effective April 3, 1989. Interest rate liberalization was delayed until May 1 because the commercial banks claimed they needed time to prepare for the increased competition for deposits that would result.[45] In August 1989, in a speech announcing tax breaks for those Mexicans repatriating capital and legalization (for the first time since 1982) of dollar-denominated time deposits in commerical banks, Finance Minister Pedro Aspe stressed the need for banks to be more efficient. In January 1990, the executive steamrolled several more changes in financial legislation through Congress. These changes gave the commercial banks more operating freedom and permitted foreigners to hold nonvoting stock in commercial banks and other financial enterprises.[46]

These moves caused speculation that full privatization of the banks might be on the horizon; few expected it to be announced as quickly as it was however. Most observers expected President Salinas (1988–present) to wait until after the 1991 midterm elections to take the seemingly politically risky step of reprivatizing banks that were nationalized in the name of national populism only eight years before. Nevertheless, on May 2, 1990, the Mexican president sent to the Congress legislation mandating the sale of the government's 66 percent holding in the nation's eighteen commercial banks. In September 1990, the Bank Disincorporation Committee began registering potential buyers, and banks began to be auctioned off on a one-by-one basis in a highly secret bidding process. The first large bank to be sold was the Banco Nacional de México in August 1991.[47]

---

of Yale University, April 6–8, 1989, pp. 13–14. This reduction was achieved in part through reductions in the rate of subsidy implied in the loans. One important goal was to try to simplify the subsidy rate schedule by equalizing rates for the many different loan categories (e.g., small farmers, small businesspeople, exporters). The rates were also indexed to the weighted average cost of deposits.

[45] "Mexico Plans Industrial and Financial Reform," *Business Latin America*, March 27, 1989, pp. 89–90; and "Mexico," *Business Latin America*, April 24, 1989, p. 128.

[46] "Aspe Wants More Efficient Banks," *Latin American Weekly Report*, August 17, 1989, p. 11; "Mexico," *Business Latin America*, January 8, 1990, p. 8; and Carlos Acosta, "El del dinero, campo abierto a la competencia entre extranjeros," *Proceso*, no. 687 (1990): 12–15.

[47] The financial details of bank reprivatization are summarized in Stefano Natella and

The legislation Salinas sent to the Mexican Congress to permit re-privatization involved amending the constitutional provision dating to 1982 that categorized commercial banking as a nationally strategic industry and reserved it for state control. As such, it was the first time since the 1917 revolution that the Mexican government proposed a constitutional change to reduce the size of the state. As a constitutional amendment, the legislation also needed to pass the national legislature with a two-thirds majority and a simple majority in thirty-one state legislatures. The PRI, holding only 263 of 500 seats in Congress, needed to find allies to secure the bill's passage. Salinas counted on, and received, the support of the Partido de Acción Nacional (PAN) deputies, who held the largest single block of minority party seats.[48]

The banking legislation passed in July 1990 permitted 100 percent private ownership of all Mexico's commercial banks with certain restrictions.[49] To prevent concentration of ownership, which was seen as one of the problems originally leading to nationalization, the law prevented individuals from owning more than 5 percent of any single bank's stock or 10 percent with a special dispensation from the Ministry of Finance. Institutional investors were authorized to hold up to 15 percent. The legislation encouraged the formation of financial holding companies whose percentage ownership was unlimited. It permitted up to 30 percent foreign ownership. The legislation encouraged the trend toward "multiple" or "universal" banking legally initiated in the 1970s. Although the number of commercial banks in Mexico fell from forty-one nationalized banks in 1982 to eighteen banks that were put up for sale in 1990, further concentration was considered necessary to prepare Mexican banks to compete directly with foreign banks. The

Justin Manson, *The Mexican Banking System* (Boston: Equity Research Department, CS First Boston, May 1991).

[48] There was some opposition within the PAN to the bank reprivatization legislation. In August 1989, after rancorous debate, the PAN made the fateful decision to support the PRI's proposed electoral law. The law drew a fine line between opening up the electoral system and guaranteeing PRI dominance and therefore limited the PAN's political potential. The party became bitterly divided over the decision to support the PRI legislation, and some feared further upheaval resulting from support of the nationalization. Furthermore, PAN deputies, together with those of left-wing minority parties, went on "legislative strike" to protest the government's refusal to investigate allegations of fraud at the government fishing industry bank (Banpesca). Nevertheless, the bill passed with a relatively high number of abstentions after the PRI conceded to PAN demands that the legislation be amended to limit concentration of bank ownership by individuals.

[49] The constitutional reforms were published in the *Diario Oficial*, June 27, 1990, and the two new laws—the Law of Credit Institutions and the Law to Regulate Financial Groups—and the reforms and additions to the Stock Market Law were published in *Diario Oficial*, July 18, 1990. Details of the legislation and government interpretation and rationale are presented in Secretaría de Hacienda y Crédito Público, "La nueva banca y las agrupaciones financieras en México," SHCP, August 1990.

legislation foresaw the opening of new branch offices of foreign financial enterprises that could perform banking functions with nonresidents but could not participate in financial intermediation in national financial markets without special authorization from the Finance Ministry.[50]

Salinas's motive for privatization was part of his larger economic plan to restore Mexican economic growth with new inflows of foreign capital. It was one of a series of moves—which included unilateral trade opening, removing restrictions on foreign direct investment, and pushing for a free-trade agreement with the United States—that were designed to create foreign and domestic capitalist confidence in Mexico's economic future. Privatization was perhaps the most effective way to signal Mexico's security for foreign and domestic investors and keep foreign capital flowing into the country and domestic interest rates low.[51]

In the immediate aftermath of the legislative changes, there was virtually no opposition to privatization. Leadership of the Mexican labor federation, the Congreso de Trabajadores Mexicanos (CTM), was supportive; the assistant secretary general of the CTM (also president of the Senate) spoke in support of the measure on the grounds that "times have changed" since the nationalization of 1982. Former president Luis Echeverría heralded the legislation as born of the "profound nationalism that has been the hallmark of the current administration."[52] The only public opposition came from left-wing congressional representatives and the architect of the bank nationalization, Carlos Tello.

Lack of opposition to liberalization and reprivatization specifically reflects both the technocratic nature of financial decision making and the distribution of costs and benefits among social groups with different organizational capacity and policy influence. The bank nationalization was decided and implemented by President López Portillo and a very

---

[50] U.S. commercial banks have long had "representative offices" in Mexico that are legally limited to performing advisory services and assisting nonresidents. The scope of such activity has been quite broad. As of late 1990, buoyed by the success of three closed-end Mexico country funds, several U.S. investment banks had set up, or were arranging to set up, Mexican offices, hoping to compensate for declining business in the United States with fees from Mexican incorporated firms desirous of floating bonds and selling stocks abroad. Among them were Merrill Lynch; Bear, Stearns; and Goldman, Sachs. Goldman won the much sought-after job of helping the Mexican government sell the state telephone company. That activity alone was not highly profitable, but it gave Goldman an inside line on the lucrative business of floating telephone company bonds in foreign markets. Further opening to foreign banks was one of the few bargaining chips Mexico had in free-trade negotiations with the United States, and it was high on the list of problem issues in those talks.

[51] This inflow and the lowering of domestic interest rates it permitted allowed the Mexican government to begin reducing its internal debt, which had become more worrisome to many potential investors than was the external debt.

[52] "Eight Years On, Denationalization," *Latin American Weekly Report*, May 17, 1990, p. 4.

small circle of advisers. Little effort was made to involve those potentially supportive of the move at any stage in the policy process. The decision was made and then, as one former Mexican financial official put it quite lyrically, "Se lo pintaron de color populista" ("They painted it a populist color"). The privatization decision was made in a similar fashion. After the decision was taken, the PRI made an effort to present it in the media in the most populist light possible. The party took out a newspaper advertisement stating that the move was part of Salinas's "project of nationalist and popular modernization," and government publications of the bill were prefaced with similar language.[53] A poll conducted for *La Jornada,* the only Mexican daily largely unsubsidized by the government, found the day after the privatization bill went to Congress that 34.5 percent of the populace had not heard about it, 29.9 percent were strongly in favor, and 20.3 percent mildly so.

Those who stood to lose directly from the cutoff of subsidized credit from the commercial banks were relatively few. Although intended to benefit small and medium-sized entrepreneurs and certain sectors of the economy, selective credit programs were never particularly effective in channeling private bank credit to socially prescribed ends. The nationalization also did little to improve the allocation of credit to small and medium-sized industrialists and other targeted groups. The cutback of subsidized credit allocated through the public development banks such as Nafinsa was more likely to be felt directly, but collective protest was unlikely because of the diversity of the beneficiaries and rise of the new targeted state aid program, Pronasol. Large-scale industrialists had ceased relying heavily on "internal" financing, as they did in the 1960s, but in seeking external financing, they shifted more toward the stock market and stock brokerages than to loans from domestic banks.

The approach outlined in the introduction appears to shed light on the politics behind the four financial and monetary policy periods just described. The response of Mexican presidents to their nation's international credit standing shaped the power and autonomy accorded central financial authorities. Cárdenas, Echeverría, and López Portillo placed little value on currying favor with international creditors. Building up or preserving the power and autonomy of the Banco de México as an international signal of creditworthiness was not important to these presidents. The two major shifts toward orthodoxy occurred only when establishing international creditworthiness became a much higher priority.

[53] Ibid.

The particular form that orthodox policy took in the stabilizing development years, however, was not strictly a hands-off policy; selective credit controls were used to achieve the objectives of stability. This stance corresponded with the political and financial power of private bankers and their relationship with the central bank. The financial weakness of commercial banks after the oil and debt boom-turned-bust provides an important part of the context for a growing government role in financial markets in the early 1980s. The new financial health of the commercial banks provided the basis for their sale in the 1990s.

Similarly, the financial situation and interests of industrialists were among the conditions shaping changes in financial and monetary policy in the 1950s and 1960s. Low industry dependence on "external" commercial bank loans gave them less financial motivation to oppose tight monetary policy or support an investment-oriented credit control program than if they had had less access to "internal" financing. Industrialists' shift to financing through the stock market and stock brokerages in the 1980s also gave them little financial motive to oppose reduction of state involvement in commercial banking.

CHAPTER NINE

Brazilian Politics and Patterns
of Financial Regulation, 1945–1991

LESLIE ELLIOTT ARMIJO

This essay investigates the effects of Brazilian politics on the choice
and implementation of national financial policies, especially policies for
industrial finance, between 1945 and 1991. The pattern of Brazilian
financial regulation during this period was broadly interventionist, with
central government policymakers playing a role in determining the
allocation and often the cost of credit. Government control of credit
was one of the three main economic policy instruments of the postwar
Brazilian developmental state, along with direct production through
state-owned enterprises and guidance of private investment through a
complex and frequently changing fiscal code.[1]

The story of the politics of postwar financial policy-making divides

I thank Jeffry Frieden, Daniel Gleizer, Stephan Haggard, Laura Hastings, Kenneth
P. Jameson, Chung Lee, Nathaniel Leff, Sylvia Maxfield, Kaizad Mistry, Carlos Ribeiro,
and the participants in the East-West Center's conference on Government, Financial
Systems, and Economic Development for their generous help and comments on earlier
drafts. I also am grateful to Wendy Barker, José Carlos Braga, Oscar César Brandão,
Súlamis Dain, David Fleischer, José Fortunati, Álvaro Manoel, António Mendes, Ary
César Minella, Paulo César Motta, Dércio G. Munnoz, Walter L. Ness, Edson Nunes,
Gesner Oliveira, Luis C. de Oliveira Filho, Luis Pedone, Luis Carlos Bresser Pereira,
Fernando Perrone, Adroaldo Moura da Silva, Juárez de Souza, and many others for
sharing their insights into recent changes in Brazil's pattern of financial regulation during
my brief visit in 1991, and to Northeastern University for funding that trip.
[1] See Werner Baer, *The Brazilian Economy: Growth and Development*, 3d ed. (New York:
Praeger, 1979); J. R. Mendonça de Barros and D. H. Graham, "The Brazilian Economic
Miracle Revisited: Private and Public Sector Initiative in a Market Economy," *Latin American Research Review* 13, no. 2 (1978); Pedro Malan and Regis Bonelli, "Brazil, 1950–
1980: Three Decades of Growth-oriented Economic Policies," Institute de Planejamente
(Rio de Janeiro: IPEA, March 1990); Working Paper and Thomas Trebat, *Brazil's State-
Owned Enterprises: A Case Study of the State as Entrepreneur* (Cambridge: Cambridge University Press, 1983).

into two periods: 1945 to approximately 1980 and 1980 to the end of 1991. This periodization is perhaps counter intuitive in that it does not coincide with the three distinct national political regimes: the semi-elite democracy from 1945 to the military coup in 1964, military authoritarianism from 1964 to early 1985, and restored civilian, democratic rule since 1985. From the close of World War II to around 1980, however, underlying patterns of national interest aggregation via the political system, insofar as they affected choices about financial regulation, remained comparatively stable. Sometime during the presidential term of João Figueiredo (1979–1985), they changed.

Throughout the first period, the central government was relatively strong vis-à-vis domestic economic elites in terms of the state's ability to control the agenda of financial reform. Three underlying structural characteristics of the national political economy allowed for reasonably autonomous central government financial policy-making from 1945 through 1980: (1) access to external financing, (2) low integration of banks with industrial firms within the Brazilian private sector, and (3) the institutional inheritance of a comparatively strong, economically interventionist state. As a result, relatively insulated technocrats within the state held the initiative, both in shaping the broad financial policy agenda and in targeting credit to specific sectors.

Central government financial policy choices in the postwar years were influenced by two elite economic ideologies: "liberalism," which in the financial sphere meant promoting decentralized, private financial intermediation and an independent central bank; and "structuralism" or "developmentalism," which advocated an activist role for the state in promoting high levels of industrial investment.[2] The developmentalist position also implied a comparatively greater tolerance for inflation as a necessary evil associated with overcoming structural supply rigidities in the economy. Despite the frequent use of "liberal" rhetoric to describe financial policy choices and the apparently sincere "liberal" intentions of some individual policymakers, especially immediately following the 1964 military coup, developmentalist industrial policy drove financial policy, which displayed a high degree of state intervention in credit allocation through the early 1990s. The importance placed on rapid industrialization as a shortcut to achieving great power status by the military intellectuals reinforced developmentalist policymaking during two decades of authoritarian rule.

Financial policies did not originate primarily in response to lobbying by private groups or as straightforward expedients to purchase wavering political support. Nonetheless, policymakers were cognizant of

---

[2] I employ "ideology" to mean a set of beliefs that are mutually consistent, plausible, and causally related, but intrinsically nonfalsifiable.

broad limits on government action imposed by the elitist class coalitions supporting both democratic and authoritarian Brazilian political regimes through the early 1980s. For example, despite the desires of successive Brazilian administrations to make loan allocation conform to state development priorities, there was no debate about bank nationalization. Decision makers understood private bankers to be crucial to the regime support coalition; therefore, technocrats designed policies to induce, but never to coerce, private banks' cooperation. Commercial banks operating under high inflation gained from legislation prohibiting interest payments on demand deposits and from guaranteed returns resulting from rediscount operations. Consequently, the private financial sector was noticeably less opposed to an interventionist state than the prevalent image of bankers in most countries would suggest. Similarly, industrial and agricultural producers received generous credit incentives in return for channeling their investments according to priorities defined by state planners. But, although it was true that state planners were relatively free to initiate credit incentives, it did not follow that policymakers possessed the power to cancel subsidies that had outlived their developmental justifications. In this sense interest group pressures mattered, as policymakers often layered new incentives on top of earlier favors, with pernicious cumulative consequences for the state's freedom of action in macroeconomic management.[3]

Around 1980, the political economic equation changed, with important consequences for financial policy-making. Concurrent democratization and economic trauma led to a breakdown of executive branch dominance over financial regulation. Interest groups, the national legislature, and state and municipal politicians asserted their right to participate in national economic policy-making. Some private and public sector elites questioned the priorities of the import substitution model itself. Although both government and opposition politicians and nonpolitical elites agreed that financial reform was necessary, society's willingness to accept technocrats' initiatives passively was no more.

I. The Semi-elite Democracy and Financial Repression, 1945–1964

The political system established during the long domination of national politics by President Getúlio Vargas (1930–1945, 1950–1954)[4]

---

[3] For a related explanation of the proliferation of bureaucratic agencies within the federal government, see Edson Nunes and Barbara Geddes, "Dilemmas of State-led Modernization in Brazil," in *State and Society in Brazil: Continuity and Change*, ed. John D. Wirth, Thomas Boganshields, and Edson de O. Nunes (Boulder, Colo.: Westview Press, 1987).

[4] Vargas was put in office by force in 1930, indirectly elected in 1932, directly elected

represented a shift from decentralized federal governments operating in the interests of agroexport elites to an increasingly centralized, urban and industrial sector–oriented national government.[5] After the international financial collapse of 1929, the central government had assumed control of all foreign exchange operations through the Banco do Brasil (BB). In 1933, Congress, responding to presidential initiative, passed two financial laws largely directed at British export-import houses and at the U.S. and German banks, which had become more prominent after the turn of the century. A usury law prohibited financial instruments from paying more than 12 percent annual interest. The gold exchange clause law forbade contracts denominated in any currency (such as gold or currencies freely convertible into gold) other than the national money, the cruzeiro. This provision effectively disallowed inflation-indexed financial instruments. The 1934 constitution stated a goal of the gradual nationalization of all banks and insurance companies, a threat that Vargas periodically raised but never acted on.

Monetary policy and banking and foreign exchange regulation were the responsibility of the Banco do Brasil. The BB had a dual existence as the largest commercial bank in Brazil and the official financial agent of the Treasury.[6] The BB was also a development bank, not only making loans to the agricultural and nascent industrial sector, but also in the 1930s and 1940s developing a strong organizational ethos that emphasized the BB's unique role in promoting progress and economic growth throughout the country.[7] The BB remained an alternative power center, allied to coffee and other agricultural interests, despite attempts by Vargas during the authoritarian period of the *Estado Novo* ("New State," 1937–1945) to subordinate the BB to executive control. Meanwhile, the activities of private commercial banks centered on financing imports and agricultural exports, with a comparatively minor role in financing production. Commercial banks owned by individual state governments handled state deposits and payments. Private industry relied primarily on internal (often family) resources for long-term capital.

---

in 1934, allowed to assume authoritarian powers in 1937, ousted by the military in 1945, and popularly reelected in 1950. In 1954 he shot himself to avoid being forced out by the military once again.

[5] For more on the political economy of 1930–1964, see Nathaniel H. Leff, *Economic Policy Making and Development in Brazil, 1947–1964* (New York: Wiley, 1968); and Thomas E. Skidmore, *Politics in Brazil, 1930–1964: An Experiment in Democracy* (New York: Oxford University Press, 1967).

[6] On the history of the Banco do Brasil during the First Republic (1889–1930), see Steven Topik, *The Political Economy of the Brazilian State, 1889–1930* (Austin: University of Texas Press, 1987).

[7] Popular Brazilian wisdom suggests that there are three persons of power in every town throughout the country: the priest, the magistrate (sometimes the mayor), and the manager of the Banco do Brasil.

Brazil fought in World War II on the side of the Allies and participated in the Bretton Woods Conference. These experiences, along with several other opportunities to interact with the central banking community of the United States and Great Britian, made a lasting impression on Eugênio Gudin, the prominent Brazilian economist, and Octávio Bulhões, his younger colleague. Before the war's end and Vargas's forced exit from the presidency, Bulhões, a senior economic aide, prevailed upon Vargas to create the Superintendency of Money and Credit (SUMOC), a consultative committee within the government to oversee the formation of monetary policy.

Bulhões was a committed economic liberal, favoring free trade and domestic free markets. He believed Brazil—which was historically prone to government deficits, financial booms and busts, and inflation—needed a monetary authority independent of the central government. He and his "coreligionists," to translate the applicable (nonpejorative) Brazilian term, had no faith in the ability of Banco do Brasil to behave as an independent central bank. If anything, the BB already was substantially independent of the central government executive but was heavily compromised with agricultural interests. At the same time, Bulhões recognized that the political power of the BB in the Congress, which was soon to be reopened, would make the effort to create a new institution extremely difficult. They chose the name SUMOC, rather than Banco Central, explicitly to soothe the sensibilities of the BB.[8] Despite this, the procentral bank lobby within the government found it necessary to modify its initial plans for Ministry of Finance dominance within the SUMOC so that three of the five members of the superintendency would instead be the president and two directors from the Banco do Brasil. SUMOC would formulate monetary and credit policies, which then would be executed by the BB.[9]

[8] See Pedro A. C. Lago, "A SUMOC [Superintendency of Money and Credit] com embrião do Banco Central: Sua influência na condução de política econômica, 1945/65," M.A. thesis, Department of Economics, Catholic University of Rio de Janeiro, 1982.
[9] The Banco do Brasil on several occasions between 1945 and 1964 showed itself to be less than fully subordinated to the central government executive. For one thing, the president of the BB, always a policymaker with an independent power base or the personal nominee of a political broker outside the central government, could refuse to comply with the wishes of the finance minister and, presumably, the president. Faced with such a rebellion, Vargas in 1952 ended up firing Finance Minister Horácio Lafer and retaining BB president Ricardo Jafet. Other times it went the other way. In addition, the technical mechanisms for restraining credit growth were also weak. A. C. Sochaczewski suggests that given the large number of branches of the BB throughout the country, it was relatively easy for local managers to ignore inconvenient central instructions. See Sochaczewski, "Financial and Economic Development of Brazil, 1952–1968," M.A. thesis, London School of Economics, 1980, p. 245. Certainly, there never was any question of causing hardship to the regional economy for the sake of satisfying the central government, much less foreign lenders, a populist position of which BB directors were, and continue to be, openly proud.

The next financial innovation represented a more interventionist approach. Vargas, reelected in 1950, warmly welcomed the U.S. offer to send a technical mission to help make an overall assessment of Brazil's industrial infrastructure needs. The results of the joint Brazil-United States Economic Commission included plans for forty-one projects in transportation (railroads, ports), electric power, and steel, which became the core of the Vargas government's economic program.[10] The Vargas administration, wary of using the extensive but politicized network of the BB to channel the expected foreign aid funds, created an entirely new institution, the National Economic Development Bank (BNDE, later BNDES). When expected U.S. assistance did not fully materialize, President Vargas got Congress to vote for a special tax. The BNDES rapidly became the major government instrument for channeling credit to industry. Control of the *distribution* of financing, particularly long-term investment credits, was a consistent aim of the state. The success of this goal is symbolized by the sectoral lending patterns of the BNDES, which were consistent with central government industrial development goals, as well as with the eventual sectoral distribution of actual economic growth. BNDES lending averaged slightly over 0.5 percent of GDP between 1952 and 1964 and accounted for the majority of long-term credit from all in-country sources.[11]

These developments overlapped with a wide-ranging debate on the role of the state in managing the economy. The most articulate proponent of the pro-interventionist position was Roberto Simonsen, a São Paulo industrialist. Gudin championed the liberal position.[12] By the 1930s, however, the institutions of the interventionist state had already progressed far beyond a laissez-faire or even a purely regulatory stance.[13] A joint cooperative and training agreement between the BNDES and the United Nation's Economic Commission for Latin America (CEPAL) was also an important mechanism for the transmission of developmentalist ideas.[14] Meanwhile, SUMOC, despite its eco-

[10] See Eliza Jane Willis, "The Politicized Bureaucracy: Regimes, Presidents, and Economic Policy in Brazil," Unpublished manuscript, 1990.

[11] See BNDES, *25 anos de BNDE: Avaliação*, Revista do BNDE (Rio de Janeiro, 1977), p. 14.

[12] See Eugénio Gudin and Roberto C. Simonsen, *A controvérsia do planejamento na economía brasileira*, 2d ed. (Rio de Janeiro: IPEA/INPES, 1978), for the most telling essays and speeches. Also see Leff, *Economic Policy Making*, and Kathryn A. Sikkink, *Ideas and Institutions: Developmentalism in Brazil and Argentina* (Ithaca: Cornell University Press, 1990). Both explore the assumptions and history of developmentalist ideas in Brazil, emphasizing their wide acceptance among various elite publics.

[13] See Nathaniel H. Leff, *Underdevelopment and Development in Brazil* (Winchester, Mass.: Allen and Unwin, 1982), vol. 1, *Economic Stucture and Change, 1822–1947;* or Topik, *Political Economy of the Brazilian State.*

[14] See Albert O. Hirschman, "Ideologies of Development in Latin America," in *Latin American Issues: Essays and Comments,* ed. Albert O. Hirschman (New York: Twentieth

nomically liberal origins, nonetheless strengthened the patterns of interventionist policy-making and executive branch initiative. Two of the most important changes in economic and financial legislation of the entire postwar democratic period were both administrative decrees of the superintendency. Instruction No. 70, dating from the Vargas years, created the multiple exchange rate system by which the government subsidized the import of capital goods and penalized consumer goods imports and agricultural exports. Instruction No. 113 (1955) allowed multinational investors to count imported capital goods as part of their total direct investment in the country, thus raising the limit of funds they later could remit abroad and giving them an advantage over Brazilian firms.[15]

The next president, Juscelino Kubitschek (1956–1961), was one of the most explicitly "developmentalist" of all postwar Brazilian chief executives. Kubitschek strongly supported the BNDES, which became the "steel bank," benefiting from a big U.S. loan through the P.L. 480 program. His visionary plans to move the national capital to the interior made him popular with both the general public and construction contractors. Kubitschek utilized the technical expertise of the BNDES to support his "executive groups," namely, sector-specific, government-organized consultative groups of state technocrats and Brazilian and foreign businesspersons, of which the best known was that for the automotive sector.[16] The executive groups ostensibly designed viable sectoral strategies; they also served to diffuse the always potent issue of denationalization associated with Kubitschek's active support for foreign direct investment. Many Brazilian businesspersons found they could prosper in cooperative or mutually interdependent ventures with foreign firms or with the state itself. Thus, the explicit Brazilian *tripé* (tripod) model of industrialization was born.[17]

While central governments of the 1950s attended to the possibilities for expanding state and foreign financing for industrialization, activity in private financial and capital markets remained listless. Inflation had by 1950 risen to over 20 percent annually, yet banks were legally bound by the 1933 usury law not to charge over 12 percent (nominal) interest

---

Century Fund, 1961); and Celso Furtado, *A fantasia organizada* (Rio de Janeiro: Paz e Terra, 1985).

[15] See Leff, *Economic Policy Making*.

[16] See Helen Shapiro, "State Intervention and Industrialization: Origins of the Brazilian Automotive Industry," Ph.D. diss., Department of Economics, Yale University, 1988.

[17] Fernando Henrique Cardoso and Enzo Faletto, *Dependency and Development in Latin America* (Berkeley: University of California Press, 1979), and Peter Evans, *Dependent Development: The Alliance of Multinational, State, and Local Capital in Brazil* (Princeton: Princeton University Press, 1979), critique the costs of Brazil's "associated, dependent development." The three legs of the tripod were national, state, and transnational capital.

a year. The consequence was financial disintermediation: the ratio of financial assets to GDP steadily fell from a mean of almost 37 percent in the years 1948–1952 to only 21 percent in 1966, just before the financial reforms of the new military regime began to take effect.[18] Time deposits disappeared as large savers took their money out of the financial system and bought land or jewels. Banks, including the BB, evolved techniques that amounted to charging positive interest rates to industrial and commercial borrowers, including requiring large "compensating" deposits (which could be 25 percent of the total value of the loan), adding substantial service charges, or exacting under-the-table payments.[19] Nonetheless, real interest rates on loans sometimes fell below the rate of inflation, and banks had to try either to recoup their losses on the spread between deposit and loan rates or to expand their branch network to capture demand deposits from small savers. Between 1944 and 1964, the total number of commercial banks fell from 509 to 328.[20] Stock markets in Rio de Janeiro, São Paulo, and several other cities, although quite long-established, did not intermediate a significant quantity of funds.[21]

Meanwhile, Bulhões, Gudin, and others in and out of government had been preaching the gospel of sound money and an independent central bank. They found few converts among the nonfinancial business community, which naturally did not favor credit restrictions, but the arguments made sense to many bankers. By the early 1960s, the private financial community, led by Brazilian-owned commercial banks, had began to organize explicitly for the purpose of seeking political action from the legislature to modernize the country's financial regulations.[22] Their principal demands were abolishing interest rate controls, legalizing innovative financial instruments (such as the discounting of trade

[18] See Comissão Nacional de Bolsas de Valores, *Introdução ao mercado de ações* (Rio de Janeiro, 1986), p. 99.

[19] Further details are in Adroaldo Moura da Silva, *Intermediação financeira no Brasil* (São Paulo: FIPE/USP, 1980); and John H. Welch, "Capital Markets in the Development Process: The Case of Brazil," Ph.D. diss., Department of Economics, University of Illinois at Urbana-Champaign, 1988.

[20] Sochaczewski, "Financial and Economic Development of Brazil," p. 134.

[21] Some sources show new stock issues to represent quite a substantial percentage of gross domestic product. Goldsmith, for example, reports that total new stock emissions by private firms averaged 5.4 percent of GDP between 1950 and 1964. This figure, however, is not quite what it first seems. Fully 3.9 percent represents the upward revaluation of permanent assets to reflect inflation; the vast majority of the remainder of the "new stock" was new infusions of capital by existing partners in family-owned firms, not capital raised in financial markets. See Raymond W. Goldsmith, *Brasil, 1950–1984: Desenvolvimento financeiro sob um século de inflação* (São Paulo: Harper & Row do Brasil, 1986), p. 305.

[22] See Ary Cesar Minella, *Banqueiros: Organizado e poder político no Brasil* (Rio de Janeiro: Espaco e Tempo/ ANPOCS, 1988), for full details of the political activities and organizations of bankers between the late 1950s and the early 1980s.

bills), and creating an independent central bank. Rising inflation, which averaged 19 percent annually from 1950 to 1954 but 61 percent from 1960 to 1964, gave credence to the financial community's complaints.[23]

In 1961 both the economic and the political situations worsened. The new president, Jânio Quadros, represented the anti-Vargas UDN (National Democratic Union), a party that had prominent bankers and newspaper owners among its visible leaders and financial backers. Quadros quit after six months, which brought to office his separately elected vice-president, the leftist João Goulart, who was an anathema to the military and Brazil's self-designated "productive classes." Under Goulart, financial legislation became more nationalistic. In 1962 the president urged the Congress to pass Law 4131, the (anti)foreign capital law, which increased restrictions on capital repatriation and dividends payment abroad for multinational direct investors but also permitted Brazilian firms (including the Brazilian subsidiaries of foreign multinationals) to contract foreign loans directly. Other legislation limited foreign banks operating in Brazil to the number that were already in the country as of the early 1960s. In addition, the Goulart administration created the Bank of the Northeast of Brazil (BNB), a new federal development bank to channel monies to Brazil's historically poor, populous, and natural disaster-prone Northeast.[24]

Finally, in the years and months before the March 1964 coup, the old controversy over credit expansion and the need for a central bank heated up again, this time in the national legislature. The Goulart administration proposed a banking reform relatively close to that favored by the economic liberals and the newly politically active banking communities of Rio de Janeiro and São Paulo. Congress's lower house instead passed a version that definitively would declare the Banco do Brasil to be the nation's central bank. Federal deputies associated with both the São Paulo Federation of Industry (FIESP, then and now the most powerful business association in Brazil) and the employees' union of the BB (historically the backbone of civil servant unionism) had lobbied their colleagues for this bill. While the banking community tried to organize in opposition, the military and their allies among the civilian politicians moved against Goulart.[25]

[23] Figures are from Francis A. Lees, J. M. Botts, and R. P. Cysne, *Banking and Financial Deepening in Brazil* (New York: St. Martin's, 1960), pp. 38–39.
[24] On the early years of the BNB, see Albert O. Hirschman, *Journeys toward Progress: Studies of Economic Policy-Making in Latin America* (New York: Twentieth Century Fund, 1965).
[25] On the role of bankers in the 1964 coup, see Minella, *Banqueiros;* and René A. Dreifuss, *1964: A conquista do estado, ação política, poder e golpe de classe* (Rio de Janeiro: Vozes, 1981). For other perspectives on the coup, see Skidmore, *Politics in Brazil;* Thomas E. Skidmore, *The Politics of Military Rule in Brazil, 1964–1985* (New York: Oxford Uni-

II. FINANCIAL DEEPENING AND STATE PROMOTION OF INDUSTRY, 1964–1980

After the coup, the new president, military intellectual and "moderate" Humberto Castello Branco (1964–1967), appointed as ministers two prominent economic liberals:[26] Bulhões, veteran campaigner for an independent central bank, and Roberto Campos, former president of the BNDES.[27] Campos and Bulhões implemented what was perhaps Brazil's only successful government-designed stabilization program. Among the costs were wage repression and a credit squeeze sufficiently severe to cause many small businesses to fail.[28] Multinational businesses and a few large Brazilian companies met their urgent credit needs by using the new Law 4131 facility to borrow abroad. The World Bank, the International Monetary Fund, and the U.S. government supported the new government with cheap credits. Other government reforms increased tax collections and raised prices of the outputs of many state enterprises.

Dearest to the heart of Bulhões, however, was the comprehensive, clearly articulated, extremely wide-ranging series of financial reforms.[29]

---

versity Press, 1988); and Phyllis R. Parker, *Brazil and the Quiet Intervention, 1964* (Austin: University of Texas Press, 1979).

[26] Economic liberals are also called "monetarists" in Brazil, which is probably a misnomer. On the wide divergence between the Brazilian military regime and the more economically orthodox Argentine, Uruguayan, and especially Chilean juntas of the 1970s, see Alejandro Foxley, *Latin American Experiments in Neo-conservative Economics* (Berkeley: University of California Press, 1979).

[27] On the political economy of the military era, see David Collier, ed., *The New Authoritarianism in Latin America* (Princeton: Princeton University Press, 1979); Evans, *Dependent Development;* Jeffry A. Frieden, *Debt, Development, and Democracy: Modern Political Economy and Latin America, 1965–1985* (Princeton: Princeton University Press, 1991); Luciano Martins, *Estado capitalista e burocracia no Brasil pos-64* (Rio de Janeiro: Paz e Terra, 1985); Guillermo O'Donnell, *Modernization and Bureaucratic-Authoritarianism: Studies in South American Politics* (Berkeley: Institute of International Studies, University of California, 1973); Ben Ross Schneider, "Politics within the State: Elite Bureaucrats and Industrial Policy in Authoritarian Brazil," Ph.D. diss., Department of Political Science, University of California at Berkeley, 1987; Skidmore, *Politics of Military Rule;* and Alfred Stepan, ed., *Authoritarian Brazil: Origins, Outputs, Future* (New Haven: Yale University Press, 1973).

[28] See Albert Fishlow, "Some Reflections on Post-1964 Brazilian Economic Policy," and Thomas Skidmore, "Politics and Economic Policymaking in Authoritarian Brazil, 1937–71," both in Stepan, *Authoritarian Brazil.*

[29] On financial reforms in 1964–1980, see José Carlos de Assis, *A chave do tesouro: Anatomia dos escândalos financeiros no Brasil, 1974–83* (Rio de Janeiro: Paz e Terra, 1983); Daniel L. Gleizer, "Government, Financial Systems, and Economic Development: Brazil," 1991, mimeo; Lees et al., *Banking and Financial Deepening;* da Silva, *Intermediação;* W. L. Ness, "Financial Market Innovations as a Development Strategy: Initial Results from the Brazilian Experience," *Economic Development and Cultural Change,* no. 3 (April 1974); L. C. Bresser Pereira, "Changing Patterns of Financing Investment in Brazil," *Bulletin of Latin American Research* 6, no. 2 (1990); D. E. Syvrud, *Foundations of Brazilian Economic*

The principal goals of the financial policy package were to increase voluntary private savings and industrial investment. The reforms embodied a curious mixture of liberal and developmentalist aims, whereas their architects, at one and the same time, preached free markets and enforced a stabilization program of unprecedented toughness while busily constructing the next generation of targeted credit lines and special incentives. Although Congress, once purged, was shortly reopened, it was clear where the power lay, and the new regime's reforms passed without extensive debate or contentious amendments. The military regime, in any case, initially was quite popular not only with foreign governments and the "productive classes" but also with the urban middle class, which was frightened by both inflation and the image of Goulart calling on workers to protest in the streets. Most segments of Brazilian opinion were happy to support technocratic innovation by the executive.

In July 1964, just four months after the military coup, the new economic team moved to recover the central government's capacity to borrow by creating the ORTN (Readjustable Obligation of the National Treasury), a new inflation-indexed government debt instrument, the first such one to be used in Brazilian financial markets since the passage of the gold exchange clause law of 1933. ORTNs were an immediate hit in the markets, particularly with such a credible new government in charge. In August, Congress approved the legislation for the housing finance system, which provided loans to builders for residential construction as well as mortgage loans to individuals. The new housing finance system simultaneously was a large stimulus to the construction industry, a benefit for the politically important urban middle class (ostensibly also for urban workers), and a new lease on life for a moribund national system of public savings banks (*caixas econômicas*). Funds came from inflation-indexed mortgage bonds and indexed savings accounts that were guaranteed by the central government through a new specialized "central bank" (the National Housing Bank) for the national network of mortgage and residential construction lenders. In addition, compulsory deposits came from a new workers' unemployment and special-purpose fund (the FGTS), which was created by the central

Growth (Stanford: Hoover Institution Press, 1974); M. Conceição Tavares, "O sistema financeiro brasileiro e o ciclo de expansão recente," in *Desenvolvimento capitalista no Brasil*, vol. 2, ed. L. G. M. Belluzzo and Renata Coutinho (São Paulo: Brasiliense, 1983); N. G. Teixeira, *Os bancos de desenvolvimento no Brasil* (Rio de Janeiro: ABDE/CEBRAE/BNDE, 1979); D. M. Trubeck, "Law, Planning, and the Development of the Brazilian Capital Market," *Bulletin*, School of Business Administration, Institute of Finance, New York University, nos. 72–73 (April 1971); Welch, "Capital Markets"; and M. L. T. Werneke Vianna, *A administração do milagre: O Conselho Monetário Nacional, 1964–1974* (Petropolis: Vozes, 1987).

government to compensate (or placate) workers for the loss of job security and had been constitutionally mandated under the *Estado Novo* legislation of the late 1930s but overturned by the economic policy-makers of the new military regime. The housing finance system had so much money through the late 1970s that its "agents" were soon allowed to lend to municipal governments for urban infrastructure projects as well.

In December 1964, the banking reform law simultaneously dere-gulated—by lifting the 12 percent limit on nominal interest rates—and reregulated—by functionally segmenting an array of special-purpose financial institutions—private financial markets. The law forbade fi-nancial institutions to own industrial companies and vice versa, annoy-ing some São Paulo bankers with incipient industrial holdings but in fact simply codifying the status quo.[30] Most important, the banking reform law transformed the SUMOC into a National Monetary Council (CMN) and established a partially independent central bank, the Banco Central do Brasil (BACEN). The BACEN's president and directors would be nominated by the nation's president and confirmed by the senate. Although the finance minister would preside over the CMN, he or she could neither dismiss the BACEN president nor force the BACEN to implement specific credit policies. Bulhões and Campos chose the new institution's president and directors and saw them con-firmed and installed. However, and significantly, Bulhões and Campos could not get even the cowed legislature to pass a bill entirely removing the independent credit creation attributes of the Banco do Brasil, which the BB argued was absolutely necessary to its mission of supporting the agricultural sector. There were limits to authoritarian control.

Policymakers expected the law on capital markets (July 1965), de-signed with the decentralized U.K. and U.S. financial markets as implicit models, to stimulate long-term, voluntary financial intermediation from household savers to private business. When, two years later, the markets remained sluggish, Bulhões and Campos offered inducements. The first and longest-lasting inducement was the so-called 157 funds (named after their enabling legislation), which is a scheme allowing partial in-come tax forgiveness for individuals (initially also for corporations) in exchange for "investment" in private commercial and investment bank-managed mutual funds. Over the next twenty years, Brazil spent in excess of US $13 billion on direct tax incentives alone to try to "educate" the general public about the virtues of investing in the stock market.[31]

---

[30] The new rules did envision that investment banks would hold minority positions in traded firms pursuant to their roles as underwriters of equity issues. Commercial banks, furthermore, could manage stock mutual funds.

[31] The figure of US $13 billion comes from a public lecture to potential foreign investors

Given this rich source of public funds, the capital markets institutions by the late 1960s had organized to lobby for the continuation of these extraordinary incentives. The 157 funds continued into the early 1980s, although the original plan had envisioned a duration of about three years. Their long life provides a classic example of how state elites created a private interest group that later blocked removal of its privileges.

The new government also took steps to meet the immediate credit needs of industry, which was hurting because of the government-induced recession. Campos and Bulhões informed the staff of the BNDES that the days of big steel were over; henceforth, the BNDES was to support private industry. The Treasury received orders not to release legally earmarked funds to the BNDES until its senior staff fell into line.[32] Castello Branco's economic team also responded to demands of specific industrial sectors, as long as these demands fell within the framework of the overall development goals. For example, capital goods producers had complained that the special incentives to import capital goods in the mid- and late 1950s discriminated against them. The now-unified exchange rate removed some of the implicit subsidy for machinery imports. In addition, the economic ministers created a special credit line, known as FINAME, within the BNDES especially to support the capital goods industry.[33]

In 1967, BACEN Resolution 63 responded to small business complaints that big firms, usually multinationals, could now borrow abroad, whereas small firms lacked that option. Through Resolution 63, Brazilian banks could borrow in international markets, on-loaning the funds to creditworthy firms that were too small or too new to be able to contract foreign loans directly. Resolution 63 on-lending was a sweet deal for private commercial banks, which earned a secure commission and passed on the exchange risk to the ultimate borrower. The bulk of the foreign borrowing in the 1970s came in under the auspices of either Law 4131 or Resolution 63.[34]

The next two generals that became president were both political hardliners who identified national security with strong industrial growth. Antônio Delfim Netto, the first agriculture but soon finance

---

by Securities and Exchange Commission (CVM) President Ary Oswaldo Mattos Filho, Boston, October 1991.

[32] See R. F. S. Pinto, *The Political Ecology of the Brazilian National Bank for Development* (Washington, D.C.: Organization of American States, 1969).

[33] On the BNDES, see Willis, "Politicized Bureaucracy."

[34] On the political economy of Brazilian borrowing, see Mônica Baer, *A internacionalização financeira no Brasil* (Petropolis: Vozes, 1986); P. Davidoff Cruz, "Notas sobre o endividamento externo brasileiro no anos setenta," in Belluzzo and Coutinho, *Desenvolvimento capitalista no Brasil;* and Frieden, *Debt, Development, and Democracy.*

minister under Presidents Arthúr da Costa e Silva (1967) and Emílio Garrastazá Médici (1968–1974), who had strong ties to São Paulo industrialists, never pretended to be a liberal.[35] Delfim saw his brief as delivery of prosperity to urban Brazil and gambled that his constituencies would resent neither politically authoritarian nor economically interventionist methods so long as the economy grew. One of his first acts as new economic superminister was to do away with the independence of the newly born central bank by forcing its president and directors to resign.[36] He expanded credit and recontrolled interest rates, as well as some prices. On the whole, the São Paulo industrial and commercial bourgeoisie loved him. He made the ministers of agriculture, industry, and commerce full members of the CMN and turned the meetings into broad economic summits. The CMN performed the dual functions of setting the extensive permutations of monetary and credit policy, on the one hand, and of interest aggregation for the business community, on the other. It became known that complaints and suggestions about the terms and availability of credit, price controls, or other sector-specific economic parameters were to be brought to the attention of the appropriate minister or subminister, who would then represent the interests of that sector before Delfim and the CMN. Nonetheless, as was traditional in Brazil, policy initiative remained firmly with the federal executive.

During Brazil's "economic miracle" (1968–1973), policymakers gave particular stimulus to the consumer durables sector, namely, the producers of air conditioners, washing machines, and, of course, automobiles. Credit expansion to the urban middle class through CMN directives to consumer finance companies played a key role.[37] Through the manipulation of financial regulations, the regime extended benefits to industrialists and the politically crucial middle class while achieving the developmentalist imperative of rapid industrial growth, which was concentrated in sectors selected by government experts. Other financial policies partly mollified agricultural export interests and less-developed regions of the country, which correctly perceived themselves to be net losers from government economic policies that favored the already industrialized southeastern states. For example, the "crawling peg" form of frequent mini-devaluations instituted in 1968 pleased the agricultural export sector by implying a central government commitment to avoid the chronically overvalued exchange rates of the 1950s. The BB continued to extend agricultural credit at well below market rates.

---

[35] This statement is strictly true only with respect to his views on the necessity for a national industrial policy. His earlier academic work had criticized excessive state interference in the growing and marketing of coffee.

[36] See Assis, *A chave do tesouro;* and Vianna, *A administração do milagre.*

[37] See Tavares, "O sistema financeiro."

Delfim apparently tried for the first year or two in office to go along with those aspects of Bulhões and Campos's mostly liberal financial reforms that did not particularly inconvenience him. But by the late 1960s, Delfim lost patience with the model based on the decentralized, and functionally segmented, private credit and capital markets of the United States, as the hoped-for surge in long-term credit and equity investments from private banks had not materialized. Investment banks proved unwilling to loan for more than six months; in 1971 a speculative boom and crash in the stock market justifiably scared off most individual investors. The new model championed by Delfim was that of integrated, multipurpose private banks. The CMN modified tax and other incentives to encourage formation of de facto financial conglomerates, usually but not always headed by commercial banks and uniting under one roof all the financial services a commercial or industrial firm might need.[38] Brazil's biggest banks delighted in being free of restrictive legislation. Delfim also altered tax incentives to encourage direct foreign borrowing by firms (Law 4131) and banks (Resolution 63). The BNDES expanded its operations into equity as well as long-term loan finance, thus completing its move into the functions private banks had declined to fill.

The 1973–1974 rise in international petroleum prices coincided with the installation of the next military president, Ernesto Geisel (1974–1979). The two ideological currents each had representation within his government. Finance Minister Mario Henrique Simonsen was closer to the liberals, whereas Planning Minister J.P. dos Reis Velloso (who had worked for three years with Delfim Netto) and President Geisel himself clearly were developmentalists. Whatever their individual preferences, the political pressures on policymakers pushed them toward greater state intervention. Inflation and external disequilibria were up, but Geisel was determined to avoid painful domestic economic adjustment.[39] Societal support for continued authoritarian rule had begun to soften. Superior economic performance was the military's only marketable justification for the prolongation of its "temporary" stewardship. Geisel continued the pattern of manipulating financial regulation to maintain high industrial investment. In 1974, policymakers transferred to

[38] See Wendy Joan Barker, "Banks and Industry in Contemporary Brazil: Their Organization, Relationship, and Leader," Ph.D. diss., Yale University, 1990; H. M. Makler, "Financial Conglomerates in Brazil: The Case of the Sorcerer's Apprentice?" Paper presented at a workshop on The Impact of the Current Economic Crisis on the Social and Political Structure of NICs, Sao Paulo, February 1985; and Minella, *Banqueiros*. A typical conglomerate united a commercial bank, an investment bank, a stock dealership or brokerage firm, and a consumer finance company, and, toward the latter 1970s, innovations such as leasing or cash management firms.

[39] See Albert Fishlow, "A Tale of Two Presidents: The Political Economy of Crisis Management," in *Democratizing Brazil: Problems of Transition and Consolidation,* ed. Alfred Stepan (New York: Oxford University Press, 1989).

BNDES management two social security/pension funds (PIS and PA-SEP) created by Congress in the early 1970s, thus approximately doubling the bank's loanable resources from in-country sources. After the mid-1970s, as Brazilian inflation made many private firms wary of contracting liabilities denominated in foreign exchange, economic planners altered detailed financial and accounting rules to push SOEs, including the BNDES, to increase their foreign borrowing, often in excess of the SOEs' own import needs.[40]

As a whole, the years between 1964 and 1980 were boom years for private industry, especially heavy industry. Between 1975 and 1977, BNDES loan approvals briefly reached the astonishing level of 4 percent of GDP.[41] Besides facilitating easy access to inexpensive BNDES credit and foreign loans, the state helped private business via extensive fiscal incentives and by promoting huge public sector infrastructure projects such as the Itaipú Dam, the world's largest hydroelectric plant. Infrastructure projects procured their inputs from, and often supplied below-cost outputs to, private industry. The construction and heavy engineering industries were especially blessed. The efforts of economic policymakers contributed to GDP growth of 7 percent from 1965 to 1969, 13 percent from 1970 to 1974, and over 6 percent in the more difficult post-oil crisis years from 1975 to 1979. Industry's share in GDP was 32 percent in 1960 and 38 percent in 1980.[42]

One might have assumed that private bankers would resent an industrial policy that, along with high growth, brought escalating inflation (up from 19 percent in 1970 to 77 percent in 1979), international debt (increasing from $5 to $56 billion), and domestic public debt (rising from 1 percent to almost 7 percent of GDP in these years).[43] In addition, virtually every month saw new BACEN regulations that altered taxation on banks' earnings from different assets, modifying maximum and minimum allowable time periods and interest rates for credit to specific uses and mandating direct quantitative targets for credit to be extended to different types of borrowers. The World Bank estimated that, as of December 1978, 34 percent of existing loans to the private sector were

[40] During Geisel's presidency, the foreign debt went from around US $18 billion, mostly owed by the private sector, in 1974 to around $ 56 billion, overwhelmingly the responsibility of the state, in 1979.

[41] See BNDES, 25 anos, p. 14; and Lees et al., Banking and Financial Deepening, pp. 38–39.

[42] Figures are from CNBV, Introdução; and Fundação Instituto Brasileiro de Geografia e Estatística (IBGE), Estatísticas históricas do Brasil: Series economicas, demograficas, e sociais de 1550 a 1985 (Rio de Janeiro: IBGE, 1987).

[43] For economic growth, see CNBV, Introdução; for inflation, see Lees et al., Banking and Financial Deepening, pp. 38–39; for foreign debt, see Baer, Internacionalização financeiro, pp. 67–71; and for public debt, see D. D. Carneiro Netto, "Passivo do governo e déficit público no período 1970/84," in Déficit público brasileiro: Política econômica e ajuste estrutural, ed. Ernesto Lozardo (Rio de Janeiro: Paz e Terra, 1986).

"highly subsidized," and only 21 percent of total loans to the private sector had been extended at free-market rates.[44] In the 1970s, 15–20 percent of the liabilities of private banks represented credits from federal public banks that were targeted for on-lending to purchasers of capital goods, small and medium-sized enterprises, farmers, residential construction, and so on. An additional 15–20 percent of liabilities of both commercial and investment banks were Resolution 63 monies borrowed abroad, the rules for which the BACEN actively manipulated.[45]

Yet Brazil's pro-industrialization policies did not imply marginalization of bankers. Although bankers professed chagrin at the failure of the project to create an independent central bank, many financial sector players soon accommodated themselves to the new order. As liberal views of financial regulation in practice lost out to interventionist ones, bankers also received concrete benefits. Policymakers constructed national financial regulations so that, in return for banks' compliance with the state's extensive programs of targeted credit, private banks received ample benefits. Several unquestioned fundamental principles of the regulatory environment protected profits. The de facto permission to form financial conglomerates meant that integrated financial businesses could protect themselves from the sudden shifts in operating costs of component units provoked by rapidly changing regulation. Rules limited bank competion by forbidding interest-bearing demand deposit accounts. Francis A. Lees, J.M. Botts, and R.P Cysne estimate the resultant inflationary transfers to commercial banks as 1.3 percent of GDP in 1970 and 2.3 percent in 1979.[46]

Retail banking was closed to most new foreign entrants, and existing foreign banks could not open additional branches. Domestic entry to the sector was also restricted; yet existing holders of licenses to operate financial institutions were free to sell their rights to the highest bidder, whose fitness to open a bank BACEN vetted only superficially. The BACEN also continued to facilitate financial concentration and conglomeration, ostensibly for prudential reasons. In 1955, the top ten banks had almost 34 percent of deposits; by 1980, this figure had almost doubled to 64 percent. Not surprisingly, the overwhelming majority of deposits (by 1980 fully 83 percent) were with banks headquartered in the already-developed southeastern states of São Paulo, Rio de Janeiro, and Minas Gerais.[47]

[44] World Bank, *Brazil: Financial Systems Review* (Washington, D.C., 1984), p. 13.
[45] See World Bank, *Brasil: Análise dos sistemas financeiros* (Rio de Janeiro: Instituto Brasileiro de Mercado de Capitais, 1985), pp. 57, 162.
[46] Lees et al., *Banking and Financial Deepening,* pp. 38–39.
[47] Figures are from Minella, *Banqueiros,* pp. 138, 158; and M. J. F. Gonzalez et al., *O Brasil e o Banco Mundial: Um diagnóstico das relações econômicas, 1949–1989* (Rio de Janeiro: IPEA, 1990), p. 147.

Another potentially sensitive issue was the market share reserved for private versus public financial institutions. Although no private banks were nationalized, the relative size of most public banks, except the Banco do Brasil, expanded. Deposits at private banks were 116 percent of resources captured by public banks in 1968, but only 55 percent in 1978.[48] Consequently, policymakers designed financial regulations to ameliorate the pressure felt by private banks, effectively reserving for them the most lucrative and visible sectors of loan markets. As a result, the share of private financial institutions as final lenders in total loans to the nonfinancial private sector almost doubled, rising from 21 percent in 1964 to 37.5 percent in 1980.[49] Public sector banks, except the BNDES, absorbed most of the pressure to loan to increasingly hard-pressed SOEs and government agencies.

Finally, the state assumed many of the risks of rapid innovation in financial markets. At first, Geisel's liberal new finance minister, Simonsen, had felt that what the private financial sector needed was a dose of healthy competition; he opposed too cosy a relationship between private banks and the state. Accordingly, in early 1974, Simonsen announced that banks that found themselves in financial difficulties could not expect the state to bail them out. In late 1974, however, the failure of one big private bank, the Banco Halles, produced such a shudder in financial markets that the BACEN rushed in to prevent a widespread panic. After the Halles episode, the central authorities treated private financial institutions, particularly large banks based in São Paulo and Rio de Janeiro, generously.[50] Once again, essentially liberal impulses in financial regulation had been undermined. Moreover, there were significant lacunae in the corpus of financial law, such that many notorious cases of gross managerial irresponsibility or outright fraud by high-flying financiers went virtually unpunished. One of the more famous of such legislative "oversights" was the rule directing that, when a financial institution went into receivership and had its operations taken over by the BACEN, the private banks' assets would receive full inflation indexing while its liabilities continued to be recorded in nominal terms. If expensive lawyers succeeded in prolonging final settlement of the case over several years during which there occurred 30–40 percent inflation, the ultimate result would be that the BACEN owed the

---

[48] If obligatory savings schemes for certain classes of wage earners are excluded from the definition of "deposits," then private bank deposits were 120 percent of public bank deposits in 1968, dipping to 106 percent a decade later. Figures computed from World Bank, *Brasil: Análise dos sistemas financeiros,* p. 56.

[49] See Welch, "Capital Markets," pp. 194–96.

[50] Assis, *A chave do Tesouro,* includes a chapter on the Banco Halles episode. See also the testimony of expert witnesses before the various congressional inquiry committees set up after 1986 to investigate possible financial reforms.

erstwhile bankrupt owners money! This (economically, if not politically) perverse law remained in force until 1986.

In sum, large private industry and big banks both gained from the style of financial management of Brazil's military rulers, implicitly exchanging political support for broadly favorable policies, although private actors controlled neither the inter- nor intrasectoral decisions about who received financing. Agricultural interests, still the country's primary earners of foreign exchange, were also part of the regime support coalition, although located on its outer fringes. Credit for agriculture was massive in quantity and very highly subsidized, being offered, for example, at a nominal annual rate of less than 10 percent in the mid-1970s, when inflation was above 30 percent. The almost "free" credit expansion facilities still retained by the BB in its capacity as rump monetary authority underwrote agricultural lending.

And what of Brazil's capital markets, the object of so much hopeful attention in the mid-1960s? The annual value of stocks traded was a respectable 2.48 percent of gross domestic product in the bullish year of 1975 and 1.26 percent in the bear market of 1979. On the other hand, stock market activity concentrated in only a few issues. For example, in 1978, 68 percent of all stock trades involved only the top ten shares.[51] By the early 1970s, the elaborate edifice of capital markets institutions and incentives created under President Castello Branco had evolved into performing four main functions. Brazilian capital markets funded and traded federal government securities; preferential (nonvoting) shares of large state-owned enterprises such as Pétrobras, the mining conglomerate Rio Doce Valley Company CVRD, and the BB itself; shares of multinational affiliates such as Sharp; and only lastly the mostly preferential shares of profitable, but usually closely held, Brazilian-owned private firms. The liberal goals of stimulating large increases in voluntary private savings, intermediated through a decentralized market in private company equities and debt securities, clearly had not been realized.

Overall, there were more similarities than differences between the political context of financial regulation under the postwar limited democratic regime of 1945–1964 and the military authoritarian period that followed it, despite quite real differences in the political support bases of the two regimes and significant variations in both economic ideology and personal style among the nation's senior financial policymakers. Similarities extended to policymakers' goals (finance of rapid import-substituting industrialization), instruments (if the private sector has not

[51] Figures from Goldsmith, *Brazil, 1950–1984;* and Lees et al., *Banking and Financial Deepening*, pp. 295, 300.

voluntarily fulfilled a desired function, then create a state incentive or state agency), and decision-making style (centralized and technocratic). Large-scale private industry, large banks, the urban middle class, and, slightly removed, large and medium-sized commercial agriculture figured among the political supporters and economic beneficiaries of both regimes. The organized industrial working class, a junior coalition partner in the semi-elite democratic period but excluded during the years of military rule, was not even a peripheral player in national financial policy-making in either period, partly because of the specialized knowledge required for making demands in this policy arena. Subnational politicians based in the state capitals and important regional cities, with the exception of agricultural export elites, also had little interest in or influence over the design of national banking and credit regulations before the 1964 coup, mainly because Brazilian credit markets were both repressed and regionally segmented. Consequently, suppression of political competition and interregional distributional conflicts during the military period did not greatly alter the center-state dimension of financial policy-making, despite the fact that financial policies clearly widened interregional inequalities. Around 1980, however, the political and economic conditions that had supported centralized, technocratic financial policy-making began to unravel.

III. REDEMOCRATIZATION AND FINANCIAL DECAY, 1979–1991

Redemocratization and macroeconomic disarray combined to undermine the model of financial policy-making that had been in place since the close of World War II.[52] The developmentalist and comparatively insulated model of financial regulation had depended on (1) a large degree of ideological concensus among policymakers and economic elites about the legitimate purposes of central government economic policy-making and (2) the rest of society's willingness to accept the decisions of "experts" in arcane policy arenas such as finance. Although faith in the activist state remained, the second of these preconditions for technocratic policy-making had come under severe strain. The political support coalition backing what Guillermo O'Donnell aptly labeled a "bureaucratic-authoritarian" regime (business elites, multinational investors, most of the urban middle class, and the military officer corps) became disenchanted with the regime's economic per-

[52] On the political economy of the early 1980s, see L. C. Bresser Pereira, "Six Interpretations of the Brazilian Social Formation," *Latin American Perspectives* 11 (Winter 1984); and Stepan, *Democratizing Brazil*.

formance.[53] Private industry and commerce remained reasonably happy until the late 1970s, when annual inflation hit the high double digits. The worsening economic situation combined with a general dissatisfaction among all elites (including the urban middle class) over continued restrictions on civil liberties and political expression.

In addition, new political actors, whose opinions gradually began to count, appeared. Beginning in the mid-1970s, first Geisel and then Figueiredo began gradual political liberalization, allowing free elections for increasingly more important political offices. Federal legislators and state and municipal elected officials began to agitate for a greater share of political power, including the power to make important national economic policies. Shortly after the peaceful return to civilian rule in early 1985, the legislature formally expanded the franchise, for the first time giving the right to vote to all citizens, literate or not, sixteen years of age and older. Furthermore, the demographic and social shifts associated with urbanization, increased literacy, and greater access to mass communications meant that a much larger share of the population in 1985, as compared with the last years of previous democratic rule in the mid-1960s, was aware of national politics and prepared to consider itself a potential participant.

Of course, the fact that the economy after 1979 or so increasingly went on the skids also undermined the legitimacy of insulated, technocratic economic policy-making. Mean annual GDP growth in 1980–1984 dropped to 1.6 percent. Although growth recovered to 4.3 percent in 1985–1989, national product contracted in both 1990 and 1991. In 1980, annual inflation hit 110 percent; in 1985, 235 percent; and in 1989, 1748 percent.[54] Stabilization was the major economic preoccupation of policymakers throughout the decade.

Under President João Figueiredo (1979–1985), the previously compelling tasks of ensuring high industrial investment and strong growth in those sectors state planners had designated as national priorities became both relatively less important to the political leaders and less feasible. Policymakers were obliged to cut subsidies. In 1975 and 1976, BNDES loans had been well over 4 percent of GDP; by the mid-1980s, they averaged only 2 percent of GDP.[55] Furthermore, in the 1980s a much larger percentage of BNDES funds went to keep ailing firms afloat. In 1984, total agricultural credit had dropped to only 20 percent of its (historically high) 1978 level.[56] Although the industrial and ag-

---

[53] O'Donnell, *Modernization and Bureaucratic-Authoritarianism*.
[54] See Lees et al., *Banking and Financial Deepening*, pp. 38–39.
[55] BNDES, *25 anos*.
[56] See Dércio G. Munhoz, "Os déficits e o reordenamento das finanças públicas," in Lozardo, *Déficit público brasileiro*.

ricultural sectors suffered (although not in silence), the financial sector did well through the 1980s, earning a large inflation bonus from demand deposits and investing funds in high-yielding treasury bonds.

Figueiredo himself was preoccupied with the coming transition to democracy, which he hoped to control and shepherd at the appropriate majestic pace. Figueiredo did not at first expect to be the regime's final military president. Nor did he anticipate that the authoritarian regime's carefully nurtured political party, given every political advantage (from campaign funds to gerrymandered rules) would lose embarrassingly in urban centers around the country in the November 1982 elections for state governors, mayors and city council members, and federal and state legislatures, the first free elections for many of these offices in over a decade. Financial policy-making was not his priority.

Under Figueiredo, government management of public banks became politicized in more visible ways. The president tried to use the intensely, even self-righteously, technocratic BNDES as a source of patronage and consequently demoralized many of the staff.[57] As the 1982 gubernatorial and mayoral campaigns opened up state and municipal politics, center-state financial and fiscal relations became more contentious. Almost every state had a state-level commercial bank and sometimes a development bank. Through most of the 1970s, these banks had been comparatively insulated from local political pressures. With the resumption of regional political competition, however, few politicians in control of governorships had been able to resist leaning on state banks for loans to pet "development projects": these resources often ended up funding campaigns. Concomitantly, the Figueiredo administration made no attempt to disguise its policy of slowing down legally mandated fiscal transfers from the center to the states in which opposition politicians had won the elections.

José Sarney (1985–1990), the first civilian president since João Goulart, came to office through the unexpected death of president elect Tancredo Neves, the skillful consensus builder who had led the victorious opposition coalition during the transition to democratic rule. Sarney lacked legitimacy both with the conservative supporters of military rule, whom he had recently deserted, and with the prodemocracy agitators, for whom he was an uncommitted Johnny-come-lately. A major feature of his political and economic agenda included redistributing government largesse to the poor northeastern region of the country and, coincidentally, the president's own political base. His first economic team included as finance minister economic liberal, Francisco Dornelles, who had links to the Rio de Janeiro financial community,

[57] See Willis, "Politicized Bureaucracy."

and a moderate structuralist, João Sayad, who was close to the São Paulo academic and industrialist communities. Dornelles wanted to stabilize the economy via tight monetary and fiscal policies; Sayad worried over maintaining industrial growth and employment. They proceeded to fight very publicly over macroeconomic policy, until first Dornelles, then Sayad, resigned. The next three finance ministers each introduced at least one drastic economic stabilization plan (involving external devaluation, a wage-price freeze, and promises to cut the public sector deficit). None of the plans held.

Sarney's government, like Figueiredo's, raised the price of agricultural loans, which had been heavily subsidized in the early 1980s. This policy raised howls from the rural areas and the Banco do Brasil. The successful efforts to increase the price of credit to agricultural borrowers contributed to loan defaults. By October 1991, the BB had a nonperforming loan portfolio of US $636 million.[58] Banco do Brasil executives and the BB "bloc" in Congress began to publicize the interpretation that the cutbacks in agricultural credit, along with the attacks on the BB's continued special privilege of expanding credit through the "movement account" (in essense, unlimited overdraft privileges with the Banco Central do Brasil, billed at negative real interest), represented a conscious plot to destroy the BB, the champion of nationalist (as opposed to foreign) financial interests. Plotters sometimes included the World Bank (which had heavily criticized the monetary role of the BB in a study published in 1985), the BACEN, U.S. bankers who wanted increased access to Brazilian markets, and the São Paulo financial community. In fact, although the BB's language was not modulated, there was some truth to each of these allegations. In February 1986, the BB lost the movement account, although its president, Camílio Calazens, was able to negotiate for the BB the right to become a financial conglomerate, thus enabling it to continue competing with private sector banking giants such as Bradesco, Itaú, or Citibank do Brasil.

Congress, moreover, had become a new locus for policy-making, including financial regulation. Legislators passed a "white-collar crime" law aimed particularly at those who profited from various sophisticated financial frauds. A specially elected legislature produced a new national constitution in late 1988. When lawmakers reinstated a clause prohibiting interest charges of more than 12 percent (real) interest a year, the new constitution appeared to signal a return to the early 1930s' model of financial regulation, which had repressed financial markets before the reforms of the mid-1960s. As with many of the other clauses in the constitution, however, this change would not go into effect until

---

[58] *Brazil Watch*, October 21–November 4, 1991, pp. 10–11.

it had been "regulated" by complementary ordinary legislation. That is, in the interests of passing the postauthoritarian constitution, the nation's representatives agreed to defer the battle over financial regulation, along with similar conflicts over wage policies, land reform, job tenure, and other sensitive issues. Although the new division of powers between the executive and the legislature remained fuzzy, economic ministers suddenly found themselves spending more time lobbying federal deputies and senators than had been the case even five years previously. Although the Brazilian Congress was activist, it was not internally disciplined or well-organized. After twenty years of authoritarian rule, political parties were not strong or deep. It was possible to arrange a coalition to block executive branch economic initiatives, but not one to pass serious stabilization programs or far-reaching financial reforms.

Yet the malignancies of Brazil's interventionist, yet permissive, system of national financial regulation could no longer be ignored. Private banks in early 1990 still earned high profits, although most other Brazilians experienced losses from inflation and, after 1989, rising unemployment. The financial sector had grown rapidly in the 1980s, increasing its share in GDP from 5.7 percent in 1970 to around 8 percent in 1980 and to 11.1 percent in 1990.[59] Despite the Congress's attempts in the late 1980s to curb abuses by financial wizards, the broad financial regulatory framework remained intact. In addition to the advantages already mentioned, many private banks in the 1980s had large earnings from investments in very high-interest government securities. Had political leaders from Figueiredo on been less fearful of alienating private bankers, they might have emulated decision-makers in many other developing countries, including Mexico, Argentina, and India: the central bank could have raised banks' reserve requirements and obligatory holdings of government debt. Instead, increasingly attractive interest rates were needed to induce banks to hold treasury bills. In turn, high interest costs fed the public debt. Government debt, which accounted for a meager 4 percent of total financial liabilities in 1965, had risen to a dangerous 58 percent by 1989.[60]

Meanwhile, many public banks were going broke. Virtually all the commercial and development banks owned by state governments were insolvent, mainly because of questionable loans made to the local political authorities in the states and municipalities associated with the elections of 1982, 1987, and, in a few cases, also 1989. Both the BNDES and the BB received fewer central government transfers, yet they had

[59] See *Conjuntura Econômica*, various issues.
[60] See Gleizer, "Government, Financial Systems, and Economic Development," p. 11.

many sour assets owing to borrowers who had fallen on hard times. The National Housing Bank (BNH) went bankrupt and in 1986 was merged with the only slightly healthier Federal Savings Bank (CEF). The heavy dependence of both private and public commercial banks on their earnings from inflation raised a policy dilemma: all commercial banks had a vested interest, at least in the short to medium term, in perpetuating inflation, despite its ravages on the rest of the economy.

In November 1989, Fernando Collor de Mello became Brazil's first elected president since 1961. As Figueiredo and Sarney had been, Collor was besieged by economic crises and political demands. His government's ability to formulate and carry through necessary short-term stabilization (which required the sharing out of costs among groups in society), not to mention longer-term reform of the financial system, was seriously in doubt. In early 1991, Collor's economic team, headed by Economy Minister Zélia Cardoso, instituted the most stringent stabilization program since the Campos-Bulhões policies of the mid-1960s. The heterodox Collor Plan came complete with the populist rhetoric of stabilizing the economy on the backs of the wealthy rather than on those of the traditional losers from Brazilian recessions, the poor. It froze three-quarters of all financial assets in the banking system for eighteen months, simultaneously angering both banks and depositors, including businesses and most of the middle class. A draconian monetary policy announced later in the year slashed credit, completing the alienation of the business community.

In 1989, the World Bank offered to make Brazil a $500 million loan, to be funneled through the BNDES, for the purpose of financial restructuring, including, it was rumored, compensating the BB to some degree for the loss of the "movement account" and perhaps assisting the central government in salvaging the commercial and development banks of the individual state governments. For political as well as prudential reasons, the BACEN had had to rescue these banks. The total debt of the state and municipal governments to the central government was estimated as of August 1991 to be $57 billion.[61] As of late 1991, the World Bank was holding its promised loan in abeyance until Brazil complied with certain conditions, presumably including guarantees about monetary restraint, limits to Banco Central bailouts, and perhaps also domestic market access for multinational banks.[62] What World

[61] "Estados que mais devem são os do Sudeste," *Jornal do Brasil*, September 3, 1991, p. 1. The three wealthy southeast states owed 53 percent of the total.

[62] The latter point has been a demand of the United States, in particular vis-à-vis semi-industrial developing countries such as South Korea, Brazil, and India, in the General Agreement on Trade in Services being negotiated within the Uruguay Round of the General Agreement on Tariffs and Trade in the late 1980s and early 1990s.

Bank negotiators might not have recognized was that the power to make national economic policy almost exclusively in the presidential palace was now gone: both the Congress and governors and state-level legislators of powerful states such as São Paulo could veto policies if they were excluded from participation in the decision-making process.

As of late 1991, some twenty-three proposals to regulate the financial reform provisions of the constitution were working their way through the national legislature, ranging from those that would immediately implement the 12 percent interest rate cap mandated by the 1988 constitution to others, backed by much of the professional economics community and virtually all bankers, that would honor the 12 percent limit by defining it so broadly that it would have no teeth.[63] There also were several proposals favoring establishment of a "truly independent" Central, Bank which variously was defined to mean an institution like the U.S. Federal Reserve, or one "independent" of the executive branch but under the supervision of Congress, a proposal that was put forward by the Banco do Brasil bloc.[64] Meanwhile, the business community as well as many professional economists worried over the fall in industrial investment and the lack of strategies within the government to cope with this.

Interestingly, despite the pressures of trying to manage the foreign debt, negotiate a pact with Congress to restore to the federal government some portion of the tax receipts distributed to the states and municipalities in the 1988 constitution, liberalize trade, and impose stabilization, the Collor government by the end of 1991 had instituted at least two potentially significant financial reforms. The more publicized was the program to end some of the state's direct responsibility for industrial investment through the sale of some big state-owned enterprises. Since early 1990, the major push within the BNDES had been the privatization program: fully three-hundred of fifteen-hundred employees were assigned full-time to this project. The other initiative was a new attempt to stimulate capital markets, this time focused on legislative and procedural changes needed to increase foreign portfolio investments. But in a move that was seen by supporters as an essential reform but by resolute economic liberalizers as caving into political pressures, Collor reversed in mid-1991 the policies of squeezing agricultural credit, which had been progressively introduced after 1980 under external pressure to cut budget deficits. Despite these initiatives, by the early 1990s virtually all Brazilians were highly dissat-

---

[63] As an example of the latter, see the proposal by Francisco Dornelles, the economically liberal federal deputy and former finance minister.

[64] See the proposal of Federal Deputy Odacir Klein, who represented the important agricultural state of Rio Grande do Sul.

isfied with both the form and the content of national financial regulation.

In the forty years following 1950, Brazil developed a modern, diversified national financial system. Loans to the private nonfinancial sector as a share of GDP rose from only 13 percent in 1964 to 51 percent a decade later, remaining near that level through the 1980s.[65] State-owned banks steadily expanded until 1980. At the same time, private Brazilian banks played an important role in financial intermediation, prospering despite the fact that substantial portions of their credit allocation were ruled by government directives. The regulatory regime limited the access of foreign private banks to a few long-established (and highly profitable) branches for commercial banks and minority positions in joint ventures in market segments other than commercial banking. In contrast to the experience of countries such as the Philippines, widespread accusations of blatant clientelism, corruption, or explicit political bias in the granting of specific loans had not been made against most Brazilian regulators or banks.[66]

The broad pattern of Brazilian financial regulation was of state, rather than free-market, direction of national and international financial resources. Sylvia Maxfield has argued that Brazil's historically loose monetary management and web of targeted credits reflects the power of an "industrialists' alliance" in Brazil, which she contrasts to the tighter money and limited credit and capital controls in a country such as Mexico, where a "bankers' alliance" captured policy-making.[67] This essay offers an alternative explanation, containing both a structural and an ideological component.

At the objective level of control over power resources, it was not so much industrialists, as individuals or as a group, that were strong in Brazil in relationship to bankers as it was the state itself that enjoyed considerable freedom of economic policy initiative vis-à-vis all private

[65] See Welch, "Capital Markets"; and *Conjuntura Econômica*, various issues.

[66] This statement, of course, is comparative. Assis, *A chave do tesouro*, describes numerous famous financial scandals. The lessons of over half of the cases, however, turn on techniques employed by sharp operators to exploit legal loopholes. That is, much of the volume is a plea for better prudential regulation rather than an exposé of corruption per se. A good comparative test case might be the lending practices of the Banco do Brasil. For many decades, it has been a heavily politically involved institution. But the BB is also renowned for its technocratic institutional culture. Entry to its ranks is by competitive examination. Its loan procedures are generally considered fair. At the operational level, it not only is seldom accused of corruption but also is often judged (particularly by individual, as opposed to corporate, clients) to compare favorably in efficient customer service with the large private banks.

[67] See Sylvia Maxfield, "Bankers' Alliances and Economic Policy Patterns: Evidence from Mexico and Brazil," *Comparative Political Studies* 23 (January 1991): 419–58.

interests—so long as the economy as a whole grew rapidly enough to ensure substantial benefits for all elite groups. Executive branch domination of financial regulation and credit allocation continued unbroken despite the shift from semi-elite democracy to military authoritarianism following the 1964 coup. Most of the major financial policy innovations came from economists and other technical specialists within the central government bureaucracy. New initiatives usually were not a result of close consultation with leading industrial or financial elites (as often was the case in Japan or South Korea). Technocratically designed initiatives, of course, could only be adopted because Brazil's institutionally powerful chief executives—at least until about 1980–on the whole were both willing and able to provide their chosen experts with the necessary resources and political support.

Three structural factors facilitated the relative maneuverability of the central government vis-à-vis both private lenders and borrowers. First, for reasons of both geography and international alliances, Brazil had more or less continuous access to external financing from the end of World War II through the early 1980s, except immediately prior to the 1964 coup. Successive presidential administrations tried to retain discretionary control over flows of direct investment and loan financing, both in order to achieve their visions of economic prosperity and as a political resource with which to reward or punish domestic elites.[68]

Second, integrated financial-industrial-commercial groups were much less prevalent in Brazil than elsewhere in Latin America.[69] Thus, both financial and industrial capital depended on the state more than would have been the case otherwise. Banks needed government support for the kinds of financial regulation they wanted (i.e., for provision of a lender of last resort, enforcement of financial contracts, and protection against "ruinous competition" from multinational banks), whereas

---

[68] See Frieden, *Debt, Development, and Democracy*.

[69] For more on economic groups in Latin America, see Nathaniel H. Leff, "Industrial Organization and Entrepreneurship in the Developing Countries: The Economic Group," *Economic Development and Cultural Change* 26 (July 1978); Nathaniel H. Leff, "Entrepreneurship and Economic Development: The Problem Revisited," *Journal of Economic Literature* 17 (March 1979); and Sylvia Maxfield, *Governing Capital: International Finance and Mexican Politics* (Ithaca: Cornell University Press, 1990).

On Brazil's historically comparatively low financial-industrial integration, see Barker, "Banks and Industry"; Carlos Halsenbalg and Clovis Brigagão, "Formação do Empresario Financeiro no Brasil," *Dados*, no. 8 (1971); and M. V. de Queiroz, "Os grupos econômicos no Brasil," *Revista do Instituto de Ciências Sociais* 1, no. 2 (1962). Reasons may include the origins of many private banks in financing agricultural exports and the historic importance of public sector commercial banks, especially the BB, Banespa (the bank of São Paulo state) and the several banks of the Minas Gerais government. Recently, this historic division has been fading. In the 1980s, financial conglomerates such as Itaú, the country's second-largest private banking group, began to diversify into related industrial ventures; a few industrial firms have fielded financial affiliates.

industrialists sought reliable access to affordable credit. Each group was sometimes satisfied, sometimes not. Under Vargas, Kubitschek, Médici, and Geisel, financial policies probably pleased industrialists more than bankers: the reverse was true under Castello Branco, Figueiredo, and Sarney.

Third, bureaucratic institutions and traditions continued from previous regimes and administrations. Brazil's state apparatus as early as the nineteenth century was, in comparative terms, economically interventionist; successive presidents and their ministers inherited both legislative respect for their freedom of action and a minimally competent bureaucracy to command. Vargas had promoted civil service reform in the late 1930s, seeking responsive bureaucracies, even while acknowledging the political value to himself and his political machine of the time-honored practice of packing the post office or the public works ministry with friends and supporters. By the mid-1950s, both the BB and the BNDES had entry by competitive examination and were relative paragons of efficiency.

There were, of course, limits to financial policymakers' comparative insulation from big business. Successive central governments proved sufficiently independent to choose their preferred new priorities for targeted credit. Yet each administration also needed cooperation from private business. Therefore, presidents lacked the power to move simultaneously against the short-term interests of all the business community—except at very high levels of macroeconomic crisis, such as in early 1991, when President Collor declared a stabilization plan that initially hit banks and large depositors very hard. In addition, various presidents, but especially Kubitschek and Médici (under the influence of Minister Delfim Netto), created ongoing formal and informal arrangements to extend to the business community symbolic participation in the big decisions of economic and financial policy-making and to receive their suggestions for incremental modifications. Another measure of the circumscribed arena for state initiative was the fact that the federal executive often lacked the strength to wind up previous administrations' financial incentives, which led over time to the proliferation of costly subsidies.[70] The financial regime thus contributed to recurrent problems of macroeconomic management.

[70] For example, in the 1970s the total value of agricultural credit averaged over 61 percent of agriculture's contribution to GDP. This level of assistance is clearly unsustainable, particularly given the extremely high subsidy component of most farm loans. The mean for 1980–1987 dropped only to 44 percent, despite the political flak both Figueiredo and Sarney took for their "attacks" on rural credits. See Gonzalez et al., *Brasil e o Banco Mundial*, pp. 125–26. Similar stories can be told about credit and other incentives to the construction industry, producers of manufactured exports, and heavy machinery, not to speak of the advantages offered to private banks by the financial regulatory regime.

If policymakers were not usually implementing long-term plans generated in consultation with private entrepreneurs, then where did the impetus for rapid innovation in financial regulation originate? Elite economic ideologies, often from abroad, were crucial in suggesting both broad goals and specific reforms to policymakers. One strand of influence was economically liberal, decentralized credit and capital market designs promoted by missions of financial experts representing institutions such as the Bank of England (particularly before World War II), the U.S. Federal Reserve Bank, the Organization of American States, the International Monetary Fund, and the World Bank. The package of financial reforms in 1964–1965 clearly reflected Anglo-American regulatory frameworks. Furthermore, whenever possible, aspiring young Brazilian economists trained at U.S. universities, which increased their job prospects at home as well as the international transmission of neoclassical economic ideology. The other ideological current was Latin American structuralism. From the 1950s through the Chilean military coup in 1973, Brazilian economists swarmed to Santiago to participate in the great debates on the future of the hemisphere sponsored by CEPAL. Brazilian industrialists, together with academia and most politicians, enthusiastically endorsed the structuralist recommendations for industrial and agricultural development banks, external trade and capital controls, and targeted finance to promote growth and national self-sufficiency. By the 1980s, Brazil's BNDES had been a center for both theoretical and empirical research in structuralist economics for decades.

Virtually all urban Brazilian elites embraced some form of structuralism and favored an activist state supportive of rapid industrial growth. Most were relatively unconcerned over the rate of money supply growth or government debt, were willing to accept efficiency losses associated with a proliferation of credit and tax incentives, and considered an annual inflation rate of 20 percent to be benign. In Brazil, as elsewhere, private bankers embraced liberal financial designs more warmly than did industrialists, who were more likely to see a need for state economic intervention on their behalf. Nonetheless, Brazilian bankers were significantly more "developmentalist" than their counterparts abroad, partly because they were not immune to dominant national economic ideologies and partly because technocrats designed the overall financial regulatory regime in such a way that both private industry and private banks flourished. Perhaps because of the conservative political cast of most postwar administrations, however, promarket rhetoric abounded, both within the government and among economic elites, except on the issue of free entry for foreign goods or foreign banks.

A qualitative change occurred around 1980. In the 1980s, although the regulatory framework of a state-led financial model remained in position, successive finance ministers under Presidents Figueiredo, Sarney, and Collor discovered that their centralized authority to allocate financial resources had seriously eroded. A majority of nationally relevant political actors were no longer prepared to accept insulated, technocratic financial policy-making by senior appointees of Brazil's president. Quite apart from the merits or demerits of the particular economic policy packages chosen, an underlying political determinant to the failures of financial regulation existed during these years. For three decades, central government decision-makers had agreed on the overriding importance of industrial growth; private business elites, foreign business interests, and sometimes military officers offered policy modifications at the margin. The transition to democracy through the 1980s undermined the legitimacy of governments performing as the "executive committee" of business interests largely based in southeastern Brazil. From the viewpoint of many business leaders, government ministers suddenly seemed to have become "unreasonable," unwilling or unable to continue to ensure the benefits to major economic interests that had encouraged the latter to acquiesce in central government economic leadership. As of the end of 1991, no new, moderately stable pattern of national interest aggregation had evolved; therefore, the political concensus necessary to once again take national financial policy-making in hand did not exist. The latter 1980s and early 1990s saw a number of awkward attempts to replace the old pattern of informal access for business leaders to senior policymakers with centrally convened "social pacts" among businesspersons, labor unions, and the central government, after the West European-Scandinavian pattern of democratic corporatism. This process probably cannot succeed in Brazil, because it still excludes too many of the newly obstreperous interests that need to be aggregated through the political system.

What does the new political reality of national financial policy-making imply for the future? One option is for policymakers to give up on state-led development, privatize or scale down most public sector banks, end BACEN balance sheet regulation of financial institutions for any but prudential purposes, and let the market allocate financial resources as it will. As of mid-1991, this option continued to be relatively unpopular, at least in an extreme form. Most Brazilian opinion-makers, despite desiring to end waste and inefficiency within the state, remained broadly developmentalist, certainly by comparison with their contemporaries in Chile or Argentina. Notwithstanding the severe problems of the preceding decade, most elites (including leftist intellectuals, who are untypically in agreement with the business community on this issue) looked back with some fondness on the achievements of the economic model between the end of World War II and the onset of the 1980s. The pattern of national financial regulation, of course, had been a significant component in that model. Construction of a stable new pattern of national financial regulation in Brazil in the 1990s may not precede establishment of a new political concensus over the future division of economic decision-making authority between the national executive and legislature, on the one hand, and the central and state governments, on the other.[71]

[71] The planned 1993 plebiscite on the future form of Brazilian democracy—presidential, parliamentary, or constitutional monarchy—epitomizes the current uncertainty.

CONCLUSION

CHAPTER TEN

Political Explanations of Financial Policy in Developing Countries

STEPHAN HAGGARD AND
SYLVIA MAXFIELD

The wisdom of government intervention in financial markets has been a recurrent issue in the debate about the role of the state in the developing countries' growth and industrial development. Much less attention has been given to the political determinants of government action or to how the institutional milieu affects its efficiency. In this conclusion, we draw on theory and the case studies to explore three questions that are of relevance to understanding not only the political economy of finance but also the broader patterns of state intervention in East and Southeast Asia and Latin America.

The first question concerns the timing, extent, and sectoral allocation of preferential credit schemes. Our cases fall into three broad groups. First are those countries with long histories of subsidizing credit to industry, namely, Korea, Brazil, and the Philippines. Taiwan and Thailand stand at the other extreme, with more limited preferential credit schemes for the private sector. Indonesia, Chile, and Mexico fall in between, with financial market policy oscillating between periods of an expanded government role in the allocation of credit (in Indonesia

This essay owes a tremendous debt to the members of this project. We received extensive and penetrating written comments from Leslie Armijo, Tun-jen Cheng, David Cole, Rick Doner, Laura Hastings, Paul Hutchcroft, Chung Lee, Andrew MacIntyre, and Danny Unger. As always, Jeffry Frieden was particularly helpful. A version of this chapter was also presented at an Organization for Economic Cooperation and Development Seminar on Financial Opening: Developing Country Policy Issues and Experiences, Paris, July 1992. Our thanks to the participants in that seminar, particularly the organizer, Helmut Reisen, and Silvio Borner, Colin Bradford, Bernhard Fischer, Peter Kenen, John Williamson, and Charles Wyplosz. Nancy Neiman provided research assistance.

through 1966 and in the 1970s, in Chile before 1973, in Mexico from 1930 to 1954 and from 1970 to 1982) and periods of relatively restrained use of the financial policy tool (in Mexico, 1954–1970 and in Indonesia, 1966–1974) or active liberalization (Chile after 1973 and the 1980s in Indonesia and Mexico).

A second question concerns the political conditions under which government policy is more or less efficient and growth-promoting. There are no easy criteria by which to judge the allocative efficiency of financial systems, and the task is, in any case, beyond the scope of this volume.[1] But we can distinguish among cases on the basis of the institutional structure surrounding credit policy and, in particular, the degree to which government policy is subject to capture and control by its beneficiaries, as this should have an influence on the efficiency of government intervention. In this regard, Thailand, Taiwan, Chile (post-1973), Mexico (1954–1970), and Korea (before 1975) show fewer signs of policy capture than do Indonesia, Chile (pre-1973), and the Philippines.

Financial market liberalization, particularly the deregulation of interest rates, poses a third puzzle. If some sector has secured subsidized finance, it is likely to oppose its elimination. Nonetheless, the cases reveal episodes of financial market reform that range from the dramatic liberalization in Chile under the Pinochet government to more incremental reforms in most of the other cases. Under what conditions do governments relinquish their control over the allocation of credit in favor of a more market-based system?

Section I is devoted to explaining patterns of state intervention in financial markets, especially the establishment and operation of preferential credit policies. We begin by looking at the international environment, particularly the availability of external finance, before turning our attention to the domestic politics of credit allocation. We expect that credit programs favoring industry—which is the main focus of the country studies—will depend on the strength of manufacturers' demand for subsidized finance and the political influence they wield relative to other groups.

We argue, however, that both the international and the sectoral approaches must be coupled with a political analysis of the policy-making structure. Where the central bank and allied "control-oriented" agencies within the state are relatively insulated and strong within the government, the use of finance as a policy tool is likely to be more restrained. We explore the conditions under which executives delegate

[1]This question is addressed in greater detail in the companion volume to this project, *Government, Financial Systems, and Economic Development,* ed. Stephan Haggard and Chung H. Lee (forthcoming).

power to such insulated technocratic agencies, as well as the conditions under which they are likely to use credit policy for political purposes.

In Section II, we explore the politics of liberalization efforts. We begin by analyzing changes in the opportunity costs of maintaining preferential credit policies and the incentives these changes provide for reform. Economic crises are an important component of the reform story, though the effects of crisis will depend on the political changes in economic team, government, and even regime with which they are associated. The cases also suggest a second source of political pressure for liberalization: pressures emanating from segments of the financial sector that stand to gain from a reduced government role. *(democratic govt)*

In the concluding section, we return briefly to the broader question of state intervention and liberalization. We argue that the effectiveness and efficiency of government action depend heavily on the "disciplinary capacity" of the state and that no general rules on the benefits of liberalization can be established without reference to the broader institutional and political milieu.

I. THE POLITICS OF STATE INTERVENTION

Before turning to the domestic political determinants of state intervention, it is important to note that changes in the cost and availability of foreign capital should have an effect on governments' financial market polices: increased availability of foreign finance provides the government with opportunities for extending preferential finance, and reduced access to foreign capital should make it more costly to do so. The logic of the argument deserves elaboration because changes in the availability of foreign credit play a role in explaining policy developments in a number of countries.

The International Setting

Even during the heyday of international commercial lending to the developing world in the 1970s, financial markets in most developing countries remained insulated from international financial markets. With some important exceptions—including Indonesia after 1970— most LDCs relied on controls on capital inflows and outflows to varying degrees. To the extent that foreign borrowing occurred, governments acted as intermediaries.[2]

[2] Jeffry P. Frieden, "Third World Indebted Industrialization: International Finance and State Capitalism in Mexico, Brazil, Algeria, and South Korea," *International Organization* 35 (Summer 1981): 407–31.

There was usually a substantial subsidy component in this process. International interest rates were invariably lower than those prevailing in domestic financial markets, but few firms in developing countries could borrow on their own, not only because of capital controls, but also because they lacked an adequate reputation. Foreign borrowing thus required a government imprimatur, for example, in the form of a guarantee. This allowed the government to control the purposes to which borrowing was put, but it also involved rationing credit among competing borrowers and opened the door to rent seeking.[3]

An increase in governments' access to foreign credit should therefore provide an opportunity to expand their role as a financial intermediary between foreign and domestic financial markets, thus providing political opportunities to extend benefits to supporters or favored activities. By relieving the constraint that is usually posed by the level of domestic savings, we would also expect the availability of international credit to strengthen the hand of the "spending" ministries within the government at the expense of the "financial" ministries, including the central bank. The "spenders" include not only the ministries of planning and industry but also capital-hungry, state-owned enterprises, which are often more powerful than the ministries that nominally oversee them.

How do these expectations fare? In the three Latin American cases in our study, preferential credit schemes date to the Great Depression. As agricultural exports and access to external finance collapsed, economic and political pressures mounted for state intervention. Building on earlier support for coffee growers, the Banco do Brasil first engaged in finance of industry in the 1930s. In Chile, where declining exports had an especially devastating economic impact in the late 1920s, the first institution to provide subsidized finance to industry was created in 1928. The imposition of interest rate controls and direct ceilings on particular kinds of credit followed in the mid-1930s in an effort to increase finance to industry. In Mexico, Cárdenas created Nacional Financiera (Nafinsa) and six other development banks in the 1930s to make up for the perceived inadequacies of private finance during a period when Mexico was engaged in acrimonious negotiations with international creditors.

In the postwar period, by contrast, preferential credit programs received a boost from international sources, including the multilateral development institutions and bilateral aid programs. In 1952 the Brazilian government launched the BNDE, the major state development

---

[3] There was often an additional subsidy component in the fact that the government absorbed exchange rate risk where it borrowed in dollars and on-lent in local currency. The government had to deal with the "transfer problem": how to access the foreign exchange required to service foreign obligations.

bank, with the blessing of the United States and the World Bank, both of which provided some of the initial capital. Kubitschek subsequently channeled foreign aid to the BNDE to finance his ambitious industrialization objectives. In Mexico, Nafinsa's operations did not become heavily focused on industrial development until the 1950s and 1960s, when World Bank loans and then foreign commercial borrowing began to flow into the country. As with Nafinsa, the activities of the Chilean industrial development bank, Corporación de Fomento de la Producción or CORFO which was founded with government funds in the 1930s, expanded with the rise in foreign financing in the 1950s. In Korea, government control over access to U.S. aid was a crucial policy and political tool in the 1950s, and the first central bank–directed credit allocation scheme in the Philippines in the 1950s was tied to the allocation of scarce foreign exchange, including U.S. aid money.

In Korea, Indonesia, the Philippines, Mexico, and Brazil, the borrowing bonanza of the 1970s had the anticipated economic and political effects: it lifted fiscal constraints, financed the growth of preferential credit schemes, and shifted the balance of political forces within the government toward the "spenders." In Korea, preferential credit was the major policy instrument used by the government to induce investment in targeted heavy and chemical industries. Andrew MacIntyre traces the resurgence of the "interventionists" in Indonesia in the 1970s to the oil boom and the influx of foreign borrowing. Paul Hutchcroft argues that foreign borrowing and U.S. support not only permitted such grandiose undertakings as the Eleven Major Projects of the late 1970s but also were permissive conditions for the entire pattern of patrimonialism he describes.

The story of the large Latin American debtors is well known. The availability of foreign finance was a crucial background condition for Echeverría's populist policies in Mexico as well as for the expansion of government financing through special state funds (*fideicomisos*). Foreign borrowing fueled the preferential lending programs that financed the industrial-deepening strategy of Brazil's second National Development Plan launched in 1975.

The cases of Taiwan, Thailand, and Chile in the 1970s, however, suggest that the availability of international credit is at best a permissive condition for the expansion of preferential credit schemes. Taiwan was as dependent as Korea on American largesse in the 1950s, yet it did not borrow extensively following the transition to export-led growth and generally eschewed the use of credit policy to achieve industrial policy objectives. Thailand introduced preferential credit for the first time in the mid-1970s, but it was directed to the agricultural sector and not tied to increased access to foreign exchange.

In Chile, the military coup of 1973 was followed by substantial re-forms of the financial system that eliminated the complicated prefer-ential credit schemes that had flourished under a succession of postwar democratic governments. A radical opening of the capital account paved the way for a borrowing boom in 1979–1980, but it was led by the private sector with little state involvement in directing the allocation of resources.

The relationship between the availability of foreign credit and pref-erential credit schemes is clearly not a tight one. Preferential finance expanded during the Great Depression in Latin America, when inter-national credit was scarce, and some countries failed to exploit the opportunities for borrowing that existed in the 1970s. External fi-nancing was at best a permissive condition and led to an expansion of preferential credit in cases that already had a tradition of using finance as a tool of industrial policy, such as Brazil and Korea. These mixed findings justify a closer look at domestic politics, though as we will see, both the interests of domestic actors and domestic political changes cannot be wholly disentangled from the incentives emanating from international financial markets.

The Demand Side: The Logic of Sectoral Analysis

The sectoral approach to public policy bears a close similarity to the Stigler-Peltzman model of regulation and the literature on endogenous tariff theory and rent seeking.[4] In these models, policy is conceived as

[4] See Helen V. Milner, *Resisting Protectionism* (Princeton: Princeton University Press, 1988); Peter Gourevitch, *Politics in Hard Times* (Ithaca: Cornell University Press, 1987); Jeffry A. Frieden, *Debt, Development, and Democracy: Modern Political Economy and Latin America, 1965–1985* (Princeton: Princeton University Press, 1991); and Douglas Nelson, "Endogenous Tariff Theory," *American Journal of Political Science* 32, no. 3 (1988): 796–837.

For applications of similar arguments to finance, see Frances McCall Rosenbluth, *Financial Politics in Contemporary Japan* (Ithaca: Cornell University Press, 1989); Sylvia Maxfield, *Governing Capital: International Finance and Mexican Politics* (Ithaca: Cornell University Press, 1990); Jeffry A. Frieden, "Invested Interests: The Politics of National Economic Policies in a World of Global Finance," *International Organization* 45 (Autumn 1991); Louis W. Pauly, *Opening Financial Markets: Banking Politics on the Pacific Rim* (Ithaca: Cornell University Press, 1988); David Dollar and Jeffry A. Frieden, "The Political Econ-omy of Financial Deregulation in the United States and Japan," Unpublished manuscript, University of California, Los Angeles, n.d.; John B. Goodman and Louis W. Pauly, "The New Politics of International Capital Mobility," Unpublished manuscript, Harvard Uni-versity, n.d.; and Stephan Haggard and Sylvia Maxfield, "The Political Economy of Financial Internationalization in the Third World," Unpublished manuscript, University of California, San Diego, November 1992; and "The Political Economy of Capital Account Liberalisation," in *Financial Opening: Policy Issues and Experiences in Developing Countries,* ed. Helmut Reisen and Bernhard Fisher (Paris: Organization for Economic Cooperation and Development, 1993).

an exchange between interested constituencies and politicians or the applicable portions of the economic bureaucracy. The analytic task is to identify the preferences of the policy-relevant sectors and provide some ex ante assessment of their political strength. The last step is particularly important; without it, this "demand-driven" approach to policy reduces to the tautology that favored sectors were, in fact, powerful.

In most developing countries, capital is scarce and long-term capital markets are thin, if they exist at all. The manufacturing sector should champion cheap credit, though the intensity of this preference will vary depending, first, on the cost of capital and, second, on the capital intensity of their planned investments at any given time.[5] As firms diversify away from investments that are relatively undemanding of capital toward investments that are larger in size, longer in payout period, and more capital-intensive, we would expect the demand for subsidized credit to increase. This process of diversification is typically accompanied by an increase in industrial concentration, which should also increase industry's political strength.

The demand for preferential credit should also be higher where firms rely heavily on external sources of finance as opposed to the owners' capital or retained earnings. There is an important endogeneity problem here: dependence on external financing may itself be a response to the availability of preferential credit. Yet the dependence on external finance will also hinge on other factors, including the prior extent of capital accumulation through agricultural or commercial activities and the presence or absence of a group or conglomerate structure that integrates manufacturing and financial activities.[6] Where groups include banks, the demand for subsidized credit from the government may be muted because of access to finance within the group.

The ability of the manufacturing sector to secure such preferential credit is not merely a function of its preferences and organization but will also depend on the power of countervailing groups. In general, there are reasons to believe that these countervailing interests are weak. Preferential credit schemes typically rest either on direct subsidies or on government control of deposit and loan rates. The most obvious

[5] On both these criteria, we would expect state-owned manufacturing enterprises to comprise a relatively powerful bloc favoring preferential credit. These firms are more likely to operate in capital-intensive sectors, and restrictions on their pricing behavior and other disincentives to profitability are likely to make them dependent on transfers and financing from the government.

[6] Nathaniel H. Leff, "Industrial Organization and Entrepreneurship in the Developing Countries: The Economic Groups," *Economic Development and Cultural Change* 26 (July 1978): 661–75, and "Entrepreneurship and Economic Development: The Problem Revisited," *Journal of Economic Literature* 17 (March 1979): 46–64.

distributive effects of interest rate controls are on savers who face artificially low deposit rates; this is particularly true in high-inflation settings. But savers, and especially households, face collective action problems in attempting to organize, and though they may have the opportunity of exit to the informal financial markets, this option has additional risks. Smaller manufacturing firms are also less likely to gain from preferential credit than are larger firms, which have the advantages of creditworthiness, collateral, and political clout. For these reasons, the concerns of small business are also unlikely to represent a strong countervailing set of interests.

The major sectoral competitor for preferential finance is agriculture. Countries with politically powerful agricultural sectors, typically concentrated export-oriented agriculture, should target a greater share of preferential credit in that direction. The institutional framework for providing preferential credit in Brazil was initiated in response to the demands of powerful coffee growers, and preferential credit to agriculture remained a component of the military's political strategy even during the "miracle" years of rapid industrialization. In both Chile and Mexico, powerful agricultural interests were early recipients of preferential state financing. The rural sector need not necessarily be well-organized and concentrated to be of concern to the political leadership, however. The case studies of Taiwan and Indonesia show that political concerns about the stability and loyalty of the countryside also affect government lending policies.

What about the preferences of the financial sector itself? As the case studies demonstrate, the structure of the financial system is typically complex. Informal financial markets play an important role in most developing countries, and as the formal financial sector becomes more differentiated, a variety of nonbank financial institutions emerge. A number of the country studies show how these different segments can have conflicting interests.

We focus our attention on the interests of the major commercial banks because they are likely to be the most important political players. Their stance toward preferential credit policies hinges in the first instance on ownership. Government ownership of commercial banks, as in Korea or Taiwan, or the creation of state-owned development banks, as in the Philippine and the Latin American cases, reflects a political interest in targeted credit policies. Although the staffs of state-owned banks may come to be sceptical of the policies of their own governments, they are poorly positioned to act against them.

The studies show that private banks can also reach a quite profitable modus vivendi with subsidized credit schemes, however.[7] Private banks

[7] See, in particular, Leslie Elliot Armijo's study of Brazil.

do not necessarily compete with state-owned ones; usually, the private and public sectors serve somewhat different segments of the market. Where privately owned banks are the instruments for preferential credit policies, their cooperation is usually bought with profitable quid pro quos such as central bank rediscounting of loans, access to inexpensive funds from government placements, and controls on deposit rates that give them a profitable spread.

There are, however, two reasons why private banks might oppose preferential credit. One is uncertainty about where the ultimate risk of such schemes will fall. Even if the government offers explicit or implicit guarantees, a question always exists of whether such guarantees are credible, a particular problem given that preferential credit schemes themselves generate moral hazard problems. A second likely objection is that preferential credit schemes are often associated with a broader laxness in monetary policy. Though the effects of inflation can be managed by indexing, as was the case in Brazil, loose money is typically a policy stance that favors debtors over creditors.

The foregoing analysis generates several simple hypotheses. The demand for preferential credit schemes favoring industry should emerge with the growing organization and political strength of the manufacturing sector and will be more intense when manufacturers shift toward more capital-intensive activities and where firm reliance on external finance is high. The extent of the state's role should also depend on the nature of the banking sector. State ownership naturally gives governments a politically useful policy instrument, although the origins of state ownership must itself be explained. A financially and politically strong private banking community is more likely to oppose active government intervention in financial markets, although they may accommodate themselves to it. Finally, government intervention in support of industry will be relatively, but not necessarily absolutely, less where the agricultural sector is politically significant.

The Demand Side: The Evidence

Table 10.1 shows the share of manufacturing in GDP in each of the country cases for the period from 1950 to 1980 and provides at least a rough proxy for the comparative weight of the manufacturing sector. The data show that industrialization began earlier in the Latin American cases; manufacturing played a larger role in GDP through the 1950s and 1960s. The Philippines differs from its East Asian neighbors in that it had a relatively large manufacturing sector in the 1950s. In Korea and Taiwan, manufacturing's share increased dramatically after the transition to export-led growth in the early 1960s. Through the

Table 10.1. The role of industry (as a percentage of GDP), 1950–1989

Country	1950–60	1960–70	1970–80	1980–89
Korea	12	17	28	35
Taiwan[a]	14	20	31	36
Thailand	13	15	21	25
Indonesia	8	9	11	13[b]
Philippines	20	21	28	27
Chile	23	26	27	23[c]
Mexico	23	25	24	26
Brazil	26	26	33	32

Sources: World Bank, *World Tables, 1990* (Washington, D.C.: World Bank, 1990); and Republic of China, Council for Economic Planning and Development, *Taiwan Statistical Data Book, 1989* (Taipei: CEPD, 1989).
[a]Data for Taiwan are for manufacturing's share.
[b]For 1980–1984.
[c]For 1980–1982.

1970s, Indonesia and Thailand were the least industrialized countries in our sample.

The cross-national data on manufacturing share of output are of some use in understanding the emergence of preferential credit schemes. As we might expect from the data, government financial support of manufacturing came relatively early in Chile, Mexico, and Brazil and has been most modest in Indonesia and Thailand. To move beyond such a broad portrait, however, demands attention to more specific features of the organization of business, including the links between industry and finance and the broader political position of business vis-à-vis the government.

In Brazil and Korea, manufacturing was organized in conglomerate groups, but these groups were not linked to banks and thus depended heavily on external financing. Byung-Sun Choi's study of Korea shows that business was perennially starved for credit. Given the government's control of finance, lobbying for preferential credit has been a recurrent feature of Korean politics. The financial links between big business and government became particularly close during the "big push" into more capital-intensive sectors in the 1970s.

Leslie Elliot Armijo's study of Brazil also shows consistent government intervention in support of industrialization, although in contrast to Korea, a state-owned development bank coexisted with a substantial private banking sector. Industry lobbied for greater state intervention in the economy throughout the 1950s, but government lending was initially channeled to infrastructure and state-owned enterprises rather than to the private sector; manufacturing benefited from these policies but secured financing elsewhere, including abroad. Direct financial support for the private sector did increase, however, as industrial policy shifted to support the development of consumer durables and capital goods production under the military.

Given that they pursued broadly similar industrial strategies, Taiwan constitutes an interesting comparison with Korea, and Mexico with Brazil. As in Korea, the state has directly controlled the "commanding heights" of the financial sector. Tun-jen Cheng shows that the government launched several preferential credit initiatives aimed at broad categories of industrial activity, such as exports or automation, and has channeled capital to state-owned enterprises. In general, however, finance has not been used as an industrial policy tool. Given the rising role of manufacturing after the transition to export-led growth in Taiwan, why doesn't that country's financial market policy resemble Korea's?

Cheng notes that one possible explanation is that the pattern of industrialization in Taiwan has been relatively less concentrated and capital-intensive than in Korea, with correspondingly less demand for longer-term bank financing. Yet this outcome was itself a function of a sustained government policy to *avoid* industrial concentration. Cheng argues that the political position of business differentiates the two cases. In Korea, the Park regime courted support from big business and fostered its growth. In Taiwan, the KMT government explicitly sought to limit business concentration and power that they believed constituted a potential threat to their rule; where special support was channeled to the private sector, it went to smaller firms.

Like Brazil, Mexico has a relatively long history of industrialization, but the larger industrial firms have typically been linked to banks through a group structure. As a result, they show a lower dependence on external finance than does industry in Brazil; large-scale industrialists belonging to financial-industrial conglomerates had access to credit without state support. Large Mexican industrialists and bankers accepted selective credit controls on bank lending after 1942, but the main objective of these controls was macroeconomic stability rather than industrial policy; this is in distinct contrast to Brazil, where stability was consistently subordinated to a high-growth strategy. When state intervention increased under Cárdenas (1934–1940) and Echeverría (1970–1976), it had less to do with sectoral pressures from business—which were, in fact, alienated by these two governments—than with the ruling party's political objective of responding to social challenges and pressures from its own left wing.

Chile and the Philippines also have relatively long histories of industrialization, and industry and finance have been linked through a group structure. Private commercial banks typically had extensive ties to commerce, agriculture, and later to import-substituting industries, in part because they were established by family conglomerates for the purpose of financing other family enterprises. In the Philippines, this group model was adopted not only by the traditional oligarchy but by the crony parvenus in the 1970s as well.

In contrast with Mexico, however, groups in both countries constituted powerful lobbyists in favor of preferential credit policies. One reason for this policy preference was no doubt the fact that the groups were confident that they could effectively influence government policy in their favor. The studies of Chile and the Philippines show how concentrated private sectors penetrated the state apparatus. Reform efforts under Frei to limit business power over financial decision-making were unsuccessful and Laura Hastings shows that even following the nationalization of the banks under Allende, the groups continued to receive favorable treatment. In the Philippines, those groups with political connections benefited from preferential credit schemes from the state-owned banks, as well as a lax regulatory regime that allowed groups to milk banks for other ends.

Among our country cases, manufacturing plays the smallest role in GDP in Indonesia and Thailand. Agriculture continues to be important in both countries, although Thailand shows a sharply rising share of industry in the last two decades. In Thailand, private banks were relatively strong and developed close links to export agriculture but were not oriented toward domestic manufacturing until quite late. Richard Doner and Daniel Unger argue that there was simply no constituency for subsidizing credit to the manufacturing sector. The small credit programs that did emerge under democratic rule in the mid-1970s were directed at agriculture.

Indonesia is also a case with limited private industry; MacIntyre argues that "one looks in vain for strategic alliances linking state and business actors in the shaping of credit policy." In comparison with the other cases, agriculture received a relatively large share of the government's preferential credit, but MacIntyre emphasizes that most state credit was directed, or diverted, to other purposes, including financing state-owned enterprises and patron-client networks.

The arguments based on the availability of international credit and the strength and weakness of the groups supporting or opposing preferential credit provide some broad insights into the timing and sectoral content of such programs. Table 10.2 attempts a schematic summary of that evidence, dividing each case into subperiods on the basis of turning points in credit policy identified in the country studies.

Yet the sectoral story leaves us with several puzzles. First, did the use of finance in support of industrial policy reflect the interests of well-organized and politically potent manufacturing sectors, or did industry

304

become more concentrated and politically powerful as a result of government initiatives? If the latter is the case, then what motivated government and, more specifically, politicians to intervene? Second, we find that the ability of sectoral interests to prevail depends not only on their own organizational capabilities but also on their *political* relationship to the government. The sectoral approach is useful for understanding the array of political forces but is less clear about the "selection mechanism" through which some interests come to be favored; thus, this approach is not well suited to explain the *timing* of particular policy changes. To gauge the actual influence of the private sector, we need a clearer picture of the political elites and institutions that constitute the supply side of the political equation.

The Supply Side: Institutions, Politicians, and Financial Policy

Under what conditions will politicians attempt to use financial instruments for political ends, and how will they do it? Some insights can be gained by extending recent analysis of the politics of macroeconomic policy in OECD countries. One finding to emerge from this literature is that the stronger and more autonomous the central bank from government, the tighter monetary policy is likely to be and the lower inflation will be.[8] An extension of this central bank–oriented approach provides some insight into government intervention in the allocation of credit. Central banks view credit policy through the lens of macroeconomic management and are likely to resist programs that threaten to result in increased government spending, loose monetary policy, and inflation. Where central banks and allied "control ministries" are well-institutionalized[9] and independent from the government, business influence on financial market policy should be muted and intervention in financial markets in support of industry less.

---

[8] See John B. Goodman, *Monetary Sovereignty: The Politics of Central Banking in Western Europe* (Ithaca: Cornell University Press, 1992); Paulette Kurzer, "The Politics of Central Banks: Austerity and Unemployment in Europe," *Journal of Public Policy* 7, no. 1 (1988): 21–48; Nathaniel Beck, "Politics and Monetary Policy," in *Political Business Cycles*, ed. Thomas D. Willett (Durham: Duke University Press, 1988); John T. Woolley, "Central Banks and Inflation," in *The Politics of Inflation and Economic Stabilization*, ed. Leon N. Lindberg and Charles S. Maier (Washington, D.C.: Brookings Institution, 1985); Vittorio Grilli, Donato Masciandaro, and Guido Tabellini, "Political and Monetary Institutions and Public Financial Policies in the Industrial Countries," *Economic Policy* 13 (October 1991): 341–93; and Alberto Alesina and Lawrence H. Summers, "Central Bank Independence and Macroeconomic Performance: Some Comparative Evidence," Unpublished manuscript, Harvard University, n.d.

[9] Peter Evans underlines the importance of internal organizational norms as a source of bureaucratic autonomy in "The State as Problem and Solution: Predation, Embedded Autonomy, and Structural Change," in *The Politics of Economic Adjustment*, ed. Stephan Haggard and Robert Kaufman (Princeton: Princeton University Press, 1992).

Table 10.2. International and sectoral influences on credit policy

Country/period	Availability of international finance	Organization and strength of manufacturing sector	Bank ownership	Credit policy
Korea				
1954–60	Aid-dependent	Emerging groups	Private	State controls
1961–75	Falling aid, increased borrowing	Increasing business strength	State	State allocation, broad categories
1975–80	Heavy borrowing	Highly concentrated, strong	State	Strong targeting
1980–90	Reduced borrowing	Highly concentrated, strong	Privatizing	Reduced targeting, gradual liberalization
Taiwan				
1949–60	Aid-dependent	Weak	State	Primarily to SOEs[a]
1960–80	Increasing trade surplus	Emerging groups	State	Broad preferential categories
1980–90	Trade surplus	Increasing business strength	Growing private role	Broad preferential categories, liberalization
Thailand				
1949–73	No borrowing	Emerging groups	Private	Noninterventionist
1973–80	Increased borrowing	Emerging groups	Private	Some preferential credit to agriculture
1980–90	Decreased borrowing	Increasing business strength	Private	Broad preferential categories, financial liberalization
Indonesia				
1949–65	Aid-dependent, balance-of-payments crisis in 1965–1966	Weak	Mixed, growing state role via SOBs[a]	State allocation
1966–73	Increased aid and borrowing	Weak	State	State allocations, primarily to SOEs
1974–82	Oil boom, increased borrowing	Increasing business strength (Chinese groups)	State	State allocation
1982–90	Oil prices fall, reduced borrowing	Increasing business strength (Chinese groups)	Growing private role	Reduced state role, liberalization

	International finance	Business groups	Ownership / state role	Policy
Philippines				
1947–72	Primarily aid	Strong groups (oligarchy)	Mixed, private dominant	Some state allocation
1972–84	Heavy borrowing	Rising crony groups	Growing state role via SOBs	Growing targeting
1984–90	Debt crisis in 1984, increased aid post–1986	Decline of cronies, strong groups	Declining state role	Reduced targeting, attempted liberalization
Chile				
c. 1930–52	Little	Strong groups	Mixed, private dominant	Limited targeting via SOBs
1952–73	Primarily aid	Strong groups	Growing state role via SOBs	State targeting
1974–82	Borrowing boom, 1979–82	Rising financial groups	Privatizing	Laissez faire
1982–90	Debt crisis in 1982, reduced borrowing	Decline of financial groups	Partial renationalization	Laissez faire
Mexico				
1934–54	Reduced access	Increasing business strength	Private dominant, growing state role via SOBs	Limited targeting via SOBs
1954–70	Increased borrowing	Strong industry-finance groups	Private dominant	Limited targeting via SOBs
1970–82	Oil boom, heavy borrowing	Strong industry-finance groups	Growing state role, nationalization 1982	Increased targeting
1982–90	Debt crisis, reduced borrowing	Strong industry-finance groups	Privatizing	Reduced targeting, liberalization
Brazil				
1930–45	Reduced access	Increasing business strength	Mixed	Initial intervention
1945–64	Increasing borrowing	Strong groups (São Paulo)	Mixed, growing state role via SOBs	Primarily to SOEs
1964–c.80	Borrowing boom	Strong groups, increased role for state firms	Mixed, large state role	Extensive targeting
1980–90	Debt crisis, reduced borrowing	Strong groups, increased role for state firms	Mixed, large state role	Attempted liberalization

aSOBs = state-owned banks; SOEs = state-owned enterprises.

This institutional approach begs a crucial political question, however. Under what conditions will politicians delegate decision-making authority to relatively independent agencies? One explanation returns to sectors: the institutional position of the central bank and the "control ministries" is itself due to international constraints—an argument to which we return below in discussing liberalization—or to the configuration of sectoral pressures. In the advanced industrial states, conservative central banks with considerable authority over economic policy have typically evolved out of and maintain close links with financially robust private financial communities. Conversely, central bank weakness vis-à-vis the government, planning and industry ministries, development banks, and the private sector might simply be a manifestation of the political weight of manufacturing interests.

We have already seen how this sectoral argument carries substantial weight in explaining long-term policy patterns. To explain changes in policy, however, it is useful to combine the sectoral approach with an analysis of how politicians respond to short-term economic and political challenges. We can distinguish two cases. Where macroeconomic instability has proven a political liability, political leaders will be more willing to delegate authority to conservative agencies, including central banks. In these cases, credit policy will be restrained. Where the greater political challenge is growth, governments are more likely to intervene. We see this behavior most frequently on the part of new governments seeking to construct bases of support.

The Supply Side: The Evidence

We begin with those cases that have been relatively noninterventionist. In Thailand, Taiwan, and Mexico from 1954 until 1970, preferential credit programs were either weak or instituted largely for inflation-fighting reasons; Chile after 1973 constitutes another liberal model that we discuss in more detail when looking at episodes of liberalization. The central banks of Thailand and Taiwan have also been the most consistently powerful in our sample, and Mexico's central bank enjoyed a golden age of substantial influence over economic policy-making as well. In all cases, the political costs of inflation were at one point extremely high, producing an institutional response.

Doner and Unger trace the origins of a conservative and noninterventionist policy stance to fears that "irresponsible" policy would prompt foreign penetration: "The potential danger to Thailand's sovereignty tempered any tendency toward expansionary financing and foreign indebtedness." These preferences were reinforced during the Japanese occupation and again in the 1950s, when an effort at state-led industrialization failed, causing substantial fiscal problems; under Sarit Thanarat and his successors (1955–1973), the government returned to a more orthodox macroeconomic policy stance. Although the Thai Ministry of Finance formally dominated the Bank of Thailand, it identified closely with the orthodox views of the central bank until the brief democratic experiment of the mid-1970s. The power of the central bank was enhanced by its governor, Puey Ungphakorn, who occupied the office for close to twenty years beginning in the 1950s and enjoyed wide respect among Thai politicians, the military, and international creditors.

Cheng argues that the delegation of substantial power to the monetary authorities in Taiwan grew out of the political lessons of the hyperinflation of the mid-1940s, which contributed to the KMT's loss to the Communists on the mainland. Taiwan's central bank comes even closer than Thailand's to the model of pure central bank independence, exercising wide-ranging influence over macroeconomic and financial policy and consistently resisting efforts to increase state credit to the private sector. This independence had a solid political foundation. The governor of the Bank of China enjoyed close political connections to both Chiang Kai-shek and Chiang Ching-kuo.

Beginning in the late 1940s in Mexico, particularly before the stabilization crisis of 1954, inflation became a serious social concern for the ruling party. As in Thailand, the Mexican central bank formally enjoyed relatively little independence from the Ministry of Finance. But, after 1954 the orthodox view of economic policy shared by the Ministry of Finance and the Bank of Mexico came to dominate the economic agenda. The credit controls initiated by the Bank of Mexico beginning in the late 1940s were introduced in part because they provided a politically useful way to increase the range of inflation-fighting tools at the central bank's disposal.

The Finance Ministry–central bank axis proved politically fragile, however, which suggests the kinds of conditions under which financial policy will be subordinated to political concerns. Urban challenges, which reached a denouement in the Tlateloco massacre of 1968, as well as increasing rural land seizures reflected mounting pressures on the "stabilizing development" model. Shortly after coming to office, Luis Echeverría quickly overturned the previous power of orthodox groups within the government, initiating a decade-long experiment with expansionist macroeconomic policies and increased use of preferential credit.

Among the remaining cases where government has intervened, we can distinguish between subgroups on the basis of the relative strength and coherence of the planning apparatus. Korea and Brazil are countries in which central banks have always been weak relative to planning ministries but in which the latter have historically had some degree of autonomy with reference to the demands of both politicians and private sector groups. In Korea, all important monetary policy decisions are made by the Ministry of Finance in consultation with the Economic Planning Board and ultimately the president. Until the 1980s, the main instrument of monetary policy was direct controls on interest rates and credit, which were facilitated by government ownership of the commercial banks; monetary policy was subordinated to the objectives of industrial development. Yet, until the heavy industry drive, and arguably during it, the government retained the ability to secure compliance and a quid pro quo from business. It was not until the late 1970s, or even the 1980s, that the concentration of the chaebol gave them decisive leverage over government policy.

The origins of this structure—a weak central bank coupled with a relatively strong planning apparatus—are closely related to the political interests of a new authoritarian regime. The Korean military seized power in 1961 on the coattails of the 1960 "student revolution" against the corruption of the Syngman Rhee government. In contrast with the Latin American bureaucratic-authoritarian regimes, the military's political orientation was populist. The government arrested businesspeople associated with the previous government, nationalized the banking system, and channeled credit to agriculture and small and medium-sized industries.

Park Chung Hee had justified military intervention on economic grounds, and when the initial populist strategy proved unviable for macroeconomic reasons, he delegated substantial authority to a new, centralized Economic Planning Board. The military amended the Bank of Korea Act in 1962 to strengthen the government's control over monetary policy. Executive power over financial policy increased even further following a new authoritarian constitution in 1973 and the concurrent announcement of an ambitious heavy industry drive. The EPB ceded power to a narrower circle of advisers around Park, thus providing the basis for the particularly close ties that Choi describes between business and the largest firms in the second half of the 1970s.

Brazil did not have a formal central bank until 1964, and even that institution had to share power over national monetary affairs with other financial institutions such as the majority state-owned commercial Banco do Brasil. The weakness of the central bank was in part simply the converse of a relatively strong set of planning ministries. Central bank weakness also reflected broader pressures connected with electoral politics and the continuing pull of the states within a federal system. To an even greater degree than in Korea, monetary stability was sacrificed to the objectives of rapid growth. Even during what Armijo calls the "semi-elite" democracy of 1945–1964, however, politicians managed to institutionalize "pockets of efficiency" within the state structure, including the state-owned development bank.

The political pressures of the democratic period did not altogether disappear with military rule. The new government did undertake a number of financial reforms, but it did not create a truly independent central bank and later weakened the one that was created. Armijo shows how the military abandoned the initial emphasis on stabilization and used financial instruments and foreign borrowing to cement the bureaucratic-authoritarian coalition between the military, technocratic planners, and the private sector, both domestic and foreign. Financial policies also provided benefits to the politically crucial urban middle class, for example, through the creation of a new housing finance system and an expansion of consumer credit. *CHILE AND DEMOCRACY*

In Chile before 1973 and Indonesia before 1966, conservative government agencies such as the central bank had relatively little power, but planning ministries were also weakly insulated. Industry's involvement in credit policy through CORFO dates to the Popular Front government of 1939 and was reinforced in the postwar period by successive democratic governments. We have already noted how the Frei administration proved unsuccessful in its efforts to disengage the central bank and planning agencies from both private sector and executive branch influence. The left-wing government of Salvador Allende undertook an even more direct and pervasive intervention in financial markets after 1970 in an effort to fulfill its electoral promise to institute a socialist order. Not until the overthrow of Allende did the institutional landscape that had shaped Chilean monetary and industrial policy undergo a fundamental change.

The Bank Indonesia had no operational freedom during the Sukarno era. Both macroeconomic and industrial policy were subordinated first to party politics and after 1957 to Sukarno's efforts at state-led industrialization. In the last years of his rule, Sukarno sought to stave off mounting political pressures on his authoritarian rule from both the army and the Communist party through grandiose domestic projects and foreign adventurism, all financed by printing money. Financial policy disintegrated, culminating in a hyperinflation that overlapped with and contributed to the political challenges to the government.

The position of market-oriented technocrats strengthened substantially with the change of government in 1966, but conflicts over macroeconomic and credit policy continued. MacIntyre distinguishes between two policy camps within the government: the economists, who supported credit controls primarily as a tool to control inflation, and the interventionists, who favored preferential credit as a development tool. The former group dominated until the rise in oil prices in the mid-1970s, when the interventionists gained influence. As MacIntyre argues, this policy pattern cannot be understood by focusing either on the influx of foreign exchange or on the central bank alone; it was symptomatic of the nature of authoritarian politics in Indonesia. Despite increased technocratic influence after 1966, Suharto and the political elite manipulated financial policies for the purpose of cementing patrimonial ties not only with emerging private sector groups outside the state but also with clients such as the military and state-owned enterprises within the government itself. MacIntyre argues that these tendencies became even more pronounced after 1974, when anti-Chinese and antigovernment sentiment bubbled to the surface, prompting a new wave of government financial intervention.

Along with Indonesia, the Philippines represents an extreme case of patrimonial politics in which state economic policy-making agencies were deeply penetrated by both political elites and private sector clients. Although Hutchcroft emphasizes the continuities in the patrimonial nature of the Philippine state, abuses appeared to have grown in magnitude during the authoritarian phase of Marcos's rule. Again, the reasons are political. Marcos subordinated foreign borrowing, industrial policy, state financial institutions, and the regulatory apparatus itself to the construction of a new base of private sector support among his "cronies" that would counter traditional oligarchic power.

Summary: Political Sources of Intervention

Understanding international constraints and the configuration of sectoral interests and power constitutes a crucial starting point for understanding state intervention in financial markets. These approaches point respectively to the availability of foreign capital and the political power of organized manufacturing interests as constraints on what states can do (see Table 10.2). Yet we have found that sectoral influence depends not only on the level of political organization but also on the strategies of politicians and the institutional setting in which they operate.

In countries where macroeconomic instability was a political liability, politicians had incentives to delegate authority over financial market policy to conservative state agencies, including central banks. Conservative central banks tended to restrain the use of financial policy instruments for industrial policy purposes.

In other cases, increased state intervention was initially associated with the political strategies of new governments. In Korea after 1961 and in Brazil after 1964, used incoming authoritarian governments finance to construct growth coalitions around a new, relatively coherent industrial strategy. Marcos pursued a similar political strategy in the Philippines but without a correspondingly coherent and insulated state apparatus. In Chile and Mexico, financial market intervention increased following victories by politicians on the left of the respective political spectrums—in Mexico, Cárdenas and Echeverría; in Chile, the Popular Front government in the late 1930s and Allende in 1970. The effects of new government were also visible in Thailand's brief flirtation with democracy—and preferential credit to agriculture—in the mid-1970s.

Intervention in the allocation of credit in Indonesia, as well as in the Philippines, was one component of a patrimonial political system in which executives used substantial discretionary powers to build personalistic networks of clients. The differences between the two countries resided in three interrelated variables: economic crisis, the relative power of social forces, and the extent of countervailing technocratic influence within the state itself. In Indonesia, the severe crisis of 1965–1966 strengthened the hands of the market-oriented technocrats who faced few organized societal pressures. In the Philippines, by contrast, there was no comparable crisis until the early 1980s; thus, the bureaucratic apparatus remained weak and the oligarchy powerful. These factors explain the strong elements of continuity in Philippine financial history emphasized by Hutchcroft.

II. The Politics of Liberalization

Financial market reform is a complex process that encompasses a variety of interlinked measures.[10] In the wake of financial crises, reform of the banking system involves determining the state of bank portfolios, consolidating and writing off bad loans, and establishing an improved supervisory regime. Over the long run, the development of capital markets is a crucial policy issue. The wisdom of liberalizing exchange controls has also been subjected to substantial debate.[11]

[10] For an excellent survey of the policy issues involved in financial market reform, see Alan Gelb and Patrick Honohan, "Financial Sector Reforms in Adjustment Programs," World Bank Policy, Planning, and Research Working Paper no. 169, March 1989. See also Yoon-je Cho and Deena Khatkate, *Lessons of Financial Liberalization in Asia: A Comparative Study* (Washington, D.C.: World Bank, 1989); and Ronald I. McKinnon, *The Order of Economic Liberalization: Financial Control in the Transition to a Market Economy* (Baltimore: Johns Hopkins University Press, 1991).

[11] We address the politics of this issue in Stephan Haggard and Sylvia Maxfield, "The Political Economy of Capital Account Liberalization," in *Financial Opening: Developing Country Policy Issues and Experiences,* ed. Bernhard Fischer and Helmut Reisen (Paris: OECD, 1993).

Although the case studies touch on all these reforms to some extent, we are concerned primarily with what we will call "liberalization," that is, the process of reducing government control over the allocation of

✱ credit. This includes raising or freeing interest rates, removing subsidies, and simplifying or eliminating sectoral credit targets and ceilings in favor of broader instruments of monetary management. These reforms are usually accompanied by a reduction of barriers to entry in the financial sector and, where state-owned banks have been dominant, by privatization.

The central puzzle of deregulation can be simply stated: why would politicians and the recipients of subsidized credit opt for a market-based system of credit allocation that typically entails higher interest rates and over which they have less control? As in the previous section, we begin by examining the role of economic factors and interests, turning next to how these are related to both the broader political setting and the contending political groups within the financial sector itself.

Financial Pressures for Liberalization

The ability to sustain preferential credit policies depends on the ability of the government to finance them. Increased availability of resources provides an opportunity to expand preferential credit schemes, whereas decreased access to savings, whether foreign or local, increases the opportunity costs of such programs and pushes the government toward liberalization. To explore this hypothesis demands a closer look at the three mechanisms through which such programs are financed: (1) borrowing on international financial markets, (2) imposing the cost on taxpayers through various direct and indirect subsidies to financial intermediaries, and (3) imposing the costs of preferential programs on savers by controlling deposit rates.

We have already outlined how access to foreign credit can provide the government with new opportunities to intermediate between foreign and domestic markets. Reduced access to international credit, in contrast, increases the scarcity value of foreign exchange and makes externally financed preferential credit programs either more costly or impossible. An external financial constraint is also likely to be associated with broader political pressures from creditors, including the multilateral financial institutions, to increase domestic savings through interest rate reforms, reduce subsidies, stabilize, and, in general, pursue more "orthodox" policies. If the availability of foreign credit strengthens "spending" ministries in the government, reduced access to financing should strengthen "orthodox" political forces at the expense

Table 10.3. Real interest rates (average discount rate), 1954–1986

Country	1954–56	1959–61	1964–67	1969–71	1974–76	1979–81	1984–86
Korea	n.a.	1	−2	3	−8	−6	2
Taiwan	−7	−11	−11	7	−3	−4	6
Thailand	3	5	4	3	1	−1	10
Indonesia	−12	−18	n.a.	n.a.	n.a.	n.a.	11
Philippines	2	3	0	−1	−7	−9	1
Chile	−38	−10	−13	−7	−75	15	9
Mexico	2	2	0	0	−12	−4	−7
Brazil	−11	−21	−33	−2	−11	−24	n.a.

Sources: IMF, *International Financial Statistics*, various issues (Washington, D.C.: IMF, various years); and Republic of China, Council for Economic Planning and Development, *Taiwan Statistical Data Book, 1989* (Taipei: Council for Economic Planning and Development, 1989).

of "heterodox" ones because of the interest in increasing credibility vis-à-vis international creditors and the need to make the most efficient use of scarce resources.

The second source of financing for preferential schemes is fiscal; governments can simply subsidize preferential credit schemes directly. The most typical form of such transfer is through the rediscounting operations of the central bank, in which seigniorage gains are in effect passed on to favored borrowers through the commercial banking system. In some cases, direct budgetary transfers are also employed. Fiscal constraints should limit the ability of the government to continue such schemes.

The final method of financing preferential credit schemes is to tax savers by controlling interest rates. Limiting deposit rates provides financial intermediaries access to low-cost funds, guaranteeing them a lucrative spread while still achieving the goal of subsidizing favored borrowers. The extent of the tax on savers and the corresponding subsidy to borrowers vary sharply depending on the level of inflation. Table 10.3 collates one indicator of real interest rates, the average discount rate.[12] Most countries experienced difficulty in maintaining positive real interest rates during the first and second oil shocks, but looking beyond these episodes, we find a sharp divergence in national experiences. In Thailand throughout its history, Taiwan since the 1960s, Korea in the 1960s and 1980s, Indonesia after the mid-1980s, and Chile after 1976, governments maintained high real interest rates, which both reflected and contributed to relatively stable macroeconomic policies. In contrast, real interest rates have been consistently negative

[12] Although the discount rate is arguably not the most appropriate indicator for gauging developments in the financial sector, the data are cross-nationally comparable and are therefore useful in suggesting broad differences among our cases.

in Brazil. They were also negative in Chile before 1973, in Indonesia in the 1950s, in Korea during the heavy industry drive of the late 1970s, and in Mexico from the 1970s through the mid-1980s, all periods of relatively high inflation in those countries.

We have already noted several reasons, including collective action problems, why governments might be able to impose the costs of subsidized credit programs on savers. But the emergence of new opportunities for corporate and household savers to realize higher returns can neutralize collective action problems and increase the pressure on preferential credit programs by increasing their cost. This may happen in several ways. As a number of the cases show, large disparities between interest rates in the formal sector and the scarcity value of capital will generate parallel markets. In addition, domestic financial markets are often informally integrated with international financial markets through unofficial channels, including black markets and the under- and over-invoicing of trade. Moreover, as domestic firms become internationalized, they often gain opportunities to borrow from abroad. Finally, partial liberalization or innovations in one segment of the financial market—such as permitting nonbank financial institutions to operate free of regulations—can have unintended consequences for the financial institutions responsible for the management of preferential credit schemes. Resources will flow toward the higher-yielding segment. Diversion into less-regulated segments places pressure on the government to bring interest rates in line with the market by making preferential credit schemes more costly for the government.

In sum, we have suggested three economic circumstances in which preferential credit policies are likely to come under economic and political strain. The first two are apt to become particularly evident during crises. Balance-of-payments and fiscal crises will directly limit the ability of governments to sustain preferential credit policies. The third route may unfold more gradually: changes in opportunities for savers—whether through the growth of parallel markets, access to international markets, or partial financial market reform—decrease the viability of state controls. To explore these hypotheses, we begin by analyzing the effects of crisis on economic reform.

Crisis and Economic Reform

We have already touched on the early crises in Taiwan and Thailand that gave rise to relatively strong central banks and an aversion to subsidized finance. The incidence of economic crises among the remainder of our country cases can be divided into two "waves": (1) those of the 1960s and 1970s and (2) those that were associated with the debt crises of the 1980s. Some support exists for the broad hypothesis of a relationship between balance-of-payments and fiscal crises and a tendency toward liberalization (see Table 10.4). But the effects of economic conditions on policy were mediated by politics: crises were usually associated with changes in the economic team, government, or even the regime. The content of the reforms thus reflected not only the severity of external and internal financial constraints but also differences in the nature of the political conflicts surrounding the crisis and the political strategies of incoming leaderships.

Populist governments in Chile, Brazil, and Indonesia pursued policies that contributed not only to accelerating inflation and balance-of-payments problems but to increased social mobilization as well. In all three countries, economic crises were preludes to authoritarian installations. The Philippines experienced a balance-of-payments crisis in 1970, and leftist mobilization and nationalist sentiment against foreign investment were on the rise before Marcos's declaration of martial law in 1972. In Korea, U.S. aid officials had become disgruntled over economic mismanagement by the late 1950s, and reversing the country's economic fortunes was the main reason given by the military for its intervention in 1961. Restoring international confidence and creditworthiness was either a motive or an immediate objective of the new authoritarian government in each case.

In all five cases, regime changes were accompanied by shifts in the conduct of economic policy, including financial market policy. With the exception of the Philippines, reforms entailed a reduction of total credit flowing to the government itself and thus a relative shift in favor of the private sector as a whole. This was true even in Korea, where the military government seized control of the banking system.

Beyond that, however, the extent and content of the reforms varied substantially. The new military government in Chile moved in the most unambiguously liberal direction. Brazil and Indonesia also moved in a more "orthodox" direction, although both governments maintained substantial control over financial market instruments. The new authoritarian leaderships in Korea and the Philippines, by contrast, *increased* control over credit allocation and sought to redirect it to new activities. These variations can be attributed only partly to the intensity of the crises; we must also look to the political challenges each government faced and the bases of support it sought to cultivate.

The Chilean military seized power in the wake of a radical socialist experiment; Argentina under Finance Minister Martínez de Hoz (1976–1981) perhaps provides a comparable case. In both Chile and Argentina, democratic governments had used monetary and credit pol-

317

Table 10.4. Liberalization episodes

Country/ period	External position	Fiscal situation	Political changes	Policy outcome
Korea				
1964–65	Declining aid	Weak	Follows authoritarian consolidation	Interest rate reform on deposits
1981–92	Either adequate or surpluses	Strong	Initiated following coup	Very gradual liberalization of rates, privatization of banks, reduced barriers to entry
Taiwan				
1975–92	Surpluses	Strong	No	Very gradual liberalization of rates, completed by 1989; reduced barriers to private entry
Thailand				
1986–92	Strong	Strong	Coup, 1991	Gradual liberalization of rates accelerated following coup
Indonesia				
1966–70	Crisis	Crisis	Coup	Decentralization of state banks, successful stabilization, and opening of capital account, but state role remains large
1983, 1989	Falling oil revenues	Weak	No	Broad liberalization of all aspects of banking system, particularly after 1988
Philippines				
1972	Improving	Improving	Coup	Efforts to strengthen banking system, including improved supervision; aborted by rise of cronyism
1980	Balance-of-payments problems	Deteriorating	No	Liberalization of rates undermined by financial crises in 1981 and 1984–85
1984	Crisis	Crisis	No	Stabilization and rescue of banks
1988	Adequate	Deteriorating	New democracy	Efforts to strengthen supervision, not passed by Congress

Table 10.4. (cont.)

Country/ period	External position	Fiscal situation	Political changes	Policy outcome
Chile				
1974	Crisis	Crisis	Coup	Radical laissez-faire program, including opening of the capital account, but instituted gradually
1982	Crisis	Crisis	No	Stabilization and rescue of failing banks
Mexico				
1982–92	Crisis	Crisis	Changes in administration, 1982 and 1988	Privatization of banks and liberalization
Brazil				
1964–65	Crisis	Crisis	Coup	Reforms free rates and encourages new instruments, but state role also increased
c. 1980–92	Poor	Recurrent crises	Gradual democratization	Very limited liberalization

icies to achieve populist objectives. In both cases, economic orthodoxy fit with the military's objective of dismantling the social and ultimately economic structure that had produced the radical challenge. In both countries, but particularly in Chile, economic teams enjoyed an unusual degree of political autonomy, which extended to even private sector supporters. These conditions allowed these new military governments to initiate far-reaching financial market reforms and in Chile to fundamentally reshape the coalitions that had sustained import substitution throughout the postwar period.

Indonesia bears a number of similarities to Chile. As in Chile, the crisis was profound; prices had accelerated to hyperinflationary levels. Technocrats figured prominently in the new military government, gaining autonomy that had been stripped from them under Sukarno. Also as in Chile, stabilization was the first priority and helped to restore the faith of external creditors and the integrity of the financial sector. Yet, unlike in Chile, the government maintained substantial control over banking. This was done partly to prevent further concentration of Chinese economic power and to favor indigenous Indonesians; partly to extend support to the rural sector, where the political challenges of the early to mid-1960s had come from; and partly as a result of the patrimonial politics already described.

The economic crises in Brazil, Korea, and the Philippines were less acute. The Brazilian military's flirtation with orthodoxy also proved to be less committed and sustained than in the Southern Cone countries of Latin America. To court political support for the government, a harsh stabilization program was modified to focus on growth. Liberalizing measures were coupled with new efforts to provide preferential credit to the private sector through state-owned banks. Nonetheless, the sweeping financial market reforms of 1964–1965 contained measures that could not have been launched under previous democratic governments, including a forced savings scheme to support housing finance, the freeing of interest rates, measures to promote the development of the capital market, and the creation of a central bank.

In Korea, balance-of-payments pressures and fiscal problems also motivated reform. Declining U.S. aid commitments and the corresponding prospect of deepening fiscal problems spurred the government's successful effort to mobilize savings into the state-owned banking system through interest rate reforms. But Korea in the early 1960s resembles Brazil in that interest rate reforms were combined with measures to sustain and even deepen government intervention in the allocation of credit. The politics of Korea's more interventionist course included initial semipopulist measures in support of farmers and small business followed by a focus on rapid industrialization designed to secure support from strategic sectors of business as well as the electorate at large.

Finally, in the Philippines, the extent of reform following the balance-of-payments and stabilization crises of 1970 was minimal, even following Marcos's declaration of martial law in 1972. As Hutchcroft shows, successive efforts at financial market reform under Marcos were subverted by the logic of cronyism and the broader patrimonial nature of Philippine politics.

The move toward financial liberalization appears somewhat more uniform in the wake of the crises of the 1980s. It is clear that the large debtor countries—which include all the countries in our sample except Taiwan and Thailand—were pressed toward more orthodox macroeconomic policy stances as a result of the collapse of international lending and the fiscal crises that accompanied it. All the countries in our study that had significant preferential credit schemes in the 1970s (i.e., the Philippines, Korea, Mexico, Brazil, and Indonesia) made some move to limit their scope during the 1980s. The hypothesis that foreign exchange and fiscal crises lead to financial liberalization seems to gain particular support from the fact that larger crises are associated with more dramatic reforms. Nonetheless, political differences across cases also affected policy responses in important ways.

After a period of rising state intervention in credit markets, which culminated with the bank nationalization in 1982, Mexico moved dramatically away from "heterodox" financial policies. As happened during earlier periods of international financial trouble in Mexican history, the efforts by both President de la Madrid and President Salinas to regain credibility with international investors and creditors strengthened the hand of economic "liberals" within the bureaucracy. The government initiated the reprivatization of the banks, reduced preferential credit distributed through public development banks and trust funds by half in 1987, and reduced reserve requirements and freed interest rates in 1989.

Indonesia is another case of dramatic financial liberalization in the 1980s, especially given that Indonesia's preferential credit program was historically more extensive than Mexico's. MacIntyre shows that when the Indonesian balance-of-payments position deteriorated in 1983, the efficiency costs of the preferential credit program became burdensome, providing an opening for reformers in the Ministry of Planning, the Ministry of Finance and the Economic Coordination Ministry. "As a sense of urgency mounted," he writes, "the authority of the liberal economists within the government grew in policy debates." A gradual decline in preferential credit followed the 1983 financial reforms and a steep decline with further liberalization packages in 1989 and 1991.

In the 1980s, Korea, Brazil, and the Philippines also had liberalization moves, albeit less successful ones. Following the economic crisis and political transition in 1980 in Korea, the new military government began the privatization of commercial banks and moved to free lending rates and to eliminate the credit schemes of the 1970s. Choi shows that progress in these reforms proved slow, despite both partial deregulation and an increasingly internationalized private sector. This might have resulted from the fact that Korea did not experience the same constraints as did other debtors; because of its export capacity, Korea remained creditworthy throughout the 1980s, and its fiscal position improved steadily. But the temerity with respect to financial market liberalization was largely due to political and economic pressures to continue subsidizing big business, particularly given that many firms in targeted industrial sectors faced severe financial distress. As political pressures on the government mounted, new preferential lending schemes appeared for agriculture and small and medium-sized firms.

In the Philippines, the financial crisis in 1981 and the balance-of-payments crisis of 1983–84 were followed by a long, slow, and complicated process of rehabilitating the two major state-owned banks that had been weakened by cronyism and mismanagement and of shoring up select noncrony private banks. A combination of creditor pressure, including pressure from the IMF and the U.S. government, pushed the Marcos government to undertake these reforms and strengthened the hand of conservative central bank governor "Jobo" Fernández. The high interest rate policy associated with the stabilization effort of 1984–85 facilitated Fernández's efforts, as banks gained from holding high-yielding government bills. Rediscounting facilities were also cut as a result of the acute financial problems facing the central bank. Further liberalization of entry and the strengthening of bank supervision were seen as the next steps in the process of reform, but progress toward these goals, particularly addressing the problem of weak bank supervision, proved slow, in part, because of resistance from the banking sector itself.

Through 1990, financial liberalization had progressed even less in Brazil, and Armijo suggests that the coincidence of the crisis with democratization holds some of the explanation. Feeling a strong financial pinch, the Figueiredo and Sarney governments cut the extent of subsidy of agricultural credits. But the transition to democracy allowed the Banco do Brasil, one of the main institutions through which such credit flows, to battle successfully against liberalization and the loss of power it would imply. State banks also became the locus of new patronage opportunities and ended up seeking support from the central government to rescue them from insolvency.

Market Pressures for Liberalization

Even where there are not distinct crises, governments may be driven to undertake liberalizing measures by pressures emanating from the financial markets themselves. The coalitions supporting intervention may shift over time as a result of internationalization, partial deregulation, or the emergence of nonregulated informal segments of the market. This theme receives attention in recent work on the political economy of finance in OECD countries. Frances McCall Rosenbluth, for example, concludes that capital decontrol in Japan was "propelled by financial institutions, acting in cooperation with the Ministry of Finance and sometimes politicians, to construct a new set of rules they need[ed] to compete in a changing economic environment."[13] John B. Goodman and Louis W. Pauly reach similar conclusions in a comparative study of Japan, Italy, and Germany; David Dollar and Jeffry Frieden underline the role of changing sectoral pressures in a com-

---

[13] Rosenbluth, *Financial Politics in Contemporary Japan*, p. 5.

parative study of liberalization in Japan and the United States; and we have extended this analysis to developing countries.[14]

As recent liberalization efforts are only now unfolding in many of the countries in question, inadequate information exists to make compelling generalizations; nonetheless, there are interesting hints for future research. Choi shows how the battle over both interest rates and the deregulation of entry pitted banks against the nonbank financial institutions in Korea; banks were increasingly disadvantaged by the looser regulations facing the NBFIs, which coveted business reserved for banks. In Thailand, Doner and Unger note that "the Thai Bankers Association's efforts to reestablish the interest rate cartel had failed by 1988 in the face of competition from finance companies, foreign banks, and smaller banks." MacIntyre attributes the liberalization of the late 1980s in Indonesia to external constraints and state choices rather than to sectoral lobbying but concludes by noting that the "reform measures have created a new and potentially potent constituency—the local private banks."

The studies of Taiwan, the Philippines, and Chile highlight another important spur to reform, namely, financial crises. In some cases, these are associated with the broader fiscal and balance-of-payments difficulties we have already noted; this was true in Chile in 1982, for example. Yet problems in the financial markets can also precede and contribute to broader economic difficulties or occur relatively independently from them. In the Philippines, the Dewey Dee scandal was crucial to exposing the weaknesses of the state-owned banks. Cheng's study of Taiwan shows how the conservatism of the formal financial sector gave rise to a dynamic, but loosely regulated, nonbank financial sector. Crises in this private segment of the market had reverberations throughout the financial system and proved to be one spur to both deregulation and a strengthening of prudential regulation. This occurred in Korea as well, where scandals in the curb market were an important impetus to reform in the early 1980s.

The Politics of Liberalization

Our cases suggest two distinct liberalization paths. One is associated with crises that result in a change of economic team, government, or even regime. In Chile, an extreme economic and political crisis granted Pinochet unusual autonomy. Liberalization was part of a broader monetarist project aimed at weakening not only the Left but segments of

[14] Goodman and Pauly, "New Politics of International Capital Mobility"; Dollar and Frieden, "Political Economy of Financial Deregulation in the United States and Japan"; Haggard and Maxfield, "The Political Economy of Financial Internalization."

the private sector as well. This project had to be modified again in response to the crisis of 1982, which in turn led to a succession of new economic teams. In Korea (1964–1965), Brazil (1964–1965), and Indonesia (1966–1970), new military governments restructured the financial sector but retained greater control over the allocation of resources. In Mexico, crises overlapped with a shift in favor of the technocratic wing of the party, represented by both de la Madrid and Salinas. Finally, the balance-of-payments crises in the Philippines in 1984 led to a change in the leadership of the central bank, bringing a more orthodox team to the fore.

In general, these crisis cases vindicate the theoretical logic we have outlined, that is, the emergence of balance-of-payments crises favors more orthodox and internationalist policy factions and pushes toward liberalizing reforms. The reason for this is not simply the macroeconomic policy justification either of increasing domestic savings or of restricting credit by raising interest rates but also the broader political concern of securing credibility in the eyes of creditors, both domestic and foreign.

A second liberalization path was more gradual and conforms more closely to the sectoral story we have just outlined. This gradual pattern of reform was visible in Korea and Taiwan in the 1980s, both countries that boasted strong economic performance. It is also visible in Thailand, though it is interesting to note that the liberalization program there accelerated following the military coup in 1991.

As noted in the introduction to this volume, the country cases present an important challenge to conventional neoclassical accounts concerning state intervention in the market. Judging from the overall growth record—which is admittedly a crude indicator—the country studies include cases of effective intervention (Korea, Taiwan, and arguably Indonesia) and highly costly liberalization (Chile), as well as cases that conform to the expectation that government intervention will spawn inefficiencies (the Philippines and Chile before 1973).

State intervention in financial markets appears to have been most efficient in cases in which politicians delegated authority to institutions that were subject neither to capture by private sector forces nor to their own meddling. In such settings, allocational decisions were more likely to reflect concerns about efficiency and growth. Insulation was not enough however; state officials also had to have the organizational and material resources to monitor business activity and to discipline it through the threat of sanctions in the case of noncompliance. In short, the government needed the organizational, financial, and ultimately political resources to extract a quid pro quo from the private sector.

These findings suggest a more differentiated set of recommendations concerning financial markets than are currently prevalent in the policy literature. Financial market liberalization may be an appropriate strategy where distortions are particularly large and institutions for formulating a coherent industrial strategy are weak and politically penetrated. In these cases, liberalization not only promises large efficiency gains, but it also serves the political function of deflecting pressures away from rent-seeking activities. Even in these instances, the state must, at a minimum, be able to formulate and enforce an adequate regulatory framework; the Chilean case makes this point clear.

Our cases also suggest, however, that the government failures attributed to developing countries are not ubiquitous, that important market failures do exist, and that there may therefore be room for a government role in the allocation of credit. The subsidization of credit to exporters in the East Asian NICs is the clearest example of government intervention in support of activities which proved dynamically efficient.

In the last decade, governments in all eight countries have come under strong pressure to liberalize. These pressures include international shocks and direct pressure from international financial institutions, foreign governments, and banks. Perhaps most important, there has been a secular trend toward greater financial market integration and capital mobility regardless of government policy. We have suggested a number of political reasons why government and private sector actors have resisted such pressures in the past. Even if the scope for such resistance has narrowed, it is clear that the path of liberalization will continue to be shaped by the play of political interests and institutions.

Index

Cornell Studies in Political Economy

EDITED BY PETER J. KATZENSTEIN

Library of Congress Cataloging-in-Publication Data

The Politics of finance in developing countries / edited by Stephan
   Haggard, Chung H. Lee, and Sylvia Maxfield.
      p. cm.—(Cornell studies in political economy)
   Includes bibliographical references and index.
   ISBN 0-8014-2892-0 (cloth).—ISBN 0-8014-8130-9 (paper)
   1. Finance, Public—Asia. 2. Finance, Public—Latin America. I. Haggard,
Stephan. II. Lee, Chung H. III. Maxfield, Sylvia. IV. Series.
HJ1301.Z6P64 1993
336.5—dc20
                                                        93-28589

Financial systems & Eco Policy in derving c's - Haggard.
HG / 195 / F 537 / 1995 X ROBA

POL'L FEASIBILITY OF ADJMT/ IN DEVELOPING C'S.
Z 2 . . ED ,, 95 - 1995 P52.

The Politics of ero adjmt/
HD 87 P65 1992

HD 82 V63 1994 ERIN AVAIL

F / 3100 / A73413 / 1988 ERIN -PINOCHET